6th Heavy Anti Aircraft Regiment
ROYAL ARTILLERY

Contents

Illustrations

_____

Foreword

by Brigadier Ken Timbers – Chairman Royal Artillery Historical Society

———————

Given my background and involvement with the history of the Royal Regiment of Artillery, it is perhaps not surprising that, when I heard that Pat Walker was writing about a Gunner regiment, I undertook to write this Foreword. I think it is important to gather together all such histories in the archives of the Regimental Museum, Firepower, not least because, despite close to 1000 individual Gunner regiments having served in the Second World War, far too little is known of their stories.

Pat Walker's book is an extraordinary history. The author happily acknowledges that he has no experience of writing and that the work began almost by accident: the enormous tasks of researching and recording his findings became a self-imposed duty as he gradually discovered the details. Reading it, I found myself completely captured by the life of the three gun batteries in this regiment. I have read no finer account of the daily grind of a Heavy Anti Aircraft regiment's wartime duties over the period from just before the start of the War to the point at which the regiment went 'into the bag' in the Far East. It is full of human interest, too, and there are some delightful touches of soldier humour.

After recounting the events of the 'phoney war' with the regiment based in England, the story deals with operations with the British Expeditionary Force and the escape via Dunkirk. The subsequent operations all over England are covered in fascinating detail, both from the technical and the personal points of view. The diversion to the Far East and the fighting in Singapore and Sumatra are particularly well covered and the latter operation provides an exciting story that is not well known in Gunner circles.

The account of the period that followed is harrowing. The dreadful stories of the infamous Burma and Sumatra Railways and the sufferings of prisoners of war being treated as worthless slaves on many other Japanese projects are all too familiar, but here they have an additional resonance as the stories of men with whom one has become familiar, knowing what had gone before. In the appendices to the book, the names of those who died are listed by battery, and a further list records the names of known survivors. It is a sad commentary on war that, of over 1000 men on the strength of the regiment, 495 died and the list of survivors found so far numbers 738.

Pat Walker deserves high praise for giving so much time and effort to telling the story of 6th Heavy Anti Aircraft Regiment Royal Artillery, and I commend his book as a valuable record of a regiment at war.

Prologue

Writing the story that follows came about totally by chance and some extraordinary coincidences. When we moved into our present house on the edge of Penn Common in 1980, there was only a golf course and wild heathland to see. However, although nothing visible remains to tell of its past, the Common hides a secret.

From time to time local people mentioned that there had been some Anti Aircraft gunners there during the war and those who were now in their seventies and eighties could remember as children seeing these gunners and talking to them. Nobody knew who they were or what happened to them. Everybody had their memories of where these guns were set up, how many and how often they fired, but all their facts were at odds with each other. No two people could agree on the details. Nothing else came to light and I just put it in the back of my mind until by chance we went down for a trip to Devon.

While we were visiting an old friend who had been in the Army during the war (RAOC) quite by chance one of his old colleagues (a former gunner) dropped in to see him. When in the course of the conversation he asked where we came from we told him Penn Common. At this his eyes lighted up and he said he knew of the area because one of his tasks during the war had been to select suitable sites for the placing of AA guns and Penn had been one of them! His job had been to knock in pegs to mark suitable gun positions.

Years later when someone else mentioned the guns but also could give no further details about them, I decided to do some 'digging' to try and find out something about them for myself. I advertised in the local papers and also the Church Magazine, and then interviewed about fifteen people. Some remembered, as children, the noise of the guns firing but still nobody knew who or what they were. I visited the local archives where I trawled through back issues of the *Express* and *Star* from 1939–45 and never a single mention of the site. The archives themselves had nothing either.

The next coincidence was when a resident in the area sent a copy of the

Church Magazine down to Penzance to a friend who he knew had lived on Penn Common as a boy during the war. Thus it was that I got in contact with Peter Cole (MBE) and he came up with a vital detail. As a lad on the Common he remembered having two of the gunners billeted in his father's house and while going through some papers his late father had kept he came across the original billeting order which stated which regiment the men belonged to. (Fig. 1)

Army Form B55.

United Kingdom.

To the LANDLORD* at   James Vincent Cole, of "Dorwyn", Sedgley Road,

Penn Common, Nr Wolverhampton, Staffs.

In accordance with the provisions of the Army Act you are hereby required to find Quarters

for ---   officers, Two {men {women} and ------ horses, of the 3rd Hy. A.A. Batt. ,6 Hy. A.A.

R.A.
Regiment for to - Night and for an indefinite period for sleeping accommodation only.

Dated the   30th   day of   November,   19 40.

                                                             Billet Master. -

The Army Act, section 106, as amended, provides that :—

106.—(1) The keeper of a victualling house upon whom any officer, soldier, or horse is billeted shall receive such officer, soldier, or horse in his victualling house, and furnish there the accommodation following ; that is to say, lodging and attendance for the officer ; and lodging, attendance, and food for the soldier ; and stable room and forage for the horse, in accordance with the provisions of the Second Schedule to this Act.

(2) Where the keeper of a victualling house on whom any officer, soldier, or horse is billeted desires, by reason of his want of accommodation or of his victualling house being full or otherwise, to be relieved from the liability to receive such officer, soldier, or horse in his victualling house, and provides for such officer, soldier, or horse in the immediate neighbourhood such good and sufficient accommodation as he is required by this Act to provide, and as is approved by the constable issuing the billets, he shall be relieved from providing the same in his victualling house.

(3) There shall be paid to the keeper of a victualling house for the accommodation furnished by him in pursuance of this section the prices for the time being authorised in this behalf by Parliament.

(4) An officer or soldier demanding billets in pursuance of this Act shall, before he departs, and if he remains longer than four days, at least once in every four days, pay the just demands of every keeper of a victualling house on whom he and any officers and soldiers under his command, and his or their horses (if any) have been billeted.

(5) If by reason of a sudden order to march, or otherwise, an officer or soldier is not able to make such payment to any keeper of a victualling house as is above required, he shall before he departs make up with such keeper of a victualling house an account of the amount due to him, and sign the same, and forthwith transmit the account so signed to the Army Council, who shall forthwith cause the amount named in such account as due to be paid.

Fig. 1 The original billeting order, the key to unlocking the name of the Regiment.
Courtesy of Peter Cole MBE.

After six months of researching for very little result, I now finally had the key to the Regiment's identity. Much further researching and more interviewing started me on the story. Trips to the National Archives at Kew gave me access to what few documents remain of their Wartime Diaries, such as they were, and slowly but surely an amazing tale began to unfold. The more I delved the more tragic the details that came out.

After contacting the Imperial War Museum and Firepower, the Gunners museum, it became more and more apparent as far as I could work out that no one had ever written up the history of this Regiment. My interest moved to not just reading about them but to trying to put down their story on paper so others could read it too, hopefully some of those whose grandfathers, fathers and uncles had formed part of this unit. It is a story of bad luck, tremendous hardships, amazing resilience and sad losses. After long hours and many months of research this is the story of the 6 HAA Regt and its three Btys as far as I have been able to discover.

In the course of researching for this story it became obvious that it was going to be a team effort to try and find the pieces and put them together in the right places. The pieces were in short supply because the records for the Regt were in many cases no longer available. Much was lost around Dunkirk and nothing survived their capture after the fall of Singapore and the Dutch East Indies. A few of the braver souls wrote up from hidden diaries of their horrendous experiences in the POW camps. These are some of the few pieces that can be put in place.

A major task was to try and locate the names of all those from the Regt who had died. Some were obvious within the CWGC records but many others were incorrectly detailed with wrong Unit or Bty names. Also during the course of the research I came across names of those who had survived and I thought it might be useful to include these too for the benefit of those looking for relatives.

I am most grateful for the invaluable help given by Robert McAllister who delved deeply into the death records and spent many hours trawling through the 'Returned POW forms' at Kew so that between us we could get as accurate a list as possible.

I am also grateful to the surviving relatives of many of the POWs mentioned who were good enough to allow me to quote from their stories:

Especially Richard Kandler whose father Reuben (of 3 HAA Regt) was brave enough to record and keep a secret diary, the discovery of which would have meant severe torture and certain death;

Also to Jaqueline Norrish for details of her grandfather, Gunner Clapp;

Chris Harrison for details on his wife's grandfather, Gunner S. Weston; John Daniels whose father George was captured in Java; Mike Hopton whose uncle was Driver Nairne; Robert Waters whose grandfather William was lost on the hell ships; Keith Jenkinson for the story of his father; Nicholas Currie for the story of his father and Elsie Pobjoy for details of her father Gnr Tart, Clare Adams on her father Major E.J. Hazel who became CO, Sue Ryding on her father Major JR. McWade who took over 3 Bty, William Boomer for details of his father's escape from Sumatra, Michael Harper-Holdcroft for the information on his grandfather Padre Capt Harper-Holdcroft and finally, to Sarah Carney whose great grandfather BQMS Cotterill she never had the chance to meet.

Many thanks also go to Jean Roberts and Frank Clark for permission to précis much of their hard work of compiling a record of the Returned POW questionnaires from 3 Bty, now to be found on their internet site 'Saigon-Thailand database' (www.fepow.org/the-database.html).

I am also indebted to those I interviewed from the Penn Common area who had lived there during the war and despite rusty memories managed to recall some of the facts from their childhood when playing tag or running about were more interesting than looking at guns.

Of these I would like to thank firstly Peter Cole MBE who provided the key to unlocking the Regt's name and Bernard Parkes for sending him the Church Magazine with my original request for help.

Others who contributed locally and gave of their time to answer my daft questions were Jim Bills, Mrs Bellingham, Rita Bailey, Hazel and Richard Turner, Tony Morrey, Stephen King, Mr and Mrs Price, and some of those on the committee of the Penn Golf Club.

Not forgetting the Imperial War Museum and Paul Evans of Firepower museum (the Gunners museum in London) for lists of the few documents held.

M.J. Jackson provided useful information on regimental personnel and organisation.

Miles Bailey and Irene Wood from The Choir Press edited and knocked my rough draft into a readable form and showed great patience in allowing late items.

Much valuable help and advice came from Angus Dunphy, local and well-published Historian and finally Major J.R.D. Hipkins, who showed me how to use the National Archives resources to find and recover what scant information was held there, especially the Records of Bravery Awards.

What started as a blank sheet of paper with the words 'AA Gunners' became an in-depth search which produced a remarkable story of hardship and harrowing details. All this started on my doorstep nearly 70 years ago and remained unknown. I hope by my bringing this story to life people will realise how much we owe to those who have gone before, for without their sacrifice we would not be free to live our present day lives.

In this respect 6 HAA Regt suffered more than most.

Reference Sources:

National Archives at Kew

6th HAA Regt	WO166 / 7595		
6th HAA Regt	WO 166/ 2337 Aug 40–Oct 41		
AIR 2 / 4768	HAA Dispositions June 1942		
3 Bty	WO 167 / 624		
3 Bty	WO 166 / 2432		
12 Bty	WO 167 / 628		
12 Bty	WO 166 / 2435		
15 Bty	WO 167 / 629		
15 Bty	WO 167 / 630		
15 Bty	WO 166 / 2436		
6th HAA Regt	WO 0361 / 246	15th Bty casualty returns	
6th HAA Regt	WO 0361 / 247	3 Bty	" "
6th HAA Regt	WO 0361 / 248	12th Bty	" "
6th HAA Regt	WO 0361 / 256	RHQ	" "
71st HAA Regt	WO 166 / 2362		
71st HAA Regt	WO 166 / 7540		
350th S/L Bty	WO 166 / 3193 Search Light Battery Aug 1939–May 1941		

Part War Diary sheets for 1st AA Regt HAA 7 June 1940–30 June 1940
CWGC records
FEPOW internet sites by Ron Taylor and Roger Mansell
Imperial War Museum and Firepower museum for advice

Suggested reading:

History of RA AA Artillery 1914–1955 by Brig. Routledge
AA Command by Colin Dobinson
Return from the River Kwai by Joan and Clay Blair
Hurricane in Sumatra by Terence Kelly
Hurricane over the Jungle by Terence Kelly

Battle for Palembang by Terence Kelly
Railway of Hell by Reginald Burton
Surviving the Sword by Brian McArthur
Sinister Twilight by Noel Barber
The Railway Man. by Eric Lomax
No Mercy from the Japanese by John Wyatt
One 14th of an Elephant by Ian Denys-Peek
The Battle for Singapore by Peter Thompson
The Sparrows by Tony Paley
History of the Royal Regiment of Artillery: Far East Theatre 1941–46 by General
Farndale
The Rising Sunset by Ken Attiwill
Dunkirk: The Necessary Myth by Nicholas Harman
The Fall of Java by P.C. Boer.
The Death Railway by Rod Beattie

Additional material:

St Bartholomew's Church Magazines 1939–45
Two original letters from survivors
Memories of some of those who lived on Penn Common during the war
Contacts with relatives of survivors and those who did not return

Glossary

ABDA	Acronym of forces in Sumatra/Java (Australian, British, Dutch, American)
ADGB	Air Defence Great Britain
A/Sgt	Acting Sergeant
Attap	Dried jungle leaf folded over sticks to form tile like system on a hut roof or wall
Bde	Brigade
Bdr	Bombadier
BEF	Shortened title for the British Expeditionary Force in France/Belgium
Bty	Battery
BSM	Battery Sergeant Major
BQMS	Battery Quarter Master Sergeant
Brig	Brigadier
Capt	Captain
CO	Commanding Officer
Coy	Company
CWGC	Commonwealth War Graves Commission (grave registration organisation)
E/FA	Elevation Finding Attachment (for use with Radar)
G/L1	Gunlaying Radar Mk 1
Gnr	Gunner
GOR	Gunners Operations Room (from where the instructions are issued)
HAA	Heavy Anti Aircraft
HE	High Explosive
HQ	Head Quarters
IAZ	Inner Artillery Zone (gun locations during the Blitz on London)
KD	Khaki Drill (light sandy/ biscuit coloured uniform)
LAA	Light Anti Aircraft (normally the Bofors guns)
LDV	Local Defence Volunteers (later to become the Home Guard)

LMG	Light Machine Gun such as the Bren or Lewis in .303" calibre
Lt	Lieutenant
Maj.	Major
ME 109	Messerschmidt 109 (one of the commonest German fighter planes)
m/m	Millimetre
NCO	Non Commissioned Officer
O/C	Officer Commanding
O/Rs	Other Ranks (ordinary soldiers)
'O' Group	Orders Group (meeting called so Officers can receive instructions)
POWs	Prisoners of War
PT	Physical training
QM	Quarter Master (provides supplies)
RA	Royal Artillery
RAOC	Royal Army Ordnance Corps
RASC	Royal Army Service Corps
RE	Royal Engineers
RDF	Radio Direction Finding (early radar)
Regt	Regiment
RHQ	Regimental Head Quarters
RMP	Regimental Military Police
'Speedo'	Japanese system for trying to speed things up
Sqdn	Squadron
TA	Territorial Army (usually the part time units)
TC	Territorial Commander
TSM	Troop Sergeant Major
Tenko	Japanese for a parade
U/P	Unrotated Projectile (early form of rocket for anti aircraft use)
Yasume	Japanese for a day off

Introduction

In Europe by the mid to late 1930s Hitler had decided Germany's destiny, as recorded many years before in his book *Mein Kampf*. Nations on his borders had traditionally had minority populations who spoke German and he had decided that it was their right to become part of the Greater Germany. He harboured a bitter resentment at the way the Allies had treated Germany and the way they had been forced to capitulate unconditionally at the end of the First World War. So too the subject of lands taken away and military quota restrictions placed on them, these were all sore points.

In the UK the Military had spent years disarming and reducing their forces after the completion of the First World War, thinking that the 'War to end all Wars' had finally meant that large standing formations were no longer needed. Inadequate attention had been paid to the giant strides that aircraft manufacture had made and the thinking was that they would never prove a real threat The good old Royal Navy, or Senior Service, had always in the past defended the realm; they had been doing it successfully for hundreds of years and so they tended to get the bulk of any defence budget. This had been kept to a bare minimum since no one was expecting trouble from abroad, but in the meantime Germany was quietly breaking all its treaty restrictions and steaming ahead in arms production.

The United Kingdom air force was very much the 'new boy'. They had had very little experience in the Frist World War other than directing the fall of shot of guns and a bit of air combat, coupled with some aerial reconnaissance. Bombing had been a bit of a novelty with very small bombs dropped somewhat haphazardly. It was considered that things had not really changed greatly. Wild estimates of the strength of the German *Luftwaffe* were expounded, in all cases greatly underestimated. The old argument had still not gone away as to whether to build up the UK forces to be defensive or attacking, and what proportion of each was needed.

Thus it was that the country's anti aircraft force and weaponry had slipped into a dangerous trough of complacency. They might not have been able to read the German mind but evidence of massive civil engineering defence projects round many major cities was there for all to see.

In mid 1936 the so-called Reorientation Committee was to try and decide what was a minimum requirement for the air defence of the UK, and had finally come up with the figures that were needed. Taking into account all bases, airfields, oil terminals and docks, the figures they arrived at were a minimum of 76 Btys of 8 guns each, giving some 608 HAA guns. They also investigated the actual number of guns available at that time and were horrified to discover the total in the whole country was just 60. This meant there were few enough HAA Regiments available as part of the Regular Army to have even the slightest chance of defending the whole of the UK should things warrant this.

But once eyes had been opened by Hitler's rhetoric, further committees were set up to write reports on what the Military really thought would be needed to give anything like a proper defence to the country in the event of an attack. Because Germany was cushioned from us by the Dutch and Belgians it meant that any attack against us would most likely come from the air, and going from past experience of their preferred choices it would be designed to be fast and furious with many low level attacks against vital targets.

While the finer details were being pored over in 1936, Hastings Ismay, in charge of one of the Government committees, pointed out that every time the RAF increased its quotas of new aircraft and airfields, then the AA forces needed to increase too, so they would be able to defend this new target. There was no clear decision on what was the most important threat. If it was to be by high level bombing then HAA guns would be needed but if by fast and low strikes then it would have to be by smaller calibre guns such as the future Bofors would be. Either way there were totally insufficient numbers.

Churchill was much in evidence giving his personal thoughts and worries about the situation and trying desperately to convince the Government of what was happening across the water, helped mainly by insider intelligence from someone who was 'in the know'.

In a little over a year since the first report the experts now adjusted their estimates to 1200 guns. The mild panic continued because what it showed was just how inadequate our forces were. Steps were immediately taken to boost production, and try and bridge the gap between what was perceived to be needed and what was actually available. Much of the equipment that was still in use was from the First World War and totally unsuitable or in many cases obsolete.

One partial solution was to take some of the old 3" guns and convert them but they still lacked the punch needed to reach high level bombers. Skilled manpower was also in desperately short supply to operate what weapons there were, most of which was controlled by part-time TA units who didn't do much more than a few weeks training a year, and many of the meagre stores they had were kept in local drill halls.

As time went on it became obvious that German aircraft were faster and flew further than first thought and therefore would be able to reach further inland to attack targets which had been considered out of reach before. Thus the cycle continued showing that now even more guns were needed to protect these new targets.

While the gathering storm clouds continued to grow, vast numbers of people were busy preparing for the worst. Hitler had already 'upped the antie' and he was quite openly helping himself to neighbouring territory on the pretext of aiding their minority populations of German speakers. He then proceeded unhindered to annex the Saarland, Austria and Czechoslovakia, after which he then sat back to plan his next moves quietly confident he would achieve all his aims. The rest of Europe looked on with growing concern but nobody liked to intervene and rock the boat; memories were still too fresh of the disasters of the First World War two decades before.

At each success, besides gaining huge areas of new territory, Hitler also gained an enormous manufacturing capacity and large pools of manpower resources, and with these came the ability to vastly increase still further his need to support the burgeoning armed forces. It should have been obvious to those at the time that he was not going to stop, but there were still the appeasers, perhaps fearful of another war of attrition like 1914–18 in which hardly a family in the land did not know of a person killed or injured.

As the West viewed what was happening on the Continent, the rate of rebuilding our armed forces gathered pace with everyone holding their breath hoping that things could be made right in time. The alarm bells were already ringing and one thing that was obviously in very short supply was anti aircraft guns and ammunition. More guns meant more ammunition and more shells meant there had to be somewhere to store them all. Working parties started to look for places suitable for storage. Once the best places had been discounted because they were already in use and well docu-mented, the hunt was on to find suitable areas for large scale dumps.

In the end, and to keep the costs to the minimum, a series of old quarry workings were settled on. It was decided to upgrade these by installing concrete or brick blast walls and chambers and narrow gauge railway tracks to service them from the nearby main line rail routes. They were graded according to the ammunition to be stored and the quantities involved, and varied from 5000 tons up to about 18,000 tons.

Their location had to be such that the munitions were safe from aerial attack and therefore some quarries were used after a series of concrete chambers had been built and then backfilled with large depths of spoil. Factories had already started to gear up to increase munitions capacity for all weapon sizes. This was quite a challenge to go from peacetime working quotas to covering the multitude of calibres needed not only by the Army but also the Navy and RAF.

After various defence contracts had been put out to tender with very specific parameters it was decided that the Vickers company would manufacture a new AA gun to be 3.7" calibre and not only able to be fixed in static defensive positions but also for a portion to be mobile and within the weight limit of 8 tons.

Thinking at the time realised that you could only install so many fixed guns in concrete emplacements and the way round the problem of numbers was to have mobiles that could be moved rapidly to any new threat to bolster the numbers needed to counter it. Once the threat had gone they were free to be moved elsewhere.

By the early autumn of 1939 Poland had worked its way to the top of Hitler's 'most wanted' list. Britain now decided it was time to stop all the appeasing and give the Poles the assurance of any previous treaties, that should things go badly we would help them out. Having so far got away with all his invasions without hindrance from outside, Hitler decided to call our bluff, and still maintaining he had been rescuing the minority German-speaking populations justifiably he prepared for his next move.

Britain's Prime Minister Neville Chamberlain had had talks with the German Chancellor over many months to try and avert what most could see was about to happen. He had warned that if Germany did not stop its aggression then there would be serious consequences in Europe. He had come back triumphantly from Munich waving a small piece of paper and claiming he had done a deal with the Nazi Chancellor and it was to be 'Peace in our time'.

He may have been deluding himself and the country as a whole, but in fact he had bought the most precious of all things: time. The time in which we could try to get into some sort of order, increase factory production, mobilise our forces and prepare for the worst. So many of the early defeats could later be attributed to the huge shortages of materials, skilled manpower and the ability of military units to work together as a team.

Steps were continuing to be taken to remedy the shortfalls and so 6 HAA Regt returned from the Far East in Aug 1939 and was stationed at Arborfield, Berkshire, manning their 3" and 3.7" mobile AA guns. It must have been considered a waste for a Regt of valuable guns to be stationed in the Far East where there was no threat at the time, whereas that all the signs were that it was about to 'kick off' across the channel.

The dependence on waiting for the warning signal was a dangerous ploy by politicians, first because in most cases they never believed it when it came, and second because their great worry was that any pre-emptive move would provoke the potential aggressor.

Not to be put off, and determined to show they meant business, on 1 September 1939 the German war machine clattered into Poland and the Poles started fighting for their lives. Chamberlain warned that if Germany did not stop and pull back then we would come in on the side of the Poles. Nothing had been done to aid the Poles so far and Hitler could see this, and since it seemed unlikely the rest of Europe would do anything either, he decided to carry on and complete the job. Sadly the Poles were left to their fate. German forces remained in occupation of Poland and it was obvious they had no intention of withdrawing so war was declared on 3 September 1939. This had rather forced the UK's hand and they had to think seriously about how to help out on the Continent and back up the treaties that were in place with the French and Belgians. Having been angered by the UK reaction Hitler was now more determined than ever and set his mind to taking on France and Belgium.

A decision was made by the British Government to send an expeditionary force across the channel to help set up a defensive line along the Belgian border, if for nothing else than to bolster morale. At this time the French were living in a world of their own and thinking they were safe behind their Maginot Line and that this would hold off any threat. This complex defence system had been built at a cost of millions of francs and was for the most part buried in tunnels. There were multiple gun positions deep underground with anti tank obstacles and wire and minefields in front of these at ground level. A lot of the surrounding countryside was viewed from observation cupolas also buried in the ground. This system stretched for scores of miles and required huge manpower resources to maintain it and was even designed to withstand poison gas attacks. However the French system did not cover the whole length of their border. At the northern end alongside

Belgium it did not exist, and their military experts always said the area round the Ardennes and Sedan was impassable to tanks. This in effect left a section of about 150 miles without any real cover should Belgium fall, something that nobody seemed to be unduly worried about.

In September 1939 Britain started sending troops as part of the general build-up of forces across the channel. They were known by the title 'British Expeditionary Force' which was shortened to BEF.

Chapter I

BEF – Dunkirk

––––––

The 6th Regt had been formed on 6 September 1935 in Hong Kong but designated as the 6th AA Brigade as was the custom at the time. It was originally composed of just two Btys, 12 and 16, and each manned 3" Mobile AA guns. Shortly afterwards on 1 November 1935 it was made up to its full complement with the addition of 3 Bty, but then on 1st July 1936, 16 Bty was replaced by 15 Bty. The Regt was redesignated as 6 Heavy Anti Aircraft Regiment RA on 1st May 1938 and thereafter kept this name.

It was thus that 6 HAA Regt, one of the few original regular army HAA units, was ordered to mobilise at Blackdown in early August–September 1939. They then became part of an estimated 106,000 men who had been mobilised although the vast majority were manning static defences around London and some of the larger cities. Many of these were TA reservists who suddenly found their services in great demand. Men were recalled and equipment prepared and ammunition scales drawn. Some of those involved had already served their time in the Army and were in the reserve and now rejoined the Colours out of patriotism. Quite a few had had spells serving in India, especially the older men, and others had been to Malaya, and it was necessary in a short space of time to bring the Regt up to a war footing.

Joining 3 Bty was BQMS Cotterill who had eighteen years of former service and among the others was Corporal Stan Newcombe who had joined up on 15 April 1932 and before this been a plasterer. He left his wife in their family home at Leckhampton near Cheltenham.

Gunner George W. Daniels was living in Birmingham and having been out of work for a while was pleased to get regular employment again. He had done three years service starting in late 1932 and been posted to Malaya as a gunner for two years. Having completed this he was transferred to the reserve but his return had led to an uncertain future and he struggled to hold down a job. Now as a married man he was recalled and took up a position in 12 Bty. Obviously it was an advantage to have gunners with previous experience to aid the core of the unit.

Another of those recalled to 12 Bty was Gnr S. Weston. Born in Pontypridd in 1907 he was to stay with the unit through all its trials and tribulations providing valuable service. He had joined up previously in 1929 for his gunner training and continued his education, passing various exams. He had specialised in the catering branch and when he left in 1932 he was highly recommended by his Officer. While he was carrying out his initial training his parents moved to Berkshire so when he left he joined them there and decided to start work in a large country house near by. This was quite fortunate since he met and married his future wife there. By 1939 when all could see how the situation was deteriorating he was a happily married man with three lovely daughters.

Gnr Frederick G. Clapp also found himself in 12 Bty; his was to be a war full of lucky escapes.

Gnr Cripps, an older man, had been a regular for many years and he was to carry on his duties as batman/driver with 15 Bty.

Gnr Charles V. Nairne, another driver, found himself attached to 15 Bty and so too Gnr Tom Evans who had done service before the war and was one of those recalled. He had originally enlisted in the Field Artillery in 1934. After home service he then spent time in Malta before leaving in 1937. He was a tough, fit man from the Midlands area of Wednesfield and had been a miner, as were many of the men now in the Regt.

Also part of 15 Bty was Sgt J.R. McWade No 833552. He had been brought up in Liverpool. His roll was as a pay clerk but he was to be commissioned and have a very eventful war. He was well educated in a Catholic school and had left with good exam results in French, Latin and Maths.

He went into the Christian Brotherhood but he was thrown out. (Family legend had it because he thumped one of them for making a pass at him!) He had joined up the day after his 18th birthday in 1934 and went off to Woolwich to join the RHA. After completing his training he was posted to 15 Bty in 1935 where he served as a pay clerk for the next few years. He progressed to Troop Sergeant and in 1939 made Troop Sergeant Major.

A member of 12 Bty and an older man was Gnr J.E. Tart No 822311. He had seen service abroad already and had spent time on Sentosa Island off Singapore and had no idea he was going to see it again.

The Regt comprised three batteries of mobile guns, making a total of 24, split between Btys numbered 3, 12 and 15, with some guns being 3" and rather old, and some of 3.7" which were the latest to supersede them. Each Bty when at full strength would contain 8 guns and these were broken down into smaller units of two troops of 4 guns which in turn were broken down into two sections of 2 guns each to form the troop.

Meanwhile Hitler's armies continued to crush Poland and had shown no sign of halting. With all this occurring across the channel on the Continent and now being able to see how successful the German Armies were, there must have been a nagging thought in the minds of the men as to whether they were actually off to a real war and what the next few months might bring.

They had been regaled for months on how good they were, how efficient their equipment was and how superior in every way. Morale was excellent, but hidden beneath the surface was the fact that this was a peacetime force rapidly recalled to a war footing and in fact cobbled together with TA reservists as part of the Regular Army, and whose equipment the politicians through their 'penny pinching policies' had allowed to become mostly inferior to that of the foe they were about to be called on to meet.

During the period of August/September hundreds of men were collecting in camps in the south of England and among these was Gnr Stanley Weston. As a devoted husband he tried to keep his wife informed as to the conditions and to try and put her mind at ease. Like most of the married men, whenever he got the chance he would send off a few lines in a hastily written letter or postcard. On 28 August 1939, while mobilising at West Firth Camp Blackdown, he sends his first letter asking if his wife has received the thirty shillings he has sent her. He notes that there are thousands of troops there and they and all their stores are being got ready. They had just had their inoculations and many were suffering from that.

By 11 September 3 and 12 Bty were assembled and 15 Bty shortly after. Advance parties had left for Southampton by road taking guns and trailers, heavy equipment, stores and ammunition, while the bulk of the men were going to join them by rail.

On 13 September Gnr Weston writes again saying he can't give his wife a destination because they just do not know. He hopes all is well with the three children but rather hopefully claims he *does not think this thing will last very long*. They had been expecting some sort of leave but the next day on the 14th they embarked on the SS *Viking* while the drivers and the road party boarded SS *Brighton*.

The heavy equipment and stores, including the guns and towing vehicles,

† Place names in italic in this chapter are the locations of 6HAA Batteries during the deployment of the British Expeditionary Force in France and Belgium up to May 1940.

were dispersed among several other ships. After an overnight crossing they arrived at the French port of *Cherbourg* and the Unit disembarked. Heavy equipment was craned off onto the dockside and then driven away. The original party who had travelled down to Southampton by train as part of 12 Bty were now marched to the area of the Hotel Sud Amerique once they had sorted themselves out at the French docks. Their transport was pulled up into a temporary vehicle park to the east of the port.

An Officer of 15 Bty complained that things were moving far too slowly and that they were angered when it was discovered that tools had already been pilfered from some of the transports by the time of their arrival. Over the next few days further lorries arrived with essential items.

By 18 September 3 and 12 Bty had moved to billets closer to their transport park, then on the 19th 3 Bty started out very early by road in convoy for *Le Mans*[†] which they reached late that night at around 2300 hrs. After halting for the night the guns were set up and manned and then their state of readiness declared. If the guns were in a state to be loaded and fired very shortly afterwards they were classed as 'In action'. However if they had a problem with the gun or with the ground that prevented it from being fired straight away, then it was classed as 'Out of action'.

By this time it had been decided that for maximum air defence the batteries would be split into four sections of two guns each and these would normally be called Section 'A' 'B' 'C' and 'D'. Gnr Weston was allocated as cook for 'B' section and would travel around wherever they went to provide their food. The Army marches on its stomach is a good maxim and his job was to maintain high morale.

12 and 15 Btys joined them via the *Le Mans* area some distance to the south west of *Vernon* and *Mantes* which were located to the west of *Paris*. By this date a trickle of first line reinforcements had boosted their numbers and these had arrived by train. To try and aid identification of where batteries were posted the sites were classed as M1, M2 etc. for *Mantes* and V1, V2 for *Vernon*. (See Map 1.)

Not long after this 12 Bty had set out and reached *Abbeville* and *L'Etoile* and they set up in farmland near the village of *Mouflers* some one and a half miles from *L'Etoile* and Bty HQ was comfortably ensconced in a Chateau in *Mouflers*. At the same time 3 Bty was 'In action' near the village of *Beaumetz* not far to the south west of the town of *Arras* with their HQ at *Gouves*. (See Map 2.)

At this time all the Btys were showing in their manpower returns they were at establishment strength which turned out to be about 302 men and NCOs plus 9 or 10 Officers. They were getting used to the countryside and

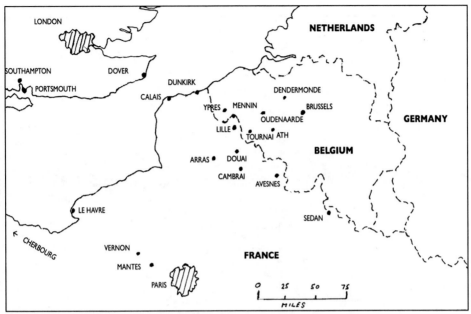

Map 1 6 HAA Regt locations as part of the BEF.

the constant moves but the weather was none too kind with periods of heavy rain.

Poland fell on 6 October after a gallant and hard fought campaign and all the while 6 Regt were continually setting up and then shifting to new locations. There was not even a note in any of their War Diaries about the news of Poland. They must have known, but perhaps they thought that this was an end to Hitler's ambitions. Meanwhile, elated with yet another success for his armed forces and his belligerent policy, Hitler now very generously decided to offer the UK peace terms as long as they kept their noses out of it.

At this time the whole Regt was set up close to the Belgian border. In early October 15 Bty was at *Ecoust* with two 4-gun positions, having shifted from *Croiselles* to *Noreuil* with one and from *Veavacourt* to *Hendecourt* with the other. Each time they set up they had had to construct pads for the guns to sit on and also dugouts for the protection of the men, and generally make the site operational. 12 Bty had been instructed to move to the railhead at *Aubigny* to protect 1st Corps. and get the men billeted in the local town. Their other task was to cover the crossings over the *Somme*.

Hardly had they arrived than they were ordered to move again via *Frevent* to *St Pol* on the *Arras* road and stop at *Savy Berlette*.

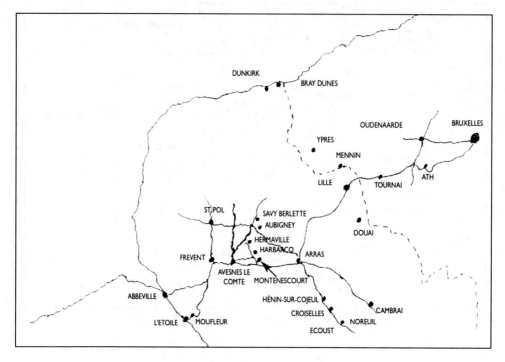

Map 2 French and Belgian border

ST POL	ABBEVILLE	MENNIN
SAVY BERLETTE	MONTENESCOURT	YPRES
AUBIGNEY	HÉNIN-SUR-COJEUL	OUDENAARDE
HERMAVILLE	CROISELLES	TOURNAI
HARBARCQ	ECOUST	FREVENT
ARRAS	NOREUIL	MOUFLEUR
AVESNES LE COMTE	CAMBRAI	ATH
L'ETOILE	DOUAI	

3 Bty had also had a series of brief stopovers as they progressed closer to the Belgian border. The villages of *Avesnes, Montenescourt* and *Tilloy Les Hermaville* were home for two weeks during which time they had reported seeing only friendly aircraft. The reason they only saw friendly ones was probably because the *Luftwaffe* had been busy elsewhere over Poland.

So too, for an aircraft to appear over their positions in the north of France meant it must have had to fly very high across neutral Belgium or fly in over the sea to the north of the Netherlands, or come in via the Ardennes region and then head northwards over French territory. Later what few they did see would seem to have been on photographic missions checking to see where the Allies were set up with their airfields; there was no need to check on the French and Belgians since their defences had been static for years and well documented already. By flying very high they knew they were almost impregnable to AA gunfire and could carry out their tasks unmolested.

At this stage the BEF had arrived at its delegated locations around the north end of the French/Belgian border. To their left flank and further north was the French 7th army. To their right flank and more south easterly was the French 1st followed by the French 9th, 2nd and 3rd Armies. It can be seen that the BEF was therefore a very small cog in a much larger wheel; in fact just a tenth of the total forces there. At this time the British Expeditionary Forces and the French troops were prevented from entering Belgium in case it aggravated the Germans and gave them cause to use this as the excuse for invasion. What it did in fact was allow the Germans to carry out their policies unmolested and thereby meant that the first strike would have to come from them and also at a time, date and place of their choosing.

In the meantime the troops had started building a series of gun positions and strong points with the usual infantry trench works to cover what they could along their section of this weak border. Through the latter part of 1939 they had plenty of time to build reasonable defences, unhindered by any action from the German forces in what became known as 'The Phoney War'.

Plans had already been drawn up, called Operation Dyle, so that any attack on Belgium would allow the BEF to advance to the river of this name inside Belgium and link up with the defending forces to repel any incursion. However during the long uneasy months when nothing appeared to be happening the Generals kept adding extra tasks for the gunners to defend, especially new airfields. All these airfields, along with canal bridges, important manufacturing bases, rail junctions, some crossroads, supply dumps and oil storage facilities and ports, would need anti aircraft protection. They realised it would be an impossible task to defend every point that was deemed at risk.

The daily routine was to man the guns from first light and once breakfast was over working parties started again on improving the defences and dugouts. Hard standings had to be prepared and defensive sandbag walls built around the guns as anti splinter and strafing protection. Access roads had to be kept in good order so that rapid moves could be made.

Towards the latter part of October whilst all the Btys were still reporting only friendly aircraft, 15 Bty had an opportunity to break the tedium. On the 26th a low flying aircraft suddenly appeared from cloud and was judged as 'a possible unfriendly'. At this time there was an instruction that any friendly aircraft at low altitude should fly with their undercarriages down when over friendly forces. Whether the pilot was aware of this odd order or *was* in fact an 'unfriendly' was never discovered, but none the less a single round was fired at it and it disappeared quickly back in the clouds.

12 Bty had also had several re-shuffles of gun positions but large amounts of rain had stopped the digging of dugouts which kept flooding. They had had to resort to digging surface drainage to try and solve the problem and channel away the continual torrents. The aircraft that they reported were all either Lysanders or Blenheim bombers and nothing hostile.

As the BEF continued to build up its forces more aircraft were deployed in France and so airfields were being hastily constructed or in some cases existing ones taken over. Many were just suitable grassy fields of sufficient size to allow aircraft to land and take off unimpeded. The necessary stores and personnel accommodation was usually provided by tentage. Each new potential target also added to the task of AA defences which were needed to protect it.

The AA gunners were spread exceedingly thin and at that stage of the campaign good radio location of hostile aircraft was almost non existent. They relied on the old fashioned method of firing by eye and at night were virtually blind.

The O/C of 12 Bty, Maj. JO Horne, besides complaining of the terrible weather also had concerns for the state of his men's boots which were falling apart. Luckily the QM's department saved the day when they rushed in replacements.

November saw little change. Plenty of rain and no real activity, either in the air or on the ground.

This false sense of security had been already dubbed 'the Phoney War' when not much seemed to be happening; however in fact although not much was happening over the Allied side, plenty was going on in the German side. Vast troop deployments were being made, armoured formations hidden in woodland, stores of petrol kept under netting, dumps of ammunition piled high, most of it quietly and without fanfare as Hitler lined up his next targets.

By the end of the first week of November long awaited supplies of sandbags arrived for the gunners. These were desperately needed to provide the anti splinter protection for the guns and equipment. No guns had been bombed as such or even strafed but the risk was very real. 15 Bty had one reinforcement in the form of Gnr 819084 R. Reynolds and at the same time A/Sgt 828981 R. Yapp left to go to the UK on an RDF course (primitive radar).

It should be remembered too that at this time most guns did not have

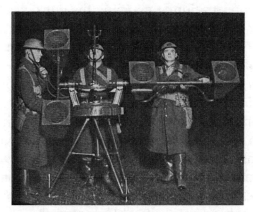

Fig. 1.1 Very primitive early sound locator.

effective searchlight location equipment for finding aircraft in the dark. There was a very primitive system of sound locators which was virtually useless even for one incoming aircraft and totally overwhelmed when more than one came. (Fig.1.1)

On 21 November one of the 3 Bty sections at *Tilloy Les Hermaville* spotted a Heinkel between 21,000 ft and 24,000 ft. This was eagerly engaged with 11 rounds fired before it flew out of range. There was no visible result seen. On the same day another Bty at *Avesnes Le Comte* witnessed another Heinkel, this time flying at the moderate height of about 11,200 ft. They fired 13 rounds and it disappeared swiftly into a rain cloud apparently unperturbed. Both aircraft made no effort to attack so were presumably out on reconnaissance. The next day several men of 3 and 12 Btys from the sites at M1–M4 also saw between them further aircraft and a Heinkel was engaged with three rounds, but like the previous ones it showed no signs of being damaged. The problem was that aircraft were difficult to see especially at high altitude and by the time the gun had been trained they were more often than not out of range.

Aircraft recognition was still an inexact science and depended on the eyesight of the observer and also his experience, though one Officer of 15 Bty noted that *'despite the height of one, the black crosses were easily distinguishable on a Junkers 87 though sadly it was out of range'*.

To boost the morale of the men and also allow senior Officers to get a feel for what it was like on the ground, visits were made to various gun sites. On 24 November 15 Bty was visited at *Ecoust* by the Commandant of the Staff College and accompanied by General Officers from 1st Corps. The site they chose was close to *Noreuil*. As with all these visits everything had to be spick and span and a demonstration of manning the guns was laid on. Even if it was hard work for the gunners at least it focused their minds on the real reason for being there. If the visitor was satisfied then a congratulatory message usually followed shortly after.

Mobile 3.7" guns were labour intensive to 'man' and on average needed 7–10 men just to fire a shell and this was without the ancillary men who worked the vital equipment to enable the range and height to be calculated. There had to be an NCO in charge taking and passing on the instructions. Two men sat on seats either side of the barrel facing rearwards, one controlling the elevation and the other the traverse. One man controlled the actual firing, two men were used on the complicated process of fusing the shells and one man loaded them into the tray. The remainder were needed to fetch and carry shells from the ready-use magazine storage. The weight of the shells was something over 60 lbs so it was not for the unfit. Besides these gunners there had to be other men within the unit for protection of gun sites once set up. Armed with rifles and LMGs and used to guard RHQ these men had a basic infantry role.

On 25 November two sections of guns from 12 Bty at *Savy Berlette* were detailed off to take over positions from the nearby 210 Bty at *Camphin* which were in 2nd Corps area. So that the vacated positions of 12 Bty were kept manned, two sections from 3 Bty were moved in. The sites in the area were designated as *Savy Berlette (M7), Villers Chatel (M8), Haute Avesnes (M2), Montenecourt (M3), Avesnes Le Comte (M5)* and *Tilloy Les Hermaville (M6)*.

Despite all these temporary moves there was still an air of unreality that they were actually at war with Germany. Men were allowed into the local villages to drink and have a meal and try the local French wines. Those who could speak any sort of French had a distinct advantage. Men were still going back to the UK for leave and for many of the others who had never left the UK before the whole experience was rather novel. Gnr Weston writes again to say he won't be back for Christmas since he has drawn the short straw but will get his leave shortly after.

The French by this time have realised that with the thousands of troops stationed over there, they have a golden opportunity to make and sell extra souvenirs. A selection of rather attractive *Carte Postale* are produced in the form of silk embroidery of flowers and birds and in some cases joined flags of the two nations, and with a short message for a loved one. These are very popular and contain a small hidden pocket in which the sender can include a secret message. Gnr Weston thinks these are perfect for his wife to whom he sends several over the next few weeks.

Unfortunately the two sections who had moved into the old 210 Bty location found things not as they would have liked. The gun platforms were set on soft ground and the guns tended to sink in under their own weight, also the sandbagging was not of a very good quality and unstable and looked likely to fall over at any moment. These guns weighed something in the order of over 8 tons and when fired the recoil would add considerably to the ground pressures and any weakness would cause the guns to settle or tilt. Large quantities of ballast were found and the guns moved out while this was placed.

On 30 November the 3 Bty O/C Maj. Revel-Smith MC left to take command of 53rd LAA Regt and his place was taken by Capt. Stokes-Rees. 12 Bty was augmented by a Lt Lowman and a section of Brigade signallers from 1st Corps.

They proceeded to run wires to the various gun positions for communications and tapped into the air-raid warning system from *Lille*.

To emphasise the need for the troops to relax when off duty, a travelling troop of performers arrived one morning, called Mr Henson's Concert Party. They went through the usual repertoire of songs and current jokes in an effort to boost morale and remind the men of home. Once it was over it was back to improving the gun sites again.

December 1939 started quietly with no serious air threats to any of the Btys.

3 Bty had an influx of 8 new gunners: Gnr 7778821 Skivington, G.; Gnr 828220 Gifford, T., Gnr 809522 Smith, C.; Gnr 1426245 Hunter, J.; Gnr 1427112 Hunter, W.; Gnr 781437 Laught, L.; Gnr 826395 Reeks, G., and Gnr 838559 Coleman, G.

Sadly Gnr Hunter, J. would lose his life in the Far East two years later and Skivington, G. would die in the UK in 1947. One further reinforcement arrived shortly after on 6 December – Gnr 798297 Davies, T., who would die on the Burma railway.

7 December was something of a red letter day with a VIP who turned out to be none other than H.M. the King accompanied by the Duke of Gloucester and various senior Officers. They inspected 3 Bty at *Camphin* and were duly impressed. (Or at least that was the impression given!)

The troops continued with their daily routines occasionally sighting aircraft at high altitude but not engaging them. Life had settled into a rather boring routine of manning the guns and fatigues. However on 18 December winter came in with a vengeance and caught the batteries by surprise, especially 12 Bty. A sudden and very hard frost did serious damage to many vehicles. They reported one Scammel gun-towing lorry with cracked cylinder liners, four 3 ton lorries with sheared pump spindles and several Commer light utility vehicles also out of action. The cold also made it universally difficult to start many of their vehicles.

The severity which lasted all day also prevented one gun in 'A' section from coming into action. Water had frozen in the traverse track and the only way to melt this was with the use of a brazier. Sandbag work was also curtailed since not only was the sand and soil frozen solid but the bags were useless as well. Then to add insult to injury a dense fog descended making it impossible to see anything let alone spot for aircraft.

At *Ecoust* 15 Bty's O/C Maj. G.A. Moxon left for a few days and Capt. G.W. Mates took over.

Shortly after yet another warning order of a move came through, this time for the guns to go to a position north of *Douai*. This involved a reconnaissance first to find suitable sites and also billets for the men, so Capt. Mates and Lt Channells drove over to look for gun positions while Lt Pain made the necessary arrangements for accommodation. This time Bty HQ was going to be set up in *Douai* itself. Christmas came at last and despite the cold and awful weather, morale was reported as good. Each Battery did its best to have a party and keep the true Christmas spirit. Whilst this move went ahead 15 Bty also moved out of their locations on the 29th from their troop site called 'E1'. The vacuum was filled by a troop from 17 HAA Bty being drafted across.

On the last day of the year Capt. Pinney joined from 1st HAA Regt and took over the O/C position of 12 Bty. By 3 January 1940 all sections had relocated to areas around *Douai*. And these had the designation letters D1–D4.

The intense cold kept a firm grip on the countryside and curtailed much in the way of improvements to the defences. The ongoing effect on the vehicles was acute, and the maintenance sections at *Camphin* were hard pushed to keep ahead of the multitude of problems. The big worry was that should a general move be ordered then there could well be a shortage of transport.

In the second week of January 1940, 15 Bty was inspected by Brigadier Milligan who coincidently had been the 6 Regt CO before mobilisation.

Sightings of enemy aircraft were few and far between possibly because of the poor weather. However from a German aircraft that had been forced to make an emergency landing during this bad weather on 11 January 1940 a complete set of plans were recovered showing just what the Germans were intending. Amazingly no one seemed to be unduly upset by this gold mine of information or if they were they certainly did not show it.

Things continued in their day to day routine, troops digging defences and putting out wire obstacles while the Engineers carried on building large numbers of concrete pillboxes as strong points, and no one interfering with the progress. The worst they had to contend with was the extremely severe winter which meant placing concrete was not very satisfactory and keeping warm was the main occupation.

By late January T.S.M. Adamson of 12 Bty had been promoted to 2/Lt and took up a post in 18 Bty.

On the weather front things improved slightly but that did not last. The roads had been severely disrupted by the cold and snow.

For the last three weeks of January all leave had been cancelled because of the military situation and the men had been ordered to draw three days iron rations, and all vehicles had been filled with sufficient petrol for 75 miles.

Manpower returns for all the batteries show they were up to establishment strength which all seemed to be around 302 NCOs and men plus about ten Officers. The Officers in 15 Bty (around October/November 1939) were listed as Maj. Moxon, Capt. Pinney, Capt. Chennells, Lts Young, Hibbert and Roe, and 2/Lts Pain, Moffat and Gilby. There was one attached Officer for training purposes called 2/Lt MacPherson. 2/Lt Gilby had originally been a Sergeant and promoted by Maj. Moxon; he was a very efficient soldier with lots of drive and would go on to win an MC at Dunkirk.

Of the others 12 Bty reported that its Officers were Maj. A.W. Webster, Maj. J.O. Horne, Capt. J.R. Stokes-Rees and 2/Lts P.A. Porteous, P.D. Morris, H.R. Martin, F.R. Gadd, W. Rouston, K. Campbell and R.G. Samworth.

3 Bty reported that their complement was Maj. W.R. Revel-Smith, Capt. J.M. Douglas, Lt A.C. Holmes and 2/Lts F.C.W. Timmins, W.L. Sherrard, D.W. Wilkinson, W.S. Clarke, G.A.M. Hills, H.B. Hare-Scott. In a fast changing situation Officers moved around quite often, especially on promotion or to replace others while on leave or courses.

Within three months 12 Bty had new Officers in the shape of Maj. B. Pinney and Capt. T.W. Gracey and some younger 2/Lts joined 3 Bty: 2/Lts P.F. Horton and D.C. Lightbody. (The twin majors in 12 Bty was a transition phase before Maj. Webster left.)

However on 7 February a tragic death occurred in 12 Bty, that of BSM F. Edwards No 1419624. His death is recorded as '*died from self inflicted injuries*'. No clue is given as to whether this was a tragic accident or a wilful act of suicide. Whatever the reason, it must have come as a bit of a shock to all those who knew him and the immediate members of the Bty. As a BSM he would have been known to a wide circle of Officers and O/Rs.

On 26 February TSM Dixon-Didier left to return to 18 Bty and the new BSM for 12 Bty was BSM Jinks.

During the first week of March the batteries continued to consolidate their gun stations and air activity was still very sporadic. On the night of 9 March 15 Bty heard two flights of enemy aircraft over the *Douai* area. No bombs were dropped on either D1 or D2 but from a height of about 1500 ft hundreds of propaganda leaflets came fluttering and drifting down to land in fields and hedgerows and parts of the town. Since neither location was equipped with either searchlights or RDF the aircraft could not be engaged.

This rather shows up the shortcomings of the AA defences at the time. This was not the only bad shortcoming in the BEF, signals equipment and the ability to stay in contact with widely spaced units was in a shocking state. Much of the time the only way to keep in contact was via despatch riders or in extreme circumstances to use the public telephone system. For some reason the French had always chosen this latter option and it would come home to haunt them in the days ahead.

Possibly as a result of this incident, or perhaps they were already worried about the situation, three lorries were despatched to *Le Havre* to collect some RDF items. On the ground tactical exercises were carried out by the troops and then on the 19th a whole load of this RDF equipment was delivered. This must have been a welcome asset for the gunners and was immediately set up and tuned by specialists and men from the signal corps. After this on the 20th all guns were manned during the night as well as the day and all Btys equipped with 'Identification Telescopes Mk 1' were ordered to hand them in and collect the new Mk 3.

The new RDF proved problematical because of its sensitivity and ground conditions and the obvious inexperience of the operators. However when it was working it did give extra cover and warning of approaching aircraft and although it meant extra work in the form of manning the guns, it did allow for night firing.

On 29 March Gnr 780837 F. Eastaugh of 15 Bty who had been in the No. 8 casualty clearing station died. Their diary does not say whether he had been injured or died from some other cause. A funeral party was gathered on the 31st and he was interred with full military honours at the cemetery in *Bois Carre* close by.

April started with a heightening of the tension and further reshuffling of the Btys. 15 Bty were instructed to move yet again and consolidate defences round *Douai* but in two new locations to be known as D4 and D5. One of the drivers attached to 15 Bty was called Cripps and with usual gunner's phlegm he derided the constant moves for no apparent purpose, roundly cursing all involved. He would feature again in the Regt's story of the Far East.

Because these were new sites they had moved into, they had to make each one into a fully manned site with gun platforms and access roads in and out, a task that by now they were getting very good at. Loads of stone were imported to allow this to be carried out along with extra sandbags.

12 Bty had the job of providing a series of mobile patrols along the *Arras* to *Cambrai* road and Bty HQ set up near *Chamblain-Chatelain*. The remaining guns were set up on two sites notated as B4 at *La Clarence* and B5 at *Pressy-le-Peanes*.

Very heavy rain made life uncomfortable and two Nissen huts complete with duck-boards were acquired and erected, which it was hoped would make life a little more comfortable.

Gnr Weston keeps up his correspondence on a regular basis, saying that the mail continues to arrive in good time and apart from the terrible rainy weather he has a cold. They are at the time billeted in a farm. He thanks his wife for her latest parcel of cigarettes and goodies but would like some of her homemade cakes. For a cook he asks rather surprisingly for some Oxo cubes and then as an afterthought requests an extra vest because of the weather.

10 April brought news of the German landings in Norway.

For the next four days the Btys were kept on 6 hours notice to move out. Because they could not take all their equipment the RDF sets, such as they were, were given to 4th HAA Regt. To add to the men's discomfort a severe storm on the 13th blew down their Nissen huts after the bolts sheared off, probably a sign they had not been erected very well. Because they now had no RDF they reverted to a system called 'Spider's Web' which worked on the fact that the GOR (Gunners Operation Room) was treated as the centre of the web for target identification directions.

On the 20th the two troops of 12 Bty both fired 6 rounds at a Dornier around midnight. Although no results were recorded it at least cheered the men up no end.

The rest of April ticked by with no hint of what was to come. On the 30th Maj. Stokes-Rees left 3 Bty and the new O/C was Capt. J.E. Bailey.

By early May, 15 Bty had been temporarily detached to come under the command of 1st HAA Regt. and they were spread out around *Hal* and *Flers* and joined the two other batteries numbered 16 and 17 which were part of 1st HAA Regt. May began much the same as all the other months but then on 10 May the Germans struck. All gun batteries were manned in the early hours. There were several raids over the 12 Bty area and they engaged the flights of bombers that came within range.

The confused situation can best be summed up by one of the gunners of 15 Bty, Tom Evans, in his recollections in the book *The Sparrows* by Tony Paley. Tom was the ex-miner from the Midlands (Wednesfield) and had joined the Artillery in the mid thirties and then been demobbed in 1937. When 6 Regt mobilised at Arborfield in 1939 he had rejoined and now become part of the BEF that had landed in France. They had been moved all over the place and spent much time at 'stand to' alongside their guns and with the lack of action had started to become very bored. However during this second week of May it all took off.

> We were sited in fields and early in the morning of May 10th all hell broke loose. Everyone was 'stood to' and manning their guns and predictors.
>
> When it became lighter we could see the sky was full of German aircraft, bombers with fighter escorts.
>
> The battery opened fire with their old 3" guns but the aircraft were flying far too high for effective fire.
>
> After some time news filtered in that the Germans had broken through.
>
> Further waiting for orders resulted in the guns being moved again with the intention of finding a place to hold up the attacks.
>
> These moves were not without risk and many times Stukas dive bombed us.

Once full daylight came it was realised that the German army had attacked the Low Countries and Belgium, not at one or two points but along much of the 300 mile front. There had long been a thought that the Germans might attack somewhere but the Allies were taken totally by surprise by its ferocity and extent.

Hitler's excuse was that he feared an attack by the Allies and Belgians against him, so he had got in first. Paratroops had neutralised the large underground fort at Eben Emael on Belgium soil and the *Luftwaffe* and *Wehrmacht* introduced the new concept of bitzkrieg. The total indiscriminate bombing of airfields went ahead, despite many of them being neutral.

This was the long awaited excuse needed for the BEF to advance into Belgium and come to the aid of this country. The Allied armies upped sticks and boldly advanced as part of Operation Dyle. As the gunners crossed the frontier into Belgium they were greeted in the villages by civilians lining the route waving heartily and handing out bottles of wine.

Continuous gunfire could be heard in the distance and at night the flashes lit up the sky from heavy action at the front. In the chaos of a fluid situation several plans were put forward and as quickly overtaken by events.

On 11 May as men were moved forward to join 15 Bty at two sites called H1 and H2 there was a casualty. Gnr J.L. Swales No. 4383007 was killed. The Bty diary says he was 'killed on the way up by lorry'. It gives no further details and although the possibility is he might have been run over and killed it is far more likely that since they were not within shelling range, he was killed by an air strike on a convoy.

Allied thinking put the German advance till it got to the front lines as about three weeks. All the carefully prepared gun positions were now abandoned as mobile AA units pushed forward as part of the advance. By evening in what was a very confused situation 15 Bty now held four sites close to *Ypres*, one section each at *Gheluvelt and Mennin* and two sections at *St Elody*. Bty HQ was at *Zillebeke* and Regt HQ at *Boezinge*. Some of these famous names must have seemed to come back to haunt them since most were known from First World War days and some of the older men may well have even been stationed there before. In the intervening years nature had not completely disguised the ravages on the countryside and in places the devastation and old trench lines could still be made out.

12 Bty made its way to the *Denderhoutem* area with their four sections split between *Liederkirke, Denderhoutem* and *Heldergem* and a further site some one and a half miles south of *Liederkirke*.

3 Bty left *Hermaville* and advanced to *Tournai*; here they set up two troop gun stations at positions called T1 and T6. Their BHQ stayed at *Port-a-Caw*.

On 12 May men from 15 Bty reported seeing a Heinkel 111 with British markings. This seems highly unlikely and they most probably misidentified another sort of aircraft as the result of jittery nerves.

During the confusion as the Allies advanced to the river Dyle they were constantly subjected to the blitzkrieg tactic. However once they reached it, it turned out to be not much better than a water filled ditch. The supposed defences, which the Belgians had not allowed the BEF to view beforehand, were equally inadequate and in many cases non-existent. Frantic work was put in hand to try and correct these defence inadequacies, forcing the gunners to set to and form new pads and sandbag walls yet again.

Having three different forces on the ground each speaking a different language and each considering they had their own area of responsibility made the situation almost uncontrollable.

The Germans continued to employ their tactic, totally new to the ground forces, of 'blitzkrieg' whereby their land forces were closely accompanied by the *Luftwaffe* whose job was to 'take out', or soften up, all strong points in advance and then carry out constant bombing of all targets in front of the rapidly moving front line. This technique employed large forces of highly mobile armoured formations in conjunction with heavy bombing raids and lightning thrusts of large troop units on the ground. Likely forming up places and vital transport systems on the Allied side were heavily bombed to prevent reinforcements getting to the front to oppose them. So taken by surprise were the BEF that they very quickly found themselves being out-flanked and this led to a series of hotly fought withdrawals.

The French like the Allies had been strictly forbidden to enter Belgian soil until the first move had been made by the German troops. There were several part completed lines of defence along the Belgian border, none of which appealed to them. They had seen what heavy fighting in the First World War had done to the northern areas of France and preferred to take on the Germans inside Belgium and let them suffer the damage.

The early advances were about as far as they got. General thinking had been that it would take the Germans about three weeks before they broke through and during this time substantial forces could be brought up; however so rapid were the Germans advancing that while waiting for orders to counter-attack, the Allies left intact many bridges for this manoeuvre and these were promptly taken undamaged by the leading German elements.

Any Allied advances were not only being held, but taken apart. Allied aircraft in large numbers bombed the advanced German positions but came up against scores of anti aircraft guns positioned as defence by the Germans around their leading units.

The attacks became a massacre and dozens of Allied aircraft were shot down by the ever efficient gunners with their 88 m/m AA guns. Initially these had been designed for AA use but against armour would turn out to be a formidable weapon.

After a few days in this position a large German armoured thrust was made in the 'impenetrable' Ardennes sector. They punched through the French lines and headed for the fortress of Sedan which was supposed to guard the gap. The French and Belgians were set in their policy of sitting in static positions like the Maginot Line and fighting off their attacker from there. They had no experience of fast moving warfare and once the line was breached they were in serious trouble.

The German Generals had cleverly avoided having to crack the 'Maginot nut' and just bypassed the obstruction leaving it to be dealt with later. This vast and hugely expensive defence line had turned out to be just a 'white elephant'.

Rapid advances on all fronts left the BEF continually withdrawing and trying to hold defensive lines against a relentless well-disciplined and well-armed foe, superior in just about every form of weapon both in quality and quantity. Just when the BEF had reached what they considered a suitable position to dig in and defend, they found themselves again at risk of being outflanked, so they slowly fell back in a fighting withdrawal towards the distant coast. The armies the Germans had met near the Ardennes sector were largely composed of old French reservists and they soon fled at the severity of the onslaught allowing armoured forces to stream through. The gunners of all Btys now found themselves targets for bombers wherever they set up.

On 13 May, 12 Bty had had an early success. 'B' section brought down a Junkers 88 when a well-aimed shot put shrapnel in its starboard engine. The aircraft came down steeply with smoke and flames belching from the damage to crash some distance away.

On the same day, between them 'B' and 'C' sections hit three low-flying Dorniers and one was believed to have come down near *Tournath*.

On 15 May 'B' and 'D' also brought down another Junkers 88.

3 Bty was also involved with air defence but reported no confirmed successes.

The mighty fort at Sedan fell on 15 May. This opened up a route for the leading German units to go hell for leather towards the coast.

This cleverly operated outflanking manoeuvre was designed to cut the Allies in two and sweep them up into a large pocket. What the French failed to grasp when the Germans broke through, was that they were heading for the coast and not to invest *Paris*, and all the troops they withdrew for its defence were just wasted doing nothing to halt the advances.

By 16 May the BEF was in complete disorder and aiming to withdraw to Bruxelles and the Charleroi Canal and by 17 May the retreat had gathered momentum as demoralised French and Belgian forces fled towards the rear. Civilians also trying to avoid the fighting and carrying their meagre possessions on carts, prams and vehicles all helped to block the only roads available for reinforcements to counter-attack.

The German advances in the south were so fast that the generals were worried about outstripping their supply routes. When someone noticed this on the Allied side in the area near Arras, a quickly put together counter-attack was mounted by two battalions and some tanks against a lightly defended side in the rear of the German advanced spearhead. It was very nearly successful and caused complete confusion for a while but the general in charge rallied his men and held the Allies off. His name was Erwin Rommel and his name would become more famous to the Allies in North Africa later.

Around 17 May 15 Bty were still heavily engaged at *Ypres*. 3 Bty moved back to *Capelle* and *Ouvignes* while 12 Bty relocated to *Oudenaarde* and were tasked with defending the bridge at *Escant*. Their HQ was by now set up in *Heirwig*.

These were a series of desperate moves from higher echelons to try and halt the onslaught and at the same time try and avoid being outflanked.

On 19 May 3 Bty moved yet again, this time to *Asuc* and *Flers* for three days.

It was now a case of trying to hold the German advances at all cost. The *Wehrmacht* always worked well in conjunction with their *Luftwaffe* and hoping to disrupt this was all the gunners could do. It had been only a matter of days and the French and Belgian forces had collapsed and were in full retreat.

Because of the way the French defences had been laid out, once the strong points had been either knocked out or bypassed the countryside behind was relatively easy going. During the relentless onslaught, every time the Allies gave up an airfield it was immediately put to use by the Luftwaffe who continued to keep up the pressure.

So hasty were the withdrawals, that in most cases insufficient demolitions, or in many cases no demolitions at all, had been carried out to render the airfields unusable.

Batteries of the 6 HAA Regt which had been dispersed within the BEF found themselves constantly under air attack. Their few radar sets were not of great quality and much of the shooting was done by old-fashioned methods of barrage fire by eye. (Fig. 1.2)

It was known that 3" and 3.7" guns were unsuitable for defence against dive bombers. This was because of their slow traverse and with the primitive radar they could not track down quickly enough. It was also known they could not cope with fast low flying ground attacks either for a similar reason. It was found best to leave both these sorts of attack to the Light Anti Aircraft weapons which were predominantly 40 m/m Bofors or as a last resort hand-held Lewis guns on mounts.

By this time 12 Bty had moved back to the town of *Harelbeke* and were attempting to defend *Courtai* with a secondary role of Anti Tank.

Fig. 1.2 3.7" mobiles firing a barrage.

As the situation became more critical one troop found themselves defending a road block against infantry and tanks. It was not usually considered tactical to fire these AA guns from the horizontal because there was a risk of damage to the mountings, although the idea had obviously been considered because there were passages in the instruction manuals on just this type of action, but needs must and these were desperate times. The 3" and 3.7" AA guns had quite enough punch to defeat any of the then current Panzer tanks. They lowered their barrels and over open sights took on the German tanks and knocked out two before they came under heavy shelling and mortar fire causing them to have to move yet again.

The effects of their heavy calibre shells against thin armour were devastating. Unable to recover all their damaged guns they disabled them so that they could not be used and then reverted to becoming infantry and hurriedly withdrew. The overall plan was for as many men as possible to withdraw to the coastal area and form a cohesive perimeter there.

Next day (20th) 'D' section relocated to *Svegegham* for the defence of the bridge that crossed the canal and had the uncomfortable experience of being there when low flying bombers attempted to destroy it but without success. Near misses threw up earth and debris but the bridge remained intact.

Guns were being moved about at short notice tying to find suitable lines to defend. They were subjected to air attacks during the day, and even at night bombers continued to drop flares to light up the country lanes and keep up the assault. 15 Bty temporarily lost one of its sections in the mayhem but by evening their CO had located them and after diverting round *Avelin* which was full of French tanks they rejoined the Bty. Not helping in the chaos were people who were going round purporting to be Liaison Officers and telling units to withdraw. It was never confirmed who they were, whether imagined fifth columnists or actually enemy agents.

A report had been circulated several times about a Lysander being flown by Germans. This was dismissed but they had great difficulty trying to convince the section commanders not to open fire on it.

The situation had now become so serious that on 21st 15 Bty were ordered to destroy all their documents with the exception of Pay Books and War Diaries.

They also had to provide some Bren gunners and eight men to go to a flank to help defend part of Vimy Ridge (a name well known to WW1 Canadians).

They were expending ammunition so fast that instructions came through not to engage any aircraft over 10,000 ft and shortly after that a maximum of eight rounds only to be expended per gun at any aircraft. Also because small arms ammunition was in short supply instructions were given that no aircraft was to be engaged with the Bren or Lewis guns over 500 ft.

However they were informed that ammunition trains were waiting with fresh supplies at three locations, namely *La Bassen, Lille* and *Marquelles* if only they could get there. On the 22nd while *Ypres* was being subjected to heavy bombing 15 Bty finally managed to get away and set out south for *Radinghem* about 6 miles west of *Lille*. Here they recorded their first confirmed 'kill'. During barrage fire 'A' section brought down a Junkers from about 8000 ft with a direct hit. A fluke occurrence but nevertheless a tonic under the circumstances.

The withdrawal to the coast was fast becoming a rout and the Bty moved again to *Armentiers–Messine–Kemmel* in order to try and protect 4 Corps as they withdrew to the Dunkirk enclave. The men would have remembered the name '*Armentiers*' since it featured in a ribald soldiers' song from the First World War and involved a certain Mademoiselle.

Some of the moves were of such a short duration that the guns did not in fact set up on their 'davits'. The gunners found the best places to hide and left them with their wheels in place. It was not recommended to try and fire in this situation but it could be done if necessary. The continual movement was always in a westerly direction and heading for the coast.

Once 15 Bty had set up again nearer to the outskirts of the perimeter they witnessed a Heinkel spotter plane flying alone. The Bty opened fire but while this was happening they noticed a bomber making repeated attacks against a Bofors gun position not far away.

We decided to switch fire to this more lucrative target and opened up with shrapnel shells. After not many rounds we hit it and it went into a dive and crashed not far away scattering debris all over the fields. The whole crews cheered loudly and later some men went off to look at the sight of the remains. Some of them came back with souvenirs of bits and pieces and even some of the aircraft instruments.

On 22 May the RAF had finally pulled out all their remaining aircraft so the Luftwaffe was relieved somewhat from the worry of air attack by fighters. This left the BEF increasingly vulnerable with a totally inadequate air defence.

During this chaotic withdrawal 3 Bty reached the village of *Recques-sur-Hem*. The guns were pulled by their tractor vehicles into a side street not far from the central square. Men and stores were hidden and spread about in any suitable location away from the road. An air of panic gripped the local inhabitants who although used to troops stationed there were not to be fooled about how serious the situation was. Gunfire had been heard for days and German aircraft seen overhead, and the roads were being choked by countless civilians trying to get away to safety with what belongings they could carry.

Late in the afternoon of the 22nd an Allied Army truck was driving about its business and passed over a crossroads on the *Zouafques* road close to the central square. Unknown to the occupants they were spotted by three German armoured cars that formed the advance party of a reconnaissance unit. These opened fire and the truck accelerated away and disappeared from the Germans' view round the corner. One of the armoured cars followed and in a skirmish the driver of the truck and one soldier who had jumped out the back were killed. The remaining troops scattered and managed to escape to safety.

The soldier killed was Gnr William Johnson No. 1071399 from 3 Bty. Both casualties were later buried in the local churchyard but this produced a mystery many years later. Three graves now sit in their own little plot (the third being of a soldier killed in the First World War). The central grave is of a New Zealand civilian called Albert J Lawson aged 24, whose headstone records he died 'serving the BEF'. What his duties were, or how he came to be there has not been resolved, unless he was driving the truck. William Johnson's grave is on the right in the row.

3 Bty reached *Armentiers* and *Kellen* on 23 May. The ever decreasing size of the enclave now concentrated thousands of troops in a strip some 15 miles long and about 9 wide.

The German forces had finally reached the coast south of Dunkirk and closed the door on 26 May. The port of *Boulogne* eventually fell after heavy fighting. There was now no way the BEF could move south to link with the remaining forces on French soil.

At this time Dunkirk was the only port that could be used for evacuation, something the planners back in the UK had in mind. They thought they might be able to rescue some 45,000 troops before the whole BEF was forced to surrender. The scheme relied entirely on the French (and some Allied units) being able to rally and produce a rear guard to allow the bulk of the BEF to embark.

As the front line shrank large numbers of troops were forced into the area of the enclave with the channel port of *Dunkirk* in the south and the town of *La Panne* in the north and amongst this mêlée the gunners had also found their way back too. It was a scene of total confusion with control being lost over much of the encircled forces.

By the 27th the order had gone out to destroy all transports and stores not associated with the guns themselves. It was specifically stated that the vehicles should not be set on fire so as to avoid drawing German attention to them. In this way hundreds of lorries and smaller vehicles had their sump plugs removed and the engines run till they seized.

On entering Dunkirk the Btys found the roads were heavily congested. Ditches and fields were full of discarded equipment and personal items such as blankets, stores and paperwork. Large amounts of destroyed vehicles gave off wisps of smoke, smashed radio equipment lay about in heaps. As they passed through the perimeter they came across lines of quickly dug slit trenches full of troops, protected by hastily erected barbed wire and road blocks. There was the usual ribald banter and exchange of remarks between regiments as they passed by.

Many of the troops had already dismounted and were making their way in on foot, long columns of men marching wearily to a fate they did not know. In the confusion many bodies lay about in the open covered by blankets since nobody had the time to worry about burying them. In the fields were the bloated dead bodies of innocent cows caught up by relentless shelling.

On the 28th the Belgians surrendered and immediately white flags and sheets started to appear on roofs, fences and makeshift poles. Whatever vehicles the locals could commandeer before they were destroyed were used to drive towards the German lines in order to surrender with columns of Belgian troops walking behind.

By a serious misunderstanding of orders from Col. Bridgman who was on Lord Gort's staff the word went out for the gunners to destroy their weapons and revert to infantry on 28th May. During the next 24 hours all those who had received this order smashed their predictors and spiked the guns. Three sections of 15 Bty 'A' 'C' and 'D' carried this out but 'B' section did not get the message till later.

After smashing the dial sights and removing the breech blocks, which they dutifully threw into a convenient canal, they then made their way north towards the dunes to join hundreds of others waiting there.

The next day a Sgt Proctor and a couple of men approached in a lorry. Tom Evans again:

> The lorry came along with the Sgt and two men in the back. He got out and asked if I would be prepared to go with them to try and rescue a gun to get it back into working order again. I thought to myself this is just crazy.
>
> We drove back along one of the crowded roads till we came to the guns still standing at the side of the road.
>
> The roads were full of retreating French troops who could only point behind them and repeat the words 'Boche'.
>
> It took some time to wade about in the canal to try and recover a breech block but we succeeded and installed it in the gun. We then limbered up the gun and towed it with us back to where we had just come from at La Panne.
>
> Here the gun was set up and ammunition found for it. It could not be fired accurately since the sights had been destroyed and there was no radar to go with it.
>
> However it was loaded and fired over open sights.
>
> For some reason the breech was not a good fit and gas escaped each time it fired ending up leaving the crew covered in soot.
>
> We continued to fire at any target we saw and even if we never hit anything at least it cheered up the troops waiting near by.
>
> We continued to fire until all the ammo was gone.
>
> The Germans must have had a spotter somewhere who had noticed us, for not long after they started shelling the area. One of their shells was close enough to burn part of the hair off driver Nairne making him look like a Red Indian. After this I ended up helping Bdr Hurst 'man' a bren-gun on one of the nearby bridges.

Once they had used up all the available ammunition they then rendered the gun unserviceable for the second time.

Around 28 May at the northern end of the perimeter in the small town of

La Panne the BEF HQ set up their base. By coincidence at *La Panne* there was still an intact cross-channel telephone cable which allowed General Gort to keep in touch with the UK and discuss matters and keep them informed of the crisis.

With radios virtually useless in most areas the other Generals had no such luxury and trying to keep abreast of what the situation really was and also to be in touch with their various headquarters was just about impossible.

For some reason the French had relied on using the country's telephone network but as lines were brought down, exchanges destroyed or overrun, the whole thing became a farce. Much vital information had to be delivered by despatch riders with the risk of being delayed or destroyed before it reached its destination.

As the situation became more critical the Generals decided that the only course open was to evacuate as many troops as they could and any equipment they could carry. In order to try and prevent a rapid collapse and ensuing panic from the other forces the whole scheme was kept secret from them for as long as possible.

Once they realised what was happening, of course, it was understandable they were furious, but they were now fighting to defend their own countries whereas Britain had to worry more about what would happen if the Germans beat the French and then went for the UK. At this stage it was pretty obvious that the French and Belgians were fighting a lost cause; it was only a matter of trying to get out what could be saved before the whole Continent was overrun. Much of the surrounding ground had been flooded and was too soft for armour so once the German guns got within range there was relentless and indiscriminate shelling.

The evacuation back to England had begun on 27 May from the dock areas of the Port of Dunkirk but proved far too slow and complicated by high tidal ranges and damaged lock gates. The senior naval officer Captain Tennant in desperation spent some time casting around for a better place and noticed the long stone mole that reached well out into the sea. He went to examine this and found it ideal because it had a timber walkway running along the top. Despite larger ships not being able to tie up right alongside they could at least anchor as close as they could get and then extend gangways across to allow for the drop in the tides.

It was also realised that men could also be taken off via boats from the beaches to the north and so large areas of sand dunes were used for forming up. The chaos continued and the situation at times was nothing short of farce. The beaches were wide and flat and were backed by tall dunes of fine sand and salt tolerant grasses. When the tide went out it went out a long way, many hundreds of yards in fact.

Queues of men four and five deep already snaked from the comparative safety of the dunes out across the beaches. Those at the front stood for hours in cold sea water up to their armpits, patiently waiting for the arrival of the next boat to carry them out to the larger ones anchored in deeper water. (Fig. 1.3)

Tom Evans became anxious at the slow progress and decided to swim out to the nearest boat which turned out to be a Naval minesweeper. Here he was pulled on board and then given a hot drink and wrapped in a warm blanket.

So too Gnr G. Daniels. When the time came for rescue he decided that the best thing was to swim for it. Being lucky enough to be one of those who could swim he made for the nearest boat. The weight of water absorbed by his uniform meant he had a terrific struggle to stay afloat and make headway. However he finally reached a boat and with his boots laced together and hanging round his neck he was pulled aboard by eager hands, a considerable struggle because of his exhaustion and having to grip the rope to be pulled out. Sadly many of those who were non-swimmers drowned just because they could not hold onto ropes thrown into the water.

Gunner Tart was also among those lucky enough to be taken off the beaches and returned to England on a Mersey ferry boat called *Royal Daffodil*. Having left all their guns and heavy equipment behind, after

Fig. 1.3 Troops waiting for rescue at Dunkirk, June 1940.   IWM NYP 68075

disabling it by destroying the vital components, the survivors from 6 HAA Regt had mostly made their way north to the beaches at the *La Panne* end of the salient.

Some of 15 Bty set up in a wood close to Bray Dunes with their last two remaining guns. It became so dangerous that they had to move out along with 1st AA's 17 Bty HQ who had also taken shelter. It was during this phase that they sustained another casualty. Hit and killed during the shelling was Gnr W.S. Orr, No 776669. He was subsequently buried in the Cemetery at *Froyennes*. It had not been long before they were spotted and the Germans started to shell the trees so they all made a dash for the racecourse at Dunkirk.

During this chaotic phase of the operations Tp Sgt Maj. McWade had followed 15 Bty to its multiple locations, even to being temporarily detached to 1st HAA Regt. It was also then that he volunteered to go back to some guns which had been abandoned and render them inoperable. For this he was awarded an MID.

Over the next few days they were eventually to get back to England via the services of a multitude of boats both large and small, mostly manned by the Royal Navy who also had their share of casualties. The RAF did their best to give what cover they could but flying time over the beachhead was limited. Much of the scene below was hidden by the smoke-filled haze.

On 30 May the lucky survivors of 3 Bty, who had also destroyed what guns equipment and transport they had arrived with, had made their way north along the coast to *Bray Dunes* too. Here they managed to find a ship and board her and were taken safely away to England.

On 1 June, at dawn, parts of 15 Bty embarked from the beaches near *La Panne* and the remainder of 12 Bty made good their escape too from the sand dunes near by.

After helping to organise the troops during the evacuation Tp Sgt Maj. McWade then found himself a place among the last thousand men to leave.

All their guns and heavy equipment had by now been destroyed, though 12 Bty did leave one mystery behind. Sometime between 28 and 30 May Gnr 1439284 John James Thackeray was killed. The mystery was that this name was an alias and his real name was J.J. Duddy. Why he preferred not to serve under his correct name is not known.

It had been an uncomfortable experience waiting around for rescue often under air attack by the *Luftwaffe* who dodged the RAF fighters to attack any target of opportunity. The whole scene was shrouded by the black oily smoke from burning storage tanks and destroyed vehicles.

Once safely on board a ship, survivors had the agonising wait while it lay at anchor just off the beaches for many hours taking on further men. These were easy targets for German dive bombers as were the mole and harbour area, and they made the most of it when the weather allowed good visibility.

Ships finally left when they felt they could no longer take on any more men and threaded their way through minefields and buoyed channels that marked the sandbanks and shallows for which the area was well known. Added to this nightmare for the captains were the multitude of wrecks of recently sunk ships, some of which were hidden at high tide and others blocking the narrow routes in. Once clear of these hazards they made full speed for the English coast to unload at any port that had room. Having discharged their valuable cargoes it was time to turn round and head back again into the channel to pick up another load. The crews worked till they dropped from lack of sleep but bravely carried out these crossings knowing that they were the only hope for so many thousands of men.

Only in the closing days did the vast array of small boats come into the equation and they manfully crossed the channel by any means, some even being towed. Once close to the beaches north of Dunkirk it was they who managed to get right in and transfer men to the larger ships waiting further out where the water was deeper.

Dunkirk became a new word in the English dictionary for 'Rescue'.

The official ending of Operation Dynamo was on 4 June and totals of troops rescued from the salient were in the order of 340,000, but what most people didn't realise was that another 200,000 were lifted from docks and piers further along the coast towards the west, ports such as Cherbourg, St Malo, Brest and St Nazaire, and men in dribs and drabs kept appearing for many weeks after as part of Operation Aerial which had been set up to gather them all in.

As the last of the rescued troops arrived back in England carrying a pitiful array of weapons, the country now faced its most fearful dilemma: how to rapidly rearm and spread along the possible invasion coasts this hotch-potch of remaining personnel. The BEF had left behind the majority of their equipment, 2500 guns, 84,000 vehicles, 77,000 tons of ammunition, 416,000 tons of stores and 165,000 tons of petrol, but most serious of all some 68,000 men had either been killed or were now captured. England now faced the threat of invasion from across just 22 miles of water. At the time they did not know that the Germans did not have sufficient boats to carry this out, let alone a navy large enough to protect its forces, but they still had a powerful air force and it was a very real threat.

Now safely back in England again, the men of the 6 Regt were sent to a temporary camp near Dover where they remained for several days, and during this time they had a surprise visit on 5 June by the Rt Honourable Anthony Eden which boosted morale.

Then on 6 June orders came through for them to go to Aberporth from where they moved on again to Aberystwyth so that regiments could try and reassemble. 1st AA Bde was going to be composed of 1st HAA Regt, 6th Regt, 60th and 85th.

In this chaotic state and still suffering from the shocks of the last few days they were granted BEF survivors' leave for ten days. Gnr Daniels was seen at this time by his brother, a gunner in another Regt who described his appearance as 'just ghastly'. Tp Sgt Maj. McWade eventually reached home in Liverpool. The last part via bus and having nothing except what he was standing up in the driver took pity on him and allowed him to go for free. His house was empty and the family were all at the cinema (probably watching the whole sorry story of the Dunkirk evacuation on the Pathe News). Sadly they had buried in France and Belgium 27 of the Regt who had died from illness, accident or as a result of enemy action.

Now that they had all returned it was decided that Btys that had been seconded to other Regts would revert to their original Units, so it was now that 15 Bty left 1st AA Regt to return to 6 Regt, thus meaning that the three original Btys were together again: 3, 12 and 15.

All along the route to the north they had been regaled by members of the Public waving Union Jacks, and who, not being completely in the picture, regarded them as heroes and part of a victory. What they heard some while later via Churchill's speech to MPs in the House was a more realistic account of the whole debacle, and what an amazing feat the whole operation had been. Far from being a victory it had actually been something of a miracle to have snatched so many troops from under the Germans' noses and got them home to face the threat of possible invasion. As some idea of how they had recovered from their nasty shocks on the Continent, on 26/27 June the Brigade held an athletics meeting which was won by 1st Regt! Many now had to start training in the use of the 3.7" AA gun in place of their old 3".

In the next few months starting in July, Hitler's tactics were to change after England refused to agree to peace terms and he gave permission for the bombing of British shipping. Targets would change to cities in August and then mainly the RAF airfields to soften up the defences prior to invasion.

At the end of August Goering would start to bomb London in reply to his heavy losses. The RAF in retaliation laid on a raid against Berlin just to show they were not immune from attack either. Having earlier declared that '... *never would a single aircraft ever reach and bomb Berlin*' Goering was left in a very embarrassing position. This attack so infuriated Hitler he ordered the stepping up of raids, but after sustained losses by day the raids altered to night time blitzes. Meanwhile preparations for the German operation for the invasion of England were still going ahead, under the code name Operation Sealion.

After the debacle of Dunkirk at which the Regt had lost all its guns and heavy equipment there was one item that brought some measure of pride back to them. Sgt Edwin Gilby of 15 Bty had been recommended in France by his Bty commander as suitable for promotion to 2nd Lieutenant and this promotion had duly came through. Some months after the chaotic with-drawal to Dunkirk he was awarded an MC (Military Cross for Gallantry), see Annex D.

Chapter 2

Reassembly and Channel Port Protection, and the London Blitz

_____

Returning now to 6 Regt, who in early July had reassembled at Aberystwyth in west Wales, the parlous state of the country after the withdrawal from the Continent meant there were precious few heavy weapons to go round. For the AA units there was a great shortage of transport, few predictors, and most serious of all very few guns to 'man'. It was very important to build up morale and unit discipline again and instil unit camaraderie after the experiences of the previous few weeks. They had had few casualties as part of the BEF but their esteem had taken a bad knock.

3 Bty had rejoined them at Aberystwyth at the beginning of July and so too 12 Bty. It had been intended for both these to go on 4 July to take over gun positions at Bishopstoke and Dibden airfields but this was later changed. Instead Regt HQ moved to Eastleigh, near Southampton, and Bty HQ of 12 Bty went to West End in the same area and closer to the coast. There was a greater need to protect channel ports and shipping. Part of the German strategy was to try and strangle Britain by cutting off her supplies and closing the ports.

So on 5 July 3 Bty started out for Falmouth. All Btys were now to become part of the Air Defence of Great Britain (ADGB). 15 Bty had no weapons with which to train so they spent the first few days on infantry drills and marches with some PT thrown in for good measure. Men went back to classrooms to learn basic drills, weapon handling and maintenance of guns and equipment.

On 4 July they had been posted to the Bristol area where they set up at two positions called Whitchurch and Reservoir just to the south of Bristol itself. They now came under the control of 76 HAA Regt, part of the 46th AA Brigade. Because of the complete lack of anything with which to fight back they had started to draw stores and vehicles for their immediate needs. Desperately short of AA guns, somebody found four old 3" semi mobile guns and brought these to site. Gun drills were started at once so the men became conversant with this slightly different weapon. Because they were a Bty used to eight guns and only four were available they split down the middle so the Left Half of the Bty had two and the Right Half the other two. In order to have somewhere to site them there was a concerted programme to build sandbag defences and command posts, and magazine storage for the ammunition.

They had to endure two days of terrible storms and lightning with heavy rain, but then on 12 July the Right Half Bty came into action in the early hours of the morning at around 0514 hrs. They had spotted a Junkers 88 and quickly trained after it just in time to fire three rounds. These burst so close to the bomber that in a panic it immediately dropped four large bombs which exploded some distance away.

12 Bty, which had been left at Southampton, split into four sections lettered 'A'–'D'. 'A' and 'C' took over Brownwich along with their HQ and the two others dispersed to have 'B' section at Southwick and 'D' at Nelson. 'D' and 'B' also came under the control of 250 Bty and 'A' and 'C' came under 252 Bty both of these were part of the 80th HAA Regt.

The great joy of being there was that they had the chance to get used to the new 3.7" AA guns. Intensive training now started with these and men were put through the latest gun drills. These weapons were well used and one Officer remarked that *'the guns had changed hands many times and were very dirty. Gun stores were incomplete and very little defensive sandbagging had been carried out.'*

These new 3.7" guns were altogether more powerful, they fired a larger shell to a greater height but still relied on a predictor and height finding equipment to be most effective. They had a brief encounter with a Dornier on 11 July which was flying in and out of clouds at around 6000 ft, and 8 rounds were fired but with no observed effect. On 15 July Bty HQ was moved to Wilderness and meanwhile the 6 Regimental HQ left by road for Tunbridge Wells to come under 2 AA Bde.

The 6 Regt's HQ soon found itself involved on a scheme called *Bovril* now it was down in Kent at Tunbridge Wells, along with two other Btys seconded to them, the 181st and 250th. Their task was to defend roads leading down to the south coast against the threat of invasion. Part of this scheme was for the Regt to make a reconnaissance of the whole area for future AA Gun positions in Ashford, Canterbury, Tenterden, Tunbridge Wells, Sevenoaks and Edenbridge. With this in mind positions were dug-in and readied in preparation for possible gun moves.

The 6 Regt was now still split up in several areas in the south of England

and the RHQ element was on its own near Tunbridge Wells controlling the two Btys which had been seconded to them, but one of their own, 3 Bty, was now down in the Plymouth area as part of the AA defence under 56 AA Bde.

12 Battery was down in Southampton attached to 80th Regt under 35th Bde.

15 Bty was in Bristol helping them while attached to 76th Regt.

Also at this time the threat of invasion was still in everyone's minds and in this eventuality 12 Bty would move straightaway and join their HQ in Kent, it being presumed that any attempt to land would come in the area opposite the shortest route across the channel.

12 Bty was still short of vehicles and struggled to carry out training manoeuvres so they borrowed some from 251 Bty. But since they were forbidden to take their instruments with them the whole thing lacked an air of reality. In the last week of July they received 8 Matador gun-towing tractors as well as some lorries. To go with these they had a few 30 cwt utility trucks and some motorcycles. They claimed the latter had *'been impressed and were quite old and very unreliable.'*

At this time a programme was started to improve rifle training amongst the O/Rs and this included the digging of slit trenches for ground defence. (The Bty O/C classed this as 'musketry training' so it is unclear what era he came from!)

In the mean time 15 Bty were suffering bad weather and heavy showers, but on 14 July during the hours of darkness they had become aware of a single enemy aircraft which promptly dropped several bombs in the region of Avonmouth. They were quite unable to fire at it because the searchlights did not illuminate it, thus showing that AA guns were still short of accurate target I/D equipment at night They too were hurriedly building sandbag walls for protection and around the tented accommodation.

Also around the same time as 12 Bty, they had been issued with 48 Lee Enfield rifles so they could train and exercise with the Local Defence Volunteers (LDV) the forerunners for what became known as the Home Guard. The rest of the month was spent building defences but not sighting any more aircraft till the 26th when at around 2300 hrs planes were seen at high level around 20,000 ft but out of range.

In fact because the German programme was initially aimed at sinking ships in the channel this area was regularly patrolled by their bombers looking for targets and many convoys suffered damage. So dangerous had it become that by 26 July the Navy had ordered that ships should only sail during the hours of darkness in this restricted water.

So too there were very worrying signs on the Calais side of long-range guns being constructed opposite to Dover and these were designed to shell convoys and were powerful enough even to reach the mainland of England.

On 30 July the Right Half of the Bty was inspected by General Pile who was the O/C AA units in the UK. He stayed for some time and they put on the usual demonstration for him and he was duly satisfied.

As August 1940 arrived and the Btys were hard at work continuing to build their defences, the sun at last decided to shine which dried out the sites to the extent of making life comfortable. What the gun crews did not know but may have guessed from the increased air activity was that what we in Britain called 'The Battle of Britain' had started. This was the attempt by Goering to knock out the RAF in a series of devastating raids, first by shooting them down in aerial combat and secondly by destroying their airfields.

From their elevated position inland from Southampton the gunners of 12 Bty witnessed a big raid against a convoy in the channel on the 6th. No ships appeared hit but several huge spouts of water went up from near misses which must have made life uncomfortable for the occupants.

Two days later on the 8th a formation of hostile bombers flew past but out of range, but shortly after a lone Spitfire latched on to the back of them and after a short sharp engagement two parachutes were seen to open from one of them. Some of the bombs were heard to explode in the Portsmouth area.

On the 13th the *Luftwaffe* bombed Southampton but neither site had more than a fleeting glimpse of any aircraft which kept flitting in and out of the cloud banks. One result of the raid was that the cold storage plant in town was hit and burnt out.

While the 'all clear' was being sounded the crews were startled to hear and see a lone Heinkel 111 at around 8000 ft. It must have been on its way home since it stayed hidden above the patchy cloud and made no attempt to bomb.

15 Bty down near Bristol were also having their fair share of action. The Left Half were based at Whitchurch (site No. 7) and the right half were at Reservoir (site No. 8). It was the Left half who engaged a bomber but once again no results were observed.

The next day it was the turn of the Right Half. They fired at the sound of a bomber which they could not see because of cloud but no results claimed.

During this period when the *Luftwaffe* were intent on going for the ports along the south coast 3 Bty had now been moved from Plymouth and set up again above Falmouth. Their HQ was in Carclew House at Perranarworthal and they were split into 4 section sites.

On 6th Aug 'C' section fired 4 rounds fuze 30 at a Dornier DO17 flying at about 12,600 ft and shortly after 'A' section fired 2 rounds at a Dornier 215 at roughly the same altitude; the bursts of the shells were observed to the right of the targets which immediately took evasive action.

The next week they were kept busy with some sort of action almost every day.

On the 8th a Junkers 88 was engaged at 13000 ft and it rapidly climbed to 20000 ft to escape. It was seen shortly after being pursued by a Spitfire, but the end result was not witnessed. Various groups fired barrage V1 and a plane was reported crossing the area with its engine shut down. A total of 22 rounds were expended, again with no visible result.

On the 12th Lt Edwards who had been promoted to Captain was cross posted to 15 Bty.

On the 13th hostile planes were detected and 'B' section fired a barrage of 9 rounds and shortly after having warned 'A' section of the direction in which the planes were flying, they too fired 5 rounds at the same flight.

BSM Donoghue was posted away on 13th to join 8th reserve AA Regt.

On 20th 'D' section fired 13 rounds at a Heinkel 111 which was flying high at around 18,000 ft; the rounds were close enough to make it veer off course. However when 'A' section fired 4 rounds at a Junkers 88 at about the same height the bursts were seen to be too low.

For the rest of the week Junkers and Heinkels were engaged most days at altitudes varying from 10,000–16,000 ft. A total expenditure of shells was 36 with no visible result.

On 15 August 12 Bty down at Southampton were detailed to select men to go to 211 Training Regt at Oswestry. Those selected were Lt Porteous, Lt Harris and Lt Davies. To accompany them were Sgts Dickenson and Townsend plus 4 O/Rs. To help while these were away Lt Whitehead joined from 81st AA Regt. [Lt Porteous left the Regt some months later and had a distinguished career winning the VC for his leadership during the Dieppe Raid as a Captain with 'F' troop of 4 Commando during the operation to silence German guns on the cliffs overlooking Dieppe town.]

On the same day in late afternoon approximately 20 ME 109s came in from the north and after opening out shot down 6 barrage balloons. They were a very fleeting fast moving target but the left troop did manage to get off 6 rounds at them before they were out of range.

Later in the early evening rounds were fired at two Dorniers and also 2 ME 109s, making a total of 14 rounds.

Right troop, too, fired at 2 Heinkels at about 9200 ft. Any results could not be seen because of the glare.

Next day, 16th August, Portsmouth was again bombed, the aircraft carefully avoiding showing themselves for too long by hopping in and out of cloud.

On 17th Lee-on-the-Solent airfield was bombed and on 19th Gosport airfield got hit too. The fighters also went for the barrage balloons again and several were destroyed. They must have had a fear of these for the cables were all but invisible and waiting to catch any unwary pilot and rip off a wing.

On 23rd an audacious pilot in a Heinkel 111 came over very low below the cloud base at around 3800 ft travelling S/E and attempted to put his bombs on the Thorneycroft Factory at Woolston. By a fluke he did not hit anything of note and the 6 bombs straddled the factory.

Sadly on the same date while digging sand from a large heap at Thornhill during the morning, Gnr 1502675 Donald David Sutton (aged 22) was buried when it collapsed on top of him. When he was finally extricated he was found to have died from suffocation. An avoidable accident with a tragic outcome.

The 24th saw a heavy raid against Portsmouth in the middle of the afternoon with the bombing being carried out from about 17,000 ft, but nothing came within range.

Again, on the 25th, just after midnight a single hostile aircraft passed close to both sites travelling S/W and released 6 bombs over Thornhill. They were so close they were heard whistling over the Westwood site and landed in Southampton Water, causing large geysers of spray when they exploded about three hundred yards beyond them. Presumably a bad shot aimed at Hythe on the west side of Southampton Water opposite to the town.

Next day further bombs dropped near Bty HQ and at the end of the month the cloudy conditions prevented the searchlights illuminating targets so that there was only one fleeting night engagement.

Bristol was also getting its share of raids and 15 Bty also had to supply a selection of men to go to the 211 Training Regt to join a Cadre Bty along with 12 Bty. They provided Lt Roe, 2/Lt Clamp, 3 Sgts, 6 Bdrs and 30 Gnrs. This was a sizable number to lose so, because men were about to go on leave because it was mid-August, a section was attached from 329 Bty to make up the numbers. Once these replacements had arrived one Officer and 42 O/Rs left to go on leave from 15 Bty.

This same day the G/L apparatus was delivered to the site at Whitchurch

(No. 7), however despite many targets being identified, none were engaged because they were not illuminated by searchlights.

Over the next few days while the apparatus was in operation it detected single aircraft on many occasions between 2100 hrs and midnight. The site did engage twice during this time but without any known results. During the day time when the G/L sets detected aircraft the Btys were often unable to fire because of the presence of friendly fighters. However the Right Half did manage to get off 12 rounds at one enemy plane. It had become the routine now for the German aircraft to come over as single planes.

The use of the G/L equipment was now improving and detecting aircraft on a regular basis and both Right and Left Btys engaged at various times. On one the aircraft dropped several heavy bombs a couple of miles to the east of the sites and some 36 rounds were fired between Nos 7 and 8 sites again without any result.

On 23 August two sections were attached from 329 Bty HAA for training purposes. To make room for them one section of 15 Bty attached itself to 327 HAA Bty at Rockingham.

Then on the 24th, shortly after midnight, about 80 incendiaries were dropped on the Right Half Bty site at Reservoir (No. 8). By good fortune there was only one casualty and one hut damaged. It was not clear whether this was a deliberate attack on the site or just a plane getting rid of unexpended bombs prior to return across the channel. Such a small number did not constitute a full load.

That same night a series of single aircraft flew near by and one engagement took place. On the following night another short engagement was fired and 12 rounds expended.

On the 27th odd aircraft were observed all day at very high altitude but one single Dornier was engaged at about 14,000 ft by both Right and Left Half Btys. All shell bursts were observed in the Predictor telescope and this caused the plane to unload a complete cargo of incendiary bombs in open fields near to site No. 8. No damage was caused to anything and the fires were allowed to burn themselves out.

Down near Falmouth where 3 Bty had its sections set to catch out planes attacking the anchorage or trying to lay mines, their attackers tended to come over at heights considerably less than at Southampton and in some cases almost at sea level. Generally the planes flew at between 6000-9000 ft but the majority were at night. 'A'–'D' sections on the 26th fired some 169 rounds but again without any appreciable results.

On 27th 'B' section fired several barrages and reported one aircraft dropped 5 HE bombs about 1000 yds west of their site.

On 28th all sections were in action again. This time they fired some 52 rounds.

So ended August and all batteries had been kept busy, but as yet had no confirmed 'kills'.

Life for the gunners was not all hard work. They were allowed into the local towns for a drink and a meal if they wanted. They could go to the cinema or attend dances laid on in local halls where they had the chance to meet the local ladies. Since by this time many of the local men of enlistment age had already left for services elsewhere they were very popular. Friendships were started in this manner and many people whose motto was 'Live for today, for tomorrow who knows what may happen' ended up getting married and many of these marriages were to be of long duration.

Life on the gun sites too had its routine. Each day the guns had to be cleaned and checked and damage repaired by the fitters. Grease had to be injected into suitable nipples and running surfaces. Ammunition had to be maintained by men of the RAOC and stored correctly. Barrels that had fired a lot of rounds had to regularly have liner changes.

The electrical ancillaries that allowed the guns to track aircraft and fire accurately had always to be held in tip-top order. At every air-raid warning the men had to man the guns whatever the time of day or night. Many times the raid was a false alarm and in others the enemy aircraft were not within range. Whichever it was, they had to 'stand to' at their guns and this could be for hours at a time in the cold and dark until they got the 'stand down'.

Early in September 1940 Hitler had given instructions for Operation Sealion which was the intended invasion of England. He was trying to get together 250,000 troops to mount this invasion and the planners were lining up all the transports they could find. These amounted to ferries, merchant ships, tugs, motorboats and large numbers of Siebel motorised barges. The latter were in the process of being constructed in large numbers and took their name from their designer. This shipping was being assembled in all ports along the channel coasts and had been monitored by RAF photo reconnaissance who flew regular sorties over the ports and harbours. There had been raids by bombers to try and destroy these transports but with limited success.

By September many of the gun sites had been re-equipped with the 3.7″ but not all.

3 Bty at Falmouth was still receiving constant attention from bombers hoping to catch shipping in the harbour, especially tankers.

On 4th two enemy planes approached from the S/E and were plotted as flying at about 28,000 ft. This was too high for the old 3" guns but they were engaged by the newer 3.7" If this fire was observed from the aircraft it might have made them think again since up till now at that height they should have been pretty safe.

On the 5th a code word, 'Cromwell', was received and because this was to warn of possible invasion all men were confined to the gun sites. The same night a bomber was heard approaching from the S/W and it dropped three bombs not far from the site and then proceeded out to sea. There was no damage or casualties.

On the 14th reinforcements arrived in the form of 2/Lts Soar and Shrives. On the same day Lt D.W. Wilkinson returned after attending a 'height finding course' which had lasted for 12 days. On the 16th No. 819139 A/BSM Hughes joined 15 Bty.

For the next few days aircraft were seen regularly but all out of range, so all the gunners could do was watch with mounting frustration.

On 22nd September things got rather tense because a warning had come in that the invasion might start at 1500 hrs. This had to be rather wishful thinking or extremely good intelligence work! At the same time Lt W.L. Sherrard left to attend a course on the latest Sperry predictor and the new 3.7" guns.

Over the next few days when aircraft were seen but could not be engaged they had a system of firing 'Pointer rounds'. These in effect were nothing more than to alert other guns to the direction of high flying enemy aircraft, giving them the chance to fire if it was within their range. Enemy bombers were fired at several times but without any visible effect.

Then on Sunday 29 September outside working hours there was a tragic accident at a place not far away called St Mawes. 5 O/Rs were drowned in the same incident, all from 3 Bty and all in 'A' section.

Their names were Gnr 4907186 John Beard (from Stoke on Trent), Gnr 788534 Albert Habbajam (from Sheffield), Gnr 797795 Charles Edward Hughes (from Tipton, West Midlands), Gnr 851198 George Kidd (from Monaghan, Ireland), Gnr 809983 Richard Mullen (Long Barton Derby). They varied in age from 20 to 33 and for the Bty it must have been a terrible shock. In such a tight-knit unit everyone knows everyone else. There were no clues given for this disaster but when I found the local paper for the time was still in existence I asked their archives to see what they could find out.

In the archives of the *Western Morning News* for the date of 2 October 1940 was a copy of the coroner's enquiry into this tragedy. It was not just gunners who had lost men but also the Army and the Navy too.

The story as given in the report says that on the night of 29 September, which was a Sunday, a group of men had gone from their camp at St Anthony on the south shore of the Helford river round to St Mawes on the other side of Falmouth Bay to attend a dance. They had stayed for several hours and around midnight nine of them made their way down to the jetty at St Mawes to catch a boat back to their camp. The boats were run under the supervision of the Navy.

On this night two sailors were in charge. They allowed the nine men on board plus another man who was a Sgt Matthews from the Duke of Cornwall's Light Infantry, making a total of twelve people. As they boarded it was very noticeable that the boat settled lower in the water. They all boarded carefully and then sat down, some observing how close to the water the gunwales were. After the usual banter with the Navy men as to whether it was safe to go they were assured that if everyone sat quietly there would be no problems. It was now after midnight and the weather was calm and they set off from the harbour. The boat lurched as the power was applied and it rocked alarmingly but the Navy men said it was still OK.

They were well outside the harbour walls when it was apparent the swell was somewhat greater than before and they noticed the skipper was having trouble controlling the heading. Under these conditions it was a disaster waiting to happen.

When well out from the protection of the harbour walls the boat suddenly took on water and capsized and they were all thrown into the sea. Those that could, clung to the upturned hull which luckily stayed afloat. Their shouting was heard by a local man who hurriedly dressed and got into a rowing boat and rowed out to find them. He came across a man floating on his back in a serious way and managed to pull him on board. He then circled round and found the hull with Gnr Nisbet hanging on and rescued him too. He then made for the shore to be able to warn coastguards and police for help.

The unconscious man was worked on but had died. Further rescue attempts collected another three gunners. These were the only ones to survive. By the day of the inquest, two days later, five bodies were still missing. The final death toll was five gunners and the Army's Sgt Matthews plus the two seamen. Both sailors had also perished and these were the skipper, William Reid, and ordinary seaman T. Elliot, both of the Royal Navy reserve patrol vessel the yacht *Nirvana*.

The names of the survivors were Gnrs Nisbet, Cook, O'Reilly and Butler. None it appeared had been wearing life jackets.

The coroner's summing up of this sad episode says it all: *"Here was a boat designed for five men but loaded with twelve. This is what caused it to founder in the swell and as a result eight men lost their lives."*

Up till the end of the month the Btys continued to fire at the odd high level aircraft when it came within range or aided by firing 'Pointer rounds', and then on the last day of the month 15 Bty received a warning order of a move closer to Bristol which was going to be around 12 October. This would give them time to pack up all their equipment and make preparations for handover to any new unit.

The month of September for 12 Bty at Southampton was not that much different from the others with a continual series of bomber attacks normally by single aircraft at high level. The weather had been sunny and visibility good. They too had received the code word 'Cromwell' and increased their readiness.

On the 7th the Left Half of the Bty at Thornhill fired a couple of pointer rounds at a Junkers 88 flying S/E. They then tried out a new technique on the 8th of 'laying' on the intersection of two searchlights which illuminated the target at night. Several targets were fired at using this method and other guns took up the same tactic from different stations. The end result was a sky filled with shell bursts but no visible results recorded.

15 Bty near Bristol were also getting attacks, nearly always at night and high level, however they reported on 2 September a detachment from the 446 Bty had set up a large 150 cm projector in the field behind their Command Post (a large searchlight). At around this time it was also noted that searchlight positions were being machine-gunned by the passing bombers as a deterrent to them staying switched on.

On 3 September there were several engagements from the Whitchurch site and one particular one at a plane flying at the low height of 6000 ft. This was seen to be most effective since an aircraft was seen rapidly losing height and also appeared to be alight. A second engagement later that night registered two hits. The plane dived after it had been attacked with 38 rounds.

On the 4th further Junkers were fired at during the early hours of the morning. Nine rounds were expended at one and 4 at another. It was most noticeable that during these raids the aircraft machine gunned the searchlights, presumably with the intention of not only causing casualties but to frighten them into turning off. The most daring was by an aircraft that dropped down to about 500 ft and sprayed one site with considerable machinegun fire.

During the course of the night no less than 30 separate raids were recorded over the Bristol area. Reservoir site engaged a Heinkel 111 after 2300 hrs and bombs dropped about 500 yds to their west. The flashes and concussions could not be disguised.

Other aircraft were affected by the AA fire and took strong evasive action, something that they could do easily as single aircraft and not so safely when in a group. They did not like to be illuminated and their actions showed this.

The same day Reservoir site had to provide 30 O/Rs to go to Portishead where they were to be exchanged with gunners from 236 Bty so they could be instructed with the new 3.7" guns. Whitchurch had a similar task to provide 18 O/Rs to go to 238 Bty so they too could be instructed in the new guns at the site called Brickfields. Several times each day and during the night both sites engaged hostile aircraft but again without any visible results.

On the 5th this offensive fire caused one aircraft to unload its bombs and a total of 6 HE were dropped but did not cause any damage.

On the 7th Maj. Moxon returned to take over command from Maj. Horne of 15 Bty.

Three enemy reconnaissance aircraft were seen during the day at about half-hour intervals from 1030 onwards, all above 20,000 ft and well out of range. The same day brought another signal from HQ to say that it was suspected that parachute troops might have landed. The whole country was in the grip of invasion fears. All troops were put on stand-to for much of the day.

Back at 12 Bty on the same day they had a warning order that they were to move shortly afterwards to London and to take with them the 212 Signal section.

It could not have escaped the notice of the Senior Officers that the raids on London had increased dramatically from early September and this was because the *Luftwaffe* had started its blitz to try and break down the will of the people. The events leading up to this had been somewhat unusual. A German raid at night on London had been intending to attack industrial areas lower down the river but in the dark and confusion they got lost and in desperation turned round and just jettisoned their loads. They had not been engaged by the air defences but the bombs struck mainly civilian housing and populated areas causing large scale damage. As a reply the next night the RAF sent a raid to Berlin to show they were not immune to being hit too. The end result was to annoy Hitler so much he agreed to step up the attacks on London in general.

On 9 September 12 Bty moved out in a large convoy towards London. They left in the late afternoon and took a route via Swathling, Winchester, Farnham, Guildford and Ripley to rendezvous with their guides at Kingston. From here they were led to their respective new gun sites by members of their new command – 105 HAA Regt who were part of 48th AA Bde.

Because of the serious threat to London they and other Btys had been moved back to aid the hard-pressed defenders and now became part of the Inner Artillery Zone (IAZ). (Fig. 2.1)

12 Bty came back with its 8 guns and was split between Eltham, which had the prefix code (ZS 7), and Grove Park (ZS 22). These were both to the south of London and on routes that the incoming bombers had used already. Their movement order stated they must come with 212 rounds of AA ammunition per gun. Also that dummy 3" guns had to be left emplaced at Thornhill and Westwood (4 at each site if possible) to try and preserve the notion that there was still an AA presence there.

Meanwhile 15 Bty still near Bristol were having a slightly quieter time as the majority of the raids were against London and the docks.

The rumours about parachutists was soon dispelled but the unit had had groups of troops out one hour before dawn till one hour after just in case in the nearby areas.

On the 11th they had engaged a single Heinkel 111 late in the evening with 7 rounds without result and later several air raids turned out to be false alarms.

On the 12th low cloud meant that the searchlights could not be used; these were still needed to be able to fire accurately at night. They had developed a system whereby two lights would cone the incoming aircraft and hold it, and the guns by trigonometry could work out its elevation and course.

On the 13th while the sites were cloud bound and without much activity a raider suddenly dived through in the middle of the afternoon and promptly dropped two large bombs south of Whitchurch.

On the 15th the sites were subjected to a series of single bombers passing overhead at high level.

In Eltham on 11 September 12 Bty was finding its feet. They were now in the thick of the bombing and could expect daily and nightly raids. Once France had capitulated all their airfields, which had been left so hurriedly, were

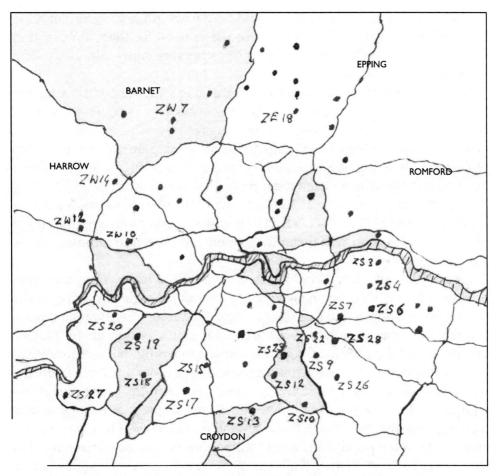

Fig 2.1 London Inner Artillery Zone (IAZ) showing main HAA gun sites.
Courtesy of D. Barton.

Site No.	Site Name	Site No.	Site Name
ZS 1	Slades Green	ZS 15	Norbury
ZS 2	Dartford Heath	ZS 16	Clapham Common
ZS 3	Plumstead Marshes	ZS 17	Mitcham Common
ZS 4	Bostall Heath	ZS 18	Raynes Park
ZS 5	St Pauls Cray	ZS 19	Wimbledon
ZS 6	Welling	ZS 20	Richmond Park
ZS 7	Eltham	ZS 21	Crayford
ZS 8	Woolwich Common	ZS 22	Grove Park
ZS 9	Sundridge Park	ZS 23	Ravensbourne
ZS 10	Hayes Common	ZS 24	Anerley
ZS 11	Brockley	ZS 25	Peckham Rye
ZS 12	Beckenham	ZS 26	Thornet Wood
ZS 13	Shirley Park	ZS 27	Weston Green
ZS 14	Dulwich	ZS 28	Coldharbour Farm
ZW 7	Chingford	ZE 18	Queen Elizabeth
ZW 14	Harrow		

suddenly available to the *Luftwaffe* and they made immediate use of these facilities. It was only a short hop across the channel for them now, instead of a long run from Germany. In many cases bomber crews could fit in two or more raids in the same day.

During the afternoon at around 1400 hrs a large force of bombers attended by fighters appeared over London. For them this was to be their first taste of mass gunfire. The two troops of guns engaged them along with a host of others. The Right Half of one troop got in some good bursts at a formation of Dornier 17s flying at about 18,500 ft and one aircraft is thought to have been hit and fallen away from the force.

Once the raid was over at 1500 hrs the O/C attended a conference at Brompton Road with Lt General Pile and many senior Officers from other units (Brompton road was the underground control centre for many of the AA guns).

Here the 6 Regt, along with others, was given the instructions that from now on all guns were to engage hostile aircraft 'at night' by firing at the sound. Searchlights in the IAZ were to remain doused. There was an uneasy fear that the lights actually helped the German crews locate valuable targets. The press and the people of London were complaining that the number of aircraft shot down was far too insignificant. They of course did not know the true extent of how hampered the gunners were with their lack of suitable equipment for locating hostile aircraft. General Pile's directions at this meeting were for the guns to fire at anything at all even if it was by sound alone; at least the population would think from the sound of the guns that the raiders were not getting it all their own way. To some extent this was to try and bolster morale among the civilians who wanted to know that the gunners were hitting back, but the ability to engage enemy planes at night was still woefully inaccurate.

'The Blitz' was of course very uncomfortable for the population on the receiving end of it all because they had no way of fighting back. They had to rely on the RAF's fighters with the help of the AA guns to keep the bombers at bay. (Fig. 2.2)

Fighters did not have the ability to find enemy bombers in the dark and successes were very few and far between. Gun laying radar (G/L1) was also in its infancy and the guns had no real way of engaging bombers accurately at high level. Balloons were tethered by cables across likely attack routes and these positions were stiffened by placing guns in groups nearby. Searchlights, too, were employed in the hope they could light up the bombers for the fighters to engage them at night, but this was a rare occurrence. (Fig. 2.3)

Fig. 2.2 At the height of a bombing raid during the Blitz.   IWM HU 1129

Fig. 2.3 Typical searchlight to aid night firing.

Once the extent of the threat to London was appreciated the task was then for the Ack-Ack commanders to try and place their precious resources to best effect. Guns were of two types, those that were static and mounted in concrete or brick positions and those that were mobile and could at short notice be switched to other locations. (Any calibre greater than 3.7" was always a static.) The trick was to try and second guess where the next wave of bombing would come, and because there was a desperate shortage of radar sets to go with the guns, the most efficient use of these was to have multiple guns working to one radar control set.

During the night of 11/12th further raids came over and the guns of 12 Bty had fired some 100 rounds each, condsiderably more than they were used to. The noise had been terrific and the amount of falling shrapnel posed a severe risk to anyone out and about in the open without a metal helmet.

The O/C Major Pinney reported that the papers next day were full of headlines such as *London's New Barrage Technique!*

On the 12th both their sites had the supposed additional help from sound locating sets attached to them. In the dark these were supposed to help locate unseen aircraft by engine noise alone, but in the past this had proved almost impossible because they got drowned out by the sheer numbers of raiders crossing over. At least they could now shoot even if there were no proven results. (Fig. 1.1)

The same day as these appeared on site there was an inspection of the guns by Maj. Gen. Crossman Cmdr of 1st AA Bde.

That night further raids came over and the guns fired about 60 rounds each but the results were not good as despite the fact it was only 50% cloud cover, the searchlight troops (who were allowed to light up again) had not mastered the idea of two lights catching the same aircraft for the guns to aim at.

The night of 13/14th there were more heavy raids as the *Luftwaffe* cranked up the pressure; the Batteries' guns again fired some 60 rounds each.

By now the situation in London was considered so serious that 6 Regt HQ was recalled from Tunbridge Wells and brought up into London to take over control of six sites in the Lewisham area under the command of 48th AA Bde.

Once the Regt HQ had reached London it took over command of these six sites and those gunners already on them and would also incorporate those about to come and thicken up the defences. The sites involved were Bostall Heath (ZS 4), Thornet Wood (ZS 26), Ravensbourne (ZS 23), Sundridge Park (ZS 9), Mitcham (ZS 17) and Southwark Park (ZS 12) (see Fig. 2.1).

Most of these positions were in open spaces, such as parks or playing fields for obvious reasons.

Two sections of guns from 250th Bty of 80th Regt were to be attached and had during the night made a rapid move, and after a rendezvous with guides been shown where to go and set up. The sites were not all the same, those of ZS 9, 12 and 23 were designed for static guns and those of ZS 4, 17 and 26 were for mobiles.

Each site had already been fitted out with a telephone line to the Gunners Operation Room (GOR) at Brompton Road from these static positions, and those of the mobiles would find their connection fixed to a wooden post within their sites and they then had only to connect their field telephones to these to receive information from control. Prior to the arrival of the guns each site had been surveyed and concrete plaques laid down with important information marked on them. These survey positions showed the position for the predictors and height finders and all that was left for the gunners to do on arrival was to collect orders from their HQ as to signals and the restrictions on opening fire and where the accommodation, water and toilet facilities were.

On the 14th during the afternoon there was a heavy raid in the offing but this was luckily turned back by RAF fighters. Once the bombers saw what sort of reception they were getting they decided it was too hot. Despite this single bombers still managed to get through and twice bombed the district round Eltham.

Later that night further single raiders came and were engaged by both troops. These raiders had not approached through the gun line but had come in across London from the north and were exiting the IAZ going south over them. There were no visible results.

On the 15th the *Luftwaffe* tried again. There were three heavy raids which started at 1200 hrs, 1600 hrs and the last at 1800 hrs. These were attacked at high level by RAF fighters. Because of the presence of the RAF none of the guns could fire, so they had the grandstand view of watching the attackers getting some of their own medicine and seeing the multiple vapour trails high in the sky as the battles progressed.

The next day the newspapers were full of the story of the battles and claimed the RAF had shot down 180 planes. This was an obvious morale boosting ploy since post-war records showed this figure to be grossly inflated. Nevertheless the bombers got a good hammering even if the RAF lost heavily too.

It is not surprising that figures were not accurate, when you consider the number of dogfights going on in which pilots were fighting for their lives, making split-second decisions and twisting and turning all over the sky, taking snap shots at fleeting targets and possibly seeing bullets strike home but having to turn quickly to avoid being attacked themselves before any positive results could be noted. The bravery of these men is not questioned and they certainly blunted the *Luftwaffe* attack.

As a result of these heavy attacks more AA gunners were drafted in. 'B' Bty from Portland, manned by Royal Marines, came up as well as another two sections from 250 Bty of 80th Regt. (Their other two sections as noted were already in London.)

Two sections from 328 Bty who were in Wales on practice shoots were called back too. Why stay and practise in Wales when you could be in London doing it for real?

On the night of the 15th bombs were dropped in a field close to ZS 7 (Eltham) and during the night the guns had fired no less than 480 rounds, of which some 120 were by the method of using searchlights together; the rest had been fired 'blind'.

Raids on the 16th were lessened, partly due to bad weather and rain but one bomb dropped close to Grove Park (ZS 22) without effect or casualties. The next night the raiders were back again, but this time mostly in streams of single bombers who dropped random bombs for about three hours. It was reported in the papers the next day that Goering was supposed to have been in one of these taking a look for himself.

On 16 September while 12 Bty was extremely busy against the raiders over London, 15 Bty was busy too down near Bristol but in a somewhat less hectic way.

Just after midnight a single bomber was attacked by a fighter and in its hurry to get away dropped at random some 20 HE bombs, all of which landed close to the Right Half Bty at Reservoir (No. 8) site. Despite aircraft flying around much of the night none were illuminated and no engagements took place.

On the 17th strong gales made life uncomfortable but during the night a high level bombing raid was made against Whitchurch aerodrome by one plane. Four bombs were dropped, one of which landed in open country and turned out to be a delayed action. This type of action became the norm for the next few days, single planes attempting to bomb from height but without much accuracy or effect. Occasionally RAF fighters came up to engage.

Some days a Recce Junkers 88 plane came over to be followed shortly after by a Heinkel 111 but there was no determination to linger in the area for longer than necessary.

Lt Holme joined the Bty on the 24th and the next day had the chance to see some action. Late morning a warning came through of a hostile raid on its way and shortly after about 40 ME 109s accompanying some 20 Heinkel 111's were sighted. The guns of Left Half Bty engaged fiercely and the formation quickly broke up but not long afterwards they reformed and proceeded to head for Filton and district, and bombed it heavily from about 20,000 ft.

Filton was an airfield north of Bristol and had an aircraft manufacturing works on site (in fact it is now the modern day site of Bristol airport). It was close enough for the Bty to see in the distance and so know what was going on there.

Low cloud hampered the *Luftwaffe* during the next night, and the next day after some intelligence warnings the Right Half Bty were warned off to move nearer to Filton in order to provide 'extra support for the Aircraft works'.

Their briefing of the 27th stated:

The enemy has made a large scale attack on Filton Aircraft Works and it is believed further attacks are likely. Two sections of 15 Bty now attached to 76 AA Regt with four 3" guns will move from site No 8 Reservoir to a new position on Henbury Golf Links. They must be 'in action' by 2330 at the new location.

Instruments, gun stores and 100 rounds per gun (92 HE and 8 Shrapnel) will move at the same time. 915 Coy RASC will provide the transport.

In order to prepare the site they are moving to, a party of 50 men from 123 'Z' Bty will move to Henbury and tools and transport will be provided by 76 Regt HAA.

The 'Z' Btys were in fact referred to as U/P launchers. This was because the rockets they fired were classed as Unrotated Projectiles. These fearsome things were fired from metal slides mounted on a turntable and pointed at an angle off the vertical and in considerable quantities at a time. They had a reputation for being of more danger to the firers than to any aircraft passing overhead. They tended to be set up in multiples of 12 launchers in a group.

Twenty tents and six marquees are to be delivered to the new site.
Further accommodation will be requisitioned in the Club House.
Water is to be available at the Club House till RE have made other arrangements.
Field Latrines are to be dug. Security of the site will be provided by 76 Regt. HAA.

There is no record of how the then current members reacted to their Clubhouse being taken over but it is expected they were clearly pleased the Army would not be using their 'loos' even if everything else was being commandeered!

On 27th the Left Half Bty, still at their old location, witnessed a friendly fighter patrol crossing their area and shortly after 34 Dorniers flying at about 13,000 ft approaching Bristol from the south. All were in flights of three in arrow-head formations. Surprisingly this bomber group was completely without fighter defence. They made their approach out of the sun and maintained height. The leader was seen to maintain a steady course while the rest seemed to take evasive action. They dropped their bombs as soon as the fighters turned to engage for they had seen the bombers and turned rapidly to get back in contact. Each aircraft appeared to drop just two bombs and then started for home diving south.

One enemy aircraft thought to be a Heinkel 111 was engaged by the Right Half Bty when it came in range of site No. 8 Reservoir. A total of 6 HE rounds were fired but these appeared to be low and the aircraft took evasive action as it flew off.

During the dog fight one enemy was seen to plunge down, obviously destroyed, and another was seen in difficulty to the south of Bristol. This one was seen losing height and leaving a smoke trail as it disappeared into cloud near to site No. 7. The survivors of the raid were harried by the fighters as they left the area.

At 1300 hrs a lone Junkers 88 flying at 22,000 ft appeared and was driven off by fire from a neighbouring 3.7" site.

Leaving 15 Bty about to make its move to two new areas nearer to Filton (it had later been decided to send both Half Btys rather than just one), we return to 12 Bty in Eltham.

On the night of 16/17th September they had fired some 75 rounds per gun, but mostly 'blind' because there had been a technical problem with the searchlights and G/L equipment.

At ZS 7 one gun had been 'out of action' because of problems with its electrical pointer gear. Other than this the equipment was standing up well to the increased fire demanded.

The night had been about 50% cloudy on the 17th with little activity. The raiders had turned before entering the IAZ thus avoiding any chance for the guns to open fire. The next night further bombs were dropped close to both sites and there was desultory action.

By 18 September the Bty was again under control of 6 Regt HQ which was stationed at Hollyhead Drill Hall in Blackheath. Large raids against London had again turned back and 100% clouds had certainly helped.

The night of 19th saw continuous activity and 3 HE and 2 loads of incendiaries were dropped near ZS 22 (Grove Park). During the day TSM Dixon-Didier left to go to OCTU camp at Llandrindod Wells.

Next night the cloud base was around 2000 ft and they might have hoped for a break but the *Luftwaffe* were blind-bombing through cloud, presumably using the method of two converging transmitted beams.

A parachute mine was dropped and exploded south of ZS 7 with a devastating concussion, far greater than anything they had so far experienced. These mines were some of the largest explosive-filled devices used at the time and it was quite normal for them to contain over a thousand kilos of filling.

ZS 22 were 'out of action' because many of their barrel liners needed changing which took till the next day to fix.

For 12 Bty, who were south of the river and some way out from the centre of London, the heavy raids were an awe-inspiring sight. Besides the tremendous crack of their own guns there was the thud of bombs and concussions from their detonation. The sky was lit up by shell fire and fires set off by the raid, the flames leaping high into the night sky, and the continuous crump of bombs some of which fell uncomfortably close to them.

In the morning the questions were of who had been hit or taken the brunt of the raid. The air was often full of the smell of smoke and burning from fires not yet put out by the Brigades and a pall of dust drifting on the breeze. Guns had to be cleaned and prepared, empty shell cases removed and fresh ammunition brought in and made ready, while the air was still heavy with the smell of expended cordite from the night's endeavours.

On the 21st a new draft of 40 O/Rs arrived to take up their places and they could not have joined at a more opportune time. The gunners were fast becoming exhausted from continuous 'manning' and lack of sleep. The guns continued to fire an average of 40 rounds each per night, creating so much wear that the liners had had to be regularly changed.

The day of the 27th saw two massed raids against London again. The first was very much a fighter affair and the gunners watched from their sites. However on the second raid at about 1500 hrs, there was plenty of scope for the guns. A very intense barrage was put up but much was seen to be low. Right troop did somewhat better and claimed one raider seen leaving the formation smoking hard as it flew over them.

What was rather disheartening was to read in the papers the scores alleged to have been totalled up so far. The RAF were credited with 190 and the AA guns just 2.

It was very noticeable that daylight raids were nowhere near the intensity of night-time ones. The *Luftwaffe* had learnt that the RAF was very good and that the guns were mostly ineffective from lack of good radar at night.

Back at Bristol 15 Bty had completed its move during the hours of darkness on 28th September without being attacked or spotted. The Left Half Bty set up at Almondsbury by 0230 and the Right Half Bty by 0630 at Henbury Golf Links.

It was hoped that adding to the defence of Filton unannounced, might prove a surprise for the *Luftwaffe*. They continued to prepare the gun pads and set up defensive sandbagging, and watched to see what would happen. Among those still in the Bty was Tom Evans who found, as most of them did, that there were long periods of boredom interspersed with short sharp action. In fact he had just returned from taking a PTI course (physical training instructor) and now found himself back in action again. It was a quiet day except for the unexpected and random detonations of bombs dropped on a previous raid which had obviously been set on time delays.

October came and life for 3 Bty still down at Falmouth did not alter much. Their warning order for a move to Bristol had not materialised.

On the 8th they engaged a Heinkel at great height and the next day fired pointer rounds at another; this time a fighter alerted to its position came along and promptly shot it down. The same day 4 bombs were dropped on Falmouth by a plane flying in cloud but their luck changed later when they fired at a Junkers 88 and after 8 rounds it was seen to turn almost upside down and seemed likely to have been destroyed.

They fired most days but without any further luck and then on the 12th 3 Bty was ordered to go to London to help the hard-pressed defenders. The advance party left from Truro by train heading for Greenwich and arrived at 1900 hrs.

The remainder of the Bty arrived on the 14th where the Right troop set up at Ravensbourne (ZS 23) and the Left troop at Thornet Wood (ZS 26). They took over the site from 328 Bty who had been attached to 6 Regt and now left to join their parent unit. The other unit moving out were the 'B' Bty manned by the Royal Marines who were going down to Watchet for gunnery practice. Most of the practice ranges were situated round the coast and kept exceedingly busy.

The site was well supplied with equipment, having 3.7" guns and the

Sperry Predictor and also a G/L radar unit and VIE (Visual I/D Equip). With the radar they engaged several unseen aircraft at night. They were now in the thick of the action.

15 Bty continued their waiting game around Filton but nobody was taking the bait. They had news of a hostile raid of 90 planes that had tried to raid Southampton but did not penetrate the defences.

They witnessed many single planes over the Bristol area, but nothing they could engage.

The G/L equipment and searchlights were ordered to move to Gordano from site No. 10, which is where Left Half Bty was, so they now had no way of identifying hostile aircraft.

On the 11th there were numerous hostile planes operating in the area but none could be engaged. Some bombs were dropped about half a mile from the Henbury site and one that was noticed did not explode so it was judged either a 'dud' or on time delay.

The 13th saw many bombs dropped indiscriminately on Avonmouth and Portishead. The weather at night had been very clear with a full moon and a steady flow of single aircraft kept passing.

The 15th saw another tactic used for the first time by the hostile raiders. It was night and a single plane flew over the Right Half Bty position leading a raid. This plane then dropped incendiaries on site No. 13 and these were followed up by the following aircraft dropping HE. It was apparent that the lead aircraft was being used to mark the target for the remainder. The general area was somewhat soft and after this particularly heavy raid a dull thud was heard close to one of the gun pits. Examination in daylight showed a hole in the ground with an unexploded bomb somewhere deep beneath. They had to wait for a captain and some sappers to arrive and deal with this unwanted visitor later in the morning.

There was another airfield not far north of Filton called Yate and here they manufactured powered gun turrets for bombers in a factory nearby. In the end, because of the continual *Luftwaffe* attentions, the production was dispersed to other areas. It was normal for many of these airfields to also be protected by Bofors guns and some were from the 79 Regt LAA. Later in the war the two Regts were to meet again in the Far East.

On the 16th the two sites were handed over to the 342 Bty so that 15 Bty could set off for London to help with the Blitz, but first it was to have a brief rest at Reservoir site before leaving.

October brought no relief for the gunners in London. Raids were almost daily and the heaviest were normally at night.

On 1 October despite there being 80% cloud cover, there was another heavy raid headed for London but luckily this time it was mauled over Kent and many of the raiders dispersed.

That day the Bty fired about 150 rounds, an unheard of quantity only a few weeks before.

On the 3rd the Left troop engaged a Heinkel 111 flying low at about 1000 ft. They were aided by a Bofors, one of several that were also on the gun sites to cope with low-flying raiders. In this instance the plane was recorded as having come down at Sidcup and in the circumstances the gunners gave it to the Bofors crew as being the more likely to have hit it. Pretty generous of them considering the rivalry between the various sites!

Some of the sites now had G/L fitted with the E/FA and this certainly allowed them greater scope for shooting more accurately by both day and night (more about this later). The only drawback was that the sets had not been calibrated by the radar section specialists, most of whom were civilians at the time.

On the 4th the site was closed in by low cloud and rain but someone was able to see because shooting was heard in the distance. On the 5/6th once the weather cleared they managed to fire about 60 rounds per gun but no results were reported. There was the usual persistent raider coming over at random times and dropping un-aimed bombs and then scooting away.

Then a new tactic was noticed on the 8th when single ME 109s started to come over, each carrying one bomb which they proceeded to drop from high level. The *Luftwaffe* made further efforts to blitz Londoners on the night of the 8/9th when heavy raids persisted for much of the hours of darkness. The gunners were still waiting for the G/L sets to be calibrated so this aid was missing, but some raids had been broken up by the RAF before they reached London.

By 12 October after further delays, in some part to poor weather and the fact the RAF had not been subdued, the German Operation Sealion was cancelled indefinitely. The promised clinical crushing of the RAF by Goering had not happened. In fact the RAF had managed to hang on by the skin of its teeth and the sheer bravery of its fighter crews. After three months of hectic action they had got the measure of the *Luftwaffe* machine, in no small part aided by the services of the radar masts of the Chain Home system along the south coast, and the ever vigilant Observer Corps crews in their exposed bunkers, and the Germans now knew that every time they came over they would get a good mauling. The morale of their bomber crews had plummeted and it was a relief to them when they knew the Operation had been cancelled.

These tall radio masts had been erected before the war as part of the defence system to give early warning of approaching aircraft. They were good for detecting the higher flying ones but had to be modified later to also be able to detect those that tried to come in much lower. If the Germans had realised just how effective they were they would have probably expended a lot more time on trying to knock them out rather than the few half-hearted attempts they made.

However Hitler had bigger fish to fry and was planning to launch his biggest attack against a supposed ally ... Russia.

On the 17th Right troop was switched to the site at Bostall Heath (ZS 4) and took all their guns with them, but left behind the G/L sets. This was the start of many short moves to try and keep the *Luftwaffe* guessing. Static guns sites could always be plotted accurately but not so the mobiles.

Lt Sherrard was cross posted from 3rd Bty and Capt. Gracey left to go to practice camp at Towyn.

3 Bty continued to 'man' ZS 23 and ZS 26 and were also being kept busy. They too were about to move and half the Bty went to ZS 34 (Addington) to take over guns that formed a 16 gun position. They had been joined by a troop from 12 Bty so met up again with some of their old mates. When the remaining half troops of 12 Bty and 3 Bty joined on 23rd this became a 6 Regt site.

Hardly had they got themselves sorted out than the whole site moved yet again to a new location at Tolworth (ZS 29). This was still part of the game of trying to keep the *Luftwaffe* guessing as to where they could expect to be fired on.

The main problem reported by the HQ element was having to try and find accommodation and billets for some 630 men at short notice. The new gun site was located to take advantage of the 'Tramline Routes' the *Luftwaffe* had been using flying into and out from London.

The guns at this new location were set up in two circles of eight and each group was controlled from a central command post using the services of a G/L radar fitted with the E/F attachment for more accurate height finding. This was in part because of the shortage of G/L radars and working with one in control and several slaves was the most economic way. In fact this 16 gun site had two G/L radars both previously calibrated and four predictors. One central predictor was connected via computer cables to each gun to control the fusing process, and by this method all 16 guns were able to fire a single salvo. This also allowed them to reload and fire a second one within 20 seconds.

They reported that if the enemy crossing point was some 2000 yards out then the whole thing worked well, but if the crossing point was overhead then there was a tendency for the radar signal to become unsteady. After three days of this shooting the personnel had become accustomed to the routine and it seemed to be working well. So fierce was the barrage from these guns when all firing together that a large number of raids had turned back and in some cases damage was recorded to individual planes. The tactic was to put up a concentration of fire in front of the IAZ before the Bombers reached it and aim if possible to knock out the leader, or at least cause him to take so much time evading the shells that accuracy was lost. When it came for 'stand down' at the end of another hectic night the guns were covered over with camouflage netting to try and keep their location secret for a little longer. A short word may help with the understanding of how the radar system worked. Up to this time radar, which was a vital component in the effective use of the guns, was still relatively primitive. The G/L 1 system, when working well, could track incoming aircraft and determine their distance away quite well. However it suffered a serious shortcoming of not being able to give an accurate height. Because of this problem the War Office had asked several companies to come up with a solution and it was the Cossor Company who devised a system which came to have the suffix of E/FA added to G/L to indicate Elevation Finding Attachment. This was in effect an electronic 'add on' ability to the original system. Originally a radar position was made up with two trailer-mounted cabins (and a large generator). One of these carried the transmitter and the other the receiving set of aerials. They were sited some distance apart and in order to get the maximum returns the receiving hut was operated from inside by one of the personnel hand cranking pedals to rotate the assembly across the expected direction of incoming aircraft. (Fig. 2.4)

Both the GL/1 and its successor the GL/2 worked on a wavelength of about 6 metres and because of this, accuracy was restricted and many of the objects on the ground nearby effectively made a clutter of ground echoes. (It was not till some time later when GL/3 came in that it managed to overcome this problem. The reason was it now worked on much shorter centimetric wavelengths.)

What they had found in practice was that the shape of the ground in front of the receiver had a marked effect on the signals on the cathode ray screens. Lots of spurious blips very often made the set unworkable, each one caused

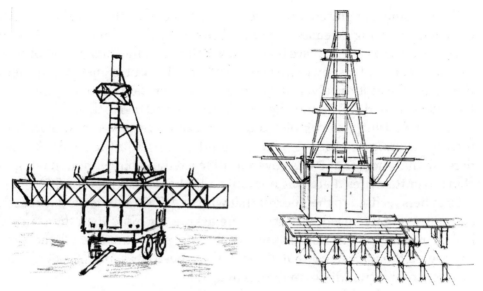

Fig. 2.4 *Left:* Sketch of G/L Mk.11 trailer-mounted transmitter. Kept separate from the receiver. The mast and aerials folded when in transit.
Right: Sketch of G/L Mk 11 receiving aerials set up with the E/FA radar mat.

by reflected rays from unevenness of the ground or objects nearby. What was needed was to try and iron these out to get a much improved surface in the form of a flat mat.

Each site where radar was to be used had to be surveyed and the details sent in for analysis. Thus suitable kits of parts were then sent out to the site to be erected by the engineers or suitably instructed civilian contractors. These kits took the form of unequal length poles to allow for ground undulations or ground dropping away to one side so that the whole thing could be set up on a level.

Once the kit arrived a large group of men then started to erect the poles. Initially it was found that about fifty men were needed and they would hopefully complete a mat in about a month. As with all things military there had to be a period of trial and error to find the best solution for the construction and a learning curve which got steeper as they ironed out the snags.

The system they finally arrived at was to set out the shape of the site and hammer in the corner posts. Using these as sight lines the rows were then hammered home in both directions working around the shape. (Some sites were circular and others octagonal and generally about 100 yds in diameter.) It was essential that a channel was left from one side that reached to the centre to allow the receiving cabin with its aerials to be pulled into position.

By this time galvanised wires were strung between all the posts in both directions by being threaded through predrilled holes near the top of each post. Once these were in place they were tensioned to the outside end of each row and then held fast by more short stakes further out, somewhat like tent pegs. Next the rolls of galvanised chicken mesh were laid out and hammered flat and then lifted bodily onto the top of the wires and tied to them.

Once the wiring was completed the cabin could be towed into place and then the avenue used for its access would be closed off too with further wires so the whole shape was covered. To reach the cabin without having to climb over the wires there was normally a timber walkway. (Fig. 2.5)

Suppliers realised to their horror that with over 7500 square yards of mesh and miles of galvanised wire they were asking for more than the country had in reserve at the time if they wished to accommodate all the sites envisaged. It had been estimated there was a need for about 600 sites, well in excess of the quantity of materials available.

Once set up though this array was a marked improvement and at last the height of an enemy raid could be deduced. Under ideal conditions and without hills or tall buildings to interfere, these radars G/L Mk2 E/FA

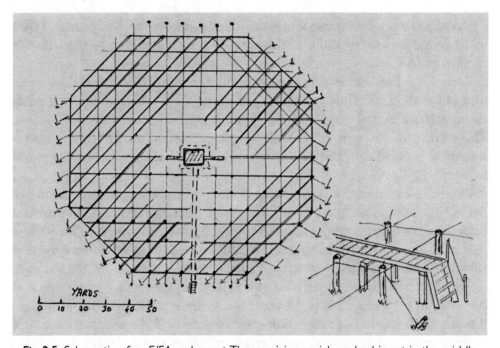

Fig. 2.5 Schematic of an E/FA radar mat. The receiving aerials and cabin sat in the middle and the operating crew reached it via an elevated timber walkway. The whole area was covered in rolls of chicken mesh tied down.

could pick up aircraft at ranges of 50,000 yards or about 30 miles. They could then keep tracking till raiders were some 30,000 yards (17 miles) and control the AA guns right down to 14,000 yards (8 miles). At this range they were capable of producing accurate fire to explode within 50 yards of the target.

The radar sets themselves had to be fine-tuned to work effectively and in many instances part of this involved using balloons from which were hung metallic arrays and oscillators. These were at known height and distance and the radar could be adjusted to these measurements. On some 'receiving' cabins there were short shafts that protruded through the side and these were for telescopes to be fitted so that the balloons could be sighted to aid the calibration. In fact these balloons were quite small being only some one to one and a half metres in diameter.

This radar was also used in conjunction with the predictors to give the gunners the information needed to fuse their shells. Predictors were an early form of computer into which had to be fed the range, height and direction of the incoming enemy aircraft and the guessed speed. (Fig. 2.6)

Fig. 2.6 Gnrs manning a predictor but on a static site.   IWM H8271

The information was then processed rapidly and fed to the guns so that they could track the incoming raid. Bearing in mind that an aircraft at 15,000 ft and travelling at some 220 mph would travel a considerable distance during the flight time of the shell, it can be seen that the lead-in of the shell would be not far short of a mile in front of the plane.

Hopefully if the calculations were correct both aircraft and shell would meet at the same point in space. In the early days shells had to be fused manually and this all had to be allowed for. (It was not till around early 1943 that the mats became obsolete as GL/3 came in and automatic fusing apparatus was introduced which allowed faster firing.)

In the early days the only way to estimate height, which was vitally important for the accurate placing of the exploding shells, was by the use of height/range finding equipment. This was in effect a long cylinder mounted horizontally on its own stand, and at both ends of which was a powerful magnifying lens. The lenses could be adjusted to aim at the same target and when the images were focused and overlapped the height could be read off or transmitted electronically to the predictor. Since the lenses were several feet apart, depending on the instrument type, the effect was either by 'coincidence' or stereoscopic, the wider the distance between lenses giving a more accurate height/range. On some of the larger instruments this distance could be as much as ten feet. (Fig. 2.7)

Fig. 2.7 Gnrs working a height / range finder also on a static site.   IWM H874

One other aid the gunners had was searchlights to try and find and hold the *Luftwaffe* at night and this added another aid to accurate shooting. These were of course hindered badly by mist and fog, and worst was low cloud (Fig. 2.3, p. 53).

The early radar sets were so sensitive to a variety of causes that it became necessary for an experienced scientist to be in attendance to try and make sure it was giving of its best. His job was then to infuse enthusiasm into the Army operatives and teach them how to operate the system and iron out the normal day to day hiccups.

General Pile had a career-long obsession with the quality of the men he was given to form into AA Regts. In his memoirs he recalled that in the early days the gunners he inherited were *'the halt, the lame and the weary from the rest of the Army Regts'*. If the man had two eyes, arms and legs he was doing well, even so he still complained many were *'Dimwits'* and in a service that involved much highly sophisticated equipment this was not helping them to be efficient. He always considered his forces were under strength and lacked sufficient guns to be able to carry out the enormous number of tasks needed but he still persisted to mould them into a fighting force.

After their three days of rest 15 Bty set out for London, and on 20th Left Half Bty reached ZW 7 (Chingford) by train, which was to the north of central London. They had come without guns or instruments and the intention was to take over the guns left by the existing occupying Bty.

On 21st the second Half Bty would arrive also without guns and equipment and they would take over at ZE 18 (Queen Elizabeth) to the north east of central London. Both Half Btys were now under the command of 4 HAA Regt.

At around this time a number of heavier 4.5" static guns were being moved in and these would require the services of the RE and pioneers to mount them. These would need substantial foundations and holding down bolts and also solid wall protection. These guns had a pretty ferocious back blast and required metal front and side screens in the form of a turret to protect the gunners and loaders behind.

It was intended that once 15 Bty guns arrived some days later they would move across to ZE 18 so the Bty would be complete again and leave the *in situ* guns for another unit to take on.

It was during this period that 15 Bty was joined by a new gunner, Walter Mear. He was a strong young man who had been working in the Welsh coal mines for several years and knew that this was classed as a 'reserve occupation', which meant he did not have to join the armed forces. However he had other things on his mind and volunteered to join up. At a time of dire need and a shortage of trained men to fill the army quotas he was allocated to the Royal Artillery and passed through his training in a few weeks, what would now be classed as a very short time. Having completed this he was then detailed off to 15 Bty of the 6 HAA Regt and here he specialised at the rangefinder predictor equipment, the vital component that allowed guns to fire accurately. Despite his young age he was very inventive and resourceful and good with his hands, just the sort of gunner the Bty would need in the months to come.

While the Half Btys were temporarily occupying their sites, the ZW 7 neighbourhood was subjected to heavy bombing. Since they had no instruments they could only engage unseen aircraft by sound alone, a notoriously inaccurate way of firing. The Right Half had a chance to rest while their other Half was busy most nights firing at single planes. They then had instructions to take over the guns at ZE 18 from 313 HAA Bty. One thing that they had noticed was that some of the bombing was being carried out by fighters carrying two bombs. They flew fast and high and were not interested in hanging around.

The Right Half now had the chance to join in once they took over from 313 HAA Bty. To aid them a searchlight and generator had been delivered so they could at least attempt to engage. After a few nights of firing, but without any visible evidence, on the 25th they fired 19 rounds and were happy to report they thought one raider had been damaged.

Left Half Bty moved briefly to Enfield and then rejoined shortly after. November came in with all three Btys set up defending London, one Bty to the north and two in the south east.

On 1 November 15 Bty was manning ZW 7 and ZE 18, both to the north side of London.

So far in the Blitz they had all been very lucky with injuries from the bombing, with only 12 Bty reporting 2 dead and 4 injured during the whole time they had been there. One of those who died was Gnr Robert Smith No. 818472 on 10 September 1940.

However while Right Half Bty was resting the Left Half was busy engaging at ZW 7. They took on several single aircraft at 16,000 ft and fired 19 rounds. At 1940 hrs during another 'stand to' two oil bombs were dropped and a 1000 lb delayed action bomb as well, all of which landed close to the site and 2/Lt M. Alberry was severely wounded. Another aircraft then dropped red flares which the gunners engaged to try to destroy them before they gave away too much information to the high flying bombers.

The story behind the injury to 2/Lt Alberry was that one of the oil bombs scored a direct hit on a lorry close to the Bty position and it happened to be loaded with 3.7" shells. These started to explode in the heat and two men (later awarded BEMs) went to the rescue of 2/Lt Alberry and managed to save his life by getting him away from the danger. The fire and explosions caused the loss of 200 rounds of ammunition.

By the 4th some of the men had been sent over to ZW 14 (near Harrow) to help with the construction of new gun pads.

Left Half Bty continued to have regular visits from high flying bombers but without any success while Right half moved to Wimbledon (ZS 19) to take over 4 × 3.7" guns.

A total of 216 rounds were fired without visible results, most engagements at heights of 18,000 ft.

12 Bty meanwhile were still to the south of London and on ZS 34, the 16 gun site, but then on 9 November their shooting improved. Using the G/L radar and its E/F attachment they managed to fire 4 salvos while an aircraft was in range, but the next day a Heinkel 111 had its tail blown off by the first salvo and the main fuselage crashed on a house in Bromley while the tail section landed in Bickley. This engagement had taken place at 19,000 ft and this was celebrated as the first 'bullseye' they had achieved.

If the gun sites were wondering where the mass formations of the *Luftwaffe* were, they would soon find out the change in tactics. Meanwhile Left troop experienced 9 HE bombs dropped near their site and a series of flares too. These they managed to extinguish by gunfire while they drifted down slowly in the wind.

Behind the scenes senior officers in AA Command had urgently demanded a rapid programme to increase the quantity of HAA guns produced each month. With so many new targets to protect and an ever increasing number of services that wanted first pick, the meagre supply had to be eked out on a priority basis of importance. Frequent switching helped to spread the resources further.

11 November saw several engagements by both Half Btys. Some 57 rounds were expended at 16,000 ft.

On the 12th one of the raiders got lucky and placed a bomb about 5 yards from the Officers' mess tents and although the damage was considerable no one was hurt.

For the next few days over 120 rounds were fired with the guns using up 50 rounds each most nights.

On 15 November they all heard the latest news from the Midlands. Earlier in the month on the 8th the RAF had flown over Germany and deliberately bombed Munich. It had not been a particularly heavy or even effective raid, but the significance of the affront was not lost on Hitler. Here was the official home base of the Nazi party and now it had been bombed. So infuriated was he that he immediately ordered a reprisal raid but it had to be on a much grander scale. Using their radio beams, which were turned on early in the afternoon of 14 November, they proceeded to aim for the centre of England. It was a clear crisp moonlit night with excellent visibility as massive numbers of bombers headed for Coventry and the air raid alarms started their mournful wail around 2100 hrs.

From then on till 0615 the next morning they continued to come, wave after wave all dropping their loads on the raging fires caused by the incendiaries from the early flights.The second wave after midnight brought HE and had no difficulty finding their target since the flames were visible from 100 miles away. The fire mains were shattered in so many places that the fire brigades could only sit and watch helplessly as the fires took hold and continued to burn all night and most of the next day. The centre of the city had disappeared and had now become a mass of rubble and broken timbers. The ancient cathedral was burnt out to a shell and the lead from the roof had melted into running streams. The death toll from the raid was some 568 and certainly the worst of the war so far.

Operation Moonlight Sonata, as the Germans called it, had been a deliberate attempt to mass murder civilians. The whole aspect of the war from the air had now changed. So delighted with the results were they that they even coined a phrase: to 'Coventrate' a place. They gloatingly said there was more where that had come from. They had used some 400 bombers which dropped about 500 tons of bombs and 30,000 incendiaries.

From earlier intelligence they knew the location of many factories that worked from the city and these were mainly Alvis who made armoured cars and Aero who made parts for the RAF. A lot of the larger factories were further out and many of those destroyed were smaller firms. Because of the nature of the factories many people lived close to where they worked. It was obvious that any mass bombing of what few factories were there would inevitably cause large scale loss of life.

The city was thought to be partially protected by its location in a dip but only had about 40 AA guns for defence and 50 barrage balloons. In fact by chance, after witnessing the heavy raids on London, the Government was concerned for the safety of other larger centres of manufacture and in the ongoing process of strengthening larger vulnerable cities an extra 8 guns had been drafted in a couple of weeks before. These had been taken from Alcester and were mobile 3.7"

In the circumstances these proved totally ineffective and records show that only a single hostile plane was brought down although this bomber crashed near Loughborough from indeterminate causes. London had suffered a severe bombing attack too but not on the same scale. The guns of 15 Bty recorded firing 50–80 rounds per gun per night and they were delighted when it was confirmed they had contributed to shooting down two enemy aircraft on the night of 15/16th. So many shells had been fired that two guns needed barrel liners changing.

On 22nd they had another move, this time to Grove Park (ZS 22) with half a Bty, but while 15 Bty remained in London and were kept busy each day, 3 Bty and 12 Bty had an order to move out hurriedly from ZS 34 to Wolverhampton.

Having seen what a large force of bombers could do to a city if they were not stopped before they bombed, the decision had been taken to move a selection of mobile guns to defend the Midlands in case of further attacks against other towns and cities. This was also to bolster the existing gunners already there. So many of the towns contained the manufacturing bases and factories for the war effort, it was vital they survived. It was realised that taking guns away weakened London's defences but it could not be allowed for another Coventry type raid to succeed and besides, London had a pretty good supply of AA guns already, not as many as Gen. Pile wanted, but enough to give a good account of themselves.

ZS 34 was therefore evacuated and left empty when the two Btys left.

The only worry that 15 Bty recorded was that their guns were out of touch with GOR because a section of telephone wire had been cut and removed. They surmised it had been 'by saboteurs'. The GPO had been called in and were replacing it. Even in the Home Counties the fear of fifth columnists was still wide spread.

While 15 Bty continued to form part of the IAZ the orders for the move of the other two Btys went ahead.

Their movement order dated 23 November stated,

6 Regt will move with 16 x 3.7" mobile guns of 3 Bty and 12 Bty plus HQ and all their instruments, receivers, transmitters, generators and stores to the Kidderminster/ Wolverhampton area. Each gun will take 220 rounds of ammunition ... also they will take 10 radar operators complete with two G/L stations.

The size of the operation to move part of the Regt from London to the Midlands is shown by the scale of vehicles involved. Just to move each Bty required 65 vehicles, and then there were another 9 on top for the Regt HQ element. In this convoy for just the two Btys there would be around 140 vehicles and for a full Regt it would have been something over 200. Each gun needed a towing vehicle and all the ammunition and men required lorries. There were more for stores and the special instruments, and despatch riders accompanied the convoys for control and message taking.

This mass of transport was scheduled to go in two convoys, each taking a different route. Partly to prevent hold ups and congestion on the roads and also to present a smaller target to aerial attack, they were ordered to drive in convoys of no more than 10 vehicles per mile so they were well spaced out.

Having set out on the 24th in the morning they arrived in the Midlands later that day and by dusk were all 'in action' at their new locations. 3 Bty were set up on an 8 gun position to the south west of Wolverhampton at Upper Penn (H 49) and 12 Bty were set up at two sites to the north west of Wolverhampton separated by a couple of miles.

Right troop of 12 Bty was at Wergs (H 51), sometimes known as 'The Elms', and Left troop were at Bushbury (H 50). The grid reference for the Bushbury guns puts them a couple of fields away from the modern-day Northycote Children's Farm. Both sites were also known in earlier times by letter codes. Wergs was 'D' and Bushbury was 'B'. (Fig 2.8)

Their Bty HQ went to Pendeford Hall, a large requisitioned mansion, which was about central to the area.

There were, in addition to the guns, sections from 352 searchlight Bty both at Coven 'A' site and one at Bushbury 'B' site. These Btys were part of the 38th Kings Regt RA (TA) which comprised 350, 351 and 353 Btys.

Regimental HQ set up in Patshull Hall near Albrighton to the west of Wolverhampton, a splendidly large country mansion set in its own vast grounds. At the time it was owned by Lord and Lady Dartmouth, who, not wishing to lose the house under requisition laws, decided to withdraw to some of the rooms and allow the Military the use of a few of the others in another wing. (Fig. 2.9)

The site chosen for 3 Bty was on the edge of a golf course at Penn Common and the arrival of 8 mobile 3.7" guns meant that some of the course had to be made out of bounds to the golfers. The guns were set up to the east side of the road that crossed the Common along with their ammunition and stores. Because the area was very rural one of the first things the Billeting

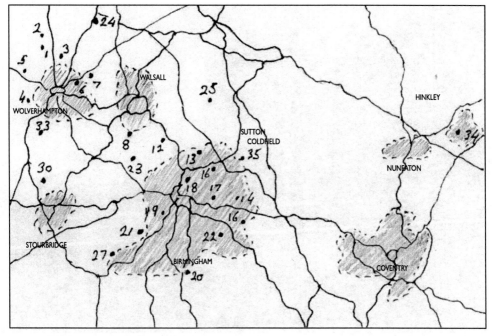

Fig. 2.8 Main Birmingham HAA gun sites 1939–45
Courtesy of D. Barton.

No.	Site name	Site Ref (early)	Later ref.	No.	Site name	Site Ref (early)	Later ref.
1	Coven Heath	A		19	Edgbaston	R	
2	Coven Heath		H1	20	Kingswood Farm	R	H 12
3	Bushbury Hill	B	H 50	21	Welsh House Farm	S	H 58
4	Merry Hill	C	H 18	22	Langley hall farm	T	H 59
5	The Elms	D	H 51	23	The Uplands	U	H 60
6	Wednesfield	E		24	Wedges Mills		H 2
7	Wednesfield		H 52	25	Sutton Park		H 5
8	Stoke Cross	F	H 5	26	Nuthurst		H 11
9	Turners Hill	G	H 17	27	Rubery		H 13
10	Mons Hill	H	H 53	30	Wordsley		H 16
11	Park Hall	I	H 6	33	Upper Penn		H 49
12	Perry Park	K	H 4	34	Warmley Ash		H 54
13	Erdington	L	H 10	35	Castle Bromwich		H 61
14	Sheldon	M	H 55	36	Glibe Farm		H 62
15	Castle Bromwich	N	H 56	37	Wylde Green		H 63
16	Olton Hall	O	H 9	38	Short Heath		H 64
17	Oaklands	P	H 7	39	Shard End Farm		H 65
18	Swainhurst park	Q	H 57				

Fig. 2.9 The magnificent Patshull Hall set in its own grounds and used as an RHQ for some months in 1940/41.
Courtesy of Mr Tim Reynolds.

Officer had to do was to secure accommodation for some of his men and he chose some of the houses that bordered both sides of Sedgley Road which bisected the Common. He placed two Corporals, Newcombe and Bagley, in number 38 owned by Mr and Mrs Cole, and others such as Gnrs Price, Rhodes and Davis in houses opposite. Men who could not be found space in the immediate area were put in tents and huts that were hastily erected on the west side of the road further down the Common. Nothing was left to chance and the movement order stating that '... *an allowance for each site to have a delivery of coal'* shows that it was a typical English winter.

For the last part of the month while they continued to build defences they witnessed on many nights the bombers passing nearby on their way to bomb Liverpool and Manchester.

The gunners' priority was to get hardcore pads made to take the weight of the guns and then build sandbag walls for protection. Once this was done the guns were towed into position and one set of wheels removed so they sat on their 'davits' (screw-down base/anchor plates). Camouflage netting on poles was draped across the top to try and disguise their location. They were never designed to be static with concrete or brick walls but had temporary stone roads leading in to each position for quick movement out.

The 3 Bty HQ was at a nearby country house called The Wodehouse about half a mile away from the bottom of the Common. This was a delightful large country house set in beautiful manicured gardens with a lake (Fig. 2.10). To allow for the influx of troops the owner had to move into some rooms in one wing and much of the furniture and fittings were removed and placed in storage in a barn at the rear.

Upper Penn site (H49) would be one of the earliest ones to have the E/F attachment for their radars. When it was installed is not clear, but it would seem to have been early in 1941, and it took up an area on what is now the 17th green of Penn Golf Club and to the west side of the road. Till then they had to rely on the G/L equipment only.

Residents alive today but who were children at the time recall that nobody knew exactly what the mesh netting was for and used it as a trampoline! (Until driven off by troops nearby.)

Penn Common is in a slight dip so a searchlight Bty position was set up at the top of Springhill Lane a short distance away to the west. This was on

Fig. 2.10 The beautiful Wodehouse used as a Bty HQ for over a year.
Courtesy of Mr and Mrs Phillips.

land known as Dicksons Farm and the Bty was close to the lane but reached by a short length of track.

On 28/29th the 12 Bty sites fired but Wergs site had problems with its G/L equipment and so could only fire by sound. After a few salvos it stopped, *'pour encourager les autres'* so their diary says. The deeper meaning behind this remark must remain forever lost.

December arrived and with it the chill weather again. 3 Bty was busily engaged in building sandbag protection for its guns and command post and also the shell magazines. Tents had been erected as well as several huts. Generators spluttered in the background and the site shook out into a wartime footing.

At some stage, nobody can actually recall when, a series of deep ditches had been dug on both sides of the positions. These filled rapidly with water since the whole area was like a sponge. Why these were constructed is not clear. They could not have expected parachute troops to come this far inland and the ditches would certainly not have prevented gliders landing.

Locals had been warned that when the guns fired they should leave their windows slightly ajar, but this might have been all right in summer but this was now the middle of a bitter winter.

The Penn Common site should have been a happy one since there were no less than ten pubs within three-quarters of a mile of it and the town was a short bus ride away where they could relax at cinemas and dance halls. The local population arranged dances in the church hall most weeks so everyone could get to know everyone else.

12 Bty at their two sites were just as busy, since these were new locations and so had no defences already built at all.

Action was limited but they continued to see on many nights high flying bombers on their way towards Sheffield where there were huge steel-making plants to say nothing of the multitude of manufacturing factories.

Towards the end of the month large formations of bombers could be seen again at night, but this time heading for Liverpool and Manchester. These always seemed to be too high and too far away to be engaged so all they could do was watch in frustration.

On 29 November the Bty put a feather in its cap when the Left Half Bty won the monthly Cup for the most efficient site in 34 Bde area, and this out of 50 starters.

Back down in London with 15 Bty who were split between Grove Park and Goddington, early December came in with the now usual engagements. Between the 1st and the 3rd they fired some 180 rounds mostly at heights of

17,500 ft to 19,000 ft but still with no further results recorded. (It was calculated at this stage of the war that for every aircraft brought down something
like 15,000 AA shells had to be fired, though this did reduce as the gunners
became more proficient and their equipment more accurate. They did get
this down to a much more reasonable 3500 or so later.) Over the next three
days they fired a further 215 rounds all at high targets.

However on the 6th they had a warning order that they were to move to
the Wolverhampton area to join up with the rest of 6 Regt again; this would
mean the whole Regt was back again under central control. Taking over
their guns when they vacated their positions would be 229 Bty of the 97th
HAA Regt.

On 11 December the whole Bty entrained at Grove Park and set out for the
Midlands and later that day disembarked at Birmingham for Sutton
Coldfield. The new sites were coded such that Left Half Bty took over 'V'
site, Right Half Bty took over 'Z' and the Battery HQ went to 'X' site.

These were three new sites and their locations can only be guessed at but
the grids suggest they were in the area of Castle Bromwich. Bty HQ made
itself at home in Sutton Coldfield at 107 Lichfield Road. At the time at Castle
Bromwich there was one of the main factories producing and assembling the
Spitfire fighter, so although the Bty had no guns yet it was in a very
important location. The remainder of the Regt were still well to the north
west of Birmingham and these new locations were to the east of the city.
Until the end of the month there were no surprises. Training started again
and they had the chance to rest a little.

The Regt celebrated another Christmas in their new locations and wondered
what the future might hold, not just for them but the country as a whole. In late
December a new man arrived to join them, Padre Capt R. Norman Harper-
Holdcroft. At a time when they were busy in the Midlands he never realised
how much his services would be needed in the months ahead.

January 1941 arrived with 3 Bty occupying Penn Common and having no
actions; 12 Bty was at Wergs (H 61) and Bushbury (H 50), to give them their
new numbering sequence. They had a brief action when they engaged
enemy aircraft with barrage controlled fire but again no results were seen.

On the 14th there was considerable enemy air activity but because of
fighters the guns could not engage, however they marked the height of the
bombers for the fighters in one instance and these managed to shoot down
two of them.

Ground defences were being dug and slit trenches started, and the normal
array of bunkers and protective emplacements, and all this despite it having

started to snow. Over the next two days it hardly stopped and then blizzards came in and they experienced snowdrifts up to five feet deep.

During early January 1941 15 Bty at last received an idea of what they were going to be called on to do. They still did not have any guns to man but intelligence reported that '... *there are recent reliable reports that reveal the imminent probability of an invasion by Airborne troops in large numbers.*' And in rather dramatic terms they were told '... *15 Bty will defend 34 Bde HQ and the GOR to the last round and the last man.*'

On receipt of the code word 'Invasion', so that they could carry out the allotted tasks given them, the battery would break down into small units which would be designated to guard certain local positions, all in nearby buildings. These had been notated as Posts 1–3 and at each of these would be one officer and ten O/Rs, complete with a Lewis gun and 8 rifles.

One of these positions was to be protected by 2/Lt Attiwill's group comprising Tom Evans and nine others. A larger patrol of one officer and 16 O/Rs would be kept as reserve and a fighting patrol of one officer and 10 O/Rs would operate in the area. Another position on the roof of the HQ building was to be guarded by 4 men drawn from the signals section. If it had not been so dire a situation it might have been funny and rather akin to *Dad's Army*.

Bomb squads were to be made up with an NCO and five men whose job it was to draw Molotov cocktails and Mills bombs. Molotov cocktails were basically any glass bottle such as that used for milk but filled with petrol and the neck stuffed with a rag. This was shaken to moisten the rag with the accelerant, lighted and then thrown as far away as possible to smash against a suitable target, where it was hoped the recipient would burst into flames. The Mills bombs were the standard No 36 hand grenade for close defence and house clearing and the final gem was '...*the Home Guard HQ. was to be found near the Odeon Cinema.*'

The Home Guard were also going to man a roadblock across the Lichfield road not far away and it was necessary to liaise with them so accidents would not occur.

At this time there was still a fear that the Germans might use gas dropped by aerial means. All civilians carried their masks in boxes or satchels slung from a shoulder strap or round their necks. As a way of warning people that there was a gas attack imminent or had actually started, men would go round, sometimes on bicycles, with wooden rattles and crank these madly, something akin to those used by supporters at a football match of the time.

Having been detailed off to protect 34 Bde HQ in the manner described, in the event nothing happened, and they were then warned they were going to take over 2 four-gun sites of 3.7" which were to the north of Wolverhampton.

In the meantime, because they were not manning guns at their present locations, four of the older type 3" mobile guns were to be delivered from 6 AA Bde and split two at each of 'V' and 'Z' sites and brought into action there.

Because the sites at Sutton Coldfield were new, all defences were still being constructed. They had virtually no interference from aircraft so as it was a quiet period, 3 Officers and 18 NCOs were detached to go to 509 Field Coy RE to be instructed in the finer arts of assembling and erecting the 'matting' for the E/F attachment to their radar.

In the event of an early move it was intended that these locations would be taken over by 168 Bty around 18 January.

On the 17th four 3" guns arrived late, having been held up by the bad weather. These were immediately manned and prepared for action. However hardly had the gunners got these sorted out when on the 19th the move took place; it was really a swop since 168 Bty were manning the two sites 'E' and 'H' already and they were coming back to change over with 15 Bty. It must have been a bit of a come down to leave modern 3.7" guns and come back to older 3" types.

It is thought that these two sites were actually in Wednesfield / Willenhall and occupied suitable open parkland in both locations. The grid reference for the Willenhall site puts it close to the modern site of Ashmore Lake.

It was during early January that Tp Sgt Maj. McWade was chosen for a wartime emergency commission and on successful completion in April 1941 he returned to 6 HAA but was transferred to 3 Bty.

15 Bty HQ stayed where they were near Sutton Coldfield during this move until suitable accommodation could be found. The move was accompanied by a heavy fall of snow which deposited around 12 inches and the road surfaces became very tricky.

It did not worry Tom Evans since his family lived near Coseley and the new location was close enough for him to get home quite easily.

Around the 22nd a very welcome report came in giving details of awards for distinguished service awarded to the Regt for operations down in London, during the period of March–June 1940 (see Annex D).

They were reported in the *London Gazette* for 20 December 1940 and included the following names for Mention in Despatches:

L/Bdr A. Andrews 7257484, Gnr B. Blizzard 784394, Gnr AG Buck 788256, Sgt Dougherty 779231, Sgt L Greystone 1426503, Bdr C Treatrix 1425040, L/sgt W Jones 819832, Gnr F Pardoe 788876, Sgt Powels 816995, Gnr W

Taylor 3649555, L/sgt Villiers 7876419, Capt AVS Chanells, 2/Lt JA Hibbert, 2/Lt BAH Pain, Gnr R Pate 3382145, Gnr Mitchell 4746410, TSM W Bancroft 808426, BQMS H Holder 1045573, L/Bdr WH Knight 3382443, Gnr AW Chapman 1517766, Gnr S Fosberry 828656, and Gnr TA Smith 1512936.

A day or so later two further awards were made for brave conduct whilst down in London: the BEM to Sgt Powels and Gnr 819108 H Orr for the rescue of 2/Lt Alberry during an air raid.

On the 19th Maj. Pinney, the O/C of 12 Bty, had been posted to Aden so at least someone was going to get to see the sun! The Bty was then taken over by Capt. Coulson who was posted across from 3 Bty. Maj. Pinney went on to win a well deserved MC for actions at Sidi Rezegh in North Africa with his new Regt but sadly was killed in action shortly afterwards.

There was quite a flurry of postings around this time. 2/Lt Magee joined 3 Bty while 2/Lt Barney left and a Capt RDM Edwards joined Bty HQ.

In 12 Bty they also had changes. 2/Lt A Moffett was detached to join the Wireless Wing at Watchet in Somerset and 2/Lt REP Balfour joined 15 Bty.

Because of the atrocious weather there was very little enemy aircraft activity amongst any of the Batteries and with dense fog reducing visibility to almost zero it was a good thing.

On 25 January 15 Bty were warned of another possible move, from their two sites 'E' and 'H' to change over with those of 3 Bty on Penn Common. This was a straightforward swop of two 4-gun sites for one of 8 guns. But because of the severe weather it was stipulated that it must go ahead only when things got better and the sites were not to be left unmanned at any time. In point of fact the swop over did not occur till three weeks later.

In early February 1941, in between manning their guns, the Regt started a school at Blackheath, which was to give a short break of two weeks to a small group from each Bty so that they could concentrate on Regimental History, PT, Aircraft recognition and Infantry tactics.

(One source, Wal Parkins, who was a despatch rider during the war and had to deliver messages to the guns at Langley Road in Merry Hill, says he thinks he recalls the word Blackheath on the fence near the entrance to the site of Merry Hill (H 18). Since this was not far from the other gun sites and would have been very convenient, it is quite possible that this was where the Regt School took place. Merry Hill was a static position of 4 × 3.7" AA guns and was a mixed battery with accommodation, offices and stores. Around this time it was manned by 456 Bty of the 134 HAA Regt. There is also an area called Blackheath not far from Dudley and Halesowen so it may well have been there.)

The intention was for one Officer and four NCOs to take part for two weeks at a time from each Bty in turn. The instructing staff were to be from the Regt HQ personnel. Not only were they hoping to broaden the minds of the men but also their chests for they had even arranged for a PT instructor to be present and it was his job to teach men so they could go back to their own batteries and continue the fitness regime there.

By 25 February they had been pre-warned of a mobilisation exercise and hurriedly collected stores and personnel to make themselves up to strength and this included all necessary vehicles. Some of these came from as far away as Glasgow and this of course took several days and the scheme was called by the code name 'Chestnut'. Many of the stores were drawn from RAOC at 10 Donnington but by 10 March the unit was almost ready except for reporting a couple of lorries short and one gun tractor. Some items were laid out ready for inspection at the parent depots to prove they were available but would not actually be issued until it became necessary.

This work had to be carried out at the same time as maintaining their duties as part of the Air Defence Great Britain (ADGB) which was the overall plan for defending the whole of the UK against hostile air attack. Because of the extra workload the Regt School was temporarily closed.

It was then that extra manpower started to arrive to bring them up to full war time complement, including an Officer, 2/Lt H.B. Windows, who joined 3 Bty at Willenhall. 2/Lt R.E.F. Balfour had already joined 15 Bty shortly before.

The Bty had reported itself at a strength of 337 all ranks including attached signallers and drivers by the end of February. They also noted that they had four members in hospital, Gnrs Hogg, Darke, Connolly and Pratt, and these were classed as on the 'Y' list. Another gunner was noted as missing: Gnr F Cooley who was being held in custody in the Military Detention centre at Chorley for an undisclosed offence, and was not likely to see the light of day for another month.

(The 'Y' list referred to men who were away from the unit sick and would not be back immediately so their places could be taken by reinforcements to bring the unit back up to strength again.)

He was to have a few lucky escapes and could have avoided them all because he was profoundly deaf in one ear from childhood and had managed to hide this at his medical.

By early March, the CO was reporting that the Regt was 1072 strong and still awaiting a few more men to bring them up to about 1100. These totals included all gunners and the attached tradesmen such as drivers, artificers, armourers, clerks, cooks, motor mechanics and one lone Battery Surveyor.

By 11 March 1941 Regt HQ at Patshull Hall had received fresh orders from 11 AA Division amending previous orders about the '*Chestnut*' plan and they now had the task of defending the defiles Banbury, Oxford and Didcot against aerial attack. Mobile exercises continued so they could continue to try and iron out problems and they also integrated with the Field Army, as it was called.

12 Bty had an influx of tradesmen including fitters, driver mechanics and gunners but the main headache was to get the contractors to complete the roadways for getting the guns out quickly when the orders came through; ground conditions were very soft and guns and vehicles got bogged easily.

'C' section under a very new but enthusiastic 2/Lt McCallum was praised for its keenness in managing to get the guns out under difficult conditions. Earlier they had had their Sperry predictor replaced with a Vickers at their 'B' site.

There was still an uneasy fear of invasion and all sorts of schemes were tried out to cover the multitude of possibilities. While the other batteries were busy with their mobilisation, 3 Bty in Willenhall was having the chance to engage enemy aircraft that appeared within range.

On 12 March they fired three rounds of HE but without visible effect. Later this was to be a busy night for them but they also suffered a serious accident during the shoot.

Just before 2100 hrs there was a premature burst of the shell in No. 1 gun. This was a 3.7" HE on fuse 207. The explosion damaged the gun and injured some of the crew and in fact so violent was the blast that men on the No. 2 gun were also hospitalised. Both guns were put out of action and the injured taken to Newcross Hospital but the guns that were left were still able to engage and fired on three more occasions that night totalling 11 rounds.

Whilst they continued manning these gun positions in and around Wolverhampton, the Batteries detached parties of Officers and NCOs to go down to the areas of Banbury, Oxford and Didcot and carry out a reconnaissance to find suitable locations for their guns should they have to move. One such recce party was carried out by the O/C Maj. Moxon accompanied by 2/Lt Steeds.

Once all these reports had been typed up they were sent up the line to 2 AA Corps for approval and the scheme was re-named '*Interim Chestnut*'.

They renewed the code words for the various scenarios such that 'Stand To' brought 6 Regt to 4 hrs notice and 'Action Stations' meant an immediate move to the areas chosen.

This would have meant that 3 Bty would take up 2 four-gun positions near Banbury along with their Bty HQ. 12 Bty would take up 2 four-gun positions near Oxford also with their HQ and 15 Bty would set up 2 four-gun positions at Didcot, also with their HQ. Meanwhile Regt HQ would move out of Patshull Hall and go to Woodstock and base themselves there.

It was the job of the Regimental Signal Sections to connect up the various Batteries to their HQs and to searchlight clusters, and also to AA command, so that they could get early warning from their network of any approaching hostile aircraft. One perennial problem of these moves was always the need to supply rations and accommodation for the troops if they were not to sleep under canvas for too long. In the initial move to Penn Common this had been partly settled by billeting some men in local houses but the rest had had to move into huts and tents on the Common.

Re-supply of ammunition also had to be allowed for, along with fuel for the transport and towing vehicles. An initial scale would be taken at the beginning of each move but would inevitably have to be replenished.

Because of the seriousness of the situation intensive mobilisation training had to be fitted in between manning their guns. All drivers had to be aware of the routes to the new gun positions in each of the three areas.

Unlike today when motorways criss-cross the country, and also many good dual carriageways, every move at this time involved an element of luck not to get lost.

All movement at night was done via the use of heavily hooded headlights with not much more than a chink of light. Most, if not all, the road direction signs had been taken down to try and confuse any German parachutists. If the route had not been marked with special signs put up by the RMP traffic sections, then every junction could be a minefield of misdirection. Despatch riders were sometimes used to lead convoys after they had studied the proposed routes. But once the main roads were left behind, trying to find a site in a field down a narrow country lane would test the best of navigators.

Like all the rest of the 6 Regt, 15 Bty was heavily engaged in the mobilisation exercises in the early part of March. What must have come as a bit of a surprise was a warning order they were to be prepared to indent for tropical clothing. The inference was that they were one month away from being drafted to the Near East.

They were inspected on 5 March by Maj. Gen Archibald, the Divisional Commander, and in fact he had been CO of 6 Regt in its early days so no one was going to pull the wool over his eyes.

They had little in the way of enemy activity to record which allowed them more time to get the mobilisation completed.

12 Bty recorded that they had a mysterious incident on the night of the 6th when the generator for the G/L broke down with a broken flywheel. At the same time a sentry had fired at a figure he said he had seen running towards the nearby woods. Fifth columnists were still being seen (with or without the aid of alcohol).

A report by the RAOC later confirmed the generator damage was not suspicious.

To keep up morale an ENSA concert was arranged and held at the Bushbury site. There had been an influx of new men that same day, 3 drivers and 16 gunners. The O/C of 12 Bty (Maj. Coulson) described rather disparagingly a dozen of these replacements from Cleethorpes as *almost useless in a mobile battery. They had no experience of any kind of mobility and should all be in a lower category then B2.'*

On the morning of the 9th 'B' site (Bushbury) was subjected to a mock invasion attack by the Home Guard. As is usual in these things the Bty won, claiming to have destroyed two armoured cars. Sadly the umpiring was not sufficiently good to decide exactly what had gone on. However later that day Defiant aircraft dummy 'dive-bombed' the battery site several times and gave the gunners much realistic experience of what to expect.

Although the 12 Bty sites had seen lots of enemy air activity in recent days none had come close enough for them to engage.

On 13 March there was considerable upheaval amongst the gunners. Four guns from 15 Bty plus all their instruments from the Penn Common site were detached to go down to the 'Robert' site south of Birmingham, thus leaving four guns behind there to maintain the site. They were supplemented by a section of guns from 400th Bty. from a separate HAA Regt.

The site reference of 'Robert' could well refer to the earlier references to gun sites by letters. 'R' had been the name for one at Kingswood farm (confusingly it was also used to denote Edgbaston).

Then on 14 March 12 Bty vacated sites 'B' and 'D' near Wolverhampton (B = H50 Bushbury and D = H51 The Elms in Tettenhall) and deployed to new sites near Coventry called 'B' and 'E'. (B = Brookfield Farm (H71) and E = Bubben Hall (H66). (Fig. 2.11)

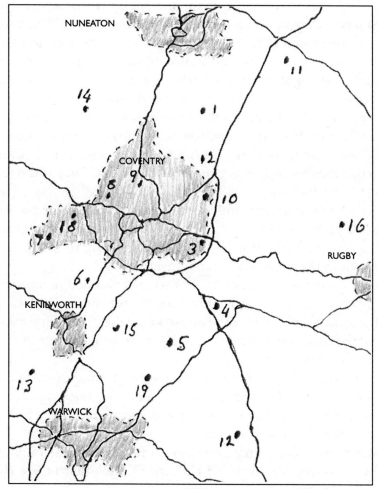

Fig. 2.11 Coventry HAA gun sites 1939–45.

Courtesy of D. Barton

No.	Site Name	Site Ref (early)	Site Ref (later)
1	Bedworth	A	H 21
2	Brookfield Farm	B	H 71
3	Binley	C	H 23
4	Ryton on Dunsmore	D	H 30
5	Bubben Hall	E	H 66
6	Gibbett Hill	F	H 67
7	Tile Hill	G	H 26
8	Keresley	H	H 72
9	Exhall	H	H 68
10	Walsgrove	L	H 69
13	Bannerhill		H 25
14	Fillongley		H 27
15	Stoneleigh		H 28

Their Bty HQ also moved with them and set up in the Arden Hotel in Kenilworth where they now came under the command of 67 Brigade. They had been at Moseley Old Hall to the north east of Wolverhampton for some weeks now, and this was a period house of some character with strong connections to the flight of King Charles II who had briefly visited and stayed there while fleeing for his life from the Roundheads.

No sooner had 15 Bty arrived at the 'Robert' site, which was occupied by 169 Bty, than their vehicles were requisitioned to tow the existing guns down to Bristol. These were to join 76th HAA Regt and it was left to Lt Campbell to organise this move which was going to take all day. They did not arrive back in fact till the 15th.

Just to make himself known and see how things were going the Brigade Major of 67 Brigade called in to the 'E' site at Coventry. While these men were settling into their new homes 3 Bty was managing most nights to fire at intruders but again without any noted results.

They might have been in parkland, but were close enough to houses for the blasts from their guns to dislodge slates and rattle window panes. However the local people were reassured to know that something was being done against the enemy aircraft even if it did mean being woken at all hours by the sudden muzzle blasts.

Coventry 'E' site had had problems with their G/L equipment, which was notoriously temperamental, and this meant they could not engage unseen aircraft. A technician from the RAOC arrived and worked on it and by the day's end they were back in business.

On 16 March the Regt Signal section returned from their mobilisation centre and moved into Moseley Old Hall which, now that 12 Bty HQ had moved out, had enough space for them.

By 20 March everyone had had the time to go down to the various possible sites in the Oxford area to work out what cable laying would be needed in the event of invasion to link up all these sites to their HQs.

The last ten days of the month were used in employing extra seconded labour to help with site work and road making to enable the guns to get in and out quickly. Because the guns were mobiles it was never intended for them to be held in static concrete positions and therefore all that was necessary when a quick move was called for was to jack them up from their 'davits' and re-fit the wheels and axle, wind the barrel down to the transit position, sort the stores and various other tasks before attaching the towing truck. The whole operation could be done in an hour including tagging on the ammunition lorry.

Lt Col. E.M.G. Brittan, the Regt CO, was extremely busy at these times and many of the routine documents were signed by his Adjutant, Capt. B.R. Emmett. One or two men were still attached to other commands and waiting to come back.

There is no breakdown of Officers, NCOs and O/Rs so it can't be determined whether they were at full wartime strength or not. But they can't have been too far off.

Because things had quietened down again and were not too hectic 12 Bty sent men off to Patshull Hall to use the range for some LMG practice (light machine-gun, such as Bren or Lewis guns).

It was not a very nice day with drizzle rain but the O/C was happy enough with the results and it was a good chance to catch up on some infantry training. Some of the men had up till then only fired the Lewis guns from anti aircraft mounts, so to do it lying prone on the ground was something of a novelty.

There was a bit of drama on 26th at the 'E' site when around midday a Junkers 88 came tearing over from the north west, hotly followed by three Hurricanes. Because of the friendly fighters the guns could not open fire but they had a grandstand view of the action. The site was elevated enough to witness the plane losing height rapidly and then jettisoning its bomb load about one and a half miles away. They did not see the final outcome but the odds were stacked heavily against the raider.

Once the practice 'Chestnut' exercise had been completed in early April the Brigade Cmdr made a special trip to Penn to inspect the Left Half of the battery there. These guns were still set up to the east of the road across the Common on the edge of the existing golf course. They were kept under camouflage netting when not in use.

During the night of 9 April there was a heavy raid on Coventry and the batteries to the south of Birmingham complained at how their radar had been affected by barrage balloons in the area.

Defences had been considerably stiffened after the calamitous raids during the previous November when the city had taken such a pounding. However balloons were not the complete answer because the raiders could still bomb from a height using radio beams. What was needed was the ability to fire well aimed barrages at seen and unseen planes and make them realise that this was a tough nut to crack. It was known that the chance of a direct hit was pretty small but if the air could be filled with sharp shards of steel which the aircraft could fly into then damage would also arise. Meeting something sharp and heavy at 200 miles an hour would always have the possibility of hitting a vital part and also making the crews extremely jittery.

12 Bty, down at Coventry on the two sites 'B' and 'E', had a good start on the 10th by scoring hits on two enemy aircraft. These were claimed as damaged rather than destroyed since without the evidence of a crash site on the ground that is all they would be credited with.

It was now that a series of moves around the Midlands were made as part of the training. Batteries were split to release troops of guns so they could be sent to different exercises, normally in sections of two. This involved packing up all their stores and equipment and sometimes their G/L gear and setting up in alternate locations sometimes for short periods only, but they had to be able to leave behind fully manned sites to cope with any raids in their absence.

On the night of 9/10 April Birmingham was heavily attacked with incendiaries and the next night the Regt was again reporting *'considerable enemy air activity in 15 Bty area on nights of 10/11 over their "Robert" site. Bombs and flares dropped to the north east of this position'*. There was *'no enemy contact'* made by the two other Btys, namely 3 and the other half of 15 who were still manning four guns at Upper Penn.

It was during this period that after a heavy raid on the Midlands one of the 15 Bty sites was visited by a large English Setter. The animal was obviously terrified and just looking for someone to make friends with. It was a lucky move since on the site was a Gnr Day who loved dogs and with its animal intuition it knew it had made a good choice. The dog gave loyalty and got it back in return and the friendship blossomed. It was to be seen gambolling about and enjoying itself, and with cotton wool in its ears could stay nearby and survive the gun blasts. It became a regular feature of the Bty and eventually became its unofficial mascot and went by the name of 'Day's Dog'.

The situation in the Wolverhampton area was now deemed quiet enough to re-start the Regt school in Tettenhall which had had to be abandoned because of the pressure of work. It was intended this time to send on each course 1 Officer, 4 NCO's and 4 OR's from each Bty in sequence for two weeks at a time. There they would be instructed in Regt history, gunnery, map reading, marching and drill, small arms drill or outdoor work in the afternoons and a good session of PT each day and most importantly too, aircraft recognition and security aspects. The instructors would come again from the CO, 2/ic, Adjutant, QMs and Battery Officers.

By 14 April the mobilisation training was still continuing, with each individual battery having to carry out an exercise somewhere. However Lt Col. Brittan went to 12 Bty area and watched a demonstration by them of driving a lorry towing a gun through a river. The CO was suitably impressed and recorded that *'using suitable winches and land anchors a Matador Tractor towing a gun could get out of anywhere'*.

Some of the men had in the past rather looked down on the Matador as an inferior vehicle since they had used Scammels in France, but this experiment, carried out correctly, proved the Matador was equally as good.

In the middle of the month extra manpower and vehicles arrived from the Mobilisation centre boosting the unit strength. These were comprised of men from the RAOC and totalled 2 Officers and 54 ORs and a selection of vehicles.

Towards the latter part of the month 12 Bty down near Coventry were visited by Colonel White and some of his staff from 11 AA Division. As was normal the gunners laid on a demonstration of coming into action and manning their guns.

Meanwhile 15 Bty was to lay on a demonstration exercise at one of their sites. Troops from the Regt School came to watch and were then used as critics of how it had gone. This suggests that the Regt School was near enough to be convenient to do this and probably reinforces the idea of it being at the Merry Hill site to the north west of Wolverhampton.

The month of May saw all Btys being split into troops and sections of guns again and spread around the areas, some to take part in exercises and others to bolster new locations.

It was during the period while 15 Bty had temporarily set up round Willenhall that Tom Evans met a pretty girl when out one evening with his mates visiting the local pubs. They danced the night away and from there things progressed till on Whit Monday 1941 they were married. At the time Tom had no qualms about his future because 6 Regt seemed destined to be part of the Home Defences.

The original scheme of *Interim Chestnut* was now implemented and batteries moved south to their positions near Banbury, Oxford and Didcot. It was a good chance to iron out any hiccups and let the signals sections lay their cables and allow everyone to communicate with everyone else.

It was considered a success and then they all moved back to their original Midlands sites. Regt HQ left their site at Oxford and moved into Bishton Manor. (Fig. 2.12) The two troops of 12 Bty returned to 'B' and 'E' sites near Coventry but their HQ moved into an area at Banner Hill which they had not used before. (This was given the code H25.) 3 Bty returned to

Fig. 2.12 Bishton Manor in Staffordshire used briefly as a Regt HQ.
Courtesy of Mr and Mrs Hollands

Willenhall/Wednesfield and the troop from 15 Bty rejoined their other half at the Penn Common site, making that a full 8 gun site once again. Not many days later two sections from 15 Bty found themselves at High Gate Farm near Halfpenny Green for a couple of days on yet another training exercise. This was not that far from the small airfield at Halfpenny Green which was under construction at the time.

16/17 May turned out to be very busy with a heavy air attack against Birmingham. The total number of guns had been reduced because some of the troops were still away on exercise *'Practice Bargain'* so those that remained had a busy time. Each site had remained manned but at reduced levels. At first it was not clear what the main target was since the bombers came over in streams. To 12 Bty in their current positions it soon became very obvious that the raid was heading for Birmingham. The guns engaged the leading aircraft of an estimated 150+ raiders.

The Right Half troop at the Coventry site 'E' concentrated on this leader using predictor control with the aid of G/L Mk2 and were so successful that it turned away losing height. Later reports suggested it may have been hit and damaged. This rather unsettled the following waves and they seemed unable to locate their target and started dropping large numbers of flares.

These flares lit vast areas and hung for minutes at a time as they slowly descended; in some cases the gunners attempted to shoot these out but they presented an incredibly small target.

The bombing was widespread covering aerodromes and power stations and Nuneaton suffered badly though not on the scale of previous attacks on the Midlands. It is possible that having lost the lead aircraft as a guide the remainder struggled to find their targets and then in desperation went for the first they came across which happened to be north of Coventry.

The Germans were trying the Pathfinder system early in the war where the leaders marked the intended target with flares or coloured markers. This is something that the Allies adopted later for the large scale raids on Germany.

They also employed a system of transmitted radio beams on which the aircraft aligned themselves prior to release of their bombs. This was not infallible since the Germans thought, and with due justification, that the beams were susceptible to being electronically jammed. This was something that the 'boffins' did find a way to do later in the war reasonably effectively.

During this same raid some aircraft spilled over into the range of 15 Bty who were split into two troops, one at Wolverhampton and the other near Birmingham. Those on the 'R' site (possibly Edgbaston) had a grandstand view of proceedings. The Right troop on this 'Robert' site fired 31 rounds of HE in four central controlled barrages at enemy aircraft flying at around 13,000 ft. There was no immediate result seen from this fire.

Meanwhile the Left troop at Upper Penn, and on their own since the rest were away on an exercise, fired 5 rounds of HE in another central controlled barrage at bombers flying much higher at around 18,000 ft. The results of this fire were very much clearer and the leader immediately released some bombs which fell some distance north of their position. These were two H.E. bombs of medium calibre and seen and heard to detonate on the ground.

The next day, 18 May, the Right troop of 12 Bty who were down close to Coventry were moved again from their 'E' site to a new site 'O' not far from Bannerhill. (Using the original code letters for the various sites 'O' equates with Olton Hall which housed a troop of 4 static 3.7".) The site itself was to the north west of Coventry but within the suburbs of Birmingham. They had hardly got there when they were in action again.

So it went on, the shuffling of troops of guns to different sites all designed to help confuse the Luftwaffe as to where they might expect to be fired on and to try and second guess where the next raid might be aimed.

On 23 May, Maj. Gen. Grove White and his staff visited a troop of 3 Bty who were involved in an exercise near Leconfield. This exercise was called a *'Bertram Mills'* scheme. The CO and the Bty Cmdr also visited on the same day. (Those of the older generation will recognise this name as that of the famous circus owners who travelled the country for many years after the war with their Big-Top Circus and animal show.)

Up to this time the 3 Bty had not seen raids to the same extent as the others but with the approach of the full moon this was expected to change. The state of the moon helped the gunners immensely. If they were lucky they might see something of what they were aiming at. However it did not always hamper the Luftwaffe when it was cloudy because they were able to use their system of 'beams' to aid 'blind bombing' through cloud.

Meanwhile back at Penn Common it was decided to reopen the Regt School yet again and this duty fell to Maj. Moxon for the first stint.

By the 25th, because of the redistribution of guns to bolster the Birmingham defences, it was decided to close the Upper Penn site (H49) for the time being. It was obvious that not a lot of action was happening there and it was necessary to remove the G/L Mk2 radar for better use elsewhere.

June saw parts of the Btys again on the move but this time much further to the north for a large exercise to be carried out in the north Midlands. This was to allow senior commanders to have the chance of controlling groups of troops and guns in a wider area and in conjunction with other units. There was an ambitious plan which involved enemy forces being played by infantry, to represent a landing of German forces by parachute and then being reinforced by further troops arriving by sea in assault craft.

Then in June one troop of 3 Bty left for Yorkshire to take part in another *'Bertram Mills'* scheme while the Right troop of 15 Bty carried out a mobile exercise to occupy the empty half of the gun site at Upper Penn. This was again for the benefit of the Regimental school for the men to watch and criticise the performance. They left their 'R' site for the day and returned that evening.

The Left troop of 3 Bty, who were still at Upper Penn with their four guns, were busy the next night when at around 0130 hrs they engaged aircraft with 14 rounds of HE. The height they were flying at was about 12,000 ft. There were no visible results.

On 7th the Right troop of 15 Bty at 'R' site again set out for another exercise, this time to occupy a two gun site near Bridgenorth. Then for a change the gunners left at Penn were subjected to an attack by the Home Guard against their positions on the golf course. This was to represent training for both parties and at the end of the day the Left troop were declared the winners. It does not bear thinking about if they had lost.

12 Bty sent two guns and their instruments for a demonstration at Wyken cricket ground, and also to be used in the anti tank role. They then set off on a 50-mile night run in their vehicles.

June and July passed in this fashion with sporadic activity against the *Luftwaffe* and the Btys were kept busy visiting several different areas around Wolverhampton including Highgate Common and Muckley Corner and as far south as Stratford, and then shortly after those on the 'R' site and Wednesfield 'E' site swopped over.

To keep up the fitness of the men a PT competition was arranged among the various sections and Lt Whale's group came second with 2/Lt Adams fourth.

12 Bty were pleased to see a new G/L Mk 2 arrive on 14 June but they still awaited the skilled technicians to set it up and tune it in. Until this happened they could only eye the equipment with envy.

The next day the new CO arrived to visit the sites and they found he was called Lt Col. Baass.

Towards the end of the month while there was an easing of air activity, fitters from the RAOC arrived to check the gun liners.

By early August 3 Bty were busy engaging German aircraft several nights a week and then they became involved with more exercises and practice shoots which involved some of the gunners going to Wales to use the ranges. Others left to go south for an exercise 'Tiger' in the Sussex and Kent area.

When these had been completed 3 Bty came back to the Midlands and took up sites near Donnington. Because of the need to release gunners to go for practice shoots on the Welsh ranges the 198th Bty was put under command and took over the empty site at Upper Penn (H49).

The life of a gunner was never dull, they were constantly on the move at short notice and each time all guns and stores had to be shipped out. During the summer months it was very pleasant and at times possible to visit the local pubs for an evening drink. However as the weather worsened and the time spent on one site increased then mud could become a serious problem.

They had to ensure that whatever the time of day they would still be able to tow their guns off the site and move to the next. Things started to get rather complicated around this time since it was necessary for 15 Bty to get away to training in Wales for practice shoots.

Yet another Bty was brought in temporarily to maintain manned gun numbers while this was happening and this was 181st Bty from a different Regt. They were all split up and the transport from 3 and 15 Btys was used to transport the incoming men to their new homes. Briefly they ended up such that 181 Bty was split down the middle and manning two sites, namely one of the two at Coven Heath (H1) and the other attached to the site at Merry Hill (H18).

The site at Merry Hill was an established static site containing $4 \times 3.7"$ but it is not clear whether they took over the guns there or just boosted its numbers.

Once the 181 Bty gunners were in place the 198 Bty who they had replaced then moved to Bushbury (H50) and Tipton, temporarily, before changing transport and moving to yet more sites, Wednesfield (H52) and an unnamed site designated (H16) near Stourbridge.

It was most important throughout these 'musical chairs ' that all guns that were left in place were manned by at least 50% of their crews.

Towards the end of August 15 Bty returned from practice camp and proceeded to return to their previous sites, and this left 198 Bty awaiting information on where it was to go.

One troop from 3 Bty came back from Donnington where they had been manning the two sites D/A and D/C complete with all their guns and moved into Rubery (H13) south west of Birmingham. (D/A was to the east of present-day Telford town and D/C to the north of it.) Their new HQ was at Nuthurst (H11) somewhat further south of Birmingham and not far from what is now the M42/M40 junction.

15 Bty now established itself again on Upper Penn (H49) with their HQ in the Wodehouse, the large private home set in its own gardens less than half a mile from the Common. They could keep in contact with their gunners by despatch rider and use the Church Hall at St Bartholomew's for messing and accommodation although there were still at this time a series of temporary huts and tents on the Common and various ancillary stores for troops.

Generators throbbed providing power to the various items although an overhead electric cable had been rigged up running down the east side of the Common and close to the duck pond. There was also a telephone linking them to the gun site at Langley Road in Merry Hill a few miles away (H18).

Around this time Dvr W. Boomer No 1568462 joined the Regt in 15 Bty along with his best mate Robert Burns No 1568466. He had enlisted in 1940 and first joined 60th HAA. He had missed the debacle of Dunkirk but served on the south coast where he used to joke they were so short of equipment that in his slit trench were three men: one with a rifle and two with pickaxe handles!

60 HAA and 6 HAA became part of the air defences for the Midlands. After sitting rather apprehensively in a lorry loaded full of AA shells during a raid on Coventry they both decided to apply for a transfer to a regiment that was going to serve overseas. He was to have a few lucky escapes and could have avoided them all because he was profoundly deaf in one ear from childhood and had managed to hide this at his medical.

By early September 3 Bty were due to go away to Aberporth for gun training and the sites they had manned were to be taken over by 198 Bty. It was intended that all 3 Bty guns be left *in situ* and taken over by the incoming battery and only a rear party left to welcome the 198 Bty, while the outgoing gunners were to travel to Wales by train.

Since they had been living under canvas these tents would also be taken over on temporary loan by the 198 Bty and all their transport would also be taken on charge.

While they were away in Wales orders came through that the 6 HAA Regt was to be drafted to the Middle East, most probably Iraq to guard the rail heads near Basra. (This was a move that had been mooted some months before when it was noted they were to draw Khaki Drill kit.) They were not told their exact destination and most of the men, helped by the inevitable rumours, thought they were on their way to North Africa. It was now they were told that all their sites were going to be taken over by 71st Regt HAA.

While they waited for their move and because of the good weather up to 100 men a day from the Regt were lent to local farmers to help gather in what remained of the harvest.

Regimental organisation now moved into top gear, for it was intended to recover all batteries from their respective locations and via three large convoys depart for the south of England to Wiltshire and Salisbury Plain. Everything had to be accounted for and handed over to the 71st Regt, from stores, secret documents and maps, to tents and beds. An advance party of 4 Officers and 40 ORs were to go to the mobilisation centre to get things ready.

71st HAA Regt had been one of the first to engage the *Luftwaffe* during their time in Scotland when German aircraft had attacked the shipping in the Firth of Forth in October 1939. This had been a sudden and unexpected attack and much of the defence were taken by surprise.

They had now had their warning order of a move on 20 September 1941 to come south and take over from the Midlands gunners. They comprised the 227, 229 and 325 Btys.

It was intended for their Regt HQ to move to Hints Hill near Tamworth while the 227 Bty HQ took over the Wodehouse. The Right troop of 227 would take over an 'Edward ' site called (H2). This is the designation of the static site at Saredon near Wedges Mills south of Cannock but would more likely have been (H52), one of the Wednesfield sites, and the Left troop would take over Upper Penn (H49). To the local population round Penn who had become so used to men and guns coming and going , it was probably a while before they realised they had new neighbours.

The left Troop of 229 were to go to Nuthurst (H11) while the Right troop went to Rubery (H13) complete with all their G/L equipment.

The 325 Bty Left troop were to move into Brookfield (H4) or Perry Park and the Right troop would man Banner Hill (H25), one being well on the northern outskirts of central Birmingham and the other to the south.

They were to take over the 3.7" mobile guns left by 6 Regt where applicable and because the radar had been removed from Upper Penn in late May they installed their own G/L Mk 2 for the 4 × 3.7" guns.

They had not been in position for more than a week when part of the Batteries were ordered to go on an anti invasion exercise in the area of High Wycombe. The first part was to be called exercise *Bumper* and once this was finished they would start the second which went by the name of *Percy*.

In fact they did not spend very long in the Midlands, only around a couple of months, before they too were drafted in December 1941. They took up locations down near Clacton to try and counter German mine-laying aircraft which were seeding the waters with magnetic mines at night. The intentions of this mine laying were to try and paralyse shipping in the Thames estuary and also to deny the use of the natural anchorages further to the north. In the early days many of these mines were magnetic and non-contact. They could sit in shallow water waiting for a ship to pass close by and then the ships natural electric field would cause it to detonate with devastating results.

Chapter 3

Leaving the UK for Iraq, but diverted to Singapore

We now return to the 6th Regt who were by now departing for Wiltshire having marched out of their various locations, Patshull Hall, Bishton Manor, Wodehouse, Moseley Old Hall, Crescent House, and the drill hall in Stafford Street where many had spent the night. They left an ongoing argument with the parish of Upper Penn who claimed over £200 for damages to their hall used for the duration of the troops' stay. This was disputed, as all these things invariably are, but nonetheless the damage was considerable comprising damaged light fittings, dents to walls, broken doors and windows and the destruction of many of the hall's folding chairs. A settlement was made much later by the War Office but it still did not cover the claim.

Having arrived safely in Bulford they then left their transport and after staying overnight journeyed back north by trains to reach Nottingham and then Yorkshire the next day. Their new address for their brief stay was GPO, Merrals Hill, Morton, Nr Bingley Bradford, Yorks. Here men were allowed to go on leave and new men joined to make up numbers.

One of those who had joined recently was Gnr H.I. Dawson No 1634325 from Yorkshire, who had, prior to training as a gunner, worked in a shunting yard with the railways.

Once they had got their pre-embarkation leave out of the way the Regt made its way to Liverpool. Here everyone had their injections and a medical and then were issued with Khaki Drill uniforms. There was much merriment among the men as to their various states of bad dress and the over-long baggy shorts. Once everyone had been attended to and their stores loaded they went to board their ship, *Monarch of Bermuda*, for the Middle East.

They had their full complement of Btys and once the ship had completed loading they sailed north to join up with further ships from the Clyde to make up convoy WS. 12. Z. This was a sixteen-ship convoy and protected by escorts.

Having moved out from harbour in late October 1941 they waited while the convoy formed up and then they set out for the Middle East early November. They sailed around the north coast of Ireland and then headed for the South Atlantic. At this time the United States had not joined the war so all the defences of convoys were provided by British ships with an occasional destroyer loaned by the US Navy. The German submarine war was going well in their favour because of our lack of suitable effective counter measures and shortage of escorts.

Up to this time the troops on board had still not been told their final destination, but having been issued with KD desert kit they all assumed it was to North Africa. They were now informed they were actually on their way to Iraq.

After plodding along for a couple of weeks they stopped briefly at Freetown (Sierra Leone) around 28 November. The town welcomed them eagerly as several thousand men went ashore from this convoy to spend their hard-earned pay. To many men this was their first sight of native Africans and the desire to convey this resulted in many sending home postcards which today would be classed as very 'non-PC' – pictures of naked 'piccaninnies' standing around holding leaves or coconuts. After this brief stop ashore to stretch their legs and buy a few souvenirs the convoy then set out for Durban in South Africa which they reached on 18 December 1941.

A letter survives from a church organisation in Durban saying they had met Walter Mear of 15 Bty and some of his mates and given them tea, and as promised sent this note to their families to say they were all well. (Fig. 3.1) This at least allowed his relatives to know where he was.

By this time it was known that on 7 December the Japanese had launched unprovoked attacks against Pearl Harbor, and Siam (modern Thailand). Hong Kong , Malaya, and the Philippines were also on the list.

The drama now started to unfold and its roots could be traced back to 1933. For years the British Government and the Military had argued over whether Singapore needed a large base and what form it should take. When it was pointed out that the Far East needed a secure base from which to guard the empire a site had to be decided on. After further dithering a location on the north coast was chosen and work started slowly on constructing this base. The Air Ministry said they could protect it adequately using aircraft alone but the Army and Navy were not so sure.

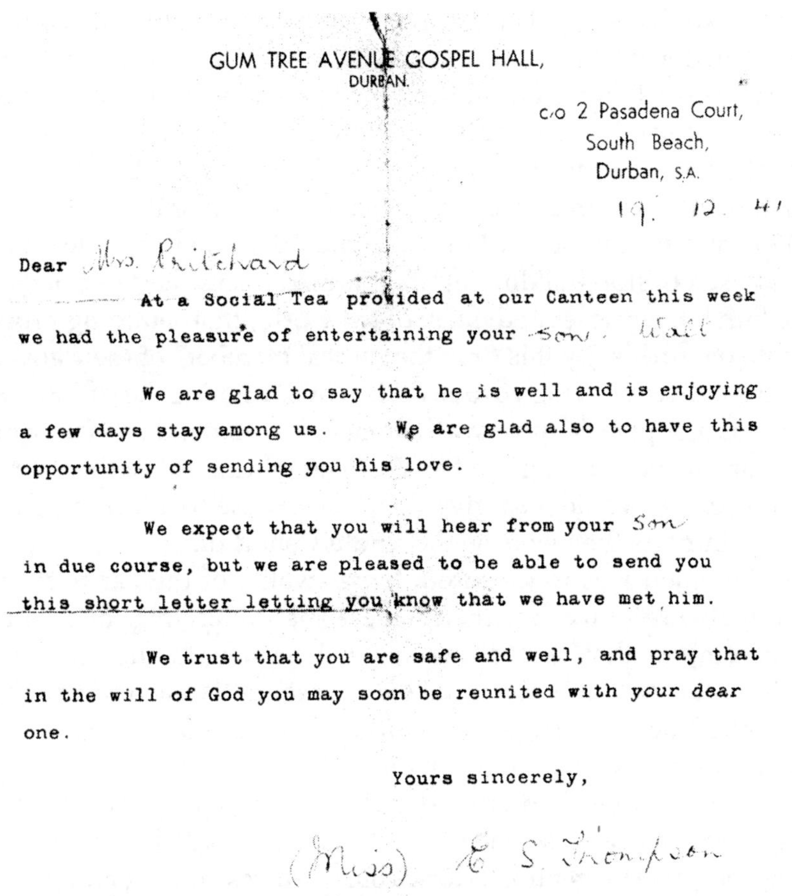

GUM TREE AVENUE GOSPEL HALL,
DURBAN.

c/o 2 Pasadena Court,
South Beach,
Durban, S.A.

19. 12. 41

Dear *Mrs. Pritchard*

       At a Social Tea provided at our Canteen this week
we had the pleasure of entertaining your *Son. Walt*

      We are glad to say that he is well and is enjoying
a few days stay among us.   We are glad also to have this
opportunity of sending you his love.

      We expect that you will hear from your *Son*
in due course, but we are pleased to be able to send you
this short letter letting you know that we have met him.

      We trust that you are safe and well, and pray that
in the will of God you may soon be reunited with your dear
one.

Yours sincerely,

(Miss) E S Thompson

Fig. 3.1 The letter from a church in Durban telling of entertaining Gnr Mear.
Courtesy of Michael Mear

An airfield was constructed at nearby Seletar and the Naval base was given its own guns for protection. Because of the thinking at the time these guns were generally large calibre. They were added to at different times but there were never as many as originally envisaged.

Around the same time as the construction work started in 1933 Japan had started to flex her muscles. She was desperately short of raw materials and the first incursion was to invade Manchuria and set up a puppet state called Manchucko. When she was accused by the League of Nations and told to withdraw, she promptly pulled out of negotiations and proceeded to start to enlarge her navy to a size that she considered suitable for her needs. The army, which was quite considerable for the time, was enlarged even further too. In the years while this was happening, the base in Singapore continued to slowly take shape. The Fortress defences were strengthened over time by the construction of three more airfields, one in the north west near the causeway called Tengah, one at Sembawang not far from the dockyard and another in the south called Kallang. With the original one not far from the docks called Seletar, this left Singapore with three airfields in the north and one to the south, and these were considered enough for the island's defence.

In 1936 at a conference in London, when the Japanese delegation were again advised to stop building up their armed forces they stormed out and, just to thumb their noses at the rest of the world, their building programme went into overdrive. By this time the radical members of their government within the military, having virtually taken over running the country with the Emperor as a puppet figure, saw their chance to expand and carry out their longed-for dream of ruling the Far East and getting rid of the 'White man' in the process. It would also give them the excuse to attack neighbours to regain the imports they were so desperately short of.

Their intention was to capture a large swathe of the Far East and gain these valuable resources for themselves. The underlying intention was to rule this empire themselves and have their neighbours as subservient countries. Malaya had at this time over three million acres of rubber trees and supplied nearly 50% of the world's tin (25,000 tons annually), and Sumatra provided vast amounts of oil.

The Japanese had looked around and the next country they wanted parts of was China. It was also the closest so they invaded. This led to fierce fighting and some horrendous stories of massacres, looting and pillaging by vast numbers of troops who had lost all discipline. Much of this unruly behaviour was encouraged by the Japanese army doctrine imparted to the troops that they were superior to the Chinese and they could treat them as sub-human. Having seen that the rest of the world did nothing to stop their expansion plans they became bolder.

Meanwhile after three years of construction the Singapore Fortress was well on its way but not completed. The Government had built into the scheme an extra stipulation that in the event of attack it had to be able to hold out for 90 days to allow reinforcements to reach them from the UK. It had long been realised that the defence of Singapore went hand in hand with air superiority and that it also hinged on the Malayan mainland being strong enough to resist any attack against it and so prevent an army marching down the isthmus.

Long-standing disagreements over the years between the Air Force and the Army had festered to such an extent that the Air Force started to build airfields in the north of Malaya in places totally unsuitable for defence. This had continued without any agreement as to how the defences would be coordinated.

There was a supposed master plan called 'Matador' and this allowed for the standing Army to move into Siam should that country be invaded to halt any advances from an aggressor from that direction. In the event when the Japanese did attack there was so much dithering and questioning of orders and whether the situation allowed for the move into Siam, that by the time it was resolved the whole thing was academic and the Japanese were already well established and moving south.

Regressing slightly the Japanese continued to hold on to Chinese territory which they had taken and because they had been warned by their economists that they would have serious shortages of raw materials especially oil, rubber, tin, iron ore and bauxite, they planned their next moves in order to secure these commodities as well.

The first plan was to invade Indochina but despite the warnings from the USA they did not withdraw. This was too much for the Americans who on 26 July 1941 immediately froze all funds and instigated a trade embargo on all goods. This basically tipped the Japanese over the edge and their master plan for the Far East was up and running again.

They were going to attack each and every country in the area and capture all the main resources that they so desperately needed in one short sharp well coordinated series of invasions.

Their main fear was the strength of the US fleet based in Honolulu's Pearl Harbor which needed to be surprised so they could neutralise the main threat against them at sea. Malaya was also to be invaded as was Hong Kong, Siam, the Philippines and the islands of Sumatra, Java and Timor. The basic plans were all in motion and Fortress Singapore was high on their list since this posed a thorn in their side if it was left without being neutralised.

Now back in the present again in December 1941, once word of the invasions reached the Allies, urgent discussions were held and the orders came through that the convoy, now anchored at Durban, would split and one part would make its way to the Far East to help bolster the defences there. The remainder would carry on to the Middle East and unload its war materials as originally intended. In a hurried change of plans troops were recalled from shore and hasty preparations made to split them for the onward voyage. 6 Regt were transferred to another troop ship called *Aorangi* and because of the muddled situation many of their stores were not loaded with them. The convoy designation now became DM-1 and around Christmas Eve it sailed for Singapore.

This part of the journey was to take more than two and a half weeks and they arrived in Singapore on 13 January 1942. The men gained a bit of a suntan on the way but no training.

By this time, the Japanese who had landed in North Malaya were busy fighting their way down the country. The attackers were well trained veterans, many from the fighting against the Chinese, and they appeared almost unstoppable. Wherever they hit serious resistance they then took to the sea or outflanked the defending forces.

Their tactic was 'strike hard and strike quickly' and where the allied experts said troops could not go because of the terrain they proved everyone wrong. One of their more unusual tactics was to mount men on bicycles for fast deployment down the few roads available. They had overcome the airfields and resistance in the north of Malaya in the first few days of the fighting, forcing the allied troops back in total disarray. Bad weather had meant that the ground defenders were without proper air support for many of the vital days. There were a variety of Commonwealth troops trying to stem the tide, including many who were Australians, New Zealanders and Indians, but try as they might they could not hold them off.

Against this fast moving army the defenders suffered from the fact that large numbers of Indian and Commonwealth troops were untried in battle and in many cases poorly trained. One of their worst horrors was when they came face to face with tanks, something many had never seen before.

Several army Battalions had been rushed in from the empire to counter the perceived threat but none of these were jungle trained or in most cases even acclimatised to the stifling humidity and the conditions under which they would have to fight. The defending forces were hopelessly out-gunned in the air and when the *Prince of Wales* and the *Repulse* were both sunk by bombing in the second week of December the naval balance changed radically.

The Japanese attack on Malaya had forced Churchill to rethink his policy on the Far East. Still under the impression of the impregnable 'Fortress Singapore', because that is what he had been led to believe by those in command out there, he had despatched the two ships from Ceylon (modern-day Sri Lanka) to sail to the Fortress and start to show their strength.

What had happened then was after reaching HMS *Terror*, the naval base on the northern coast of Singapore island, they resupplied and then set off up the east coast of Malaya with scant escort. They had been promised air cover but at the last minute the RAF said this could not be supplied. Nevertheless Admiral Tom Phillips felt they should do something, so they set off despite this. He was quite confident that the ships and escorts had enough fire power to hold off any threat.

Having sailed north for a day and found no sign of any Japanese invasion fleet, which was in fact considerably further north, the task force turned around only to be told (erroneously) that attacks were at that moment taking place on the coast of Malaya near Kelantan. They altered course and as bad luck would have it a Japanese scout plane on its last sweep of the day caught sight of them through the cloud cover.

It was 10 December 1941 and the scout radioed back the information to the 22nd Air Flotilla who immediately started changing some of their bombs for torpedoes. Early the next day 85 aircraft took off in waves and searched for the two capital ships. At around 1030 hrs in the morning they finally sighted them and the battle began. Before they knew it the two capital ships were being heavily attacked by bombs and torpedo-carrying planes. The attacks were relentless. Having turned at high speed to 'comb' the tracks of torpedoes they then found themselves under bomb attack and having jinked to avoid these they found even more torpedo planes coming at them from all different angles. The ships absorbed several torpedo strikes but it was obvious they were gravely damaged. Japanese torpedoes were considerably more powerful than the then current British types and damage was considerable to the hull below the water line, and the 12" armour belt did little to help because it was primarily designed to stop shell fire.

Later that same day the orders were given to abandon the ships and they both sank with heavy loss of life and Admiral Tom Phillips was among the casualties. It had taken just a few hours and the pride of the Navy's Far East fleet was lying on the bottom. So quick and efficient had been the attacks that the myth started that the Japanese were invincible in the air, on the sea and land and it would take some time before it was proved this was not the case.

So much for sabre rattling, the little 'yellow men' had provided a classic example of how it should be done. To be fair to the capital ships much of the disaster was caused by not having adequate air support and this in turn let the Japanese aircraft have a clear run at the ships.

After this success, slowly but surely the Japanese on the mainland continued their advance pushing all before them down the isthmus; they now knew that their fleet was no longer at risk from heavy naval units.

It was into this scenario that the convoy carrying the 6 HAA Regt Gunners docked in Singapore past smoking sunken ships, during an air raid and in a tropical storm on 13 January 1942. What the new arrivals could not possibly know was the extent of the disaster unfolding further north or for that matter the bitter rivalries amongst the senior generals and commanders on the ground. The Australian General Bennett thought he should be running the whole show and had bitter arguments with his fellow Officers and much back- stabbing had gone on.

On the British side, despite an Army General being in charge, the position was even more bizarre, since with the Civilian Governor and his Government staff still in place, neither could decide who was in overall command and whose instructions the troops should obey. The Navy took umbrage that they might be controlled by the Army and tended to stay out at the Naval Base which was some thirteen miles from the Army GHQ at Fort Canning. There was so much 'in-fighting' going on in the background that the situation gradually slipped beyond anyone's control.

On 4 January 1942 shortly before the convoy's arrival, General Wavell had taken overall command as Supreme Commander ABDA forces (Australian, British, Dutch and American). He had visited and made assessments of the situation and it left him horrified and his immediate response was to try and get General Percival to realise how serious the true situation was.

It could be seen how quickly things had progressed and that the original idea that Singapore would face its main threat from the sea was now not the case. Many of the guns had been sited for this eventuality and a desperate race was on to find which guns could be trained towards the Malay peninsula. Engineers worked all hours to remove concrete walls and if possible roofs to allow guns to train to the threat. Side walls were broken out and the anti bombing roofs were now a liability and prevented many guns being of much use.

At the same time ammunition checks had been made and found the stocks woefully short. The peace time scales had never been upgraded, and because of the expected threat from out at sea, most ammunition for the larger guns was armour piercing. Hurried orders were sent out for as many of the large calibre HE shells as could be found to be shipped in at once. Sadly none of them ever arrived in time. The army still thought the 'little yellow men' were inferior soldiers and not really a problem and this under-estimate was part of the undoing of the whole campaign.

So the convoy disgorged 4000 men, part of the 18th Division, with some of their stores to join the defenders. Unfortunately because the original intention had been for the gunners to go to Iraq, and then spend some time training and acclimatising, many of the stores had not been loaded tactically so a lot of the Regiment's equipment had gone to be unloaded in the Middle East and those who had landed in Singapore had to be hastily re-equipped from local supplies. Amongst the stores in some of the ships' holds were some 50 Hurricanes for the RAF, in crates ready to be assembled and put into action to aid the hard-pressed defenders, sadly too little too late and many were still in their crates weeks later.

The ships had berthed at the main wharf of the Empire Dock and efforts were made to unload as quickly as possible. Troops stood around in large groups on the dock amidst huge piles of stores and equipment awaiting someone to tell them where they were to go. Valuable transport ships such as these were in great demand and it was intended to turn them around as quickly as possible.

Not helping in the chaos were the queues of civilians, mostly women and children who were trying to escape from the wharfs and eagerly awaiting passage in what few ships were available going in the other direction. The escapees were desperately aiming to reach either Colombo (in Ceylon) or Australia.

The gunners finally moved off to take over part of the defence of Singapore city which was on the south coast of the island and furthest from the advancing Japanese. By this time there was a steady stream of civilian refugees coming onto the island fleeing the fighting on the mainland. Those that had relatives in local Kampongs (villages) settled there but many who did not just set up tents in parks and open spaces.

Singapore had continued to live in its Colonial past, complacent in its belief that with all the additional defensive works it was impregnable. There were well over 80,000 troops spread around the island and it had a large garrison force to man the gun sites. These guns ranged from the enormous 15 inch right through 9.2 inch and down to 6 inch. They were predominantly around the perimeter of the island, or sited on islands nearby, and positioned to cover approaches from the sea and in their hardened concrete emplacements would have been more than a match for any hostile approaching ships. However, surprisingly, all was not what it seemed, and there were only about 30 shells each for the 9.2 inch guns.

There were the four airfields with fighters and bombers but unfortunately many of the latter were almost obsolete and out-gunned. The stories being peddled by intelligence about the quality of the Japanese air force were about to come home to haunt them and they soon discovered they were totally out-gunned and out-manoeuvred by skilful and experienced pilots. Some intelligence briefings by senior RAF officers claimed that '*Japanese planes are a joke, they are held together by string and bits of bamboo, and there aren't too many of them either*'.

Other items protecting the island included a special anti submarine mine boom defensive system on the approaches to the Dockyard, huge Naval guns and searchlight batteries and over 80 anti aircraft guns at strategic locations, many of the guns being controlled by basic Radar. Along much of the coastline there were wire entanglements and minefields, with the exception of large areas of the north and north west where mangrove and creeks made this difficult.

Added to this was the unerring belief of General Percival, who was in overall command, that the onslaught would come in from the north east. It was pretty obvious by then that Singapore was going to have to fight for its survival. One of his worst blunders was to ignore the advice of his Chief Defences Engineering expert who tried desperately to get defences built along the north and north west shores only to be told *'extra defences are bad for the morale of the civilians'*.

Thus the scene was set and a very large chink was left in the defensive armour of this supposedly impregnable fortress. The whole defensive strategy relied too on the defenders being backed up by superior airpower.

By this time the advancing Japanese were well down Malaya and to the north of Johore Bahru and still pushing all before them.

Some of the LAA gunner units from the convoy had been sent immediately across the Causeway into the southern part of Malaya to link up with the hard- pressed defenders and they found themselves in action almost immediately.

Within the next few days 3 Bty had set itself up a couple of miles inland from Keppel Harbour in the south with some guns close to a golf course and awaited the onslaught, integrating their borrowed guns with those of the existing defenders as part of the outer ring round the city. (Map 3)

15 Bty were also set up on the Keppel Golf Course close to the top of a hill with the men's tents lower down the slope. There were, not far away, a group of smart European houses and from the site they could see the sea and numerous small islands off the coast. Equipment was sparse and air raid warnings notoriously inadequate.

This was hardly the best way of acclimatising when going to a new posting and for many of the men involved it was a totally new environment. None had had the time to get used to the hot temperatures and high humidity, there was the constant nuisance of mosquitoes but above all the fear of being thrust straight into combat. Most were wearing desert uniforms, which were suitable for where they expected to be, but the QM stores had not had time to re-issue them with jungle greens. Much of their equipment was sand coloured as were their camouflage nets. They now found themselves manning guns in unfamiliar surroundings. Around them

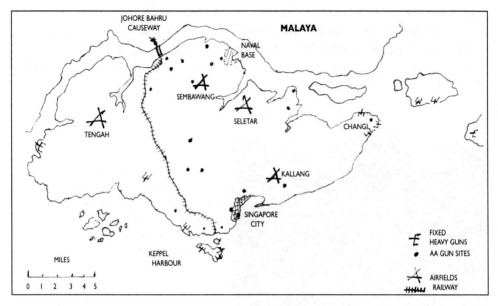

Map 3 1939–1945. Singapore Island.

there was much uncertainty as to what was happening and Officers spent hours attending briefings to find out the general situation and how they were to react to it.

The high humidity and almost daily rain made life exceedingly uncomfortable. Dry hard packed ground soon became a morass of mud. Weapons rusted almost overnight and ammunition had to be kept scrupulously clean and lightly oiled. Positions had to be protected by walls of sandbags and even in a short time these tended to sag and rot.

The constant threat of air attack meant they were manning their guns much of the time and all the while the news was not good. The rapid progress of the Japanese troops could not be kept secret and it was obvious that troops were being withdrawn to the island from the mainland while the Regt carried on with their manning of the 3.7" guns spread out around areas thought to be at most risk.

On 21 January 1942, hardly a week after arriving, they suffered their first casualties. Two men travelling in a vehicle from the north of Singapore back to HQ in the city were subjected to an attack by a Japanese aircraft. The vehicle was bombed and badly damaged and A/Bdr Oakley R.H. No 1063227 was killed instantly. His companion Gnr Anstee W.E. No 8200116 was seriously injured and died some ten days later. Both men were from the RHQ.

It was now only a matter of time before things were to get desperate, almost daily attacks from the air showed how things were developing.

Among those who had disembarked and part of the HQ element of 3 Bty was Sgt Newcombe who had been promoted before leaving the UK. (Fig. 3.2)

Fig. 3.2 Sgt Stan Newcombe No 819125, one of the lucky survivors from the Burma Railway.
Courtesy Peter Cole MBE

Fig. 3.3 Left: Gnr Arthur F.B. Luffman. Right: Gnr Trevor Davies, 3rd Bty 6th HAA Regt RA Singapore, 1942.

Chapter 4

12 Bty and 15 Bty in Sumatra and Java

While 3 Bty continued to defend itself on the island the two other Btys 12 and 15 after a brief stay of about a week on shore were hastily re-equipped with what could be put together and put back on ships and set sail for Sumatra late January 1942, but not before some men had had the chance of a few days to go ashore and enjoy the sights and sounds of this exotic colony. In fact, just long enough for 6 men to catch gonorrhoea. (This would become problematical later when they ended up in a POW camp and there were no medicines to treat it.)

True to form Gnr Weston managed to find a telegraph office and sent a quick message. '*Arrived safe, address same Regt, base post office Malaya.*' Dated 26 Jan. 1942 the same day they arrived there. This must have created some surprise for his wife since no one knew where anyone had gone. Gnr Tart was able to write a short letter home which passed the sensor because he was able to say he knew the place well because he had been there before.

The Regiment's CO Lt Col Baillie accompanied these two Btys along with Regimental HQ.

Up till a couple of months before he was known to his fellow Officers by the name Baass, but he had placed an advertisement in *The Times* on 19 September 1941 along the following lines:

The London Gazette 19th Sept 1941
I , Geoffrey William Gray Baass residing at Bishton Manor, Albrighton in the county of Salop, a Lt Colonel in his Majesty's Royal Regt of Artillery, a natural born British subject, give notice that after the expiration of twenty one days from the date of publication hereof, I intend to assume the surname of Baillie-dated this 16th day of September 1941 (in) G.W.G.Baass Lt Col R.A.

Fig. 4.1 Gnr Walter Mear No. 1818076, the Welsh miner who
survived the Sumatra Railway.
Courtesy of Michael Mear

Thereafter any reports he wrote were in his new name.

Still amongst the gunners of 15 Bty was Tom Evans, who had been through the hell of Dunkirk, and the Welsh miner Walter Mear. (Fig. 4.1)

They were accompanied by gunners of Light AA units and troops being hastily evacuated from Singapore, many of whom were unarmed and in some cases injured. Many of these were not front-line soldiers but RAF ground staff needed to maintain the aircraft either already on Sumatra or about to be flown down there.

The large string of islands to the south and south east of Singapore, including Sumatra and Java, were predominantly Dutch colonies and had some Dutch soldiers as a token defence. They were bolstered by Ambonese and Achinese troops who were in reality not much more than an armed Militia controlled in the main by Dutch officers.

This little convoy including the SS *David* and the 'Spon' ran the gauntlet of bombing and threaded its way round the multitude of islands as it sailed

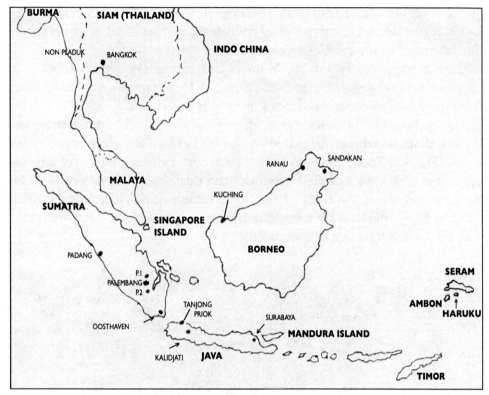

Map 4 Singapore, Sumatra and Java campaigns.

for Palembang on Sumatra, a town towards the eastern end of the island and where the port was situated on the north east coast. The town was sited some 70 miles inland and reached via a tidal estuary of the Moesi river. (Map 4)

The gunners were not on the only ship making a hasty exit. By this time it was obvious the situation in Singapore was extremely serious and everyone who could was trying to make their escape to the islands further south, or those lucky enough to be on larger vessels were looking to reach India or Australia.

Viewed from the air a multitude of boats of all sizes were sailing in groups and individually, heading mostly south east towards Sumatra. Many had civilians on board who had worked and lived in the Far East for many years. Others were loaded with service personnel advised to get out and many more were being sent away from the fighting because they were non-combatants such as fitters or armourers and of much more use on the airfields of Sumatra. Sadly some of those on the boats were deserters who had commandeered whatever they found, sometimes even at gunpoint, to the detriment of the existing occupants.

They arrived safely on 30 January and immediately unloaded their supplies and what guns they had managed to scrounge and drove away from the docks to occupy positions around two airfields.

Also included in the defensive strategy were several oilfield refineries and the installations which were sited on the far bank of the river opposite the town. (Fig. 4.2) These consisted of a vast array of storage tanks set out row upon row and a mass of pipe networks and machinery. These two facilities were spread along the river bank and although quite close to each other were in fact separated by a smaller tributary of the river. They extended well back from the edge of the water.

Fig. 4.2 Refineries at Pladjoe/Soengei Gerong under attack. Sumatra.   AWMP 02491256

Palembang was extremely important because it produced some 60% of the oil in the Dutch East Indies which amounted to some 4 million tons a year and this oil was classed as particularly 'sweet' and suitable for refining. Besides this the islands had large resources of tin, rubber and copra, things the Japanese were seriously deficient of in their own country.

Because of the chaotic nature of their departure from Singapore the Btys had arrived with only 6 × 3.7" mobile guns and very little ammunition to go with them, just some shrapnel shells. Much of their ammunition had been lost when a ship carrying it had been bombed by the Japanese and sunk and this had also caused great loss of life.

While the various troops went off to their respective locations RHQ set itself up in Palembang town in the Methodist mission. They did not know it at the start but were soon to realise that they overlooked the local brothel.

Up to this point the airstrips had not really had any sort of coordinated defence system except for some Dutch Bofors guns, but with the arrival of some 40 hurricanes and an assortment of bombers such as Hudsons and Blenheims from various sources it now became a necessity.

The two airfields had the code names P1 and P2. P1 was situated at Pangkalan Benteng close to and north of Palembang while P2 was at Prabumulih some 40 miles further south. P1 like P2 was only defended by some 150 native troops and a couple of armoured cars. The arrival of the gunners and RAF personnel increased the logistic problems enormously.

During the chaotic situation in Malaya and Singapore it was now very apparent how serious the situation was. Many of the aircraft had been flown down from Malaya and Singapore when airfields had been captured and also additional ones had flown up from Java as part of 232 and 258 Squadrons. Some had been moved away from the airfields of north Singapore to avoid the dangers of bombing and shelling by the attacking forces.

Prior to the gunners' arrival it had been routine for aircraft to be flown up from Java, refuel at P2 then land in Singapore. The men and machines of 232 and 258 had had a rather unusual journey to reach the Far East anyway. They had been at Gibraltar in October/November 1941 and it was decided to transfer them to the carrier HMS *Ark Royal*. The idea was for 258 Sqdn and half of 605 to remain in Gibraltar while 242 and the other half of 605 embarked on the carrier and she set sail for Malta.

When it was judged close enough they were all to fly off and land to aid the defence of the island, a trip not without risk since the distance would be at the extreme range of their flying time. As is turned out they reached Malta in varying stages of unease since many were down to their last gallons of fuel slopping around the tanks.

The *Ark Royal* turned about out of the wind once she had launched her aircraft and set off for the return to Gibraltar with the intention of picking up the remainder of the squadron and carrying out a similar tactic. Unfortunately she was found and shadowed by U.81 who managed to get inside the escorts and put torpedoes into her. On 13 November 1941 she slowly settled and then sank. The survivors were returned to Gibraltar where a change of plan had to be hatched.

It was now decided because of the Japanese threats to the Far East that the surviving pilots from both squadrons should make their way there and form part of the defences. Thus they started a long tortuous journey across the width of Africa to eventually pick up the carrier HMS *Indomitable* which was waiting in the Indian Ocean. She then set off to Java with the intention of offloading her charges to fly to the airfield of Kemajoran (near Batavia) which they did successfully some days later.

Having landed and got themselves and the ground crews sorted out they then flew on up to Singapore where they became operational by 1 February 1942. It was not long after that they flew back to the fields on Sumatra in disarray. The airfields they arrived at had been built by the Dutch for just such an emergency and the Japanese knew exactly where P1 was. However for whatever reasons they did not seem to know about the existence of P2. Of the two P1 was mainly used for Hurricanes while P2 was predominantly for bombers such as Blenheims and Hudsons with the odd Buffalo thrown in. A large number of Australians crewed and serviced these aircraft, but many of the LAA units with their Bofors who were supposed to provide the defences were desperately short of ammunition.

The ground was predominantly dense jungle interspersed with some clearings and much swampy ground and along the coastal regions there were vast amounts of impenetrable mangroves and creeks which stretched for a considerable distance inland. Roads were few and far between and in many places constituted little more than rough tracks. The airstrips had been carved out of the surrounding jungle and relied on rolled dirt runways. The jungle canopy came right down to the edge of the dispersal areas and although aircraft could not be hidden in the tree line because of the swampy nature of the ground, they were set inside bays made from either bricks or sandbags which was considered more than adequate. In the surrounding areas there were plantations of rubber trees and pineapples but much of the rest was thick primary vegetation with occasional stretches of paddy fields.

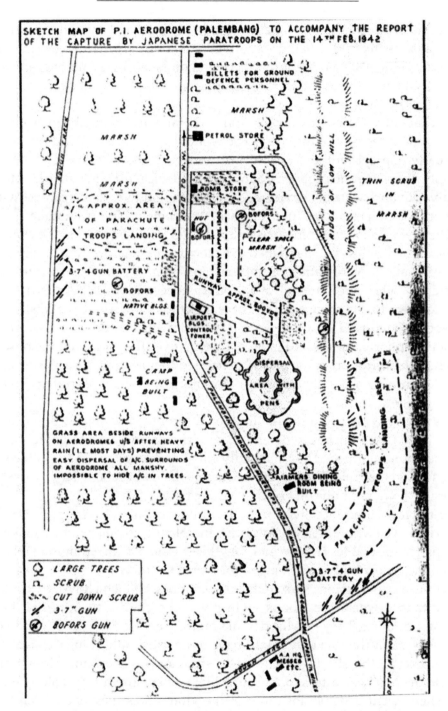

Fig. 4.3 Sketch of the airfield at Palembang, Sumatra, known as P1.

P1 had been constructed in a cleared area of jungle and contained just two runways, the main one being some 1400 yds long and the shorter angling across it being 850 yds. At the southern end of the north/south one, and set to one side, was the flight control building such as it was, made from brick and concrete. (Fig. 4.3)

The lack of facilities was very obvious. Aircraft were routinely pushed into bays built at the side of the strip to be worked on by fitters. Buildings were virtually non existent and any sort of transport was in desperately short supply. There were no proper radar or homing devices for returning aircraft or to give advance warning of approaching enemy raiders. Radio contact with airborne aircraft was at best poor and at certain times useless from static.

The main air-raid warning was to hoist a red flag up a pole on the control building and unless you happened to be looking in that direction you got no warning at all. Notification of approaching aircraft came via a system of 'watchers' who were stationed at various distances out from the airstrip and had to telephone in their reports. These watchers were situated at distances of about 50 and 100 kilometres away from the airfield. Because they were generally poorly trained and in most cases natives they were not the best at aircraft identification. In the past this had led to no end of false alarms and a lack of confidence in their abilities. A more flawed defence strategy could hardly be imagined.

Having been pitched into this situation the gunners frantically dug in and constructed slit trenches to defend these airfields and tried to get to know the surrounding area. They hurriedly filled sandbags to make protective walls round the guns. There was a lull before the main action started, mostly sporadic bombing raids on an almost daily basis.

In the meantime they lived in tents while local natives completed their *attap* huts. The whole area was swampy and plagued by mosquitoes making life pretty miserable. Hardly had they been issued with Straights Dollars when these now had to be changed for Dutch Guilders.

Because of the serious shortage of AA ammunition, which was to last for more than a week, the troops were given the chance to improve their infantry training. They practised 'tank' hunting and section attacks and got to know about the role they might have to adopt should things go wrong. The reason for this shortage was that the ship carrying the ammunition from Singapore had been attacked and sunk by Japanese aircraft, and along with the shells went a whole lot more of the vital stores they needed and so without sufficient ammunition, initially the gunners were mere witnesses to the unfolding events.

Hurricanes took off and landed and did their best to attack and break up the bombing raids, however the lack of warning meant they were more often than not caught taking off or going flat out to try and gain height from where they could engage the enemy formations. Invariably the attacking bombers were accompanied by large numbers of fighters. Strangely the Japanese bombers had the habit of flying in tight formation in groups of three with raids often comprising twenty-seven aircraft.

At P1 they had set up some of the HAA guns well to the south of the strip with Bofors gun positions between themselves and the runways. At the northern end was a large bomb store and still further north beyond a small access track was a large fuel dump. The remainder were set up to the west, outside a local road and also supplemented by Bofors guns sited closer to the main runways. Some of these Bofors were supplied by a section from 78 LAA Bty and aided by others from a troop of 84 LAA Bty.

It was intended for the Bofors to take on any low flying attackers while the 3.7" were to engage the higher ones. The shortage of Bofors ammunition was temporarily overcome by using shells borrowed from the Dutch which although of the same calibre were different in composition.

Communications were also problematical. No lines linked the guns to the control building and the control building was only connected to the town of Palembang by a very erratic telephone link and Palembang was where many of the personnel were actually billeted. The lack of transport would also make it very difficult for any personnel in the town to get back to the airstrip in an emergency or even to cover the long distances between points around the airfield where aircraft and materials had been dispersed for security.

A few days later another $10 \times 3.7"$ guns were about to be delivered on the SS *Subadar* when she was attacked and seriously damaged off the coast not far from the entrance to the Moesi River. The Captain managed to beach the ship while damage was assessed and then with sterling work from the engine room crews and engineers on board they managed to limp up the river to unload at the wharfs. These were the balance of the Regt's guns and the eagerly awaited supplies of ammunition were also unloaded. Everything with the guns was hastily distributed between the two airfields and some of these additional guns set up close to the refineries on the other side of the river.

This resulted in the dispositions being such that P1 had eight 3.7" of 15 Bty while P2 had four belonging to 12 Bty. The remaining four of 12 Bty were split to cover the areas of the two refineries of Pladjoe and Soengei Gerong, which included not only the machinery installations but vast areas of tank

Fig. 4.4 Dvr/Gnr Charles Vincent Nairne No. 797907. A survivor from Japan.
Courtesy of M. Hopton.

farms. Attached to the HAA guns at each location were a section of guns from 78 LAA Bty and aided by others from a troop of 84 LAA Bty.

Among those of 15 Bty was Gnr C.V. Nairne, he who had been burnt those months ago at Dunkirk. (Fig. 4.4)

The only way to get the guns across the river to the refineries was via a small ferry which had a maximum capacity of between four and six cars. On the waterfront in the refinery area there was also a small harbour with jetties and all the necessary unloading facilities required. As they unloaded stores they found much of the necessary equipment for controlling the guns and range finding was missing, having been sent to Iraq.

Because the Japanese already knew about P1 they had started to bomb it on an almost daily basis in late January1942. This continued into the first weeks of February and the attrition rates of aircraft shot down or destroyed on the ground resulted in more being flown up from Java.

1 Squadron RAAF (Australian) from P2 maintained their sorties over the mainland of Malaya bombing Alor Star and Kluang and any shipping seen. Targets of opportunity were often attacked in an effort to aid the troops on

the Malayan mainland.Tropical weather conditions often obscured the targets and made flying extremely uncomfortable especially when trying to locate P2 for the return landings.

Unknown to the Allied Officers in charge, the Japanese were setting in motion the beginning of the softening up process of the airstrip prior to an air and seaborne assault and many of these Japanese bombers were taking off from captured airfields on the Malayan mainland and Borneo. They had already set the date for the invasion of Sumatra and had postponed it once at the request of the Navy, and one of the prerequisites was the neutralisation of the allied airpower.

During this period the gunners were kept on their toes and the lack of efficient radar location meant that sometimes the first they knew of an impending raid was when the enemy aircraft were sighted overhead and bombs started exploding on the ground.

The state of the defences were seen to be short of small calibre AA weapons for the troops, so four Browning guns were removed from the Hurricanes so these could be fixed on special mounts to be constructed by a local metal workshop. The removal of the guns marginally improved the performance of the planes and the loss of firepower was not considered a problem by the pilots.

By the second week of February the situation was so critical in Singapore that flights were arranged for the Hudsons to fly up and try and pick up as many of the key senior RAF and Army personnel, and evacuate them to the supposed safety of Sumatra.

These were risky operations because they had to run the risk of being spotted en route and were in the main unescorted by friendly fighters.

Chapter 5

3 Bty as Malaya Falls and Singapore Capitulates

———————

In the meantime the forces on the Malayan mainland had finally decided they could no longer hold out and withdrawn back to Singapore across the world-famous causeway. Long columns of transports and troops cluttered all the routes funnelling into Johore Bahru, the Malayan town at the northern end of the causeway, coming from both east and west coast roads.

The causeway was blown up at the end of January 1942 by the Engineers just as soon as the last of the troops had crossed. The aim was to try and hold off the advancing hordes.The last to cross over were a detachment of the Argyll and Sutherland Highlanders led by their piper playing a jaunty reel as they marched the three-quarters of a mile along the embankment. The bulk of the causeway was solid stone with a rip-rap face but at the northern end there had been a small bridge to allow small fishing boats to get from one side to the other without having to go completely round Singapore island. The causeway carried a rail track and large water pipelines on concrete plinths and also a two lane road.

The Japanese arrived shortly after in Johore Bahru and dispersed into the jungle and rubber plantations towards the west. They needed time to catch their breath before the next phase.

The gap formed by the demolition was no more than a token delay and of course severed the only water pipeline bringing supplies onto the island; from now on the defenders would have to rely on their own reservoirs.

The Japanese had bridged the gap within a short time and then using spotters stationed in the tower of the Sultan's palace in Johore started to direct artillery and mortar fire onto the island's defences. Despite the obviousness of this high point being used for artillery spotting it was never shelled and served the Japanese well. (There was a rumour later that the Australian General Bennett who had been a firm friend of the Sultan of

Johore had said he would make sure no damage occurred to the Palace.)

The Japanese artillery spotters also used baskets suspended from balloons and from this vantage point much of Singapore could be viewed.

The situation for the defenders was not helped by the fact that the vast majority of the larger guns on Singapore were sited with the intention of preventing a sea-borne attack and faced out to sea in various directions. A few, near the dockyard area, could actually train onto the Japanese positions but only had armour piercing shells which were not of much use.

While these events were taking place at the north end of the island, 3 Bty to the south, close to Singapore City, was being bombed daily and attacked by Japanese aircraft, and the perimeter of the defences was put under extreme pressure.

Once the advancing Japanese had got the north of Singapore within artillery range they had shelled the airfields making them untenable. Those aircraft that could still fly withdrew to Kallang in the south and what few sorties that were still flown were from here, till around 10 February when all aircraft were withdrawn to Sumatra, and this in effect left the defenders without any air defences.

As the Japanese racked up their pressure the perimeter started to crumble and then after a sea-borne assault to the west of the causeway the Japanese made their landings at night. Once onto the island and after fierce fighting the attackers reached the Naval Base to the east, from where dense clouds of black smoke emitted from partially demolished oil storage tanks.

The Japanese were astounded to find that many items had been abandoned intact, the Navy having done a rapid exit some days before, handing the dockyard straight into Japanese hands. What damage there was had been carried out hastily after they had left by the Public Works Dept engineers. The attackers took over complete workshops of machine tools and vast amounts of ammunition and supplies. They soon overwhelmed the northern airfields which could now be used by them to mount further attacks against the shrinking perimeter.

Because of the need for gunners to help man the AA defences in the north some of those from 3 Bty had been moved there once their weapons had been made inoperable in the south. A few were sent to the Changi area where they spent a couple of days prior to the collapse and then were withdrawn to the south again.

Gnr G. Smith recalled spending a few hectic days at Sembawang close to the airfield where the Bty HQ was stationed in a local Chinese High School. Once this became untenable they also withdrew. After this the defenders continued to withdraw back towards the city, coming under intense fire the whole way. They kept withdrawing to new lines of defence hastily set up in a futile effort to stop the rout.

Constant artillery shelling and mortar fire and vicious hand-to-hand fighting left little doubt what the outcome was going to be. The gunners tried desperately to counter the Japanese air strikes but by now most of the defending air force had been neutralised and they were running out of time. Some aircraft had been withdrawn to Sumatra but the bulk of the rest were smoking heaps on Sembawang and neighbouring airfields such as Seletar and Tengah.

Eye witnesses record that during the last days as they grimly defended a tightening perimeter they were dug in on both sides of the Keppel Road. Many who no longer had guns to man were deployed as infantry. Survivors had been marched by Maj. Bailey, the O/C of 3 Bty, to an area called 'The Gap' where they took over some defensive trenches along the line of a ridge. They were spread very thin and joined on their left by Malay troops.

It was while holding these trenches that during an air raid they received a direct hit which killed several men. Lt Barney and Gnrs Morgan W.C., Mercer W. and Jones N. were killed and Lt Wilkinson D.W. was severely wounded from shrapnel and blast effects. He had to be rapidly evacuated from the position towards a first aid post further down the Pasir Panjang road but had been mortally hurt. The whole episode had been witnessed by another gunner nearby called W.G. Smith.

By this stage of the war, not only were the gunners having to contend with multiple air attacks each day but the Japanese had brought up long range guns which could shell the distant perimeter while being controlled by artillery spotters from the balloons over the Johore coast.

Two men, Gnrs Teal and Schofield, saw Gnrs Ginn and Bdr Peppin nearby and they had also been hit by splinters from the bombing and hit in the legs. Both Ginn and Peppin had volunteered to help man a Bofors gun at a nearby location shortly before but had now returned.

They witnessed Gnr Bennison who was a 'well-built fellow' driving a 15 cwt truck loaded up with wounded and also making its way to the clearing station, weaving in and out of the shell and bomb holes in the road and avoiding piles of debris. (Gnr W. Bennison No. 826800 was to turn up safe at the end of the war having by some means arrived in a POW camp in Taiwan. He seems to have been exceptionally lucky since he also appears on the rescue roll from the sinking of the Japanese Hell ship the *Hofuku Maru* in which many hundreds died on 21 September 1944.)

Later in this confused action they took two others with them from an anti tank unit and set up a defence with a Boys anti tank rifle and a Bren gun just to the side of the Pasir Panjang road. (A Boys A/T rifle was an infantry weapon comprising a special rifle with a long barrel and padded butt, but with an enlarged calibre of .55 inch. Using bullets with hardened tips it could penetrate the armour of vehicles or the skins of light tanks. When armour became too thick for it to penetrate it could be used to disable tracks instead. It had a pretty formidable recoil when fired and was not for the faint-hearted.)

While holding their positions here, and amid the chaos, they saw Gnr E.T.G. Robinson No. 826502 who had been shot through the neck, being taken to the medics further down the road.

By the morning of 14 February the defenders were loosely dug in all round Keppel road. What remained of the unit was ordered to consolidate wherever they happened to be. It was during this last final phase that Maj. Bailey on 14 February got together a hastily gathered bunch of about a dozen gunners and acting as infantry they set off over the hill to try and do something. None of these were seen alive again after they had entered the jungle fringes.

Fig. 5.1 3 Bty 6HAA Regt Officers, Lt H.B. Windows, 2/Lt L.D. Andrew, Maj. J.E. Bailey.

Also in the area was a driver attached to 3 Bty called Hammond No. 1059482 and he was hit too and had to be evacuated to a field medical post.

The constant shelling and bombing had fractured water mains all over the city and these spouted fountains at each break. The only water pumping station still working was at Woodleigh and this was losing two-thirds of its supply through these breaks.

Because they had had no food or water for some time Schofield and his mate went scrounging and came across a trench manned by Sgt Riley and two others, Dean and Murphy. They had between them a Bren gun and a couple of rifles but shortly afterwards they reported that the position of Sgt Riley was seen heavily obscured by bomb blasts which had straddled it. A few minutes later Sgt Dunkely, who had been close by, came and reported that he thought that Sgt Riley and Dean had been killed, but he did not know about Murphy. (Sgt Riley in fact survived the war.)

A/Sgt Ward had been last seen sitting at the side of the road, resting.

Fig. 5.2 The grave of Maj J.E. Bailey (O/C of 3 Bty) in Kranji cemetery, Singapore.

There did not appear much they could do amidst the utter chaos of the situation. During these actions Gunner Carpenter was seriously wounded in the face and left leg and had to be helped on his way to the medics. Though seriously injured he did make a good recovery.

The perimeter continued to shrink till it was full of wounded and injured troops and many dead. There were also thousands of injured and terrified civilians. Food and water were in short supply and the chaotic situation was exacerbated by indecisive military leadership.

Roads and streets had been continually bombed and shelled and many buildings had collapsed into heaps of rubble blocking them. Hospitals were struggling to cope and it was only then after contacting his senior advisors that General Percival made the decision to capitulate to save further casualties.

Sadly what he did not know was that the Japanese had also reached the end of their resources and were about to stop. They were seriously short of ammunition and supplies and had completely underestimated how bad the situation was, that they had created within the perimeter. Those of 3 Bty who had survived thus far suddenly found themselves as POWs and were rounded up.

On 15 February the island capitulated. It had been a very rude introduction to war for within 6 weeks of starting the survivors had all been captured. They had no idea of the treatment to follow but having to bow to any Japanese soldier whatever his rank must have given some idea.

They might also have got a better idea of Japanese brutality if they had heard about the massacre of patients and staff at the Alexandra Hospital on the 13th where a few Japanese soldiers went berserk. These men had stormed into the hospital buildings and proceeded to murder the occupants by bayoneting them or taking them outside and shooting them. None were spared despite their non-combatant profession. At the end of the bloodletting there were some 323 dead and one of these was a soldier undergoing an operation who had been bayoneted while under the anaesthetic.

Not content just to win militarily the Japanese wished to rub the Allies' noses in it in a final act of humiliation. Many thousands of the POWs who could be mustered were forced to line the roads leading to the centre of Singapore city while the Japanese generals drove sedately past. Among those who were forced to stand and watch were the survivors from 3 Bty.

In order to make the most of this victory the whole episode was captured by Japanese film crews and then shipped back to the homeland where it was viewed as massive propaganda of the invincibility of the Japanese armed forces.

Some of those who went to the Changi area saw at first hand about a week and a half later the extent to which the Japanese would go with their atrocities. The Japanese had rounded up as many Chinese as they could and accused them of being 'undesirables'. They took them to the beaches and machine gunned them to death. British and Australian soldiers had to watch and then dig the pits to bury the corpses in. This must have been a salutary warning of what might be coming.

Into the bag had gone Sgt Newcombe (he had been promoted shortly before leaving the UK), Gnrs H. Dawson, Rhodes, Davies, Price and Waters (see Fig. 3.2, p. 110).

During these last chaotic hours before surrendering, the troops had been instructed to destroy as much of their valuable equipment as they could. Some idea can be gained from Japanese records made at the time of the weapons and items they found after their examination of gun sites, as to how thorough this scorched earth policy had been.

The majority of the huge naval guns had been blown up using either special demolition charges fired within the breeches or effectively spiking the barrels using other shells or tamps. Special charges of up to 250 lbs of gelignite had been detonated in and around the guns to destroy them but if someone had gone back to check they would have found that one of the huge guns had been left intact. In fact it was still in working order over three years later when the island reverted to Allied control again.

The controlling radar and motors and sights had been smashed beyond repair. However during this rapid exercise many guns although badly damaged could be put back into working condition by the simple expedient of cannibalising parts from other guns.

Most of the anti aircraft guns had been deliberately destroyed by firing charges in their barrels or breeches creating such pressures that the steel ruptured. However four 3.7" AA guns had survived and although the strikers and sights were useless on most of the others, the Japanese found among the captured stores many spare barrels with which they fixed the damaged guns.

Out of the 70-plus HAA guns, mostly 3.7" but also 3", many were mounted in fixed defences and some must have been disabled during air raids or their crews killed so it is not known how many of these guns may have belonged to 3 Bty. Hopefully none if they had had time to deal with them before capture.

There had been far too few guns to defend every likely target on the island but what guns there were, aimed to protect the airfields and docks with another ring outside Singapore City. There had been eight near Nee Soon which was close to the airfield at Sembawang and also close enough to be of some use to defend the Naval dockyard, six at Ayer Hitam, another eight to protect Kallang airfield and some to guard Tengah. The rest were mostly in a ring round the city and a few scattered on nearby islands to protect the oil tanks.

Sensitive electronic equipment such as predictors and height finders had for the most part been smashed beyond all use, so too electronic sights for some guns. Searchlights which came in several sizes were captured including over 100,000 spare carbon elements and along with these was a massive haul of ammunition of all calibres.

The immediate Japanese response was to try and take control of the vast number of men and they had also to make plans for the large number of civilians and service families too. Initially once they had been paraded in open areas such as the Padang, not far from the sea front, they were marched towards the east side of the island to Changi.

Here many were deposited in the jail but the sheer quantities were too much for them. Others were put in the former army barracks called Roberts, India, Kitchener and some at Selarang. More went to an area called the Great World Amusement Park which was close to a former bar and red light district. Even this was not enough and many more were held in open camps at Changi, not far from the beaches and warned that trying to escape would bring the severest retribution. The camp at River Valley Road was also put into use, and those civilians attached to the POWs and government officials (women and children) were segregated into the other half of Changi jail. Still confused and shocked by the heavy fighting and sudden capitulation, short of water and food, they all sat down to await what might come.

Japanese guards were in very short supply because of the rapid ending of the fighting and no one in their wildest dreams had imagined such vast numbers of prisoners. The Japanese high command had also banned large numbers of Japanese troops from entering the city centre to try and avoid a repeat of drunken soldiers running amok, raping, looting and pillaging in scenes seen already in other captured towns. In effect the captives were put on trust not to attempt anything since they outnumbered their captors many hundreds to one.

Another and rather nasty event had occurred towards the end of hostilities when several hundred Indian troops turned traitor and started to work for the Japanese, in part believing they were going to get independence from the British for their help once the Japanese had won the war. Many were later to be used as guards for the POWs and this caused obvious resentment.

During the chaos of the fall of Singapore some men of 3 Bty managed to escape to Sumatra by boat, L/Bdr J.T. Adamson No 1073090 being one of them. They were picked up by a British organisation and moved onwards to Padang. Despite all their efforts and ingenuity in getting that far the Dutch refused to give any craft for their escape and they were all captured shortly after by the Japanese.

One of those left behind on Singapore was Dvr J. Byron No.3707408. He had been seriously wounded by a mortar shell and his wounds required the amputation of a limb. He thus spent all the rest of the war in Changi.

Chapter 6

The Defence of Sumatra and Java

————

Regressing slightly, while this was all happening in Singapore, on 13 February the alarm bells had started to ring further south when a large Japanese convoy was sighted approaching the northern coast of Sumatra. Bombers had been dispatched and those that found the convoy had limited successes, hitting a couple of transports and damaging others with near misses.

Further air attacks were planned for 14 February and these were intended to be by bombers from P2 and escorted by fighters from P1. Their instructions were to search for the convoy and then bomb it again.

On this date, while the garrison of Singapore was about to surrender, the Hurricanes at Palembang (P1) were awaiting their escort duties late morning, but for some reason the bombers did not show (low cloud and mist had made take-off unsafe.)

Thus it was that the fighters took off through low cloud and mist from P1 and set off to find the convoy by themselves. Whilst gaining height and flying generally northwards they briefly sighted below them through gaps in the clouds and heading in the reverse direction what appeared to be a large number of Hudson bombers. Assuming them to be friendly they did not turn to investigate. In fact this time they were Japanese and carrying paratroops and about to drop them on P1 while others also went for Pladjoe and Soengei Gerong where many of the valuable oil depots were. Hudson aircraft which had been bought prior to the war were also made under licence in Japan, and were cleverly disguised by having RAF roundels on them so confusing the defenders as to their real intent.

Amongst this air armada were a series of Kawaski KI-57 transports which were almost indistinguishable from the Hudsons. Two waves flew over dropping about 150 men each time on P1. (Figs 6.1, 6.2 and 6.3)

Fig. 6.1 Japanese paratroops parading shortly before loading.
Courtesy of I.D. Skennerton

Fig. 6.2 Japanese paratroops waiting for the green light.
Courtesy of I.D. Skennerton

Fig. 6.3 Japanese paratroops dropping.
Courtesy of I.D. Skennerton

Accompanying them were a group of Ki 21 bombers which proceeded to drop supplies for this first wave of troops. Another separate wave made for the area close to the Pladjoe refineries and dropped men there too. Once on the ground these troops formed up quickly and set about their tasks. They formed into about three separate groups, each having its own agenda. One lot went for the airfield and the others went for the AA guns to the south and west sides.

The Japanese plan had been to drop paratroops on P1 in two areas on the strip but as close to the tree line as possible. These troops would then form up and fight their way round the airfield in both directions and meet at the area of the hangar, clearing guns and defenders as they went.

Those dropped at the refineries were supposed to be within the perimeter so they could disrupt the planned demolition.

In fact because the pilots were inexperienced and not used to being under accurate ground fire they had wandered from the proper line and also risen much higher than normal for the drop.

This, aided by the slow exits from the planes, meant many of the attackers were widely scattered and landed in trees and much of their equipment was also lost or hung up.

Because intelligence had warned of such a likely attack several ground defence parties had been trained. As part of the initial attacks Japanese bombers dropped many anti personnel bombs on gun positions and any signs of buildings. During the very first contacts bombs were dropped near the cook house of the Regt, killing Gnrs J. Lupton and F.W. Davis before they had a chance to take cover in a nearby slit trench. A third, Gnr Coates, was seriously injured by shrapnel in the back but survived.

Ground troops at P1 now engaged in a fierce fire fight with the invaders and managed to inflict heavy losses on them. Most of the gun pits came under small arms fire and it was not long before casualties mounted.

In the pit containing No. 2 Gun of 15 Bty was L/Bdr L.N. Oliver and amongst the others were gunners Emery and W.J. McVey. About 15 yards away was No. 3 Gun being manned in part by A/Bdr T.H. Baxter and Gnr L. Waterhouse.

Emery was hit in the leg by a bullet and during the confusion they managed to evacuate him by vehicle to the hospital in Palembang. While he was there others came in during the day who had also been wounded and announced that both Baxter and McVey had been killed during the attempt to move out and several men wounded including L/Bdr Oliver.

While chaos reigned amongst the multitude of fierce actions taking place Sgt T. Graystone was hit by a burst of machine gun fire across the stomach and seriously wounded. He too was evacuated to Palembang but died the next day.

The guns were firing a large number of shells and it was deemed necessary for an ammunition party to go down to Palembang to bring up more. Lt Bird took Gnrs Haran, Harris and Renton for this duty but while they were away the situation deteriorated and they never made it back.

In the early stages of the attack 15 Bty had engaged the aircraft flying overhead and were credited with destroying three of these bombers, but once it was clear that the landings had finished they then directed their guns at ground targets.

Gunner Mear recalled later that the *'skies were full of parachutes and the air full of bullets'* as they manned their 3.7" guns. *'It certainly wasn't advisable to raise your head too high over the sandbag walls.'*

Of the three aircraft shot down, one was carrying equipment for the raiders at Pladjoe and it crashed nearby and another was so badly damaged it made an emergency landing on the strip still containing its troops who made a hurried exit.

Lt Simpson commanding one of the guns later complained that their biggest problem was trying to shoot at aircraft without the necessary radar and gun control equipment; all they could do was aim over open sights. They also had to protect themselves from infantry attack by groups of Japanese who were stalking their positions, and one gun position was heavily sniped at from the surrounding tree line which made life difficult.

Fig. 6-a Lt Simpson who survived the paratroop attack on P1. Courtesy of Clare Adams.

They found the novel answer to the problem of the snipers was to train the guns at the ground below the area of the sniping, set the fuses for .15 and after a few rounds of HE the incoming fire was stopped.

Shortly after, the Japanese some distance away managed to over-run a Bofors position which had been in place to defend the airfield against low flying aircraft. This position was between the gun line of the 3.7s and the runways and all the occupants had been killed. Having made a show of hoisting a Rising Sun flag they then turned the gun round with the intention of attacking the 3.7" gun pits which were sited further out. Luckily once the danger had been realised the 3.7" crew trained their barrel onto the Bofors pit and opened fire. This was an unequal fight and the Japanese position was soon knocked out.

Further raiding troops were seen to be examining some of the sparse G/L equipment and these too were silenced along with the destruction of the equipment by a few well placed shots. Because of the proximity of the raiders, fuses could not be set for such a short distance and therefore the guns fired rounds directly at the area and its equipment, trying to set it on fire.

As the battle ebbed and flowed with fleeting glimpses of the attackers appearing in the edge of the jungle, the guns to the south of the strip at P1 started to run short of rounds. They normally carried a supply of shells for ready use stored around the inside of the defensive position in small ammunition bays but when these ran low they had to be replenished from the main magazine nearby.

Because they were hard pressed they enlisted the help of RAF ground crews to go to this magazine and bring back shells. What made this an interesting enterprise was the gunners were being shot at by raiders hidden nearby and could not locate them. The working party found that the best way round this problem was to crawl along cradling one shell each and so keep below the line of fire.

The confused action went on for much of the morning but then the order had come through to take the guns out of action, that is those that were still in a condition to be fired, and move them off the airfield and down to Palembang itself, a distance of about ten miles.

Once the paratroopers had started to jump there was a state of total confusion. Dvr W. Boomer No 1568462 of 15 Bty recalled that they appeared to jump from quite a height and were very vulnerable to air burst shells which they fired as fast as they could load them. Shortly afterwards he and a section of men were detailed off to form an ambush party and hurried off into the vegetation to find a suitable location.

Once they had found a clearing with the track running through it they took up positions and anxiously waited. It was not long before a Japanese patrol came into it from the other direction. They all hugged the ground hardly daring to breathe and allowed the patrol to get very close. Then at a given signal they all blazed away with everything they had. Several paratroops fell dead and the rest withdrew.

It then went deadly quiet until one of his patrol whispered 'I think they have all gone'. Dvr Boomer then replied that he did not think so, but the other man said he meant the rest of their own patrol. Telling him to go back down the track and find the others he agreed he would cover him and then join him. However, a few minutes later when he went back there was nothing to be seen of any of them. He never saw any one from the regiment again until after the war.

Unknown to those involved in the fierce fighting on the airfield, some of the surviving Paratroops had managed to capture an armoured car belonging to the Dutch and with this they took off for Palembang down the only road heading south. They came across various vehicles which they shot up, killing or wounding the occupants. They then proceeded to attack any vehicle that approached and after a while these were overturned and formed into a road block.

Thus it was that back at P1 any vehicle that could be found was pressed into use. One of the first to leave was a utility truck used by the gunners and this was well loaded with a mix of personnel and set off down the road to try and reach Palembang. It had only gone about two miles when they drove into the road block and were badly shot up with all the occupants becoming casualties.

By this time word had gone out to abandon P1 completely and make for the town of Palembang. An Officer who knew something of the situation declared '*This is a no prisoner situation, so everybody make their own way off the airfield,*' and thus many of the personnel were fleeing by whatever route they could find. There were many who had no weapons and also a large party made up from RAF ground crew and these all eventually became part of a convoy.

Rumours had already come back about the fate of the first vehicle and this decided Gnr Walter Mear and his best mate Gnr Robert Digg (who was a cook by trade) that it was not the best way to evacuate the area down this road. By this time Walter had no weapon since his Bty Sgt Major had requisitioned it claiming he needed it to protect their Bty O/C. So the two of them made their plan to get back to Palembang on foot by taking to the jungle to the south of the airfield, and this they did. But first they made a visit to the abandoned cook tent where they filled their pockets with cans of corned beef and whatever else they could find. The problem they found on the route they had chosen was the jungle was predominantly swampy and the only way to progress was to wade through the fetid water up to their armpits in places and struggle ever southwards.

Behind them the growing panic continued and unfortunately because there was only one serviceable purpose-built Matador towing lorry it was to take a bit of time to hitch up the guns, but after some anxious minutes two guns had been limbered up and removed from the immediate area with the aid of another vehicle. Guns that could not be moved were disabled by having their strikers removed and then abandoned and by this time the few predictors had been rendered unserviceable.

Once they had gathered enough men the small convoy set out, with the lorry towing a mobile gun in the lead. This Matador was driven by Gnr Earland and was heavily loaded with more than twenty men squeezed in the cab and the back, mostly gunners but with some RAF personnel as well.

Other men still looking anxiously for some sort of transport to get away had grabbed a petrol bowser and this was loaded with as many men as would fit inside the front and standing on the running boards and behind the cab. This set off after the gunners' Matador and following behind them was yet another truck carrying wounded from the various actions in a vain attempt to get them to Palembang hospital.

The Matador was going well until they suddenly came across the damaged vehicles across the road on a bend. They were taken by surprise and in the seconds trying to work out just what had gone on the vehicle was attacked by automatic weapons and riflemen enfilading the road from the sides.

In the initial burst of firing Dvr Earland was hit in the chest severely injuring him and several others were killed. There was a panic to get out and into the safety of the roadside ditches during which further casualties were taken.

Of the gunners who comprised the group within this Matador, Bdr J. Brackley and L/Bdrs S.H. Legg and F. Seabrook were killed, so too Gnrs J. Rennie, D. Hollingsworth and W. McVey, making a total of six.

Of the others the driver R. Earland was seriously hurt, E. Owles was hit, Dvr W Finch was injured in the head and hand by splinters, H. Blackburn had shrapnel in the leg, T. Morrissey was wounded in the stomach by a bullet fired from the captured armoured car, P. Walsh was hit, so too T. Bishop and Baines. L/Bdr L. Oliver received serious wounds, as did Dvr E. Coates. Out of this sorry party of eighteen men no fewer than six were dead and ten wounded and only two men escaped uninjured.

For some the wounds were not life threatening and they did their best to aid those more seriously hurt in the ditches and beside the road or trapped inside the back of the truck. Those that could returned fire and Gnr R. Branter got out and positioned himself with a Bren gun to one side to give covering fire which he did as best he could. Sometime during the exchanges he was hit and killed at his gun. So having escaped unhurt in the initial exchange he was now dead too.

The order 'Every man for himself' went out so Gnr H. Towhills who was unhurt throughout made good his escape into the jungle along with other walking wounded and got back to Palembang later that day. (See annex E for casualties.)

Meanwhile into this mayhem drove the petrol bowser, crewed predominantly by RAF personnel and Armourers and this was similarly attacked from the front and sides. The driver was killed by a grenade causing the vehicle to slew into the ditch and turn on its side. Some of those men hanging on to the outside were thrown clear and shaken up, but several were trapped beneath the tanker and at least two were dead and another dying.

Gnr Bishop, who had been in the first vehicle, had been wounded but escaped into the bush where he claimed to have shot two Japanese and then returned to take cover in the roadside ditch. It was then that he was hit by the second vehicle as it crashed and he was badly crushed by it. (He and Morrissey were later taken by lorry to hospital and then moved to the Hospital in Batavia (Java) along with others who had been injured in the fighting. From here they were evacuated to Ceylon and survived the war.)

The vehicle following which was carrying the dead and wounded from P1 met a similar fate. The driver was killed in the first bursts of fire and it came to a sudden halt. Japanese troops appeared from out of the scrub at the rear and ordered the survivors out, shooting wildly all the while and killing some of the wounded.

Those who were able to, clambered into the ditch and lay down expecting the worst. Then quite suddenly while the Japanese were obviously thinking what they were going to do next, a party of Dutch troops appeared and opened up on them killing most of them. A survivor ran off into the jungle pursued by a Dutch trooper who reappeared shortly after with a satisfied smile on his face.

This roadblock effectively cut the road to Palembang and prevented any chance of the guns being withdrawn or reinforcements getting through from the town, and was still being defended by Japanese infantry using a light machine gun as well as the cover provided by the captured armoured car. The road block continued to repel any attempts to advance along the road and repeated attempts to outflank it caused casualties to the ground troops because they were exposed to many snipers that had taken up positions in the nearby vegetation. This was a narrow road and did not allow for the 3.7″ gun to be turned round such that it could engage the enemy block and so as a precaution the sights and strikers were removed.

Under orders from Lt. Col Baillie, who had learnt about some of the action, troops were sent off into the bush to both sides of the road with the aim of trying to get close enough to silence the LMG on this road block.

Also in the mad rush to escape was Lt A.J. Steeds of 15 Bty travelling with an RAF officer in a staff car. When they came under fire they hastily decamped to the roadside ditch and tried to see what was happening. The scene was total confusion but during the move to outflank the Japanese gunners' position Lt G.H. Crawford No 79855 was hit in the back and died shortly after. Lt K. Attiwill immediately took over Crawford's men and started to move away from the road.

Some of the men of 15 Bty under the control of their Officers split into groups and with small numbers of men from attached batteries such as the 78th and 89th LAA began to make their way through the bush in the direction of Palembang.

At length the Japanese had brought up a light mortar to reinforce the blockade and things were getting serious. However with the help of some

Dutch soldiers and after a sustained firefight the LMG was finally silenced in the late afternoon.

Two unsuccessful attempts had been made to get troops past this block from the Palembang direction but been repulsed each time. The Japanese then tried coming down the road using the captured armoured car and men from 15 Bty set up to stop it.

'Geordie' Allen from this battery manned a Bren gun and managed with some excellent shooting to disable it and kill the Japanese occupants. ('Geordie' was one of the lucky ones to survive his captivity.) This allowed troops to advance down the road and finally clear away the debris, and once the road was open again medics had the chance to treat and escort the wounded away to Palembang, some in an armoured car that had been brought up for the purpose.

Examination of the two HAA guns which had got this far revealed that one had one of its tyres badly shot up. Attempts were then made to tow it but after a short distance the damaged tyre caught fire and the gun had to be abandoned and so the sights and striker which had been replaced again were removed. The remaining gun was now towed along till they came to Palembang where it was set up in defence of the local ferry point.

Lt. Col. Baillie was very disheartened by the whole affair and claimed that had they had just three more Matadors then at least six guns could have been recovered. As the day drew on, and in the tropics darkness falls very quickly, he set about forming a rear guard to the location. He then set off for a visit to 12 Bty who were some miles away at their sites near Pladjoe and Soengei Gerong which is where most of the oil refineries were located. Initially it was thought about 200 Japanese paratroops had also landed close to these with the primary aim of seizing the oil refineries before the defenders had a chance to set them on fire.

The gun positions of 12 Bty were not attacked in the initial phase and had thus been free to engage enemy aircraft all day, in fact claiming, with the help of the Bofors, to have shot down sixteen.

While driving along the road to get to 12 Bty Lt Col. Baillie ran into Maj. Moxon (who at one time had run the Regt School back in Wolverhampton). Maj. G.A. Moxon No 13435 was the unit second in command and an older man, being 43 years of age. He had seen service in the First World War and been Mentioned in Despatches three times. He had also retired in the rank of Captain and been put on the reserve only to be called up to join 6 HAA for the BEF in 1939 with the rank of Temp. Major.

They had a hurried discussion on the situation and it was agreed to try and enlist the help of the Dutch forces to attack a new LMG position which the Japanese had set up close to the previous one. There was also a light mortar firing from somewhere in the area. However in the gathering dusk it was not possible to positively pinpoint where the two actually were. The perennial snipers, too made it dangerous to try and walk around in the open or show yourself for long. The Dutch were unwilling to try and attack in the dark but agreed to hold their positions and their commander agreed he would advance at first light to try and locate the Japanese lines and then put in an attack.

Lt Col. Baillie then left with the Dutch commander at around 1900 hrs in order to report the situation to the Territorial Commander who was in Palembang. Here he was given reassurances by the TC that things were well in hand and they would all hold their positions in the line and counter-attack in the morning. The TC did not seem overly worried that paratroops had landed at both Pladjoe and Soengei Gerong, perhaps because he did not know the true situation.

At the start of the day 12 Bty had had a section of guns at each location and these were set up to defend against any possible aerial attack on these valuable installations. Because the Japanese had aimed to capture the refineries first, the guns had been left to carry on their main task of AA defence unmolested. However once the fighting entered the refinery complexes, which covered many acres, Dutch troops and others from the squads set up in advance for anti-paratrooper operations went in after them.

There was a delay next morning while they waited for Dutch reinforcements, who had been promised, but they did not arrive, so an attack was made against these Japanese forces by gunners acting as infantry and during the initial advance Capt. Sherrard and one other man were killed. These small scale actions continued for much of the day as men met or stalked each other within the confines of the complex.

Capt W.L. Sherrard No 74545 had been commissioned in 1939 when he joined the unit and eventually found himself in 12 Bty. He had been part of a hastily formed infantry squad to try and winkle out the paratroopers in the refinery. Sadly he left behind a widow after less than a year of marriage.

Fig. 6-b Capt W.L. Sherrard who died leading his men at Pladjoe, Sumatra.
Courtesy of R. Flory.

Later that same day while Lt Col. Baillie was at the 'O'group (orders group) meeting in Palembang he was assured by Air Commander Hunter that it was intended to re-occupy P1 once the situation had stabilised.

RAF personnel who had been evacuated to the south side of the river Moesi into a new rearguard location were now brought back across the river to the north bank. Men were still arriving in dribs and drabs as they managed to break through between the Japanese positions.

Walter and his mate still struggled gamely on unaware that the orders were about to be given for everyone who could to make their way to P2. Those men who had injuries had been transported back to several hospitals in Palembang. The minor ones were treated and returned to their units while the more serious ones who could be moved were prepared to be sent out by sea to Colombo or India using a ship called *Orcades*. The very serious were left in care at Palembang where they of course were captured a few days later. They were not to know it at that time, but those evacuated because of their injuries were to be the lucky ones who avoided capture and three and a half years of hell at the hands of the Japanese.

Lt Col. Baillie's visit to Pladjoe earlier in the afternoon had shown that the situation was 'contained' within the refineries although the Dutch troops were still engaged in action against the paratroops in some areas as were gunners acting as infantry. The guns were untouched and still able to fire, their defence on the ground being assured by fighting patrols who were searching for Japanese troops who might be trying to get closer.

At the end of what had been a hectic time the defending gunners had lost 1 Officer dead and 16 ORs killed with 36 wounded and another 6 men missing and unaccounted for.

The Japanese paratroops had not had it all their own way and also been badly mauled.

[One odd incident has surfaced from researches. Apparently there was a bit of a loose cannon in 15 Bty called Gnr C.D. Yates No 816925. He was caught whilst part of a three-man guard duty asleep in the back of a truck by his Troop Officer, Lt Steeds, and in the early part of February 1942 he had been awarded 14 days C.B. (Confined to Barracks). In order for this punishment to be carried out he had been transferred to 12 Bty for them to supervise this at Pladjoe. He arrived and was found a space to sleep by BSM Hawkins. It was noticed at Roll Call the next day that Yates was missing and then the Japanese attacks started. No sign of Yates could be found and besides this the BSM was far too occupied with other matters. It was thought that Yates had on his own account taken himself back to 15 Bty but his name does not appear again and neither is he shown in the Commonwealth War graves lists. We can only surmise that somehow he survived.]

Lt Col. Baillie reported that the men had fought well, in what had been their first combat for many of them, and had taken well to their new role as infantry when the guns had been lost.

After a very anxious and confused night in which it had been agreed that the plan was to recapture P1 the next day, he visited the HQ again. This time he found at HQ Brigadier Steele of 2nd Australian Corps who being the senior rank had taken over command, and they planned their next move.

It came as a bit of a shock to be advised that the new orders were for all troops to be evacuated to P2. The gunners of the units were to form the backbone of the defence for the withdrawal.

Sadly once they had finished engaging enemy aircraft at Soengei Gerong, because there was no way of retrieving their guns from across the river without the use of a ferry, 12 Bty destroyed their two guns. The gunners then withdrew and became infantry.

Bombardier East of 12 Bty later recalled that at the time of the paratroop landings he had been in charge of a stores party working on the steamer *Ipoh* tied up in the port a short distance from the refinery. They had heard the air-raid sirens and seen the Hudson bombers go past and thought nothing of it till they saw Japanese fighters strafing the refinery positions. It was then they realised exactly what was happening.

Shortly after this paratroops were seen descending. Their Company Commander Maj. Coulson hurriedly acquired arms and ammunition, and gathered up as many men as he could find and made for the area where these troops had landed.

A series of sharp engagements followed over several hours during which many of the raiders were killed. The paratroopers had dropped a short distance away from the refinery and as is normal with these sorts of operations, some had landed in trees and thick scrub and then had to disentangle themselves and find the rest of their troops before forming up. The tall grass and shrubs hindered both sides but did afford cover to the raiders and they had to be located and winkled out and then eliminated.

After several hours of this chaotic situation rumours started to be heard of an impending seaborne assault and it was decided to set demolition charges to destroy the infrastructure. Because the defenders were not demolition experts they had to be shown how to set explosive charges and the most vulnerable points to attack. Once this was done and while the paratroopers were still fighting for control of the refinery, the charges were fired. (Fig. 6.4)

Fig 6.4 Burning fuel tanks at Palembang.

Large quantities of burning oil gushed out from the tanks and flooded into the fast flowing Moesi river. The current carried this fiery raft down-stream covering everything under a pall of thick black smoke. Another witness from 12 Bty, Gnr Roberts, said they had dealt very well with the paratroops and they had certainly managed to hold them.

It was at this point that they were ordered to start a withdrawal in stages back to the river, and this was when they sustained many casualties from Japanese machine-gunners who had managed to climb on top of some of the remaining tanks. However to the surprise of these machine-gunners further charges were set off causing massive fireballs which removed the threat and incinerated the Japanese on the top of these tanks. The flames and heat were tremendous from these fires and could be felt on the other side of the river. At another 'O' group meeting A/Cdr Hunter advised that all RAF personnel were being withdrawn and this had been in progress for some hours.

In these chaotic hours it had been forgotten to advise the RHQ of the gunners and therefore it was not till later in the morning that the rear guard had been put in position and by this time many of the RAF personnel had gone across the river by ferry.

With limited resources Lt Col. Baillie had to make his plans. The last remaining 3.7" gun of 15 Bty was set up in action on the north bank of the

River Moesi to guard the ferry crossing. Two further 3.7" guns recovered by 12 Bty from Pladjoe by ferry were sent to guard the railway station and also the station at Katapati. These were vital points and so too a road bridge nearby to the east of it. All guns remained in action while the troops crossed over to the south side.

Because of the chaotic situation and the dire need to get people away and down to P2 nobody had thought to include the gunners in the evacuation scheme. It was thought that the dismounted gunners, now in the infantry role, would have to march to P2 a not inconsiderable distance of over 40 miles. However training kicked in and with initiative to the fore the Officers managed to get places on an RAF train for them all – probably helped in no small measure, by the thought of having to march that distance in the heat and humidity.

The bottle neck to the whole operation was the fact that everything from stores to personnel had to be carried across the river by the single small ferry. By this time there were many seriously wounded on stretchers who also had to be transported as carefully as possible. The Padre, Capt Harper-Holdcroft, was seen making himself useful by driving an ambulance and others tried their best to get the transport, both military and civilian, into orderly queues.

At this time there were all sorts of rumours going the rounds about Japanese troops having landed at Pladjoe by boat and to scotch them and also find out the truth for himself, Lt. Col. Baillie took a trip there to find out. He ascertained that this was pure speculation and proved to himself that all troops had left along with many civilians who were frightened of what might happen to them when the Japanese arrived.

The two guns of 12 Bty had withdrawn from the railway stations to P2 by towing tractor but the last remaining of 15 Bty could not be taken across the River Moesi and had to be abandoned on the north bank. The reason given for having to abandon this valuable resource which had been nurtured for two days was a lack of suitable ferry to get it across the river. With its loss came the last chance that the gunners of 15 Bty would have to fire a 3.7" mobile again during the war; they now reverted to being part of the infantry. It fell to Sgt Burdett, the No 1 on the gun, to remove the breach block after all the ammunition had been thrown into the river. Claiming in disgust as he always did 'Every time we destroy ammo or equipment we are lengthening the war'. It was getting to be like Dunkirk all over again, a chaotic withdrawal leaving all their heavy equipment behind.

Eventually all personnel arrived at P2, some 40 miles south of Palembang and up till then the airbase still appeared to be undiscovered by the Japanese forces. Because of this it had not been attacked and the guns had had a quiet time. Admittedly they were missing some of their equipment and the frequent low mists and clouds meant they could not often see too much anyway.

Once rumours started that the Japanese were advancing along the roads some of the guns were pulled out to form and hold a road block to the north of the airfield.

RAF fighters and bombers continued to harass Japanese forces wherever they could find them, and the Japanese still did not realise where the airfield was. What made this more mystifying was the Japanese claimed to have knocked out many of the aircraft at P1 either on the ground or in the air, and still they were meeting fighters and bombers which logic should have told them were coming from elsewhere and presumably another airstrip.

A/Cdr Hunter had managed to husband his few remaining aircraft and intended to carry out one last sortie on 16 February with the bombers before they flew off to land elsewhere. They would not return to P.2. Unless he received orders to the contrary, he said, they were all making for Oosthaven (modern-day port of Bandar Lampung).

They had had some success in bombing the invasion convoys in the earlier sorties, hitting several transports and damaging others with near misses but the pilots' main gripe was the size of the bombs they were having to use, which they considered, with good evidence, were just not large enough to do serious damage. However the withdrawal operation did require at least some sort of AA protection so the guns were put into action there along with the surviving Bofors of the LAA regts.

By this time all surplus RAF ground crews had left, many by air. It was intended for the HAA guns to leave at dusk that night and the light guns to leave once the sortie was airborne the next day.

During the morning of the 16th the telephone exchange at Palembang was destroyed to prevent its use by the Japanese and so all communication with the outside world was cut.

Shortly after A/Cdr Hunter changed his orders and cancelled the last sortie for the bombers. It had been decided to evacuate the last of the RAF personnel by air during the afternoon. This meant there was now no need for the gunners to hang about and they could make their way south. It was all set up to be started later in the day until a report arrived that said Japanese infantry had been seen in barges advancing up two rivers nearby, the Salang and the Telang to the north. [The Japanese plan had been to secure the airfields and refineries by the use of paratroops and then follow up quickly afterwards with seaborne landings of thousands more infantry.]

This development, mostly rumour at the time, resulted in the whole scheme being brought forward. This further increased the chaos and it was clear that everything was going to have to be transported by road or train to these small and overworked docks. At this stage the guns that were available were still in a fit state to be fired so with the only two remaining Matadors some were limbered up and towed away.

There were not enough aircraft to transport all the remaining personnel by air so as many as could be gathered together were sent to the train station. These were non-essential to the operation and surplus to those needed to man the guns. In fact, ludicrous as it may seem now, many were unarmed having had their weapons and ammunition taken off them by the Dutch troops who had said they could find a better use for them amongst their own troops. It was hoped they could, or as many as possible could, be transported to the port of Oosthaven, where further plans for defence were to be put into action.

It was a chaotic situation, for everyone who could was trying to escape. Many of these were injured and even more were actually unarmed and thus just passengers to the events. Amidst the heat and humidity, the dust and the flies, a mass of humanity, servicemen, native coolies and civilians had only one thought in mind, and that was to put as much distance as possible between the advancing Japanese and themselves.

The rumours still persisted that the Japanese had moved from P1 and were now in Palembang but this was obviously incorrect because at this time, mid morning, the ferry was still in operation carrying people and supplies across the river.

The reported landing at Pladjoe by seaborne troops had also surfaced again but this too was incorrect. In the circumstances it only took one careless word for a rumour to spread like wildfire. Up till then it was everyone's aim to get away from the Japanese and find an escape route to the south. Nobody it seemed was putting much effort into resisting the invaders or finding out the true size of their forces. Vast amounts of stores, ammunition and fuel dumps were destroyed to deny their use to the Japanese, who eventually took over P1 not by force, but rather the fact that everyone had left and just abandoned it still in an operational condition. The paratroopers had no further supply drops or reinforcements and relied on what they could secure.

Some of the locals who had been under the occupying force of their Dutch masters for so long were not at all unduly upset by their removal and some people aided the new arrivals, sadly ignorant of what was about to come.

While all these panic moves were being instigated Walter and his mate continued to struggle on through the jungle and swamps. Subjected to leeches and mosquitoes and falling into submerged holes under water and having to clamber over obstructions, progress was very slow. By the time they eventually reached Palembang some while later the place was almost deserted and most of the service personnel had already left.

By chance they had come upon a railway track which they continued to follow going in a southerly direction and as luck would have it they found in the dark a hut into which they flopped exhausted. They had eaten all their food and drunk the contents of a small whisky bottle they found in the hut and were awoken some time later after daybreak by the sound of voices nearby. Fearing for their lives in case they were Japanese they cautiously peered through gaps in the hut walls to find they were British service personnel.

While Lt Col. Baillie sought out Headquarters to find out his orders he arrived to find utter confusion and Brig. Steele had just issued his latest order. This was for the complete evacuation of Sumatran forces and to head for Java, an island further to the east in the chain of Dutch East Indies colonies.

Lt Col. Baillie, as O/C the gunners that still remained, then left to go to Oosthaven to make a survey of the area and see what it would take to set up a defence. Having no information at all provided by the Dutch as to what he might find he set off in the early afternoon. This was not just a short drive but a journey of nearly 300 miles along narrow roads with in many areas the jungle coming down to the road edge on both sides.

They had not gone more than 10 miles when the first obstacle was met. This turned out to be a thirty foot bridge south of Moelih. The bridge was quite strong enough to carry the weight of the guns but had the unfortunate feature of a timber roof on supporting columns. The height was obviously too low to admit passage of the guns and towing vehicles underneath it and so all those present hastily set to with axes and saws and eventually managed to remove this obstruction.

However after travelling further south along this same road they came to yet more bridges, this time there were two and considerably longer than the first and also having roofs. A quick meeting was held and it was judged too difficult to cut these off in the time available, so the order was given to destroy the guns. This came as a heavy blow to those men of 12 Bty who had nursed their guns and overcome many difficulties to keep them in service-able condition. Now after having got this far they had no choice but to lose them. As was the usual practice, sights and strikers were removed for safe keeping and the guns immobilised.

What they did not know in the general panic, since nobody seemed very intent in trying to stop the Japanese, was that a convoy had arrived at the southern end of Sumatra carrying 3400 Australian troops comprising Pioneers and machine gun units and also a number of light tanks. These were off Oosthaven but before they could unload, their ship was diverted to Java thus denying the defenders this valuable resource.

Many of the remaining troops and gunners who had been left at P2 were desperately trying to reach Oosthaven. [Large numbers of personnel were being transported via the railway which was the quickest mode of transport.]

Had better intelligence been used it would have shown the true extent and numbers of the raiders and possibly more could have been done to resist them.

All the guns that had survived thus far were to be destroyed and every man possible was to be collected and be prepared to evacuate. Enough lorries were found to pick up 12 and 15 Bty too while the gunners of the 78th LAA had sufficient transport of their own to reach the station near P2.

At this time everyone was streaming to the south and the scene must have been familiar to those who had been at Dunkirk – long files of people trudging along the roads, large numbers of abandoned vehicles, both military and civilian.

Amongst this tide of humanity was Gnr Tart. He had been to the local hospital to see his best mate who had been wounded at P1 and wish him all the best. His last words to him were that they were headed for Java and were to be armed as infantry. Beyond this they did not know what their duties were going to be. His best mate was lucky to be evacuated by Hospital Ship shortly after and he in fact survived the war. As many as possible of those who had been wounded from the actions at

Fig 6-c Gunner Tart who died at Kalidjati. Courtesy of his daughter Elsie Pobjoy.

Fig. 6.5 Destroyed vehicles on the approaches to Oosthaven, Sumatra.

Palembang were evacuated to Oosthaven but some of the more seriously injured were left in Palembang Hospital to an unknown fate.

When Lt Col. Baillie finally reached the port many vehicles had been either driven into the docks or as close as they could get and then abandoned. A large part of the day was taken trying to clear a route through but in the end the task was too great. The attached 78th Bty LAA who up till then had managed to get two guns to within three-quarters of a mile of the docks were now forced to destroy them because there was just no way through. (Fig. 6.5)

The situation was absolute bedlam, men trying to load ships with stores and personnel and get as much away as possible before the Japanese arrived. Trains had been driven into the marshalling yard near the docks and abandoned, leaving carriages and freight strewn all over the tracks. Personal belongings and suitcases lay in heaps as the civilian Dutch population also tried to escape. There were also large quantities of petrol and ammunition still on their wagons, just abandoned and left in the sidings.

There seemed little co-ordination between one group and the next. Ships were sailing at random, many times at the whim of their masters. In fact the one designated for the use of the 6 Regt survivors left the quay without all its stores on board. While the QM (quarter-master) was below detailing the storage arrangements it set sail and left behind a valuable lorryload of equipment which included a few predictors and height finders.

It later transpired that these were destroyed on the dockside the same day, where a hasty demolition programme had been carried out to try and deny anything of value to the Japanese. (Fig. 6.6)

While the rest of the British forces had been hurriedly trying to reach

Palembang and then Oosthaven, Dvr Boomer, having been separated from his patrol, went north west and set out for Padang. It is possible that along with other stragglers he joined up with Dutch forces who were conducting a fighting retreat away from P1.

During their escape they had each night dug a small 'X'-shaped scrape for four men to lie in so they could keep all-round surveillance and with their feet touching in the centre so they could alert each other without any noise.

They were involved in skirmishes with the Japanese and during one of these Dvr Boomer received a bullet wound to the leg. He was sent to an aid station for treatment where soon after his arrival a doctor announced that the Japanese were close and that anyone who was able to leave could do so and be given a 'chit' to verify that they weren't deserters. Along with five or six other men he left the hospital and made it to Padang.

Fig. 6-d Dvr W. Boomer in Ceylon after his lucky escape from Sumatra.
Courtesy of his son Bill Boomer.

This port was the end point of the Indragiri river escape route from Singapore and there was total chaos as large numbers of civilians and service personnel tried to find berths on ships to Ceylon. The other men he was with all embarked on the *SS Rooseboom* but he was turned away and embarked on another ship. Sadly, shortly after sailing the *Rooseboom* was found and sunk by Japanese aircraft with heavy loss of life, but the ship he was on eventually reached Ceylon and he went into hospital for treatment to his wound.

From here he recovered and later in 1942 he was returned to active duties and joined 8 HAA in Burma where he spent the rest of the war and survived to return home.

Back near Palembang Walter and his mate had emerged from their hut and found the senior Officer of the troops who turned out to be a Navy man. They reported to him their unit name and asked for instructions on what to do next. Apparently these men had found a steam locomotive parked up in a siding not far away and the Officer asked if anyone knew how to operate it. Walter stepped forward saying he had some idea because he had worked

Fig. 6.6 Oosthaven oil fuel tanks and docks deliberately destroyed in the hurried withdrawal.

in the mines in Wales. Thus with Walter in charge men scampered around collecting firewood and topped up the tank with water. Once a good fire had been started they anxiously watched the pressure gauge to see if it would rise. After several hours there was enough steam to get going. Everyone who could clambered aboard and with great care they set off. By this time they had acquired the help of a local driver.

There were a couple of empty flat bed wagons behind which also soon filled up and the great adventure began. They saw no sign of Japanese troops as they trundled southwards and with the personnel keeping the fire well stoked with logs they spent most of the day travelling south east towards Oosthaven where they reached the area near the docks and disembarked, just in time to become part of the chaos and mayhem that was all around. From here they joined the queues of men trying to board and it was not long before they got a place on one of the ships and ferries being used in the hasty evacuation. Many of the Regt had boarded the SS *Yoma* for the short trip across the straights and in the company of various other ships arrived at last in Java at the port of Batavia and waited to unload their cargoes. By this time rumours were flying around that the Regiment might be sailing on to Australia. In fact 15 Bty spent two days anchored in the outer harbour awaiting further instructions but then their hopes were dashed and they came alongside and hastily unloaded. 12 Bty by this time had already disembarked from their ship and dispersed inland.

Because the Btys no longer had any guns they had reverted to infantry and were immediately assigned to airfield defence. They had to be issued with small arms and ammunition from whatever sources could be found. The survivors of 12 Bty were allotted the airfield of Kalidjati and Walter and his mate in 15 Bty went to Tjililitan, both of which were in the Batavia area (modern Jakarta).

Because of the chaotic situation and the dire lack of transport 15 Bty had some difficulty in reaching their destination airfield but 12 Bty joined with elements of 78 LAA Bty, 35LAA Regt and 89 LAA Bty and finally got to Kalidjati.

Here the most immediate problem was to get the defences into some sort of order. Trenches had to be dug and sandbags filled and placed, but on a site of such size only local positions could be formed to cover what were considered the most vulnerable points. The defenders were again spread very thin.

Some of the Dutch troops whose job it was to defend Kalidjati had been away on extended exercises and were not due back immediately.

On 1 March the Dutch commander of the airfield, Lt Col Zomer, arrived hurriedly from the nearby town of Bandoeng. He had been advised via a telephone call on the very erratic phone lines that the Japanese in the early hours of that morning were actually landing troops and some small tanks on the beaches some 75 kilometres away as the crow flies. Because Japanese transport ships had been observed off the north coast some days earlier, a hasty demolition plan had been drawn up should this be necessary.

What few surviving aircraft there were from Sumatra had all been flown down to these two airfields (and another further south) but there were of course no guns brought by 12 or 15 Batteries since by this time these had all been destroyed. To help remedy the dire situation of guns to defend these airfields, orders had been given that some were to be brought in from further east to redeploy at these locations. 49 LAA Bty had arrived in the area and now manned 10 Bofors guns which did at least afford some sort of anti aircraft defence and also a few 3.7" of 77 HAA Regt. were due. Both airfields were typical of the time and cut from the jungle, and had hard rolled strips for runways.

Whilst all these panic measures were being taken, the Australians had already decided by the middle of February that it was a lost cause to try and hold Java. They could see how the Japanese onslaught had become unstoppable and now, worried for the safety of Australia, they started to withdraw a large portion of 1st Corps to the homeland. This severely depleted the defences of Java and resulted in much redeployment to fill the gaps so left.

By 21 February there were only about 40 fighter aircraft left to the defenders as well as a few bombers.

The Australians had not taken their entire forces but left behind a couple of battalions of infantry and machine gunners, with some pioneers and transport echelons too, all under the command of Col. Blackburn VC. He was a typical Australian soldier and well used to hard times and fierce fighting having won his VC at Poziers in 1916. This force now became known as 'Blackforce'. Like the others he was considered subordinate to the Dutch commander Lt Gen.Ter Poorten who along with other Dutch commanders each had a responsibility for the Naval and Air sections across Java still in existence.

'Blackforce' was basically of Brigade strength and along with the Dutch contingents it was only possible to defend a few of the likely points of invasion and even then with very limited forces.

The Dutch commander was adamant that most forces should be placed around the ports at Batavia and Surabaya and this was not popular with the Allies who wanted to defend other areas too. At least a compromise was reached but it was not a complete solution and two LAA Btys were moved.

The Allied General Wavell, who had been thrust into the mess with instructions to sort it out and hold the line, had visited Singapore and been horrified by what he saw. He had briefly contacted the defending forces on Java. After rapid consultations to gauge the situation from the local commanders he signalled his findings to the UK and Churchill.

Basically he considered that if Java fell it would not be the end of everything, but trying to prop up the defences would be a waste of manpower since they would inevitably be sacrificed too. His opinion was that the whole scheme relied on air power and this was in very poor condition and in short supply. With this he was given instructions to get out and away to safety. He had flown out on 23 February 1942 and made his way to India leaving all the forces behind to their fate. The last unhappy signals to the Commanders stated that reinforcements or rescue could not come for some considerable time, which in effect meant they were going to be left to their own devices to try and hold for as long as they could.

Intelligence had already suggested to General Sitwell, who was now in overall command, that the Japanese were about to invade North Java. He was frantically re-distributing his meagre forces to try and guard this area. Troops and guns were brought in from other parts of the island to bolster the north in places where the most likely attacks would come in. The trouble was there were too many possible suitable places to land and too few troops to defend them.

While the defenders were busy digging in and trying to form as strong a line as they could on 27 February the Naval forces available were sent out to sea to try and stop what had been seen of a large Japanese fleet. There was a combined force of British, Dutch and American ships, everything that could be scraped together from the meagre resources locally. HMS *Exeter* (of Battle of the River Plate fame) HMAS *Perth* and USS *Houston* and the Dutch cruiser *Java* were among the largest, together with a series of destroyers and smaller ships.

They sailed out into the open sea and found at long range the Japanese fleet which was nearly 100 ships strong. A long range gun duel took place at the extreme ranges of each force and this was mostly ineffective but HMS *Exeter* received a hit in her engine room which slowed her down, resulting in her having to be escorted back to port.

The other downside to the engagement was the loss of two British destroyers, HMS *Electra* and HMS *Stronghold*. These were both elderly ships but vital for the fast defence of convoys or as naval escorts. HMS *Electra* had, only a few weeks before, been part of the defence of the task force that included the *Prince of Wales* and *Repulse*. She had been heavily committed to rescuing survivors from the *Repulse* after it sank. So ended their careers, outgunned by heavier Japanese warships and sunk. There were survivors who were picked up many days later by an American submarine. Those picked up by the Japanese were transferred to POW camps. The only compensation was one Japanese transport hit and left badly on fire.

Some distance away the American carrier USS *Langley* was sailing on 27 February at full speed towards Java to unload her cargo of P-40 fighters to help boost the flimsy defences on the island. She was an old cargo ship hull converted to a carrier and one of the very first carriers in the US Fleet. She was found by Japanese aircraft and heavily bombed and sustained severe damage. The damage was so severe in fact that they decided to abandon her and so she was scuttled. Thus her cargo went to the bottom and another valuable resource was lost.

On 28 February the actions resumed and the now repaired *Exeter* left port to join the others. In this part of the action one Dutch and two British ships were sunk after damaging several Japanese ships including sinking two transports.

Later the *Exeter* in the company of the others sailed west and ran into the main Japanese surface force. Another fierce action ensued but this time the results were catastrophic. They were completely out-gunned by heavier weaponry and air attack and all were sunk by the larger cruisers.

Thus the *Exeter, Perth* and *Houston* went down and it was only very much later that the true story of what had happened was actually found out from survivors. With the sinking of the Allied naval forces completed, Java was now wide open and there was now nothing left to prevent the Japanese invasion.

Compounding the dire situation on the ground, on 1 March the Dutch decided to pull out some of their forces without warning and withdrew to an airfield at Andhir further inland from Kalidjati.

The Dutch commander had pulled back his aircraft as well and left instructions for the Allies to make ready for actions later that day but also without making it too obvious that they might have to pull back too.

The defenders of the airfields now had to reorganise and fill the gaps. They were an impromptu group comprising members of 12 and 15 Btys

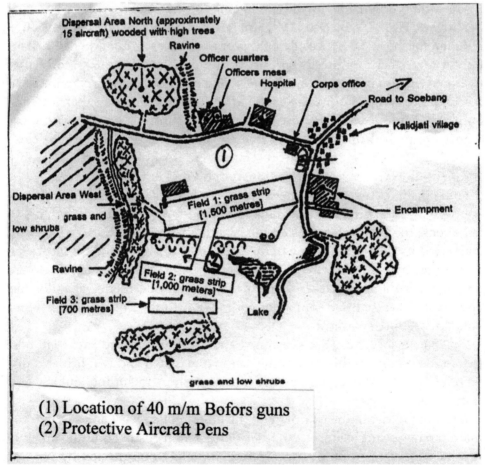

(1) Location of 40 m/m Bofors guns
(2) Protective Aircraft Pens

Fig.6-e Layout of the airfield at Kalidjati, Java in 1942. Courtesy of P.C. Boer.

and men from RAF personnel and two batteries of LAA Bofors gunners. There was also not too far away a detachment of the 3rd Hussars with their light tanks. These were small and almost obsolete and in great need of servicing.

Maj. N. Coulson and the survivors of 12 Bty, numbering some 140 men plus some 30 men of 84 Squadron defence section, had arrived mostly in the days before and many in the dark so were totally unfamiliar with the layout of the airfield or the surrounding terrain.

The LAA gunners under Maj. Earle were detailed to set up their 40 mm Bofors guns around the northern part of the airfield.

Maj. Coulson's first priority had been to assess the situation and deploy his limited forces accordingly and link in with the LAA gunners.

Others from 15 Bty of the regiment had been deployed to different airfields such as Tjililitan, Tjimahi and Andir where they of course were also to be used as infantry for their defence. For them it was an uncertain existence since they were kept on the move from one airfield to another, in most cases arriving to find few aircraft and vast expanses to be guarded, so vast there was no hope of doing anything very constructive.

Communications problems were the least of the O/C's problems with those RAF aircraft that were left behind.

While Allied forces were still in the process of organising, early on the morning of 1 March the invasion fleets had closed the land. They had attacked three different areas of the coast: in the north west at Merak (near Batavia), in the centre at Eretenwetan and also Surabaya to the east.

The Japanese 16th Army accompanied by a Shoti (about ten light tanks) got ashore in the centre.

Gp Capt. Whistondale at Kalidjati arranged for the Blenheims and Hudsons to be scattered around the perimeter while spare crews were moved to Bandoeng, another airfield further south. The remaining crews were put on immediate standby.

Aircraft from several airfields took off to bomb and strafe the invading forces in the different areas of operations. Lack of transport made manning the aircraft very difficult since they were dispersed at considerable distances from each other.

To aid Maj. Coulson the Dutch had loaned him some jeep-type vehicles and a few lightly armoured assault vehicles and he had dispersed some of his men around the airfield on likely approach routes for the Japanese.

There were as part of the airfield defences four widely spaced pill boxes now manned by RAF personnel. These were surrounded by barbed wire but were poorly designed, having the firing slits only on the sides facing the grass airstrips, so they were blind to any attacking force from other directions. There were also a few imitation pill boxes made of canvas containing a machine gun mounted on a concrete block in the centre.

By mid-morning Coulson and Earle had formed two forces with Bofors guns and infantry to make up two defensive road blocks on likely routes leading to the airfield.

Other men had been formed into mobile patrols to try and find out what and where the Japanese troops were up to. Spare transport was parked to the south of the strip to await developments.

The Dutch had by this time gathered some of their forces and pushed these out in an outer ring to protect the town of Soebang to the east.

By 0800 hrs the Japanese advance guard was nearing their positions and the first warning they had was when one of their mobile patrols rushed in with the Japanese hard on their heels. The opening shots were fired shortly after.

Elsewhere RAF and RAAF personnel who had started to move out after some of the last of the aircraft had flown off were now ordered to grab whatever transport they could and make their way back to Kalidjati again.

Some civilians had decided to move too from Soebang to avoid the conflict but there were nurses in the local hospital who could not leave their patients, many of whom were RAF, RAAF and Dutch service personnel.

The Dutch outer ring resisted briefly before retiring to Kalidjati and this resulted in all those in the hospital falling into Japanese hands. The majority of these were murdered or executed shortly after. The Japanese advance party having cleared Soebang then regrouped and settled down to await the remainder of their forces.

Meanwhile back at the airfield there was total confusion caused in no small part by poor communications but also by different groups all with their own agendas who were trying to round up personnel, collect stores, carry out demolitions and generally make off southwards towards Bandoeng and Andhir, in most cases without relaying their intentions to others or even advising what was happening.

At around mid morning at Kalidjati the station officer was in the station HQ building situated some hundreds of yards from the airfield. The defending gunners were closed up at their weapons anxiously awaiting what might come. 12 Bty men acting as infantry were dug in to defend what they could.

Not long after that the building came under fire from Japanese motorised units which had infiltrated the airfield and tanks and armoured cars could be seen in the areas around the strip and in the jungle nearby. There were only a few tanks and armoured cars but they were attached to a motorised column of heavily armed infantry and they were going flat out.

So sudden was the attack that many were caught by surprise. A few of the Hudsons which were nearest the runway managed to get airborne and flew off to Andhir, but unfortunately most of the Blenheims were caught on the ground and either captured or destroyed.

Frantic attempts were made to evacuate the main body of personnel back to Andhir and the gunners and RAF ground staff were left as a rearguard to allow them to escape. The majority of these gunners were from 12 Bty and LAA gunners.

While all this was happening at the airfield, those groups being used as mobile patrols and road blocks were also having a busy time.

15 Bty were also in the infantry role but stationed at two airfields called Tjimahi and Tjililitan. Whereas they were yet to encounter Japanese ground troops they had to endure countless air-raids from Japanese high flying bombers and ground strafing attacks by fighters. The bombers were out of reach of the Bofors and made the most of it. 15 Bty were to be joined shortly by survivors from 12 Bty who had escaped and gave them firsthand accounts of what had occurred.

The Japanese attack on Kalidjati had been swift, but the defenders put up a stout defence and fired everything they had. So successful were they that the Japanese were taken by surprise. The LAA guns were even depressed to act as anti tank weapons.

In a series of short sharp engagements lasting most of the morning the Japanese overran the airfield and its defences, with heavy casualties amongst the defenders and the LAA Regts. Much of the fighting was at close quarters and hand to hand but by midday the defenders had been overwhelmed. The Japanese tactics were to take no prisoners and those who were unlucky enough to be wounded were very often bayoneted where they lay. Their sacrifice had allowed the others to get away but sadly it made little difference to the final outcome.

It was thought that there were few survivors from the defending rear party at Kalidjati and this was apparent when, after the airfield had been captured, the Japanese used men captured elsewhere to go back and clean up the debris. They found all over the airfield among the detritus and in the jungle skirting it, scores of bodies not only of Allied troops but also Japanese soldiers.

It was during this bitter fighting that Maj. Neville Coulson the O/C of 12 Bty was killed leading his men.

Also amongst the casualties was Gp Capt Whistondale who was killed with his driver when their car was ambushed while they were escaping.

Sadly amongst those killed was Gnr Tart and in the chaos of the withdrawal his grave is not known. Whether he is one of the unknowns in the mass grave or still in an as yet to be discovered grave near the airfield we don't know. Far worse was the fact that a complete airfield in operational condition was now in the hands of the Japanese.

[It transpired after the war that witnesses told of men surrendering with their hands up only to be murdered and many were reported as having their hands tied behind their backs when the bodies were collected for burial. Those in the hospital fared no better; soldiers and civilians were also massacred. At the War Crimes Tribunal Col Koshihinge Shoji, who was the Japanese commander, was accused of allowing atrocities but lack of evidence meant no one was ever prosecuted. The bodies which had been buried in a mass grave were exhumed and buried in individual graves where identity could be confirmed, but this left the majority as unknowns.]

General Sitwell commanding troops nearby had lost contact with the airfield and decided to send out patrols to discover the true situation. Sadly they came back with the news that Kalidjati airfield was now in Japanese hands and that by 4 pm all resistance had ended.

The 6th Regt is also recorded as having 'lost' their CO, Lt Col. Baillie (formerly Baass), but in fact he was not killed but had escaped. He had obviously not been too popular since two Officers commented on his departure.

Lt Attiwill notes *'We are a reasonably happy family since our late Regimental Commander left us bushed in Andhir airfield and got himself flown out of the mess under the impression that he was needed elsewhere. He certainly wasn't wanted here.'*

Later the Brigade Major, a career soldier, commented on the episode: *'I'm glad it's not on my conscience to be one of those who ran away. It's a soldier's job to escape after surrendering, but not to anticipate it while the rest are busy fighting.'*

Baass had been born in Australia in 1895, one of four children and then been brought to the UK and spent much time on the Isle of Wight.

He was an old established Officer having served in the First World War as a 2/Lt in the 8th Bat. The Hampshire Regt TA (known as Princess Beatrice's Isle of Wight Rifles) and then transferred to the Royal Artillery, and gradually worked his way up through the ranks to command the 6th HAA Regt in mid June 1941.

The Regt emerged from these engagements having lost over forty men killed and many injured, and a necessary reshuffle of Commanders was needed such that Maj. Hazel took over as CO of what remained, Maj. Moxon took over as 2i/c and Maj. Allpass took over 15 Bty.

The 49th Bty of the 48 LAA Regt was decimated and many of the gunners who had been fighting as infantry along with men from the 6th Regt had been killed too; particularly hard hit were 12 Bty. Survivors withdrew inland towards the south coast and regrouped waiting for orders.

Fig. 6-f Maj E.J. Hazel who took over as CO in Java.
Courtesy of his daughter Clare Adams.

By 2 March plans had been set in motion for 'Blackforce' to move westwards with the aim of counter-attacking the Japanese forces now advancing down the roads from Merak.

The tanks of the 3rd Hussars had as yet made no contact with the enemy.

The whole plan was scuppered when they found during their advance that by the time they had reached Luewilling the only bridge had been blown prematurely by some local home guard unit without orders. This meant they had no way of crossing in force to advance to make contact. Some troops managed to get across and probe to find signs of the Japanese but without results.

Investigations at the time showed that the Japanese were still some 30 miles away and Brigadier Blackburn VC was quite obviously furious.

After this serious setback the Dutch commander then settled for Plan 'B'. This was for the Australian force to turn about and head back for Kalidjati with the aim of attacking the Japanese and forcing them from the airfield and re-taking it.

By mid afternoon of the 2nd 'Blackforce' had not started on its way and the plan was to take part in the counter-attack with elements of Dutch forces in the early hours of the 3rd. By this date the airfield at Kalidjati was swarming with Japanese planes hurriedly flown in after its capture. This was a somewhat optimistic plan since they had a considerable distance to travel, well over a hundred miles across difficult terrain and hills and of course much of it in the dark. Gen. Sitwell visited the Dutch commander at his HQ and made known his disquiet at the plan saying he thought it had a very small chance of success. The men would be tired and there would have been no time for a detailed reconnaissance of the Japanese dispositions. The Dutch Commander agreed and cancelled the order.

Meanwhile back at the blown bridge 'Blackforce' had guessed that the Japanese would arrive some time the next day. In this they were quite correct and having also guessed the Japanese tactics which were to outflank obstructions, they had set up a large scale ambush at the site of the bridge and also another at points where they anticipated the Japanese would try and cross.

The Japanese duly arrived and 'Blackforce' kept well down in concealed positions. They watched anxiously as the advance party reached the far side of the remains of the bridge. Here there was much discussing and further vehicles arrived carrying a senior Japanese officer and his subordinates. Some light tanks pulled up further back down the road along with infantry in trucks.

Completely unaware of the waiting Australians the outflanking party started to try and cross the river. At this point the defenders opened up a devastating fire catching them by surprise. Those at the bridge also opened up at the troops they could see on the far side.

After a fierce fire fight which left several vehicles and tanks on fire and numerous dead bodies lying about, the Japanese withdrew in confusion and then started to mortar the Australian positions. They in turn ordered counter fire from American artillery which had been set up in the rear. This completed the rout and gave the first round to them. During the rest of the day further skirmishes took place against the few Japanese who had managed to cross the river further south of the bridge site.

Meanwhile Gen. Sitwell had ordered all AA units to withdraw from Batavia to the Bandoeng area.

Dutch counter-attacks against the Japanese advances in the central area had failed and the non-arrival of Maj. Gen. Schilling's Dutch forces meant that the Kalidjati operation did not go ahead either. The Dutch attacks on the right section did succeed and gains were made round Soebang, but a determined Japanese counter-attack against them drove them back out and they lost all their gains. These losses were felt hard by the Dutch and morale seemed to take a turn for the worst.

In the west the fighting continued around the demolished bridge site through 4th/5th and then the forces withdrew behind their rearguard towards Buitenzorg. By this time anti aircraft units were still on the move or in position defending the few remaining airfields from which RAF and a pitiful few Dutch aircraft were still flying. Many of the Dutch planes were obsolescent and also heavily outnumbered.

That evening of 5 March the Dutch C. in C. Van Tooten called an 'O' group to discuss the situation with most of the Allied commanders. Despite the wish by the British and Australians to carry on the fighting by starting a guerrilla campaign he was not at all in agreement. Dutch morale was at a low point and there seemed no enthusiasm to continue the fight. What came over strongly was their fear of what might happen to the civilian population once the Japanese took over if the Allies had continued to fight on. They still had an underlying notion that even if the Japanese took over they would allow the Dutch to carry on in a supervisory role.

The possibility of withdrawing to the south to continue the campaign was discussed but although there was no hope of evacuation from there it would at least make a strong point. There was an airfield at Tasik Malaja and so it was decided to try and congregate all surviving forces in that area and around Garoet in the south. Road blocks were set up and forces deployed to the flanks.

Once Kalidjati had been lost the survivors were instructed to form into convoys and head south. As many stragglers as possible were gathered in and these joined up with those of 15 Bty who had as yet not been in action. This large convoy of varied transports and mixed service personnel started out. 15 Bty in the lead under Lt Steeds with 12 Bty miles away in the rear. The close spacing was designed to help speed up the progress but was a dangerous ploy. The rear of this column was bombed by Japanese aircraft who could not have failed to notice the tightly packed vehicles. During one of these attacks a gunner from 12 Bty was killed (possibly Gnr Hawtin No 822186 from 12 Bty). It was a narrow road with, in many cases, jungle close to the edges, and it climbed up and down the mountainous terrain.

The situation now descended into a confused withdrawal from one airfield to another, much of the time without all the units knowing any overall plan or where the other troops were.

Those at Tjililitan were sent to boost Tjimahi with the intention of them all then going to Andhir. By the time this had taken place around 7 March Lt Col. Hazel (6 HAA Regt) and Lt Col. Macarthey-Filgate (CO of the 48 Regt LAA) were busy reconnoitring yet another location for their guns and gunners acting as infantry near the airfield at Tasik Malaja. Hardly had they completed this than orders sent them back 30 miles along the road they had already advanced down.

Sadly yet again the remaining 3.7" HAA guns were ordered to be destroyed. This time it was the unenviable task of the 77 HAA Regt who had come over from locations in the east to help out. Survivors continued to drift into the defences but it was never going to happen.

Throughout the 7th and 8th hasty defences were set up and then when the Dutch declared they were going to ask for a ceasefire it was all over. They had already stated to the Japanese that several towns were now classed as open and non-combatant. These were Batavia, Bandoeng, and the latest being Garoet.

This rather forced Gen. Sitwell's hand since it was obvious that the Dutch had no further interest in fighting on, even though the Allies were quite happy to do so. Being subordinate to Dutch orders they had no choice. Gen. Sitwell ordered in his last proclamation that all forces were to stop fighting and be prepared to hand over to the Japanese. The surrender document delivered to all the troops was signed by Capt K. Campbell of 6 HAA, and a harder task for any military commander would be difficult to imagine.

Surviving troops and gunners were by this time drawn up in long convoys to the south of Garoet and heading towards the coast. They had it in mind that if they could get there then they would find boats with which to escape to other islands or Australia. At this time they had seen no Japanese or even been attacked by them, so life took on a leisurely air. They reached the coast and the men then sat around on the beaches realising that there was going to be no escape from there.

Some of the more adventurous got into groups to make their own escape and left with the usual banter in their ears. They were back again a few days later having been short of food and water and unable to communicate with the locals and then found no way to get off the island, let alone a single boat.

By 10 March Allied commanders met with Maj. Gen. Maruyama, the Japanese commander of 2nd Japanese Guards division, and it was agreed that troops would stop fighting and stay where they were. The Japanese promised they would treat all those captured under the rules of the Geneva Convention but their subsequent treatment of POWs made this a total travesty.

Thus the last of the surviving gunners went into captivity and started three and a half years of hell. Amazingly Gnr Weston had managed on 6 March to find a Cable and Wireless telegraph office amidst the total confusion to send a two-word message to reassure his wife: *'Safe, Well.'* They had no way of knowing how much those back in England actually knew of the war in the Far East. In fact it was very little and the situation remained very confused for a long time.

The gunners and defenders of Kalidjati could take some consolation in the remarks made by the Japanese commander who accepted the surrender. He commended the actions of these men and showed his admiration for their courage in the defence of the airfield against his troops.

Orders were given for the motor convoys to turn round and head for Batavia but some hundred miles short at the town of Trogong they ran into a Japanese road block manned by soldiers with fixed bayonets and very twitchy fingers. By this time much valuable equipment had been disposed of into rivers as they crossed them, including a Boys anti tank rifle carried by Gnr Williamson.

Having dismounted from the trucks, the instructions were then to leave the vehicles behind except for taking one for the wounded and another for rations and water and then start marching north. The men started to march with Lt Attiwill accompanied by his driver/batman Cripps. Also joining them was Sgt 'Darky' and another gunner 'Gypsy' Lewington who had a choice turn of phrase. When he met up with another roadblock and saw the size of their captors he stated: 'Gaw Blimey! Is that what we have had to surrender to? Look at 'em, they've even got cleft feet like cows.' (This was an observation on the footwear of the Japanese soldier, which comprised a jungle boot in which the big toe was separated somewhat like modern flip-flops.)

Their guards had to hurry to keep up the pace which was deliberately kept fast and they had to keep going to the front to try and slow things down. The marching was kept up for several days and then the Japanese changed their minds. The whole group was entrained at the nearest station and set off for Tanjong Priok on the north coast.

By this time some fifty-odd men were squeezed into each carriage and they were joined by a large contingent of US Field Artillery and some Australians. Once at their destination station everybody dismounted and marched off to the camp. Most men were carrying what personal belongings they could, including hard tack food. The US gunners were struggling under the weight of huge kit bags containing all their kit and as these became too unwieldy they started to jettison items, leaving a trail along the roadside.

After a chaotic time while they were counted, they then got allocated their new huts within a wire perimeter fence in a former Dutch camp, later to be known as the Bicycle Camp from the number used by the previous Dutch occupants. 15 Bty troops ended up in camp 8 and 12 Bty in another complex not far away but all within the same perimeter wire.

Once the surrender had been accepted the Japanese wished to round up as many stragglers as they could, just to make sure they were not going to be involved with guerrilla fighting, and they started a programme of flying over the mainland and nearby islands dropping leaflets to warn the inhabitants and Dutch not to hide or assist escaped service personnel under pain of death. The Dutch seemed to think that they were not going to have any problems with the occupying Japanese and in many cases handed Allied soldiers over. However it was not long before they realised their mistake and they were to be treated in just the same callous way as the rest.

By this time it was well known that Singapore had fallen and while 3 Bty was going through a similar process of becoming POWs 12 and 15 Btys awaited their fate.

The camps had water and electric light and although crowded were not overly so. Food at this time was reasonable but still below what was needed to maintain good health.

Among the gunners who had been swept up in the surrender were Walter Mear and his mate Robert Digg who had managed to stay together, but this was the start of over three and a half years of hell working on various war projects for the Japanese; of being perpetually hungry and overworked and at the hands of brutal guards where daily beatings were the norm for any perceived infringement. Unknown to them they were to have some amazingly lucky escapes.

At this time the Japanese had refused to disclose the names of all the POWs they were holding. Those back in the UK had no idea whether their loved ones were even still alive.

One of the Japanese daily rituals was to march large numbers of POWs along the streets down to the docks for their forced labour details. By a strange twist of fate many passed each day close to a school run by local Dutch nuns, who had made it quite clear that if the men could pass them their names and units they would do their best to pass as many of these as they could on to the International Red Cross. Thus it was that by furtive whispers, names were passed over and among the lucky ones was that of Walter Mear. The proof of this was when his parents received a letter (still in existence) from the Red Cross saying that they had had information that Walter was alive and safe in a POW camp in Java (Fig. 6.7). Of course this was a tremendous relief for his parents and family. Sadly this was one of only a few names that got through and for the rest there was no such luck.

Their relatives had no news for more than three years as to their fate until the war had ended.

Walter never knew that he had been reported as safe because although his mother wrote several times to Java the letters were never delivered and were returned with a stamp on the envelope saying the Post Box was closed.

Also among those captured was Gnr Stanley Weston and he ended up in Tanjong Priok. He would spend some months there before being shipped to Kuching. Once there he again was lucky enough to be able to fill in a POW postcard giving the briefest of details. He claimed he had received four letters and was in good health and in a POW camp in Borneo. (This was confirmed by the War Office to his wife some time later.) The postcard in itself was an unusual occurrence with the Japanese and many POWs never having any contact with home for the whole of their imprisonment.

At Kuching the main duties comprised going down to the docks each day and working to unload and load up cargoes for the Japanese war effort. This was a routine they settled into and as usual the scroungers managed to pilfer various materials in order to try and make life better. It is more than likely since Stanley was an accomplished cook that he was involved with providing the cooked meals each day.

It was not long after this that the Japanese demanded a large force to go to the east of the island to a place called Sandakan with the intention of constructing an airfield. In a situation where fate dictated who lived or died, Gnr Weston was one of those detailed off to go along as part of a group of some 2700 men. What he did not know was that he would not return, and neither would most of the others. (There were just 6 survivors, all Australians, out of these 2700 and they only survived by escaping.)

Once again he sent another rare postcard from Sandakan with the cryptic comments allowed: '*I am in Sandakan; My health is usual; I am working for Pay; please see that the children are taken care of. . . Stanley*'

Regressing slightly, while these forces had been busy conducting their own short little war in Java the Japanese had attacked the next large island to the east, that of Timor, on 19/20 February 1942.

There was not a great force defending this island; mostly Australians, some Portuguese, the British 79 LAA unit and a very few Dutch with some American artillerymen. Many of the Australians had not long arrived and had been sent to try and stop the island falling. It was vitally important that it did not fall into Japanese hands since capture of the airfields would have allowed the Japanese to be within bombing range of Australia.

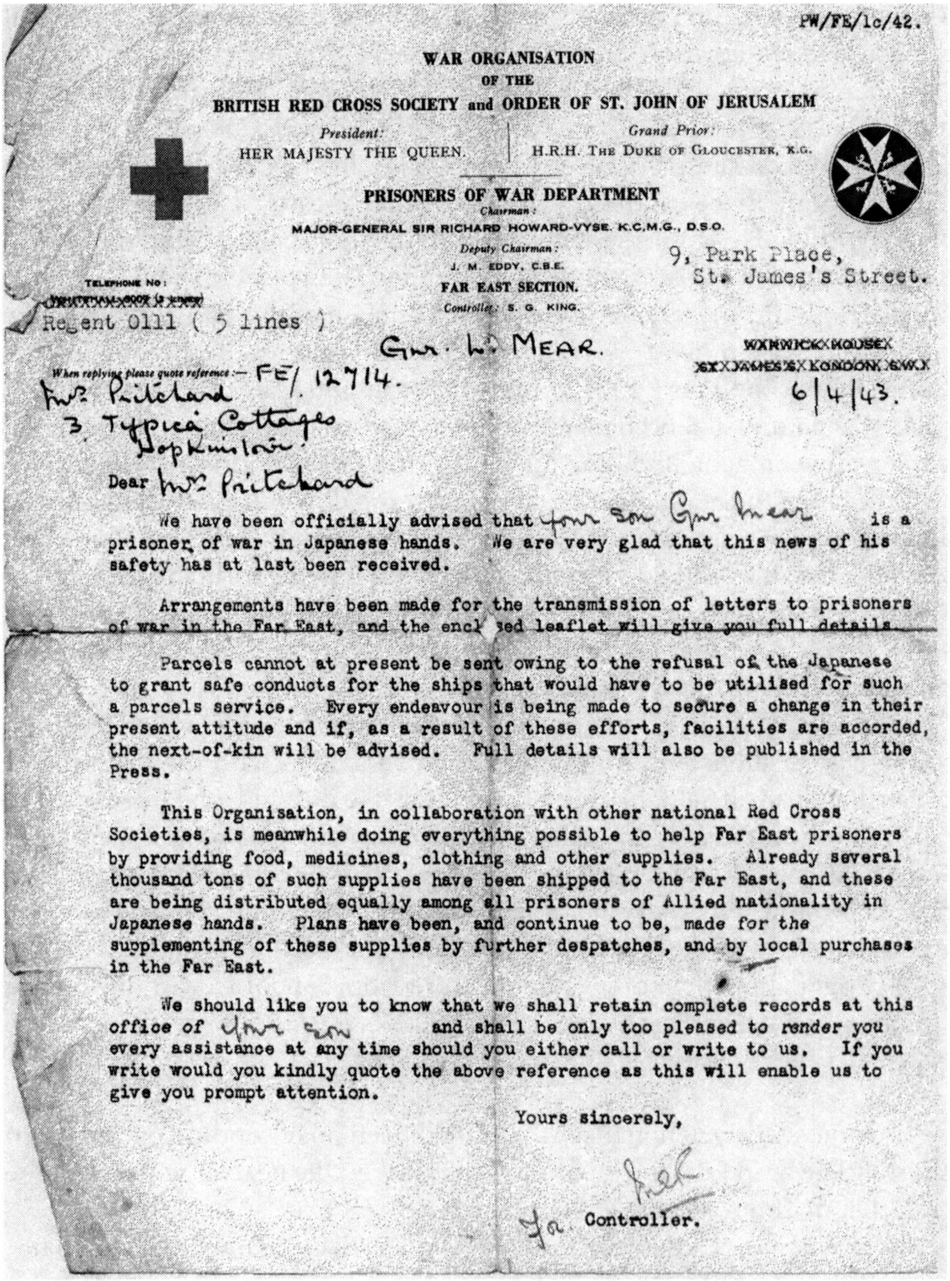

PW/FE/1c/42.

WAR ORGANISATION
OF THE
BRITISH RED CROSS SOCIETY and ORDER OF ST. JOHN OF JERUSALEM

President: HER MAJESTY THE QUEEN. | *Grand Prior:* H.R.H. THE DUKE OF GLOUCESTER, K.G.

PRISONERS OF WAR DEPARTMENT
Chairman:
MAJOR-GENERAL SIR RICHARD HOWARD-VYSE. K.C.M.G., D.S.O.
Deputy Chairman:
J. M. EDDY, C.B.E.
FAR EAST SECTION.
Controller: S. G. KING.

TELEPHONE No:
~~XXXXXXXXXXXX~~
Regent 0111 (5 lines)

9, Park Place,
St. James's Street.
~~WARWICK HOUSE~~
~~ST. JAMES'S, LONDON, S.W.1~~

Gnr. W. MEAR.

When replying please quote reference:— FE/ 12714.

6/4/43.

Mrs Pritchard
3. Typica Cottages
Hopkinstow.

Dear Mrs Pritchard

We have been officially advised that your son Gnr Mear is a prisoner of war in Japanese hands. We are very glad that this news of his safety has at last been received.

Arrangements have been made for the transmission of letters to prisoners of war in the Far East, and the enclosed leaflet will give you full details.

Parcels cannot at present be sent owing to the refusal of the Japanese to grant safe conducts for the ships that would have to be utilised for such a parcels service. Every endeavour is being made to secure a change in their present attitude and if, as a result of these efforts, facilities are accorded, the next-of-kin will be advised. Full details will also be published in the Press.

This Organisation, in collaboration with other national Red Cross Societies, is meanwhile doing everything possible to help Far East prisoners by providing food, medicines, clothing and other supplies. Already several thousand tons of such supplies have been shipped to the Far East, and these are being distributed equally among all prisoners of Allied nationality in Japanese hands. Plans have been, and continue to be, made for the supplementing of these supplies by further despatches, and by local purchases in the Far East.

We should like you to know that we shall retain complete records at this office of your son and shall be only too pleased to render you every assistance at any time should you either call or write to us. If you write would you kindly quote the above reference as this will enable us to give you prompt attention.

Yours sincerely,

for Controller.

Fig. 6.7 The letter from the Red Cross advising that Gnr W. Mear was still alive.
Courtesy of Michael Mear.

The Japanese main landing took place at Dilli while others landed to the south of Koepang and true to their previous methods were escorted by carrier- borne aircraft. Somewhile later they also dropped paratroops inland.

Greatly outnumbered, some of the defending forces formed a group called 'Sparrow force' and managed to resist for four days before being forced to surrender. Others retreated to the east end of the island where they continued to attack anything Japanese using true guerrilla tactics for over a year before being withdrawn to Australia.

Fighting had long since ceased for the most part by late March 1942 in the whole area and it was now time for the Japanese to decide what to do with all their prisoners, and including those on Singapore there were something like 150,000 to be sorted. Those who had been captured were rounded up and then marched away to the coast where they were told to build a camp for themselves. This was done over a period of weeks until some semblance of order was restored. The numbers increased later when survivors from HMAS *Perth* and USS *Houston* arrived.

By September a large contingent from the camp was assembled ready to set out for Java. They arrived at the docks and were herded onto a battered old tramp steamer called the *Dai Nichi Maru*. Conditions on board were horrendous as always and the men were crammed into the areas below decks. Many were suffering from malaria and dysentery and various tropical diseases. They set off for Dilli where unfortunately the ship was bombed by the Australian Air Force but luckily not hit. Having survived this incident she sailed on to Surabaya in Java, which took about six days.

Once there they all boarded a train which took them along to Batavia, a considerable journey right across the length of the island. From there they were transported to the main POW camp at Tanjong Priok and met up with many lost mates from different regiments. Here the British gunners were segregated and marched off some miles to another camp at Makasura, which was only a temporary stop-over till the main dispersal of POWs started. Tom Evans, veteran of Dunkirk in 15 Bty had already been there for some time.

Over the next few days the Japanese managed to issue every prisoner with a number and even had them all paraded so they could be instructed in 'how to salute any Japanese soldier whilst wearing a hat' or 'how to bow when bare headed'.

The Japanese were not long in ordering men to be used for work in the nearby docks and each day they were paraded and then marched down there to work unloading and loading ships. The harbour was full of sunken ships but a steady stream of barges were loaded and made their way further out to more ships anchored nearby. Those that had the chance to go to the docks noticed several large Sampans in a creek and ideas of trying to escape emerged again, so in between loading rice and scrap metal they formulated plans of how to get hold of them. As was the norm the Officers did no work but were more often used in a supervisory role.

Some time later extra manpower was forced to go each day by truck to an airfield where they spent much time shifting barrels of high octane fuel for Japanese planes. It was galling to know that their work was going to aid their captors but there was not a lot they could do. What they did when the Japanese were not too observant was to carry out small acts of sabotage, such as leaving the caps of some drums slightly loose so they leaked their contents on the ground. If the drum was left with its cap facing inwards then it might go undetected for quite some time.

For those left in camp boredom was a problem and the fittest ones started to play football games on a cleared area.

In a camp where most normal hygiene requirements were denied, it was not long before diseases started to make an appearance. The daily ration of rice was totally insufficient and the lack of vegetables for vitamins did not help. The 'black market' appeared and for those with money or something to barter there was the chance to obtain little comforts such as eggs, a tin of evaporated milk or even a jar of Marmite. The diseases they were suffering from were all preventable had the necessary medicines been available. Men suffered from prickly heat rashes, jungle sores, scabies, foot rot, dermatitis, ringworm and dysentery. In extreme cases the first signs of beriberi occurred – deficiency of Vitamin B1. Sadly for those troops who had contracted a venereal disease, and now numbering 30, they were isolated from the rest of the camp. The Japanese refused point-blank to provide medicine so they languished on their own as some sort of lepers.

As the daily routine continued, the opportunity to pilfer stores from Japanese sources was always welcome. Much of their time they spent rolling barrels of oil along the jetties or humping sacks of sugar, rice or dried fish. There was even the chance occasionally for swimming parties to be allowed out to go to the nearby beach.

The sick parade men were kept isolated in their own hospital hut but some showed how the diet was affecting them. Bdr Frostick could raise an arm to show a huge scab covering his armpit and to avoid startled stares Gnr Ward started to grow a beard to hide his rashes (not perhaps a good idea). Careless hands and the ever present blow flies spread germs and there was never a time when the MO and his dedicated staff were not fully occupied trying to help the patients. New fevers appeared such as dengue and these could take a fit man down virtually overnight.

Needless to say as men got weaker then they very often just gave up the struggle. The first to have died in 15 Bty was Sgt R.V. Burdett. The surprising thing in his case was he had been on an outside working party the day before and then within 24 hrs he was dead.

Captured in Java with the rest of the 6 HAA Regt men was their Padre Capt Norman Harper-Holdcroft. He too found himself at Tanjong Priok. He worked tirelessly for the wellbeing and spiritual needs of the men at a time when the last thing on many of their minds was religion. Nevertheless he set out and with their help they built a small chapel to be named St George's which did provide solace for some. He was later to find himself transported to Japan to a camp at Mitsushima from where he was released at the end of the war, deaf in one ear as a result of a heavy blow during his captivity.

Fig. 6.g Capt R.N. Harper-Holdcroft the Unit Padre after his award of the MBE.

Courtesy and copyright of his grandson Michael Harper-Holdcroft.

A perennial problem was the presence of large hordes of mosquitoes which came out in the cool of the evening to gorge themselves where they could. They also brought with them malaria and despite repeated requests to the Japanese for nets none were delivered. This left well over a thousand men unprotected. In order to get perks two gunners had volunteered for fly swatting duties in the Japanese part of the camp. Gnrs Turrock and Connolly made the most of this because the work was not hard and at the end of meal time the leftovers were given to them. These they carefully brought back into the main camp and had distributed among the sick.

It was shortly before a large influx of new POWs that the Japanese decided to move 500 men to make space and many gunners from 15 Bty went with them. The incoming men were all from Timor and brought their own tales of hardship, many arriving carried on litters by their mates and showing all the signs of malnutrition.

Then one day to everyone's surprise the Japanese handed out back pay.

This was supposed to have been issued to all men before, but only now did it get paid. It was in Dutch Guilders which meant that at least the locals would accept it rather than the occupation money, which they didn't like at all, and of course the black market started to flourish again. The irony of the situation was when the men checked what they had been paid they were somewhat short of what they were due. The Japanese explanation was: *'One guilder a day for fooding and bedding, fuel and lighting.'* Ten per cent was taken for tax and a further chunk for something called *'Compulsory Japanese Savings'*. For sheer downright arrogance and meanness it took some beating.

It was during this period that Walter Mear and his mate met up with and formed a close friendship with a Dutch soldier called Albert who had also been amongst those captured.

It was shortly after the mass influx of POWs that men started to be dispersed to other areas, some ended up in Kuching while others were shipped to Japan. Many from the Regt ended up at the POW camp at Batu Lintang near Kuching. This was a very large camp in two parts with captured Dutch civilians and other nationalities in one camp and POWs in the other. The main task the POWs had to work on was an airfield close by. The Japanese pilots had complained that the approaches were made difficult by a small hill and several planes had crashed or made bad landings. The task was now to remove the top of this obstruction and level it off. Conditions within the camp were similar to those elsewhere: severe treatment, arduous work schedules and as always inadequate food or medical supplies.

Many of those in Singapore had already been distributed by this time as the next chapter shows. But while 12 and 15 Bty languished in Java in far from comfortable conditions, those of 3 Bty, much further north, were not enjoying their captivity either.

Chapter 7

3 Bty and the
Burma–Siam Railway

———

Back in Singapore, which had capitulated on 14 February, the survivors of 3 Bty had been rounded up too and put into temporary camps, a large one being situated near Changi. Many of the men were seriously wounded and in need of medical help but got nothing other than what the medics could do with minimal supplies.

The Japanese never signed up to the Geneva Convention which laid down minimum conditions for the treatment of POWs so they felt quite justified in using and treating them how they wished. Thus it was that this huge pool of manpower was immediately put to work on military projects. After the disappearance and presumed death of Major Bailey, Lt McWade was given a field promotion to Major and took command of 3 Bty. He was now to serve with them for the duration of the war.

Many were selected to work in the docks in Singapore unloading their supplies. Large numbers were set to clearing the streets of debris and pulling down unsafe buildings in the city. They would go out each day under the watchful eye of Japanese guards who seemed to delight in humiliating their charges. Even the civilian population was not exempt; the Japanese had a terrible hatred for anything Chinese too.

It was in April that a large number were assembled and detailed off for Saigon, in fact around 1100, many of whom belonged to 3 Bty. They had all been assembled on the parade ground and then a Japanese Officer had walked along the ranks pointing out each man he considered fit enough to go. At this stage of the war most were still reasonably fit.

This large number of POWs were shipped to Saigon to work on the docks and this is where Gnr 1634325 Harry Dawson found himself along with Sgt Newcombe. Harry had enlisted in 1941 so he had avoided the debacle of Dunkirk and by the time he had finished training he joined 3 Bty of the Regt just as they were starting their embarkation leave for Iraq on 12 September 1941.

This first party had left Singapore in what was to become the usual method of transporting POWs, crammed in the holds of ships with the barest of their needs catered for. They reached Saigon after a few days and were billeted in an old French Foreign Legion camp, close to the docks, where the 3 Bty men tried as far as possible to stick together.

Their first job was to clean up the camp which had been derelict for many years and heaps of rubbish and years of dirt covered every surface and had to be shifted.

Shortly after they had arrived about 100 men from the camp were selected and sent to work in Hanoi. Those remaining had no idea what they had been sent to do but in fact it was the construction of an airfield and after some six months these men returned to Saigon.

Meanwhile BQMS Cotterill, Sgt Newcombe and his fellow gunners found themselves working on anything the Japanese deemed necessary to aid their winning the war in the Far East. Because of the vast numbers to be guarded the Japanese system was for Allied Officers and NCOs to be in charge of the various working parties to control them while they did the general over-seeing from a distance. The men had jokingly referred to themselves as the Saigon Battalion and amongst the thousand POWs were at least 220 belonging to 3 Bty.

It was not long before dysentery and disease spread again and men started to become seriously ill or in extreme cases to die. In order to keep control of this vast workforce the Japanese showed just what they were capable of and beatings and torture were a daily occurrence.

Work was centred on the docks and in nearby rubber plantations and also an airfield not far away. Those that remained in the docks were employed in unloading and loading stores and munitions for the Japanese Army and Air Force. They were not to know it but they had another year of this work in front of them. The work was hard, the amount of food was minuscule, the conditions extremely arduous and sickness rife. Although the food quantity was not sufficient to keep men fit at least it was edible despite it being composed mainly of rice as the basic ingredient.

It was a warning of the dangers of trying to escape, that when two gunners from 3 HAA Regt did in fact get away and received some help from local Thais, they were caught by Railway Police some miles away on a train. The two men were returned to camp and then shortly afterwards police came and took them away to Cholon Prison. They were never seen alive again. In fact they had been systematically tortured by the guards for several weeks and then been taken away and executed. It was only some weeks later when another POW died from illness and had to be buried in the local cemetery that the cortege party came across two freshly dug graves which locals said belonged to two white men.

What is not well known is that there was another POW with the two unfortunates who were murdered and he was Gnr Garry No. 1492995 of 3 Bty. He managed to escape back into the camp via the same hole they had used to get out through the fence in the first place.

They had, in Lt Col. Hugonin, the O/C of the camp, a first class Officer. In the POW reports after their freedom many of the men wrote about his perpetual attacks on the Japanese and his attention to the men's well-being. He stoutly encouraged the endless acts of sabotage while sniping at the Japanese himself. He even risked severe beatings and threatened shooting by the guards but they always backed down and lost face afterwards. (None was quite brave enough to shoot an older Officer.)

Whilst enduring the long days of hard work in the docks the POWs were not idle in trying to sabotage Japanese war material. Much of what they were forced to unload was for the nearby airfield and included spares and parts for fighters. In fact many fighters arrived crated up and it was not too long before the men had worked out how to get into the crates without giving away this fact and systematically smashed vital components such as gauges. More subtle damage was done by cutting or removing wires and fuel pipes on the engines.

There was so much going on in the docks and so few guards that it was not difficult to do this damage when their backs were turned. Items of ammunition were dropped over the dockside into the water as were valuable ingots of tin. The fuselage panels of aircraft were punctured by sharp objects and ripped.

Vast amounts of aviation and vehicle fuel were unloaded and transferred to waiting lorries or flat bed rail wagons for onward transit. Much was stored in piles at the airfield and hidden in the surrounding rubber plantations and the secret here was to loosen the bungs enough for the fuel to leak out unobtrusively into the ground. Just to make sure the Japanese did not find it too quickly the drums were hidden in the heap underneath and with the bungs facing downwards. Drums were also loaded onto flat bed wagons and had the caps loosened enough for the petrol to leak while the train travelled to its destination, thereby ensuring many arrived empty.

Looting became a way of life to stave off hunger and provide extra food for the sick. Large amounts of rice and foodstuffs came through the docks daily, including sugar. It was not difficult to tear a sack or puncture a drum of cooking oil or seasoning so it was spoilt. Despite the eagerness to pilfer extra food for themselves much of the sugar was used to doctor the fuel in tanks and drums and along with sand must have caused no end of headaches for the Japanese fitters.

Vehicles left at the dockside or in the holds of ships were also tampered with. Wiring looms were slashed or pulled out or even stripped so they would cause short circuits. One day several captured 25-pounder guns arrived and these were disabled by a Sgt armourer who removed cover plates and disabled components underneath before re-fixing them. In extreme cases complete breech blocks were removed and thrown into the sea. As well as this type of damage, dial sights were destroyed on other guns to make them totally useless until they could be replaced.

A continual stream of thousands of acts of sabotage were done daily that may not have been major on their own, but must have been a nightmare for the end user. It gave the POWs great satisfaction under the circumstances, to be getting one over on their captors. So good at their sabotage were the POWs that things became so desperate at one airfield that the Japanese ground staff even refused to allow POWs to work there any more. In one rather more amusing incident a whole shipment of bicycles arrived and these duly had their tyres punctured with a nail and then the valves removed. One can't imagine the Japanese soldiers being too pleased to have to spend the rest of the war riding around on the rims!

The scale of these wanton acts was so great that they began to wonder why the Japanese never complained but it was thought they did not have correct manifests to work out the shortages. With regard to the physical damage, which must have been a little more difficult to explain away, either they had to accept it as an occupational hazard or put some of it down to damage in transit.

Wherever men were allowed access to the stores then damage was done. However they were not always attempting sabotage. The men were constantly on the lookout for medicines and useful medical stores and because these were also in short supply to pilfer, two gunners, J.P. Murray and Purcell, both from 3 Bty, took it on themselves to sneak out at night from the camp and find and collaborate with Thai civilians to purchase what medicines they could using local currency from the camp reserve. This was an extremely dangerous act because to be found out meant torture and probably death at the hands of the guards.

Both these gunners became known for their daring in raiding the warehouses on the docks and managing to come back with all sorts of 'goodies'. So good did they become that after the war Maj. McWade wrote in his 'Returned POW report' that they deserved some sort of recognition for their undoubted bravery and resourcefulness.

Another man who was remarkably successful, but in another direction, was Bdr Currie. On one occasion when a man fell in the dock at Saigon while working on a ship he ran round and jumped in to rescue him and saved Gnr Greathurst (who was from a searchlight unit) from drowning. He must have been a good swimmer because he did the same for another man some while later; this was L/Bdr S. Harrison of 3 Bty, but sadly this time there was no happy ending and the man died.

This natural ability also probably helped save his life for he was one of the few survivors of the *Kachidoki Maru* incident over a year later.

Their days were long and at the end they just wanted to get back to camp and have some food and then get to sleep, however Saigon docks were extensive and it was quite common for several ships to dock at once and when one had left another would arrive at all times of the day or night. This usually meant another *Tenko* (parade) and then the men were led back to the docks and had to work through the night on unloading the ships. Eighteen-hour days were not unusual, but the darkness did give better cover for the pilfering.

Part of the overall Japanese strategy had been to capture Hong Kong, Malaya, Singapore, Thailand, Philippines, Borneo and Burma plus a multitude of the Dutch islands. These would have guaranteed their supplies of raw rubber, tin and oil which they were deficient of in their homeland. They had engineered the military side of things so well and prepared for it for so long that they were rather surprised at the rapid advances and capture of all the territory they wanted.

One thing that they still had to take was Burma and in a densely jungle covered country with extremely long supply lines they needed some way to overcome this problem. The ideal way they thought was to build a railway along which vital supplies could be carried. Japanese engineers had looked at the project and after much debate decided it would take about 5 years. The Japanese military were not satisfied with this and said it must be done quicker. Their latest estimate was about 18 months and this is what they now ordered.

They had estimated that they could transport some 3000 tons of supplies via this railway each day to support their troops in the Burma campaign (a tonnage that they never ever achieved). They had already taken large numbers of Malay, Tamil, Burmese, Sumatran and Chinese civilians to work as forced labour on a multitude of other projects and were now short of manpower. Someone looked around and the obvious pool of men were the POWs. These were mostly British, Australians, Dutch, Indians, Singapore volunteers and later a few Americans.

The Japanese wanted the railway to run from Ban Pong in Siam (modern Thailand) and connect to Moulmein in Burma where there was an existing track, a not inconsiderable distance of 415 kilometres.

Because of the vast distance ships had to sail from Japan to get to Rangoon, well over 4000 miles and the effect being produced by submarines from both Allies attacking this weak line of supply at choke points, the railway was considered vital.

The idea of a connecting rail link was not new, it had been thought about decades before but never implemented by the two countries concerned because of the costs and the geography. The terrain was primary jungle with many rivers and large limestone outcrops and subject to a monsoon that dumped unimaginable quantities of rain for several months of the year. There were a few small native villages but generally the area was uninhab-ited and very inaccessible. By this time the Japanese had decided that the track gauge was going to be a metre wide and this would determine the size of the rolling stock. Most engines were to be steam and fired by woodburn-ing boilers. Basic work in the form of Japanese survey parties had started in April 1942. These men had set out route trace markers and level guides in the form of bamboo 'rugby posts'. It had been decided that the track-bed would be a fairly constant 19 metres above the level of the river Kwei Noi (Kwai) and generally follow the course of the river and its flood plains.

It was to be a difficult project and had to be broken down into sections based on the complexity of the terrain or obstacles found within each stretch. It was intended to set up a series of camps in the jungle from which the teams would work left and right forming the track-bed till it joined the section on either side. Then the teams would be moved further along to start the next section and the process would be repeated. In total there would be over 70 camp sites of varying sizes some of which would of necessity have large hospital facilities for the sick.

In order to complete it in the best possible time the railway was to be worked on from both ends as well as from the intermediate camps. (Map 4)

Once the plan had been decided the Japanese started to bring men in from

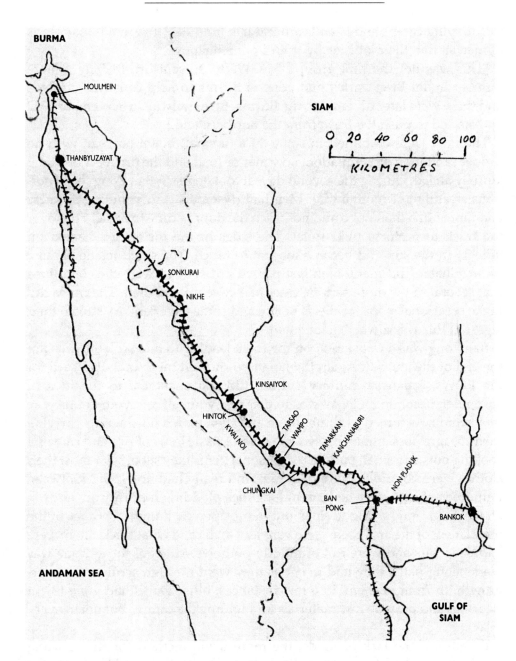

Map 5 Burma–Siam Railway from Non Pladuk to Thanbyuzyat, 415 kilometres.
Showing a few of the more than 70 POW camps.

the outlying camps and islands around late June 1942 and many thousands of men started their journey by train from Singapore.

[This was not the first group of POWs to be sent off. In May a large number under Brig. Varley had gone to Burma to help construct airfields and these were later diverted to the Burma–Siam railway in September 1942 and started to push the track from the northern end.]

The men were crammed in some 30 to a small metal box car, with no proper sanitation or ventilation, no water or food and the prospect of a long journey ahead. During the several days it took to reach Ban Pong the conditions steadily got more awful. Men had dysentery and vomiting sickness and more often than not could not reach the door in time to be held out over the track to perform their toilet. The sides of the metal cars heated up quickly in the sun and became too hot to touch. The smell inside became unimaginable and many men just passed out. So bad were the conditions that several of the more serious cases just gave up and died. The trains did make occasional stops for meals of rice and some water and to 'stretch their legs' but this was always inadequate.

Ban Pong was a rail station on the track leading to Bangkok but was not the end of the journey. Again the Japanese showed their total disregard for the POWs. Japanese military culture did not subscribe to the idea of surrender, becoming a POW was to disgrace yourself and your country, so they were now forced to climb down and then march northwards carrying their meagre possessions. They were given a basic issue of rice and carrying cooking pots and small bundles of personal items they set off. For most their clothes were not much more than rags and many had no proper footwear. Hundreds of men stretched out in long files plodding forlornly onwards in all weathers and having to sleep out in the open each night. Because of the remoteness of the area there were very few roads and what tracks there were had deep ruts and were full of muddy potholes. Much of the journey was made along paths they had to cut as they went through scrub and under-growth. In front of them, in a few instances, other gangs had gone to cut clearings and provide raw materials for building the camps, but not in every case.

Because of the lack of roads, the more usual method for transporting goods was via the river using boats or by boats pulling small barges. Some of the luckier later groups were taken up river by boat so avoiding the worst of the long marches. In fact the river was the main highway and very much subject to the rainy season where it carried dirty brown water in swift currents for several months of the year and then in the dry season the levels dropped dramatically revealing sandbars and rocks. The river also carried vast amounts of debris and diseases especially the deadly Cholera bacillus.

Having marched for days the large groups of POWs then split up taking tracks into the jungle to where in some cases a clearing had been formed with attap huts. Attap was a form of dried leaf folded over sticks so that it overlapped the row below to shed rain water, just like roof tiles. It was also used for walls.

Some of those sent to the furthest reaches had more than a hundred miles to tramp before reaching their destinations. However in most cases they had to clear the area themselves and it was the first priority at the end of an exhausting day to get the sick under cover, get the cooking started, dig sanitation trenches and then erect basic hutting. They also had to erect huts for the Japanese guards before their own.

By the time they had arrived at a camp site carrying rucksacks or cloth bags tied up with all their worldly possessions it was most often raining heavily. There was no fence around the camp to show where it ended; there was no need. What was the point in trying to escape, where could they go? Many of the natives were unfriendly and if they were caught trying to aid an escaper it was death for them both.

The Japanese guards were generally second rate soldiers and not front line and mixed up with them were the feared Koreans who could be far more sadistic. They all seemed to delight in abusing the hapless POWs and any dissention was dealt with by a severe beating. One thing they all had in common was their total disregard for human decency. What the POWs were fast learning was the idea that a Japanese or Korean could stand all sorts of dreadful conditions but the worst thing for him was to lose face. The Japanese despised the Koreans and in turn they both hated Europeans.

Any attempt at arguing or trying to point out some problem was immediately answered by face slapping or beating the person making the comment. Some of these beatings were severe and could put a man in hospital. Once they had settled their rage they could quite easily walk away as though nothing had happened.

It seemed that within the Japanese psyche was a long-standing hatred of the 'White man'. They had invaded the East and taken control of the countries they had come to and made them into their colonies, which they then continued to run with the original inhabitants' help as servants. They imported their way of life, sat back and ran the colonies in a very laid back European style. This grated badly with the Japanese who tried to emulate their ancestors way of life, in the style of Bushido which was very much a style of the Samurai and their code of honour.

Once they got the chance to be masters over the 'White man' they were going to show him who was the boss and really make him suffer; his life was worthless as far as they were concerned. The fact that many of those they now controlled were service men who had surrendered made the situation even worse. Although greatly outnumbered by their charges they would instil discipline by showing what they were capable of. Murder and beheadings were just a part of the possible punishments that would be meted out to any offenders who dared to disagree, especially trying to escape. Withholding food and medicine was another way.

Among the other problems the prisoners had when first arriving at camp was to find enough water for cooking and drinking and, if they were lucky, washing. Almost without exception their water had to be taken from the river which was already contaminated with diseases, silt, sand and debris. Any village upstream used the waterway as a toilet so this was also carried down to them. There was no way of filtering the water so this meant that before it could be drunk it had to be boiled, and for over a thousand men this amounted to many hundreds of gallons. This dirty taste of silt and water came to taint everything they ate or drank and along with second rate rice was something they would never forget.

The basic staple food was the rice which had to be boiled. If they were lucky they might get some additional vegetables or dried fish or seasoning to make it palatable. Salt was a vital commodity and also used for barter. On some occasions by the time the vegetables arrived from downriver they had started to rot so they were left with just the rice and any foodstuffs they might be able to barter or scrounge from local sources. Whatever it was, it was never enough, and for men expected to carry out hard physical work all day, the diet was little more than starvation.

The huts they lived in were generally bamboo framed with 'attap' roofs and walls, with a door at each end and one in the middle of each long side. Sleeping arrangements were on raised platforms of split bamboo down each side. They were so tight for space that each man had just enough to lie on but could not turn over properly and when full you could only get out of bed by shuffling to the end of your space on the platform to drop your feet into the central passageway and stand up.

The floors were just beaten earth which soon became a mud bath from driven rain or even worse the 'night soil' from those who could not help themselves. These camps were never free from disease, many men had dysentery or malaria but the one they all dreaded was cholera. It could strike without warning and spread like wildfire and with no medicines to combat it, it normally proved fatal.

The other worries the men had were injuries or wounds that they had picked up and which would not heal and then became septic. One of the worst types was ulcers which became large open sores like volcanoes filled with pus and in many cases these resulted in amputations after gangrene set in. What frightened the men with these sores was that in the event of an amputation being required it would be done in the jungle camp by one of the doctors and most probably without proper anaesthetic.

Those in the various units would try their best to keep together so that when they reached a camp they would at least have mates around them. The idea was to have a close friend and you could look out for each other, and this proved a very necessary way to maintain morale. However because of the way groups were split by the Japanese, many ended up in different camps.

It was normal to have a *Tenko* twice a day during which every able-bodied man had to appear. If they could not stand or were too sick then these had to be accounted for as well. At the morning *Tenko* the Japanese allocated the work parties and the remainder were then split up to carry out the cooking, camp maintenance or look after the sick. Poor diet from the lack of sufficient food meant that the inevitable sick list got longer and longer. Many of those that were sick just got sicker and as the maltreatment continued they just quietly faded and died, in many cases just a handful of skin and bones.

Once the work quotas had been decided the men then went to the tool store and collected a selection of digging implements which were never in sufficient quantities and in all weathers the men marched out each day to do heavy manual labour. When they reached the intended work area they would find pegs and level markers from the surveyors showing how high the embankments needed to be formed. Material had to be dug from local sources and carried in rattan baskets or on sacks slung between two poles and then dumped on the alignment and rammed down and compacted.

In the early days the Japanese allowed the men to work at their own pace without too much interference, however later when things were not going as fast as they wanted a quota was instigated by measuring the size of excavated holes to see if the required daily amount per man had been achieved. The POWs were up to all sorts of tricks to fool the simple-minded guards and in many cases got away with it.

Even later a system was started called 'Speedo' which really made life difficult forcing men to produce more and more each day. This was also aided by shifts working at night under the glare of oil lamps and arc lights But in the early days the quota was set at about one and a half to two cubic metres per man per day (up to four tons).

The gangs worked in a coordinated sequence. Once they had reached the marker pegs the clearing gang went ahead to cut down undergrowth and remove small trees and shrubs, leaving a cleared width for the track-bed. Bamboo clumps which could grow to fifty feet or more contained extensive root systems and also had a thick covering of sharp hairs which would penetrate the skin and go septic. Bamboo was also a favourite feeding place for large red ants which if annoyed or disturbed went on the attack. Trees had to be felled by hand, which in the case of large diameter ones was a major undertaking.

The bulk of the men were used to move vast amounts of fill and areas that were low were made up with an embankment. When they came to streams and gorges these were generally spanned with timber bridges, however the one at Tamarkan was made of steel trusses on concrete piers. These trusses had been manufactured in Java and then shipped over to Siam. [This was the bridge that gained fame in the mostly fictional film *The Bridge on the River Kwai*. In reality there were two bridges at this location, a timber trestle one used while the main one was constructed and the concrete permanent one a short distance away.]

Where sections of the ground were high in relation to the future track bed levels they would be reduced by forming cuttings using large long handled *changkols* (an item somewhat like a mattock).

In other places where bedrock was encountered the arduous task of drilling shot holes was carried out using forged metal bars about two foot six inches long, and hammering and twisting these into the rock till a hole was formed using sledgehammer blows. This task was referred to by the POWs as 'Hammer and Tap' and took many hours to produce a useable hole. They also had to try and avoid hitting the rod holder on the fingers or hands.

When a series of these holes were deep enough and normally at the end of the day Japanese engineers came along, loaded them with explosives and lighted dozens of fuses, and then they all withdrew hurriedly. There was not a lot of care taken with regards to flying rock and many men were seriously injured during the project, some even killed. The broken rock was removed with bars, hands and *changkols* and then the process started again on the next layer down till the correct level had been reached.

On rare occasions when large amounts needed blasting, rock drills and a compressor were brought in and in extreme cases where limestone cliffs dropped into the river the blasting had of necessity to start at the top of the cliff and be carried on down in multiple stages till a suitable ledge had been formed; there was never any intention to construct tunnels.

Every day from dawn till dusk the work went on. Occasionally, dependant on the Officer in charge, the tenth day was classed as a *Yasume* day (a day off). The POWs were expected to carry out this arduous work on starvation rations and in all weathers and for many who had no footwear the work was carried out in bare feet, a highly risky method when working on sharp rock.

When they arrived back at camp exhausted it was very often to find that the heavy rain had flooded the latrine trenches and the surface was covered in raw sewage. 'Night soil' from those unable to reach the toilet in time at night was now washed about the camp and into huts creating a stench and health hazard. Areas used for the latrines were covered by large black flies which carried the contamination to everyone. Huge maggots also lived among the faeces and thrived in it as they wriggled about in their daily lives.

Another common illness was beriberi, caused by the lack of vitamin B1. Organs started to fail and pools of liquid built up in various parts of the body under the skin. This made it difficult to lie down safely and if it reached the lungs then death followed.

Malaria caused by the ever present mosquitoes was very common and very debilitating. Men who had this lay on their beds with uncontrollable shaking fits and suffering from hot and cold sweats. Because of the lack of drugs to treat it most had recurring bouts for their whole time in captivity.

The general lack of medicines and ointments allowed skin infections such as scabies and ringworm to thrive and the lack of essential vitamins created an uncomfortable condition known as Changi Balls where the whole scrotal area became grossly enlarged.

Among the natural hazards were the ever present leeches. These were everywhere and could be collected from undergrowth or working in the water. Although these did not kill people directly they would attach themselves and after filling up with blood would drop off. The resulting puncture would then bleed uncontrollably for several days until the anti coagulant the leech had injected had dispersed. For the puncture to heal properly it required to be kept dry, something that was impossible. The result was the puncture would very often go septic and then develop into a jungle sore which in turn could get larger until it became an ulcerous crater.

Snakes were not a problem although there were records of people being bitten by centipedes or stung by scorpions. Neither of these would prove fatal but just painful and unpleasant.

The Japanese rarely issued Red Cross medicines, preferring to steal the contents for themselves and so medication for a vast array of ailments was not available. Bandages and antiseptic creams which would have controlled many of the illnesses were sadly missing too.

Food parcels made up by the Red Cross with all sorts of useful items which would have helped to sustain the men's bodies were also withheld, in many cases being looted as well or just stored elsewhere out of reach.

Surprisingly despite all their other faults the Japanese did actually pay the working POWs for each day's work, the money owed being paid every ten days. The currency was divided into Ticals and Sattangs. One Tical equalled one hundred cents or Sattangs. Locals refused to accept Japanese Occupation printed notes but the ten cents a day for other ranks went some way to helping to buy medicines and food from local traders.

NCOs got 15 cents and officers considerably more although in most cases the officers did not have to work. This was a continual bone of contention because in many cases they just shut themselves away and played endless games of bridge, or read. Despite being 'in the same boat', many still tried to maintain their traditional segregation from the other ranks. In the worst cases they made no attempt to try and alleviate the hardships for the men.

In some places, where there were no traders locally, they came up river in small boats to sell wares such as limes, sugar, salt and vegetables or dried fish and duck eggs. In others where there was a local village nearby men were delegated to go and barter and bring back what they could. A priority was to try and get enough fresh greens or medicine for everyone, especially those who were sick.

Never one to miss a trick the Japanese guards demanded a commission from these traders for the privilege of being allowed to sell to the men. There was an unwritten code that a small percentage of the wages was to be put aside to buy suitable food for the sick to help them get better. This went on greens or eggs to provide valuable protein.

For the men in most cases there was never any mail in or out for the whole of their captivity so no one at home knew whether they were alive or dead or even where they were and similarly for the POWs they did not know what was happening back at home. Sadly many a man went home hoping to pick up where he had left off with a girlfriend or fiancée only to discover she had already married someone else.

However as the demands of the work increased, more and more men became seriously ill. The Japanese in charge, always reluctant to feed extra mouths that were not producing, tended to have them shipped out downriver to one of the camps that had hospital facilities. That way they managed to avoid having too many men die under their command.

In some of the worst areas so many men became sick or injured that work began to get behind schedule. This problem was eased by sending in further POWs from elsewhere and in February 1943 a system called 'Speedo' was instigated. Basically this meant even longer working hours and arduous work and still no improvement in the food ration.

The health situation amongst the men degenerated to such an extent in mid 1943 that in some camps the Japanese even brought in medical men to give injections against cholera in order to try and keep the workforce alive. The one disease they all feared was cholera for its potential to kill so rapidly and spread indiscriminately. The Japanese never seemed to realise that if they had treated the men better then they would have got more from them, they preferred to maltreat them; instead as part of the humiliation.

Having been sent down river to seek treatment many men were thus separated from their units and if and when they got better they could be sent back upriver to any of the many camps, so units became jumbled up. In the early days the Japanese had segregated men by nationality such that Tamarkan was predominantly Australian whereas Tarsao and Tonchan were British. Kanchanaburi, one of the lower camps on the river, and known to all by the name Kanburi , was a huge camp with large medical sections (see Map 4, p. 113). It had a very mixed bag of most nationalities and as time went by many of those who were desperately sick ended up there. This not only made the task of the overworked doctors greater but also meant that the death lists were very high.

As well as these camps that were full of military POWs , but not often seen, there were a number of other camps full of civilian enforced labourers, mostly Malays, Burmese, Tamils and Chinese with some Filipinos. These were very often there under duress or having been lied to about conditions. When the Japanese realised the scale of the project they had advertised in the local villages attractive rates of pay and conditions and that men who took them up would be able to go home after three months. Many had joined but others, fearing the true nature of the scheme, had hidden away in the jungle or with distant relatives.

When the Japanese realised they were not getting the numbers they needed, one rather underhand method used had been to advertise a film show for free in the local cinema and when it was full the doors were locked and all the men of suitable age frogmarched away to work camps.

When cholera struck, and it frequently did, not having the same organisational system as the military, these coolie camps suffered badly. Thousands died from disease and overwork and when petrol was not available to burn the corpses they ended up in unmarked mass graves close alongside the railway. There are no records of names and quantities so they just remain as a vast army of unknowns.

What is known is that they numbered well over a hundred thousand.

Chapter 8

12 and 15 Btys move to Japan, and the *Singapore Maru* Incident

_____

In October 1942 large scale movement of POWs took place in Java from Tanjong Priok. There had been a big influx of more prisoners, mostly Australians, and the Japanese had now found a new use for those captured earlier.

With one day's notice the order was given to evacuate the camp and leave behind the Australians and Indians and prepare to go to the docks. Their ultimate destination was not disclosed. Men were moved on a regular basis from Java to Singapore or other islands and from Singapore to Japan in convoys. Sometimes the move was quite short but the dangers were just as severe.

The men fell in outside the camp and marched the two miles down to the docks carrying their most valuable belongings, and amongst these possessions was one of the rare radio sets constructed by the signals and RAOC men from bits and pieces and scrap parts. It had been broken down into convenient-sized pieces to evade disclosure.

The gunners from the Btys managed to stay together which was good for morale but once at the docks they went through the laborious process of counting, which the Japanese soldiers never seemed to master. What threw them were blank files in the ranks where either one or two men stood but never the three in the files alongside. Under ordinary circumstances men 'fall in' in files of three men. If their numbers create a total that is not divisible by three then the spare men form a file towards one end of the ranks which will of necessity have either one or two men only in it called a 'Blank File'. Looked at from the front someone trying to count the files using the three times table would have to realise that in one particular file there was not a full quota of men. This situation could be used to advantage by the men to confuse the count, either intentionally or not. It would also confuse a guard who might not be too bright.

The ship was a rather old and rusting cargo carrier called the *Yashida Maru* of about 5000 tons. After being shepherded up the gangway by the gentle prodding of bayonets and rifle butts some 2000+ POWs were squeezed down in the holds. (Among this vast number was Gnr Frederick G. Clapp, who by this time was already suffering seriously from malnutrition and dysentery.) The camp guards then dispersed and new men took over their duties.

The deck areas were cluttered with sacks, baskets of vegetables and other gear and of course ship's tackle. The crew were pretty untidy in dress with ragged shorts and sweat bands and for the most part seemed uncommitted.

The numbers of POWs the ship could carry had been increased by the tactic of installing timber shelving in the holds to make a mezzanine floor. The hold covers were left open with the result that once at sea rain squalls pelted down on the inmates and drenched them. The holds were alive with vermin – beetles, cockroaches and even rats, which scampered over everything.

On deck were the *Benjos* (squat toilets) crude timber structures mounted outboard of the sides. There were a dozen of these and just eight urinals for two thousand men, many of whom were very sick and suffering the effects of dysentery and vomiting upsets.

Meal times were chaotic since everyone had to queue in the limited space down each side to have his food slopped into a mess tin or homemade container and then struggle back to eat it in the hold. The air in the holds below was steadily fouled by the number of men and their tight packing. There was no proper ventilation.

After three days of this hell they arrived at Singapore and anchored off the harbour and many of the men were just grateful for the break to get over their seasickness.

When they reached the upper deck they could see what remained of Singapore docks. The Japanese had made scant effort to repair the damage and many of the cranes lurched drunkenly from the abortive scorched earth policy to demolish them before the capitulation.

Huge warehouses still retained missing panels and roofs. The harbour was still partially blocked by sunken ships including *The Empress of Asia*. Sturdy weeds had managed to push up through concrete and asphalt wherever they could and there was the smell of rusting metal and decay.

After the usual delays everyone disembarked only to have to stop on the quayside. Here they were ordered to undress and then ignominiously hosed down from a fire hydrant. If this was some sort of cleansing it was a joke. However for the men who had had no such luxury as washing this was in most cases a blessing to get rid of some of the dirt clinging to their bodies.

They had up till then not been advised of their final destination. It was always a forlorn hope that if they could stay around in the southern regions then by good fortune they might be rescued by Allied troops when they came back.

After a brief meal of rice again they left all their belongings behind and queued up in a double row in a nearby open area. Then under the watching eyes of the local population they had to come forward two at a time. When they reached a table, behind which sat a white coated doctor, they were obliged to drop their trousers and bend over in full view of the masses. In an undignified motion a glass rod was forced up their rear ends to take a sample for checking to see if they had dysentery. This would show later in the sampling dish as having blood in it if they did. After this totally unnecessary public humiliation they returned to their ship.

This was followed by more days of waiting around in the stifling heat and then another trip onto a different ship where they had to undress and this time all their belongings and themselves were sprayed with disinfectant powder.

Back again to the *Yashida Maru* and more delays. Then quite suddenly after dark Japanese guards were heard shouting 'Speedo. Speedo.'

The whole thing was repeated with a scramble to make sure nothing was left behind. However this time they boarded a different ship called SS *Singapore Maru*. It was somewhat larger but not in any better condition with regard to rust. The next day she sailed as part of a seven ship convoy and after clearing the Singapore Roads headed northwards.

Despite all the protestations from the Medical Officers and senior Officers that sick men should not be carried in those conditions, the Japanese ignored them. By this time many men were suffering badly from dysentery and diarrhoea, malaria and various fevers. Packed in like sardines it only took one fly or carelessly placed hand on a rail for germs to be transmitted to a healthy man. Water was in short supply and there was none for washing.

Also sailing on this ship were some 500 armed Japanese soldiers and a few women of dubious character – geisha girls who had been part of the comforts enjoyed by the Japanese soldiers but now returning home.

The Japanese called the MO and told him to go and collect his medical stores, which he had ordered before they left.

When he got there he was totally disgusted to see that all they had found for him were some Bismuth tablets, some Andrews Liver Salts and a small first aid kit, and all this for 2000 men! True to form the promised new clothing to replace the rags being worn by the men was not provided either.

Men continued to get sick as the ship sailed ever northwards and still no destination had been disclosed. The rumours had already decided the final destination was going to be Japan and this meant there would be no hope of rescue there till the war's end.

They had departed in these very unsanitary conditions with some foreboding. Men were already sick before loading and under these conditions things could only get worse.

It was not long before men started to go downhill with the dysentery and before long they had their first death, Gnr C. Stewart No. 1738111 of the 15 Bty (Left troop) whose body was committed to the sea.

As the voyage progressed at a slow plod of about 9 knots things got steadily worse. Lack of food and medication meant men were too weak to fight diseases. By the time they reached Formosa after two weeks they had to 'heave-to' for a typhoon with all the hatches closed and this exacerbated the whole situation.

As yet another sign of the sadistic Japanese nature a small dog that had been brought aboard happened to brush up against one of the soldiers who without a thought threw it over the side. He and his mates then laughed and giggled as they watched it trying to keep up behind the ship. A more horrible death could not be imagined.

By this time while waiting for the storm to blow itself out, one of the Officers who had been seriously ill for some time died, Lt M. McCallum of 12 Bty. Along with several other bodies of those who had also died during the night he was removed to shore and later their ashes were returned to the ship in metal tins. Seven in all.

At this point, as the storm finally blew itself out, about 100 Japanese soldiers disembarked and another 500 were intending to get on. In order to accommodate this number, a horde of carpenters arrived and started to fit out another hold with shelving for the POWs. Once this was completed men were moved around into the new hold and the life of sardines started all over again.

Amoebic dysentery had taken a tight hold in the ship and so bad were the conditions that the Japanese officers would have nothing to do with the POWs. They were petrified it would spread to them and even the guards would only come as close as it was necessary in order to look down into the holds, holds whose atmosphere was by now foul smelling, rancid and fetid.

Every day more men succumbed to their illnesses and the total neglect of their captors. The bodies were raised to the deck and laid out ready for the Padre to read the final service. They were wrapped in rice sack paper coffins and weighted by shovelfuls of sand brought up from the ballast below. They could only be committed once the ship was under way again.

Three more men from the Regt were amongst them, all from 15 Bty: Gnr F. Cooley No. 847924 who was the one held in detention at Chorley all those months ago, considered fitter than most and stout hearted, and two others, Gnr H. McLatchie No. 1774707 and Gnr E. Dwyne No. 1725591. This time the burial service was for seven men, three of whom were from 15 Bty.

The ship plodded on its way northwards with Japan now known to be the final destination.

Death daily stalked the lower decks and the toll rose as men could no longer maintain the will to live. Hardly a day went by without more corpses.

Gnr Clapp like so many others got steadily weaker, as without proper medicines his dysentery worsened. Like many of the others he was also suffering symptoms of beriberi and fever. On this next stretch of the voyage there were several more deaths in the Bty. One of these was L/Sgt W. Baker No 812965.

Eventually the ship arrived to the south of Japan and anchored and a new experience greeted the survivors. It was now the end of November, they had been at sea for 35 days and the weather was bitterly cold. They were still in their tropical shorts and shirts and not much else. Any pieces of material that could be found were used to tie round themselves to try and keep warm.

Gnr Cripps had a new friend from 15 Bty called Gnr Field. They shared the same area of shelf and took it in turns to help each other get through another day. Both men were skin and bones with sunken eye sockets and covered in sores. Skin was pulled tight over their bones making them look like mobile skeletons.

While they were at anchor a Japanese doctor came aboard and after a cursory look round declared nothing amiss. He wouldn't even descend into the holds because of the overpowering smell.

He had been summoned by the constant protestations of the Senior British Officer to the Japanese Commandant. In fact there were over a hundred seriously sick men in the hold which had been converted into a sickbay. After further remonstrations he finally agreed to allow 21 men to be offloaded to the hospital. With the usual unbelievable Japanese logic the men were tested again for dysentery by the glass rod up the rear. Just about all the men were suffering from dysentery so this would prove nothing.

Later that night there was a deathly quiet around the ship, and no one was quite sure what was happening. However the more astute ones discovered that most of the guards had left to go ashore and the prisoners were on their own. In fact there was just one corporal and seven soldiers to control the whole ship.

Almost as one the men descended on the food lockers and broke open the locks. Inside there was a large supply of tins and vegetables and even alcohol and Saki. For a few frenzied hours everyone got his fill and many got drunk on the alcohol. Many a stomach which had not tasted food for a long time rebelled and men were violently sick all over the place on deck and also in the holds making the stench even worse. The guards deemed it prudent not to interfere and pretended nothing was amiss. They stayed at their end of the ship and kept their heads down.

By morning all sorts of goodies were hidden in whatever places they could find, but then the Japanese guards returned. They discovered the situation and went absolutely crazy, running about shouting, and the Commandant ordered the Officers to see him and explain. Nobody of course had seen anything which made him even more angry. He demanded all food to be returned and the culprits listed. Expecting the food to be returned was a forlorn hope since it had been eaten.

After a long period of stand-off a list of names was presented but there were too many for him and he wanted it shortened to just a few. Further wasted time and then a coordinated search was made by the guards who were very reluctant to go anywhere near places occupied by the POWs, but they turned up pitifully few items. Most of the tins were empty.

Then as suddenly as it started, by evening, all went quiet and the men were told to disembark. The Japanese ultimatum was for all men to get out, anyone left behind could expect to die in the hold. After such a nightmare voyage and the terrible smell and conditions below the men did not need urging. No sooner were they off than more stretcher cases were loaded back on, this time mostly Americans and all in poor condition too.

Those of the Btys too ill to be removed were left to their fate; some were taken to a hospital at Moji, and many were left below in the festering holds. One of these from RHQ was Gnr Barnbrook No 230114 who died two days later in Moji Hospital from the effects of the voyage.

It was during this period that Gnr F.G. Clapp No 5616255 managed in his debilitated condition to clamber out of the hold and find his way onto the dockside. Here he collapsed and was removed by stretcher. He ended up in the hospital at Moji where luckily he got some attention, and with his strong constitution he eventually recovered.

Those fit enough to walk were taken to the docks and gathered in an open space at the end of a wharf. They were split into four groups and some boarded a coal barge for a three-hour trip to the mainland.

After landing at a small dock they once again disembarked with great difficulty, those who were sick being helped by their mates to get out from the depth of the barge's hold. Then there was another walk through silent streets of a town with small houses on both sides until they reached a wooden walled compound containing some huts. The separate parties knew nothing of where the others had gone but in fact they were all in separate camps around the area of southern Honshu. Some of the lucky ones ended up in a camp with decent huts all containing mattresses of straw on the floor. They were given their first good meal and then collapsed into oblivion. They found themselves in four camps at Ube, Ohama, Motoyama and Omine, all on the same part of the mainland on the island of Honshu. Across the water lay the town of Moji and its hospital where some of the worst cases were taken. They then waited to see what the future held for them.

By the time they had arrived, there had been 63 deaths on board, all preventable, but now they faced the risk of hypothermia from the biting cold of a Japanese winter.

6 Regt's losses from this trip and from the immediate aftermath would be 65 men.

12 Bty lost 7 died on board and 14 shortly after.

15 Bty lost 11 died on board and 19 shortly after.

RHQ lost 4 died on board and 2 died shortly after.

Attached ranks lost 5 died on board and 2 shortly after.

A sad indictment of complete indifference from their Japanese captors.

During this nightmare voyage, which lasted for more than four weeks, the huge casualty rate could have been prevented by the Japanese taking basic precautions instead of just packing them in and allowing the prisoners to die in the unsanitary holds.

Sadly one of those carried ashore too ill to walk from 15 Bty was Lt Gilby (MC) and a few weeks later he died. The cause of death was given as 'acute enteritis, beriberi, tropical diseases and severe malnutrition'. Despite surviving the attacks in France and Belgium and during the Blitz he was not killed in action but brought down by the atrocious treatment of the Japanese.

The only small light in this dark episode is two reports that survive written by officers from the regiment after the war of special praise for two men and their terrible ordeal during this voyage.

The first is by T/Maj JS Allpass No 73393.

'Dvr F.Pardoe No. 788876 (15 Bty) carried out the duties of medical orderly under trying and arduous conditions from March 27th 1942 until Sept.13th 1945. He performed particularly outstanding work for five weeks on the Singapore Maru (Java to Japan Oct 22nd–Nov. 27 1942) under filthy and inhuman conditions and as result of this voyage it is estimated there were over 200 deaths out of 1100 POWs.

He showed great devotion to duty during this epidemic as indeed he has shown throughout. This man was under my command for the period mentioned.'

Pardoe was to be awarded a BEM after the war for this valuable service.

The other report is by Capt K. Campbell MC No 85544 and appears in his returned POW questionnaire form.

Fig 8.1 Gnr A.R. Barnbrook No 230114 of RHQ. Sadly to die from his treatment on the *Singapore Maru*.
Courtesy of his grandson B. Barnbrook.

'Bdr W. Fairfax No.545131 6 HAA Regt. :- Nursing the sick personnel under extremely bad conditions on the ship *Singapore Maru* 21 Oct. 42–25 Nov.42. He died shortly after the voyage as a result of his devoted work.'

When morning came they still had no idea of what they were going to be required to do. The other camps were in a similar situation but it was obvious that they were going to be used as slave labour yet again.

After the preliminary parade and count it was made clear to them what they were going to be involved with. The camp at Ube held something less than 200 men, many of them gunners from the 6 HAA Regt. They had no news of those they had to leave behind on the *Singapore Maru* or even those who were unloaded at

Formosa and these had been the ones too sick to continue.

The camp itself was made up of barrack style houses with traditional sliding doors across one end. These were a bit of a problem to begin with because they had paper windows and these didn't take much to rip. The Officers and NCOs took up rooms at one end of one hut and the men filled the rest of the accommodation. Since it was winter the huts had a traditional charcoal stove (*hibachi*) in the middle for warmth.

The ever present sickness and diarrhoea was still prevalent, but at least there was now the chance to get on top of it with the marginally better conditions. However, within a few weeks there were another six deaths. The bodies were wheeled away on handcarts and some while later a small tin for each containing their ashes was returned. One of these was Gnr E. Frostick No. 1525610, he of the oversize scab in his armpit. His cause of death was attributed to colitis, malnutrition and severe neglect along with other tropical diseases. By that time those at Ube had over a dozen such tins.

Lt Attiwill caught up again with his batman Cripps to find out the latest news. It was not good, for he found out that his friend and helper Gnr E. Field No. 824967 had died from malnutrition, even after helping each other for so long.

Eventually after repeated complaints to the Japanese about the lack of fruit and vegetables for vitamins, a small supply of oranges appeared.

The routine continued unabated for over a month with people just kicking their heels but then one morning they were all marched out of camp into the town. By this time the snow had mostly melted. They marched through the streets now filled with people going about their daily chores, who stared at this strange mix of men with unabashed curiosity.

They had been issued with Japanese style army uniforms to combat the cold and none were a good fit.

It was not long before this that the Japanese had again demanded that all prisoners sign a special form saying they would not attempt to escape and they would obey all orders without hesitation. Where they were going to escape to was not obvious. Odd extra questions had been added to the questionnaire such as did anyone have a title? and what did they intend to do after the war?, rather showing up the serious Japanese lack of understanding of the European mind. After the usual haggling with the Commandant about this and having been assured by their Officers that it did not constitute anything because it was signed under duress, the men signed. Never has there been such a collection of Ronald Colemans and Gary Coopers and even Donald Ducks outside Hollywood.

Ube was a medium-sized town whose main existence was coal mining, though there were other factories in the surrounding area. There was not much more than a single main street with shops and large numbers of poor quality timber houses in the surrounding area as far as the eye could see.

The gaggle of men stopped outside the local mine and then were given a lecture by the owner through an interpreter. They were then introduced to the mine proper entering via a pressurised airlock system. The main roadway was lit by electric lights but at the end of this the only lighting was via helmet-mounted torches. The coal seams were at the end of the main roadway and reached by a mile walk and at that point well out under the sea.

The POWs were organised into two working shifts so that as one finished the other would take over. They had found that the journey from camp to the coal face took about two hours. The Officers would not be required to work but in order to maintain discipline one would accompany each shift. There was as always the language barrier to overcome and although the Officer was in charge of the work party, there was also a Japanese overseer known as the 'Gaffer'. Although the men had to work to certain quotas it was generally free from the face slapping and sadistic treatment.

As each shift clocked on they had to comply with the Japanese ritual of praying for good luck from the gods of the mines. These seemed to reside in small Shinto shrines in the main hall and had to be bowed to and a mumbled prayer said.

The main seams were reached by a lift which lowered the men some 500ft and then they started their walk out under the sea. It was during this walk that men could again summon up the strength to sing bawdy ballads or snatches of music hall songs and two Welshmen, Davies and Jones were especially good at this.

Once at the face the routine was to collect picks and shovels from a store and then pick at the underside of the exposed face to undermine it and then to give the top a good clout and with luck the face would crumble into a heap of coal ready to be loaded up. It was then shovelled into small skips and these were pushed on rails into the main gallery where they were hitched to an endless steel hawser which pulled them back to the lift cage for hauling to the surface.

Food was taken with them at the beginning of the shift in small wooden boxes, plain rice as always and hardly enough to sustain Gnr Johnny Lobb who was still recovering from a serious illness. He was notorious for always being hungrier than the rest and no left-overs were safe from him.

So started a routine that happened each day unless a *Yasume* had been ordered and continued round the clock. Month after month and, for most, with no real idea of what was happening in the outside world in the war. Annoyingly all the coal that was cut was going to help the Japanese war effort.

Amongst the others who had arrived earlier at the surrounding camps, many were set to work in industry. Here they were dispersed among factories and used once again as free slave labour. Some of the tasks involved working long and dangerous shifts down other coal mines still being fed less than enough food to survive in a fit condition.

Once Gnr Clapp had recovered some of his fitness he was released from Moji hospital and forced to start work at Branch 6 Omine-Machi mine. This was a drift coal mine which meant it was approached from the surface via a sloping roadway which led down to the working faces below. This was dug into the side of a hill not far from the actual camp site, which comprised a collection of poor quality timber huts with hard packed earthen surrounds.

Other camps such as Fukuoka 14 were actually inside an ironworks and the men had to work sorting scrap metals and breaking up heavy castings. As in all other cases the care of the POWs was not high on the Japanese list; they were not supplied with safety goggles or gloves and the inevitable injuries from sharp edges and dropped items could not be treated.

Men were also put to work in shipyards hoisting and unloading stores from the holds of merchant ships, transporting them to waiting lorries on the docks, and yet others at Mitzushima had to endure long hours working on Carbide furnaces. Here the fumes and lack of suitable safety measures made life very unpleasant and their long term health suffered again.

The camp at Ube happened to be close to an airfield and it was not unusual to hear the fighters being run up and then take off for patrols elsewhere. They were a constant reminder of the combat going on but as yet no Allied bombing had been heard.

This existence continued for months and although there was no radio contact from the outside world or even contact with other POW groups they did have access to two Japanese newspapers produced in English. The first of these was called *The Nippon Times* and the other *The Mainichi*. These were brought in so that the wartime propaganda could be absorbed by all, and in the hope the POWs would see that Japan was all-conquering and continuing to win everywhere they fought. Obviously the news items were slanted to show the Japanese in the best light and any hint of a setback was carefully avoided.

However *The Mainichi* was published by its editor Mr Tochi Go who delighted in trying to use English phrases to convey how educated he was but frequently got them hopelessly mixed up. He was also struggling to convey that things were still going well on all fronts but by his weird choice of language and avoiding the truth when it hurt, he had ensured the POWs had learnt that by reading between the lines a lot of useful information could be gleaned. Such comments as 'A famous British General once said, the battle of Waterloo was won on the football fields of rugby' and 'The victorious German army is rapidly advancing behind its strong rearguard' at least raised a smile or two. They might not know the full story but at least they were getting a rosier picture than that which the Japanese were trying to suggest.

The Japanese considered there were actually three separate wars being fought at the same time and did not try and connect them together as a world struggle. The Germans and Italians were fighting the British in the Middle East, the Russians were fighting in Europe and the Japanese were fighting the Americans in the Far East. They did not seem able to associate that all three were the West's struggle to beat off the combined aggression.

The Japanese continued to withhold the Red Cross parcels but did allow the men to start growing vegetables in cleared patches of ground. The soil was so poor that the only way to get fertilizer into it was to empty the cesspits into trenches. The smell and flies were pretty awful as a result but at least things did grow. Not content with this generosity the Japanese sat back and waited and then helped themselves to the best tomatoes and sweet corn when it was ready.

Morale went up when news of increased air raids on Germany was rumoured. The year dragged on and a hot summer came round and then another winter set in. They noticed that the younger guard soldiers had disappeared and that older men had come in, more the Japanese Home Guard types, a suggestion that fitter men were needed to replace losses elsewhere.

The first mail from the UK came in. It was months old but most welcome. This was a most unusual event and not available to all camps. Those on the Railway never had any correspondence from home for the whole of their stay there. It had always been a serious bone of contention that the Japanese had refused to notify the Red Cross how many POWs they had and who they were. Many of those back in the UK had assumed the worst because of the lack of information about husbands and sons and even boyfriends.

While 12 and 15 Btys worked their monotonous routines they were totally unaware of the desperate events happening to 3 Bty in September 1944 or even that the Allies had invaded the Continent in mid 1944.

There were at last signs of hope. The camp at Ube had a distinct advantage when a doctor arrived who had taught himself how to read Japanese so local Nippon papers were now worth their weight in gold. He translated for the whole camp and they found that the Germans had long been booted out of north Africa, Italy was no longer involved and the Russians were making bold progress on their front. The routine at Ube now took another turn for the better.

Col. Hazel and Lt Attiwill (who had been something of a writer before enlisting) now wrote a pantomime-type show to be put on for the whole camp: *Cinderella*. Everyone was most enthusiastic and those that dressed as girls were well received. Surprising unexpected talents were revealed and Dvr Nairne (he who had been badly burnt during the retreat at Dunkirk) showed he had an aptitude for scenery painting on a large scale and it was he who did many of the stage backdrops. Scrounging from all sorts of places produced rope to be plaited into wigs, material for clothes and props. The whole affair was a great success and plans were made to repeat it with another more ambitious production. Cpl Pilcher who took the lead part of Cinderella was so successful dressed as a glamorous girl, that it was a miracle he survived with his honour intact! The effect on morale was amazing and men now walked with a lighter step. This was the first of several shows written by them with the accompanying music provided by 'Freddie' Powel who also wrote much of the dialogue. They managed to put in many pointed remarks such as 'there's a nasty nip in the air tonight' which always produced much laughter to the puzzlement of their captors. However much later once they had 'cottoned on' to the meaning every time it was used, so the stage was stormed and there was much sword bashing of the cast.

There was one setback around this time when the Japanese assembled the senior Officers and they marched them off to another camp: the final destination or the reason for the move was not disclosed.

When things took a turn for the worse on the war front the Japanese suddenly withheld all newspapers, desperately trying to avoid any bad news getting out. What they didn't realise was that Dvr Marshall, who volunteered to work in the Japanese mess, managed to get out a copy of the local paper each day while the Commandant was having his siesta in the afternoon. The doctor who had taught himself to read Japanese managed to gather much needed news of the war's progress. More to the point Dvr Marshall also managed to return the paper before the Commandant woke up to discover the 'theft'.

Chapter 9

Burma Railway and Return to Singapore; the *Rakuyo Maru* and *Kachidoki Maru* Tragedies

————

While those of 12 and 15 Bty were contending with their conditions in a much cooler climate in mainland Japan their compatriots in 3 Bty had been struggling still in the Saigon docks for over a year.

All this was to change in the middle of 1943 when the Japanese needed still more men to try and complete the Burma railway on schedule. Thus it was that in June 1943 they selected 700 men from the 'Saigon Battalion', those whom they considered the fittest, and transported them to Phnom Penh by barge, a journey that took two days in tight, overcrowded conditions and with insufficient food and water. From here they went by rail through Indochina (modern Vietnam) to the Burma–Siam railway where the tropical temperatures and constant rain made life a complete misery. For them the Japanese brutality would take on new dimensions and their death rates would soar.

By this time the railway was over three-quarters complete but due to the attrition rates and sickness among the labourers and POWs the Japanese needed hundreds more replacements. They were taken by rail after a few days stopover along the line to the camp of Tarsao where they disembarked and had to make their own temporary camp site. Here they met the existing men who had been on the railway for many months and the shock and horror at their condition was profound. These men were in many cases skeletal, covered in sores and stumbling around in bare feet, and what made it even more horrendous was they knew many of those already there as mates from months before and in those days they had been fit young men. On many their uniforms had long since rotted away and they made do with a thing like a large adult nappy which went by the name of a 'Japhappy'.

This was the realisation of what working on the railway was really about. The unsanitary conditions of the workplace, coupled with the severe sickness of most men meant that only those of extra strong mindset were ever going to make it through.

When they arrived all the multinational gangs of forced labour were still being used to construct the railway. They had bravely struggled on through the last months of 1942 and well into the middle part of 1943 but the bulk were only intended to be used labouring to form the track-bed. Once it was completed to the correct levels in their area they were moved on to the next section to start again.

The new arrivals were thrown into the novel routine of railway construction having had no experience of this type of work before. They spent about two weeks there, going out each day in pouring rain to walk some 4 kilometres to the actual work site. Here they were involved with digging earth from one source, carting it by sacks to another and depositing it onto an embankment.

While they were involved with the earth-moving side of things, a large group of the existing men were also busy on several small bridges which were needed to cross ravines and link the various sections together. Other men were being used to prise boulders from slopes higher up as part of the infill and scant safety measures were in place to protect those working below from this potential hazard. There were the inevitable injuries and the man had then to be carried or taken back to camp for the medics to try and help him.

After this brief introduction to the railway the Japanese felt a greater need for these POWs' services elsewhere and they were moved further up the line. This was accomplished by barge on the nearby river and they chugged slowly upstream till they reached Kinsaiyok. This move involved a short stay in a camp they had to build for themselves before being moved on to the camp of Kinsaiyok Main. The usual huts were put up and many men were left to sleep in tents which were by now rotting and permanently damp inside. Because of the leaks all their meagre clothing and personal belongings got wet too. Nothing ever had the chance to dry out, even the blankets they had to wrap around themselves were in a soggy state and covered in mildew and smelt of decay.

Where it was obvious there was going to be a need for a structure then temporary sawmills were set up by the river. They were pretty basic affairs with a motor mounted on a base driving either a circular saw blade or a bandsaw via a thick belt. Cut down timber was carried to these mills or cut and thrown into the river higher up to drift down to the mill where it was captured and dragged ashore. All sizes of timber sections could be produced at these mills from sleepers to bridge trestles and cross bracings (Fig. 9.1), the more exact joints being formed by teams of Siamese carpenters. Along with the structures came the need for concrete bases and retaining works and these sawmills turned out planking for use as shutters. In some of the busier sections Siamese mahouts were brought in with their elephants to move large logs and load these up for processing.

Sgt Newcombe and Gnrs Rhodes, Davies and Price had all ended up in the same camp, as did Gnrs Waters and Dawson. By this time work and sickness were taking an increasing toll of the men and Gnr Rhodes was in very poor health. Things were only relative since everybody was suffering to some extent and it could only be judged against the health of the others.

The work progressed through all weathers including the monsoon where it rained for days and weeks on end. The work was always dangerous and the ground treacherous, but any lack of enthusiasm by the POWs was rewarded by beatings and brutal treatment. The worst of this treatment was

Fig. 9.1 One of the many bridges built on the railway near Hintock.   AWM 122309

meted out by brutal Korean guards carrying sharpened sticks who seemed to delight in inflicting their torture. They were despised by the Japanese so took out their frustration on the POWs.

While the POWs struggled to stay alive and be able to walk to the work site each day, the back-up teams were busy behind laying track and sleepers and catching them up. (Fig. 9.2) The teams that did the track laying were controlled by Japanese engineers from a Railway Construction Unit and helped in some cases by Dutch POWs; however many units provided men for these duties including the Australians who were distinctive in their bush hats.

The system used was for the rails to be loaded by hand onto two sets of boggy wheels bolted together about a rail length apart. Flat cars carried sleepers and all tools and the necessary fish-plates for securing the rails to each other, also boxes of spikes for holding the rails securely into the sleepers. When the train was made up it then set off down the track pushing these goods wagons in front. With the usual Japanese ingenuity the majority of these trains were not in fact 'locos' but road lorries which had had the tyres removed and were fitted with steel wheels which ran on the rails. They very often carried a bamboo frame and *Attap* leaves over the cab, partly for shade and partly for camouflage. Because of their weird look the troops did not take long to name

Fig. 9.2 POWs laying track on the Burma railway. AWM P00406034

Fig. 9-a Hybrid railway vehicle nicknamed 'Flying Kampongs' by the troops.
Courtesy of Rod Beattie, Director of the Thailand-Burma Railway Centre.

these hybrid vehicles 'Flying Kampongs' (Kampong being the local word to describe a native village made of bamboo and *Attap* huts). When they reached the end of the track the men unloaded and centralised the sleepers and then manhandled the heavy rails into place. Here the gauge was checked and then the rails held in position by driven spikes. In the meantime the train had returned to the nearest store area and was collecting further lengths of track. It was an efficient system that got better with practice and by the end they were laying up to 900 metres of track a day.

At last around the end of October 1943 the two ends of the tracks met in the area to the north of the camp at Nikhe (see Map 4, p. 168).

As a tribute to how hard the men had been pushed, by October 1943 some 415 kilometres of track had been laid and over 685 bridges of all sizes constructed. By best estimates the embankments had needed some 4 million cubic yards of material and cuttings had required the removal of 3 million cube of rock and spoil. The work had taken 18 months but at the cost of thousands of lives. It was estimated that more than 12,500 POWs had died and many thousands more of the local coolies.

Once the bulk of the work had been completed a large contingent were held back for maintenance. Maj. McWade was one of those kept back to control the men on this maintenance. One other vital duty he was involved with was to keep records as far as possible of all the men from 6 HAA. While they were in Saigon a Bdr Kandler of the 3 HAA Regt and a clerk by trade had suggested it might be a good idea to keep records of all the men in the camp, whatever Regt they came from. They knew to be caught keeping a diary was completely against Japanese orders and the punishment would be severe beatings, torture and most likely death.

Thus Bdr Kandler with the help of the officers and NCOs made out lists in notebooks stolen from Japanese sources and also on loose sheets. These lists gave the men's name, rank and number, age, unit, civilian employment and details of next of kin.

In order for the lists to have the greatest chance of surviving they were spread among suitable officers for safe keeping. Kandler's book was kept in many different locations often under the noses of the Japanese guards and its vital information survived the war. So too Maj. McWade's which for the most part covered men from 6 HAA. Being originally a pay clerk McWade was used to keeping exact records and liking everything neatly in its place the notes are still easily legible 70 years after they were made. Although heavily involved with the men's welfare Maj. McWade taught himself basic Japanese which did come in very useful on occasions.

[The story of Bdr Kandler's book and his life as a POW can now be read in a book published by his son after a series of interviews with his father and called *The Prisoner List*.]

By this time it was obvious to the Japanese that things were not going well in the war and they decided to ship out as many POWs as they could find who were fit enough to work in the mines back in Japan. They also had a desperate need for labour to work in war industries as vast numbers of their men were already away at the front. When choosing who was 'fit' the criteria meant those that could just about stand up.

Recorded deaths on the Burma Railway for the Regt are Kanchanaburi, 37, and for Chungkai, 17. Added to these were another 6 from subsidiary camps. This makes a total of 60 men and these were accumulated over the whole period of just four months while the camps were occupied by them. This gives some idea of the attrition rates from the conditions and the appalling treatment.

So around March 1944 the camps were being emptied and the men who could, marched out, with many of these being survivors from 3 Bty. The first the POWs knew about what was happening was when the guards came in one morning and said *'All fit men go work Nippon!'*

Sgt Newcombe and Gnrs Dawson and Price were kept back for maintenance duties connected with the railway. Sadly by this time Rhodes had already died some months before and Davies had died only a few weeks previously. Gnr Price was very ill but still hanging on. Another of those chosen to move out was Gnr Waters.

They were all suffering from various ailments including malaria and dysentery and most suffered sores and ulcers. The permanent malnutrition meant these ailments would take much longer to heal, and in many cases they never did.

The first stage was to get to the nearest railway station which involved a march and then to be forced into the same metal boxcars as before. They were still without adequate food and water as the trains started their journey to Saigon where it was intended the men would be transferred to ships for the journey to Japan.

They reached Saigon some days later and were marched down to the docks. Here there was the usual chaos and they hung around all day in the sun. After standing looking at a suitably large Japanese transport ship all day its Master refused to take them on board. This rather upset the Japanese plans and the men were transferred to a camp outside the dock area. Here they spent many weeks continuing each day to form working parties for the tasks the Japanese thought up. These were mostly loading ships with rubber and tin and unloading large sacks of rice, drums of petrol and also munitions. Because the hardships were considerably less and the quality and quantity of food somewhat improved, supplemented by the ever resourceful thieves, their strength and health began to improve. They knew their way around since many had already been there before.

Compared to the railway camps this was a whole lot better but they had left many of their mates behind still living in the deplorable conditions. Many were lying seriously ill at hospital camps such as Kanchanburi and even the ordinary work camps still had large numbers unable to work through disease and injury.

After several months it was realised that there was going to be no ship from here so the Japanese made alternative plans to transport all the men to Singapore, many hundreds of miles further south. With the usual strange attitude of the Japanese Command, men were now issued with new clothing to replace worn-out and ragged shorts and shirts. It was too much to hope they were embarrassed by the state the POWs were in and so needed to smarten them up for return to civilisation again. They were paraded one morning and all the POWs were subjected to a search for contraband, but with their hard won experience they managed to conceal a vast array of items. Once this laborious task was over, including the usual delays while they were counted, the large contingent climbed aboard the standard metal box-cars and the trains set off for Singapore.

By this time the fighting in Burma had been continuing for many months and reinforcements and stores were travelling north daily. Their train spent much time being shunted into sidings to allow these troop trains to get past. After nearly five days of this stop-start routine they reached the station in Singapore near to Keppel Harbour around 4 July 1944, not far from where they had originally been involved in action with their guns.

After climbing stiffly out of their metal boxcars they were lined up for yet another count and then marched into two transit camps, one in Havelock Road and the other in River Valley Road in the downtown area of the city of Singapore. These camps were again totally unsuitable, many of the buildings were falling down and there was waste everywhere including open drains, which attracted large numbers of vermin. The huts were filled with double tiered bunks and the food was still held at starvation levels.

The men were again formed into work parties each day and sent to the docks and other locations. At least working in the docks allowed them to see some of Singapore as they made their way there each day. The living conditions for the local population were just as indescribable as theirs and there were only glum faces. Life under the Japanese was one long nightmare.

Large parties of POWs were still regularly being transferred south by rail from the camps in the north and in amongst these was one contingent, composed mainly of Australians, who were transferred to an island off the south coast of Singapore. From this camp they travelled each day back to the mainland and joined other POW's to march down to the docks in Keppel Harbour. The scheme they were to join was run round the clock in shifts and was the construction of a gigantic dry dock facility large enough to take a battleship.

It had been running for over a year and the finished size was to be 1500 ft long by 200 ft wide and about 50 ft deep. Also amongst this labour force were hundreds of coolies press ganged into working on this monster of a hole. For the most part either press-ganged into it or believing that they would actually get paid.

Their daily existence continued for another period of weeks until one day they were told they had a ship. It was now early September 1944 and all their meagre goods were again packed up and they marched down to the docks. Several ships were tied up and loading supplies but they were ordered to stand around and wait till these operations had been completed. These ships were to be part of a convoy to Japan taking war supplies and injured men and with them would be a large group of POWs including men from 3 Bty. However, many of the Bty had been left behind because they were considered too sick to travel.

As was typical with the Japanese, when they transported prisoners they made no effort to mark their ships to show they were carrying POWs or injured men and in many cases their own wounded as well. A simple red cross on the side would have sufficed.

This large group of POWs sat down to await further instructions and were still desperately short of any water to drink. Some of the best scroungers made off to explore the warehouses and try and find any source they could. The lucky ones came back with water bottles filled from inside taps and even from pipes leaking at bad joints. Meanwhile the ships were not ready for them and stores were still being loaded so they continued to lie about and try and rest most of the day.

Two ships had already been allocated for the POWs who now numbered about 2300, and of these many were British and the rest predominantly Australians. The ships were quite large freighters called the *Rakuyo Maru* of about 9500 tons and the *Kachidoki Maru*, somewhat larger at about 10,500 tons. (Figs. 9.3 and 9.4) They were about twenty years old and used for carrying both passengers and cargo. The latter was loaded via derricks fore and aft of the central accommodation blocks into the cavernous holds. There were about a dozen lifeboats which was satisfactory for the usual number of passengers but nowhere near enough for the large amount of POWs carried as well. There were also a few cork and timber floats to supplement these. Much of the cargo was rubber which was in the form of sheets about the size of a small attaché case with a handle at one end also formed out of the rubber. Once the cargo had been loaded it was the turn of Japanese passengers including women to go aboard.

Meanwhile it had been decided how many men were to go on each vessel; the *Rakuyo Maru* would take some 1300 plus, split roughly at about fifty per cent British and fifty per cent Australians. The *Kachidoki Maru* would take about 900 plus, most of whom were British. As a final insult to those about to board, when they asked about life jackets they were told to pick up a rubber 'sheet' and told this would float if required. They proceeded to embark with each man carrying a 'sheet' which had to be deposited in the holds. Many questioned the ability of these 'sheets' to float because of their weight which was some 30 lb, but nevertheless they all

Fig. 9.3 The infamous hell ship *Rakuyo Maru*.

Fig. 9.4 At 10,500 tons the slightly larger hell ship *Kachidoki Maru*.

carried one up the gangplank, and then under brutal treatment from the guards were forced down into the holds.

Those first to board could see how awful the accommodation was. The original holds had been designed for half the number of men, about 450, mostly Japanese soldiers trooping on them. These holds had now been fitted with a mezzanine deck that afforded about four feet of headroom so that men could be packed in on two levels. Considering that many had dysentery and other ailments including vomiting, the conditions were going to be horrendous.

The only ventilation to the holds was when the large wooden planks were removed from the hatches at deck level. Temporary toilet facilities had been rigged on the outside of the upper decks by hanging timber 'long drop' boxes for the men to use (*Benjos*). There was a never ending queue to use these since so many were sick, and water was again in short supply and so too any suitable food. Complaints by the Officers in charge on the *Rakuyo Maru* to get better conditions were basically brushed aside. It had been stipulated that all men were to be confined below decks unless they wanted to use the toilet, but a concession had been wrung from the Japanese that sick or injured could spend time on deck and during the day a third at any one time would be allowed to lie on the top areas.

Things were no better on the *Kachidoki Maru*, and although there were fewer POWs, there were also a large number of injured Japanese soldiers in one hold accompanied by numbers of Japanese nurses to look after them. The more observant of the POWs noticed with some surprise the name on the ship's bell: The SS *President Harrison*. In fact she had been captured by the Japanese and renamed as *Kachidoki Maru*.

Eventually after the seething masses had found some sort of space below, the ships sailed. They did not go far, only out into the anchorage where they dropped anchors. Other ships continued to load war stores and after two days at anchor the convoy left harbour to form up.

On 6 September they sailed out into the China Sea and formed into two columns comprised of four cargo ships and two tankers, and their escort of four ships made up of frigates and corvettes. Once at sea it was possible to stay topsides and view the world as it went past, anything to get out of the stifling conditions in the holds. They passed another convoy in-bound to Singapore after they had left and this was accompanied by an unusual small carrier with no superstructure (the *Unyo*).

Water was, as always, in very short supply and various ingenious ideas were in action even to the extent of condensing a steam leak from one of the winches.

For the next few days thing went well, they sighted no other ships, just Japanese aircraft giving them air cover while within range of land bases. The usual scroungers had come across a load of life jackets in the hold, around 500, but nowhere near enough to give everyone one each.

However on 10 September they entered a heavy rain squall. The men came out from below to dance and jump up and down and let the water wash some of the grime from their filthy bodies. They did not waste any opportunity to gather rain from every source by putting out containers.

On 11 September the convoy had reached an area to the east of Indochina and was joined by a small convoy of ships coming from Manila. This added another three freighters and also three more escorts. The ships shook out into three columns and the escorts scurried around the outside. It was on this day that the air cover ceased and the Japanese started to talk of the Submarine blockade by the Americans. Convoys in the past had been severely mauled by this unseen menace and because of this risk some men started to work out what they would do should things get desperate. They carried a lot of sick and weakened men and these would not be able to abandon ship very easily or even at all.

By this time in the war the US code breakers were reading most Japanese signals so knew when and where convoys were sailing from. Because of this three submarines were on their way to the area to stalk the convoys. Later in the evening everyone was brought up short by the sudden explosion of one of the escorts. It had been torpedoed by the submarine USS *Growler*. This escort had discovered the submarine on the surface and had swung round to attack. Showing remarkable coolness the skipper of the *Growler* waited his chance and fired a fan of torpedoes, one of which despatched this escort in record time as it tried to run down the submarine. Within minutes of being hit it just blew up and rapidly sank. This created panic among the other vessels and the escorts immediately fanned out to try and locate the intruder.

Other torpedoes which had been launched went on to strike two further ships in the convoy. In the dark and not knowing exactly where the attack had come from ships altered course in a free-for-all and in an amazing stroke of luck one tanker struck the *Kachidoki Maru* a glancing blow near the bow whilst going on a reciprocal course but did no serious damage. The POWs were now wide awake and wondering what the night held for the rest of the ships.

After some chaotic scenes the escorts managed to get their charges back into some sort of order and the convoy turned north west towards the coast of Hainan and plodded on. The POWs were delighted with the outcome of seeing a Japanese ship going down, but some stopped to think that they might also be in line.

Despite losing three of their number the remaining ships were now steaming north westerly and unbeknown to them into the sights of another lurking US submarine USS *Sealion 2*. Her skipper, Capt. Reich, had time to line up several of the larger transports and chose a freighter which he fired at. A gyro malfunction caused the torpedo to miss and this disclosed his presence to the escorts who proceeded to put him down and depth charge the area.

During the night engineers worked on the problem and in the dark *Sealion 2* surfaced and put on full speed and managed to get round in front of the slow moving convoy again for another try. This time the Captain aimed at the starboard column and chose the second ship, a tanker, and the fourth ship, a large freighter (the *Rakuyo Maru*). He also aimed at another ship in one of the columns beyond.

The hits on the tanker and the other ship beyond it were watched by the POW's and gunners who were getting a grandstand view. However while they watched they saw to their horror two trails of bubbles coming straight for them from out of the dark. There were two loud explosions and the ship lurched violently. One had hit near the bow and the other amidships. Because of the 'way' on the vessel this caused the bow to bite deeply into the sea and large amounts of water came flooding over the remainder of the ship, completely soaking some of those on the upper deck.

There was no disguising what had happened and the first impulse of those below was to get out and up onto the top deck. It was a mad scramble with many men being trampled underfoot. The ship's gun crew who had been 'closed up' on the field gun on the bow had been obliterated. Meanwhile the Sealion 2 had dived to avoid the escorts and was trying to get deep.

As the Rakuyo Maru lost momentum the Japanese started to try and launch the boats. Armed guards prevented any chance of the POWs getting near, and any who did were beaten off by rifle butts and sticks.

Thus far few if any of the gunners had been killed in the blast, but once the Japanese had left the ship the prisoners had to make the best use of what they could find. Many just jumped over the side with or without any life jackets. A steady stream departed from the upper deck in this way. It was realised that the ship was not in immediate danger of sinking so men started to look for anything that would either make a raft or would float. Sadly some started throwing these rafts and crates and baulks of timber over the side without looking and many men in the water were killed by being hit on the head by these heavy objects.

Many of those from the Japanese passengers and troops in the forward hold were already dead but there were almost 1300 prisoners untouched. The life jackets that had been found earlier were now put to good use though this still left about 800 without any buoyancy aids. Men searched the ship and came across some Japanese who had still not left. With old scores to settle none of these survived.

In the water Japanese who were already in lifeboats or on rafts made strenuous efforts to thwart any attempt by prisoners to get on board with them. In other actions men who came across soldiers or guards made short work of forcibly drowning them. Under the circumstances nobody could blame them.

As the exodus continued very few men made any effort to take water or food with them. The rafts had none and the lifeboats very little. In groups the men slowly drifted away from the wreck, some floating in their jackets while others clutched rafts and the ropes hanging from them. As time went by it was obvious that the ship was not going to settle soon; possibly the large amount of rubber in the holds was keeping the water out so she stayed afloat.

After a couple of hours it was estimated that ninety per cent of the prisoners were in the water. Some were injured in the fall, some were harbouring old injuries and many were in shock. It was a mild early morning and the water was not unduly cold. In their dazed and shocked state they witnessed another escort being torpedoed and blowing up. The cheering at this was muted when one of the escorts came back into the area and started to drop depth charges. To the men in the water this was a death sentence and many died from internal injuries caused by the concussions. Those on the rafts fared better because they were actually out of the water.

By 0700 that morning the subs had slunk away unscathed and were reloading their tubes. Two ships had sunk and another was badly on fire giving off dense clouds of black smoke. The *Rakuyo Maru* still showed no sign of sinking and in daylight they had a chance to look at her carefully. She had settled somewhat in the intervening hours but was still steady. By this time there was a pool of burning fuel oil on the surface which had escaped from the hull and the main effort was to paddle the rafts away from this. Many of the men who were keeping afloat by hanging onto ropes from the rafts were obviously at most risk.

It was around this time that people started to consider re-boarding the ship to try and find water and food before it was too late. Those that had the energy paddled back and climbed the rope ladders and were amazed to find quite a contingent who had never left. Many of these were injured men or men who could not swim and had no buoyancy aids.

While they searched all the compartments that were still accessible above the water line they found some food and water which was taken. Others looted cabins looking for anything to take. Cigarettes were high on the list but any souvenir was considered.

Meanwhile at water level the various groups were making the best of things. The currents had separated them into two main sections. Amongst these there were Japanese sprinkled around, some having commandeered boats or rafts to the detriment of the prisoners already on them. There was a lot of floating debris of all types and many dead bodies too supported by their jackets. The old service rivalry between the 'Aussies' and the 'Pomms' was now shelved, and survival was the name of the game, survival at all costs. Men helped each other to lash bits of wood and rafts together so that they kept in groups and formed larger platforms for protection. Where Japanese were found they were either avoided or if possible dealt with. While the survivors were coming to terms with their predicament the convoy had steamed on and continued towards the north west, in the general direction of Hainan.

Late in the afternoon the *Rakuyo Maru* finally started on her last voyage. With hissing from internal fires and a sudden dip at the bow she settled into a forward dive until she was standing out of the water and then she gracefully slid beneath the waves. The whole thing had been watched in silence by those in the water and then the full enormity hit them. They were now totally alone and hundreds of miles from anywhere.

Not long after she had disappeared two frigates appeared along with a merchant ship and started to nose about through the tide of floating debris. The men's spirits soared because they thought they would at last be rescued and taken on board. However it was a rude awakening when they noticed that the ships kept stopping and collecting Japanese soldiers and crew and nurses, but deliberately leaving behind any of the prisoners. Prisoners who attempted to climb the rope ladders were clubbed off when they reached the top. This went on for some hours till all the Japanese they could find were aboard and then the ships turned and left.

The prisoners now collected the recently vacated lifeboats and rafts and started to pick up from out of the water all those they could find. Boats and rafts were tied together to try and keep everyone within reach and the motley array of rafts and bits of hatch covers and tables slowly continued to drift. It was now estimated there were about 900 men left and many of these were from the 6 Regt. It was a good mix of nationalities with a large contingent being Australians.

Later in the day it was obvious that the floating masses were in two distinct groups several miles apart drifting on the unseen current. The one comprising about 200 men and commanded by Brig. Varley was almost out of sight near the horizon and many of those were being carried in lifeboats. (It was Brig. Varley who had been with the first party to leave Singapore and taken to Burma to construct airfields. They were subsequently taken off this work and transferred to the railway but to start at the Thanbyuzyat end.)

While the survivors were trying to make the most of a terrible situation the convoy had made off in a north westerly direction over the horizon but unknown to them within the sights of yet another US submarine. This time it was another from the 'wolf pack' called USS *Pampanito* under Capt. Summers. The convoy by this time was about 50 miles off the Hainan coast and still steaming north westerly. Despite being within the range of the shore based aircraft none spotted the submarine. Once it was dark he surfaced and started his stalk of the convoy. By near midnight he was ready and had selected ships from the port column. The intention was to fire four torpedoes at a large freighter (*Kachidoki Maru*) and another two at a medium sized freighter beyond. Then by a swift turn he wanted to bring his rear tubes to bear on two further freighters in the starboard column, a total expenditure of ten torpedoes.

Just at the moment of firing one of the torpedoes started early and was running at high speed within the tube, a very dangerous situation. This was cured by the torpedo engineer and the remainder of the salvo left safely.

At this time those on the *Kachidoki Maru* were settled down for the night after all the excitement and the vast majority were inside the hold. Japanese ships generally had no radar except in the case of some of the escorts and so they relied totally on sentries with binoculars for their early warning. For some strange reason the exploding torpedoes were very muffled and many on board did not realise the ship had been hit. Those who were more aware made immediately for the one ladder up from the hold. By the time they reached the deck the Japanese were shouting and screaming in panic. This rather focused the minds of those around on the top deck.

She started to sink so rapidly that anyone who had not got topside within the first ten minutes was never going to get off. The escape attempts were a carbon copy of those on the *Rakuyo Maru*, everything and anything that might float was jettisoned. The Japanese took to the boats and left all prisoners to their fate. The same fights took place and the same settling of scores. Many of the Japanese wounded were unable to get out from their hold so were left to drown by their comrades. Within a short time the ship had sunk leaving a trail of oil and debris covering the sea.

It was estimated that about 600 of the prisoners had managed to get away and these were clinging doggedly to any bit of wreckage that would take their weight. Many of the rafts and planks were so heavily overloaded that the men were actually sitting waist deep in the water. Men had already started to die from injury and shock and they were quietly pushed over the side, where once their jackets were removed they just sank out of sight.

While they were coming to terms with being adrift those to the east of them, survivors from the *Rakuyo Maru*, were suffering even more having been without water for quite some time. Those that were incautious enough to drink sea water very soon succumbed. Many had become crazed and a danger to their comrades, some hallucinated that they were at home or with friends, and a few who could stand it no more just got up and said 'Farewell' and jumped into the water where they sank like stones. The temperatures were baking hot and no wind. Mouths dried up and tongues swelled. Lips split and faces burnt. There was no cover from the sun and all the time they slowly drifted with the unseen currents.

Later on the survivors in the *Kachidoki Maru* group saw two more frigates in the distance but these too stopped to collect only Japanese personnel. While the ship was close to one group they could distinctly see and hear a heated argument on the bridge and after a while the ship stopped and men beckoned to those on the rafts to get closer. At last they started to pick up the survivors but made no effort in helping to gather them up. It was left to the men themselves to go round the various groups and haul them out of the water into a lifeboat, then row to the ship and unload and then go back again for more. In this way some 300 men were rescued but suddenly an alarm sounded on the frigate. They were obviously worried about submarine attack so they just stopped and got under way leaving a large number of men still in the water.

Some while later another frigate arrived and proceeded to collect only Japanese survivors. These were troops, crew and some of the nurses who had been attending the wounded, plus of course surviving guards. Once she had all she could find they made off.

Luckily a small Japanese trawler came along and she was much more humane and hauled out an estimated 160 men. These were laid out like sardines on the limited deck space in various states of dehydration and sickness. She had done her best but could take no more without risk of capsizing. In order to aid those she was going to have to leave behind, she collected a string of lifeboats and towed them closer to those in the water so they could at least have some security. By this stage it was thought about 150 men were still alive and they watched forlornly as the trawler sailed west towards Hainan with the intention of unloading at the nearest port.

Meanwhile back towards the east the survivors of the *Rakuyo Maru* struggled to keep afloat in their widely separated groups. Brig. Varley was in command of his section of boats and rafts containing some 200 men and they had obviously decided to try and sail to China. They gradually disappeared into the far horizon. The rest in their groups tried to maintain morale because by this time many were just giving up and slipping away.

Early on the 14th and two days after they had been torpedoed , they saw the smoke from ships over the horizon and shortly after heard the distinct sound of small arms firing and machine guns from the direction of the Varley group.

Not long afterwards three Corvettes appeared in line astern and one of these peeled off and came towards them. Having heard the shooting and formed their own conclusions they realised it was now their turn. Rather apprehensively they awaited what was about to come. However the ship hove-to and signalled them to come closer and identify who they were. Once it was established they were British they allowed them to climb aboard, but as usual giving no assistance to the weakened prisoners, and placed armed guards all round the top of the gangway. After collecting all they could find, which was estimated at about 136 men, they turned to the west and steamed for Hainan. During the voyage they were given a small supply of water and food, the first they had had for several days. The ship probably did not have the resources to provide for so many over and above their normal complement, but the prisoners were grateful for that small kindness.

The next day as they continued to steam west they suddenly came to an area of floating wreckage and the hulk of a tanker still on fire but well down in the water. This had been one of those ships from the convoy torpedoed by the USS *Pampanito* the day before. The Corvette steamed round in a circle looking for anyone in the water but found none and then no doubt wary of further submarine attacks speeded up.

Eventually they reached a small port on 15 September and the prisoners were unloaded and transferred to a tanker in the harbour where they were accommodated on the open decks. To men who had seen the result of torpedo strikes against tankers this must have been a further harrowing experience.

For whatever reason the Japanese then decided to move the prisoners to another ship, which turned out to be a large whaling factory ship converted to carry oil in tanks below deck (the *Kabibi Maru*). The men were in dire straights, many with dysentery and malaria, some with open burns and lacerations. They were directed down into the hold and had to make the best of it. By this time they had joined the other survivors picked up from the *Kachidoki Maru* who had been dropped off by the Corvettes and the trawler at the same port shortly before. Out of the original 900 men it was estimated that only about 520 had been saved. Combined with the 136 from the *Rakuyo Maru* they were all now destined for Japan as forced labour.

Of the Brig. Varley party there was never any sign and their fate is unknown but those who were rescued from the other party present were always convinced that the firing had been an indication of what had befallen them.

The whale factory ship left on 16 September but due to bad weather and suspected submarine presence did not reach Japan till 28 September. The men were then split into separate parties and taken by train to two camps at Sakata and Fukuoka.

Meanwhile, since the time of the picking up of the survivors on 14th/15th two US submarines from the Wolf pack had continued to try and find the remnants of the convoy. They had agreed to comb the possible area and keep in touch.

Thus it was that having decided to turn east they steamed on into the area where the first attack on the convoy had taken place. It was not long before they came across large fields of floating debris and bodies in life jackets. Many of the bodies were Japanese and others so covered in oil that they could not be recognised. There were a lot of floating crates and rafts and all manner of drums and timber planks. Two empty lifeboats were passed which they presumed came from one of the sunken ships.

A little later the lookouts on the bridge sighted a raft with men on it. Because they thought these would be Japanese and one man might provide useful information on which ships they had sunk, they approached it with the intention of capturing a man. However when they got closer they were astounded to hear a man cursing them in English. It was not long before the whole situation was clear. These were survivors of the *Rakuyo Maru* sunk several days before.

A frantic operation was set in motion to get these men aboard and cleaned of oil. The submarine went from area to area collecting men from the water and rafts and getting them down inside the boat. There was the ever present risk of air attack if they were discovered on the surface.

After several hours it started to get dark and they could see no more and besides they could not carry any more. Their medical facilities were very restricted and having suddenly to take on a large number of very sick men pushed them to the limit.

After eventually contacting another submarine USS *Sealion 2* to come and help they left for Saipan some days away. By this time they had collected no less than 73 men; the other sub had collected 54. There were others who had to be left because they just could not cope with any more. With this valuable haul they both set off for Saipan but before they managed to get there two of the more seriously injured had died and these were buried at sea.

They had arranged a rendezvous with a destroyer on their way back to Saipan in order to unload these seriously sick men, but the weather transpired against them and such a swell was encountered that they had to abort and make for Saipan themselves.

Two other subs had also got the message about the survivors and were making their way from 150 miles away to help. These were the USS *Barb* and USS *Queenfish*. During the time in transit they made efforts to make extra bunk space and sort out places for men to sleep on the floor and get ready medical facilities. However on their passage they had a radar contact at extreme range of a convoy. With this terrible dilemma it was decided to go after the convoy first.

USS *Barb* closed and lined up two ships. The result was a tanker sunk but shortly afterwards a much larger ship was hit. This turned out to be the small 20,000 ton Japanese carrier *Unyo*. She was despatched in a well executed attack by three torpedoes.

Their work done the two subs then turned again to the south west to try to reach the site of the survivors still afloat. By now the weather had worsened and there was a strong wind and high waves. They plodded on till they reached the area on 17 September where they both set out search lines and trawled up and down.

By this time a sea was running and they wondered if they would find anything. At about ten o'clock in the morning one of the lookouts suddenly called out that he could see debris. They altered course and saw it stretched to the horizon. Then slowly they both followed the trail and kept coming across dead Japanese, British and Australian bodies kept afloat by life jackets.

They started to wonder if anyone could still be alive after five days but at midday a shout went up of two rafts with men on board. These were quickly recovered and got below. They were in a shocking state, covered in sores, dehydrated, badly burnt by the sun and had had no food or water for the whole time. Many were liberally coated in fuel oil which had got into their eyes and so temporarily blinding them.

Both subs went about their task collecting what few they could find alive. Most survivors were too weak to be able to get across to the subs and had to be lifted by willing hands. After hours of searching it was decided there were no more in the area and it was imperative to get those they had to a hospital, so they wheeled and turned for Saipan, which all the survivors reached some days later and where they went into intensive care.

Amazingly there were another 32 more rescued to go with those already there. After much treatment and when considered healthy enough to survive the journey, they were sent to their respective countries. Those for England went by ship to Hawaii and then on to the States where they were taken by train across to the east coast and then by ship to the UK. They arrived on 9 November 1944.

It had been the most traumatic of experiences, with many from the 6th HAA Regt. not making it. Sadly during these terrible circumstances the Regt lost 15 men in the actual sinkings and several more died shortly after in captivity from illness and the effects of the experience.

All the casualties were from 3 Bty and amounted to six on the *Rakuyo Maru* and nine from the *Kachidoki Maru*. Among those who died during these horrendous events was Gnr William Waters. It is not possible to say exactly how or when, but his name did not appear on the list of survivors. Having joined up from Tottenham from his job as a garment cutter, been through the hell of Singapore and then Saigon and after time on the railway, to die being transported to Japan beggars belief. He must have had a strong determination and will-power just to make it that far.

The only small consolation was that 3 Bty had twelve men survive the *Kachidoki* experience.

Back in the UK in early 1944, Foreign Secretary Anthony Eden had happily announced to the House that postcards had been received from the missing POWs in the Far East about whose fate nothing had been known. It appeared on the surface that they were all in good hands and being well looked after and even being paid. Since these were pre-typed postcards where the man could only cross out one of several choices and was not allowed to add anything of his own that might betray his condition it was judged prudent to accept what was stated but with reservations. In Germany POWs were treated well and kept in good camps and there was no reason to suspect any difference in this case.

However when one Lieutenant in a Japanese camp managed to peel a card in half and write a message inside and then glue it back together again it got through to its recipient. His curiosity was aroused by the wording and the fact his name was misspelt. The key to unlocking the code was fathomed out and the card peeled again to reveal the message, which gave the real state of the POWs and that men were being worked to death on the railway, something that up till then was completely unknown.

Now with the survivors of the two ships able to give their side of the story it was finally confirmed exactly what had been going on, and the terrible conditions on the railway. Their physical condition did not need any further proof of how the Japanese were treating their captured men.

Chapter Ten

The End for Ube and the Japanese Camps

In late 1944 those at Ube still had no idea that there were hundreds of fellow POWs all working as slave labour in outlying areas and other islands of the Japanese chain. The Japanese had put the POWs on any work that needed doing which freed up their own men for the front. The tasks the men found themselves working on were many and varied. Some spent their time loading trucks with supplies, others transferred coal from barges into trucks and vice versa while many were employed catching and dismantling floating log rafts and then transferring the timber to special rail wagons for onward shipment. There was obvious anxiety among the Japanese and work quotas had to be increased. They brought in Korean labour to help speed things up in the mines.

There was then a tragic accident involving Gnr Brandon No. 1426949 who was killed. What had happened was never satisfactorily resolved but it was thought that one of the Koreans had left a charge in a part drilled hole. When Brandon started drilling to increase its depth the charge exploded, killing him. It also left two other gunners who were aiding the drilling, blinded.

The Japanese just took a bottle of Saki and some sugar to the location in the mine and held an impromptu service. Everybody clapped hands and bowed and that was it. The Japanese claimed to have sent money as compensation to Brandon's family but this must have been a cruel ploy. How could they know where they where, or even transmit money to them?

One man's life extinguished for a simple mistake.

As winter turned to spring for their third time, it became apparent that the Japanese were seriously rattled. Newspapers had been withdrawn some time before, but this could not hide the contrails of high flying aircraft, and these were not Japanese. Fighters from the nearby airfield were routinely launched but to little effect. There were signs all around of shortages for the

Nipponese people, signs that could not be hidden from the men as they marched daily to work in the mine.

However uneasy the POWs might be they would not have been pleased to know that an order had been issued by the Japanese High Command some time before which went out to all camps and units.

> Extreme measures to be taken against POW's urgent situation. Whether they are destroyed individually or in groups or however it is done, with mass bombing, poisonous smoke, poisons, drowning, decapitation or what. Dispose of prisoners as the situation dictates. In any case it is the aim not to allow the escape of a single one, to annihilate them all and not to leave any traces.

How a supposedly civilised nation could honestly expect this to be carried out without a trace beggars belief. If they were worried about a mass uprising by the POWs when they realised the end of the war was near, then common sense and looking at the emaciated men would show this to be unlikely. It smacks far more of the need to destroy the evidence of how they had been treating the men as well as a large helping of spite.

Meanwhile the locals practised air-raid alarm drills, running about banging gongs and tin cans and loudly blowing whistles. Even at the mine they had their own 'warbler'. The raids by American aircraft were heard in the distance but the local Japanese seemed to have no effective defence against them. Quite suddenly in April the Officers and men were called out for a parade.

They were marched in columns along the road for a couple of kilometres to a nearby cemetery. Here after a short service the tin boxes of ashes were reverently buried in a small vault. Only a little stele-type stone remained to mark the spot. By this time there were no less than 17 tins, each containing the final remains of one man.

The surprise of the day was to meet up again with many others from neighbouring camps, men from the Regt who had not been seen or heard from for years. Although no contact was allowed during or after the service, it was heartening to see so many survivors. They too brought their tins of ashes and all were safely stored in the vault.

In the days that followed, the Japanese attitude darkened. It became known that Germany had surrendered unconditionally but they would carry on the fight regardless until the Great Asia Co-Prosperity Sphere was attained.

The rumours from the mine, brought back by the outside working parties, claimed that American fleets were all over the Pacific south of the islands. In a bid to overcome these forces Japanese pilots had volunteered to become human bombs by being strapped in their aircraft which had been loaded with explosives and bombs. The planes were designed for a one-way trip with no weapons and enough fuel to get there but not back again. These were desperate measures and signs that the end was in sight.

The camp at Yokahama was destroyed by Allied bombing in April and the occupants were moved on yet again. Sadly many allied POWs were killed in these attacks for there was nothing to warn the airmen there were prisoners there.

June came in hot and dry but still the men had to go to the mine each day to work. Shortages become more apparent each day. Tokyo was bombed heavily and so too Osaka and Kobe. Aircraft on their way to raids were seen high up in large numbers. Much time was spent in the camp air-raid shelters where Japanese guards with rifles and fixed bayonets stood outside. Where they could escape to was beyond most of them; a white skin in an oriental scene would last but a few minutes.

Then in July during a raid the sound of bombs falling was heard, very close by, bringing back memories of the times spent in London during the raids of the 1940s when it was a different foe. This time the bombers were friendly but they just hoped their aim was good.

Desultory anti aircraft fire could be heard but it was totally ineffective and without direction or coordination. The bulk of the bombs were incendiaries and those that landed in the town soon started serious fires. One or two landed in the camp and huts caught fire to be put out quickly by fellow POWs with Japanese running about like headless chickens.

This was all new to them and something they could never have envisioned and so had little preparatory training for. War on their own doorstep was unthinkable and unheard of. It was quite frightening, especially to the civilians who had been suffering from the shortages of food and materials for the last few months. From the roof of a hut it could be seen that much of Ube was burning and the main building of the mine had been blown apart and destroyed.

Daylight brought the full scene of devastation. The town was empty of people, the survivors have fled to the safety of the paddy fields, while their homes were just turned to heaps of ash.

Shortly after this the camp was paraded and marched out to the rail station, and then by electric train transferred to another camp called

Motoyama some twenty minutes along the coast. Here they swelled the numbers to something under 500 men in total, each man carrying his worldly goods by whatever means he could.

Many old faces met up again. Despite the hardships of three and a half years of neglect, spirits were high. The turn of events suggested that the war may be coming close to an end, the evidence was clear to see. What worried many of them was what the effect would be on their captors when they realised it was over.

The camp contained a mix of units and nationalities, many from those bombed out during the raids on Kobe and Osaka. They had previously been based in other camps and then sent to work in the shipyards of Kobe.

It was possible to see Moji from the camp by looking across the sea to the far distance and hear and witness further raids on Kyushu and its surrounding areas. Factories that had survived the earlier raids were now pulverised. Night after night the assault went on.

However not to be outdone the Japanese still demanded their pound of flesh. Men were sent to work in a different coal mine where the conditions were considerably more arduous. The seam of coal was quite small and much of the work of necessity had to be done while lying on their sides. Food was still in very short supply and made up from the basic rice diet.

Towards the end of July American fighters were seen overhead and since there were no airfields close enough on land for them to have come from they must have been carrier launched. They met no opposition.

The worrying thing for the POWs was that many camps were situated in or around industrial areas, harbours and docks and there was absolutely no painted identification anywhere so the Allied airmen had no way of knowing which areas to avoid.

Even at this late date the Japanese were still withholding Red Cross parcels and when they were reluctantly forced to hand them over they had already been pillaged and robbed of useful items.

5 August 1945 dawned as just another day with its anticipated hardships in the camp at Hiroshima. This was not much more than a few miles from the city centre.

During the morning a lone high flying B-29 (US bomber) was observed crossing over the city, a bomber considerably larger than many had seen before. Flying at 30,000 feet it was seen to drop a large black object attached to a drag chute. This fell for some considerable time and was clearly visible shining in the sunlight. When it reached a few thousand feet from the ground there was the most monumental flash which was followed by a blast wave which damaged many of the camp structures killing some of the POWs, most of whom were Dutch.

The noise followed shortly after on a scale never heard before.

In that one instant the city centre ceased to exist. Thousands of people going about their daily chores were just vaporised. A whole contingent of Japanese soldiers carrying out their daily PT sessions in a nearby barracks disappeared. Anything that could burn, did, and the city, or what remained of it, was one large fire storm.

A huge mushroom-shaped cloud rose into the sky. It sucked up dust and debris as it went, carrying this to thousands of feet into the upper atmosphere and then deluging the whole area in a black rain. Nobody knew or could tell what had happened but the panic among Japanese guards told its own story.

Unknown to the POWs Japan had been given the chance to surrender after this warning event but the military leaders, whose vocabulary never contained the word 'Surrender', just voted to continue the war.

Thus on 9 August 1945 the POWs in the camp at Nagasaki where there were extensive shipbuilding yards woke to another day of gruelling work schedules. Another lone B-29 flew high over the city, having been diverted there from its original target which was obscured by cloud, and dropped another bomb. The city of Moji, the intended target, had had an amazingly lucky escape and so too the many POWs who were in camps in the area. This bomb was slightly bigger than the previous one but not dropped with such accuracy.

However the result was just the same; this time the city of Nagasaki disappeared in another fire ball of destruction. Thousands of people were killed either in the blast or the fires and devastation that followed. Those in the camps must have considered themselves most fortunate since they were situated between both of the cities destined to receive the bombs. In fact the men from Ube saw the planes flying over to carry out a bombing raid but they disappeared in the direction of Kyushu over the horizon. It was not long afterwards that while they were watching they saw the enormous mushroom cloud rise up from somewhere over the horizon.

Much debate resulted among the men as to what had been hit that could cause such a large distinctive cloud and the general consensus was it must have been some sort of chemical works. Since they were over a hundred miles away it had to be something pretty substantial to create the effect and also the rumble of thunder from the blast. They would not know for a little while that Nagasaki had been selected.

What they also did not know was one of the Camps, Fukuoka 14, was only 1850 yards from Ground Zero (the point considered directly below the point of detonation). Several POWs died in the blast and many more from extensive burns to exposed flesh.

The Japanese military were still unwilling to surrender and fighting continued in many areas for several days. The army had ideas that the whole population would be mobilised to defend the homeland by whatever means they could. Ultimately they realised they were beaten by something they could never have envisaged and against which they had no defence.

The dropping of the two atom bombs rescued all the remaining POWs whom the Japanese had had ideas of murdering before they would give up the fight. Those who were in the closest camps knew first-hand that this was the end, but the many thousands spread about the Far East in other camps would not know for some days.

The Japanese soldier was not used to being beaten and this was a bitter pill.

It was several days before the Japanese nation admitted defeat on about 15 August and during this period the POWs could only wait and pray.

The first POWs to be released were rescued by American forces, who were horrified at what they saw.

A rapid programme was instigated to find as many of these camps as possible and lay on air drops of food and medicines and new clothing. Sadly, even during these mercy missions men were killed by containers or pallets landing on them.

The POWs had languished in their camps still emaciated and sick and in most cases not knowing how the progress of the war was going.

Many had had no inkling that after the total success of the Japanese war machine pushing aside all defences for months, at last in June 1942, not that long after their capture, a key event had occurred, a chink of hope.

Using information obtained from 'cracked' Japanese coded messages the battle of Midway had been fought by two major carrier based forces and the Japanese had come off worse. The two sides never caught sight of each other but by luck and good planning the Japanese were caught reloading their planes when the American bombers arrived.

Four of their latest carriers were eventually sunk and their invincibility was now in doubt. Although they continued to advance in Burma the Allies had got their measure.

Shortly after, in August 1942, the American fightback began at

Guadalcanal. This was to be the long awaited move to take back the islands that had been so easily won by the Japanese. Taking them back would prove considerably harder to do, compared to the ease with which they had been lost originally.

All the while the POWs worked at their tasks, unloading war supplies, building airstrips, constructing roads and the two railways in Burma and Sumatra. They were forced to labour in factories and coal mines as slowly the Allies clawed back lost territory. North Africa had been cleared of German forces, Italy had surrendered and the long struggle of the Battle of the Atlantic was well on the way to being won.

The Allies had invaded northern France in the middle of 1944 and were desperately fighting to clear France and Belgium and then ultimately get across the Rhine to finish the German armies off. The Russians were squeezing hard from the East and the German war machine was in the jaws of a vice and being beaten everywhere.

In the Far East the Japanese were being slowly squeezed back towards their homeland from where their Militarists had had the audacity to claim they were entitled to the Greater East Asia Co-Prosperity Ring to enable them to be self sufficient. By April 1945 these Militarists had become ever more disliked by the average Japanese civilian. Allied air attacks were increasing, food was in short supply and so too housing.

The home defences were incapable of stopping the bombing and so too were the fighters.

As the Dutch East Indies were invested the oil supply line had dried up. The same situation that had caused so much worry and one for which they had gone to war in the first place, was now repeated.

Large Allied fleets roamed the seas and landings were taking place one after the other and creeping closer. The Japanese were powerless to stop them and still they persisted in maltreating the POWs, even though in their hearts those 'in the know' must have realised they could not go on like this much longer. As late as April 1945 last desperate attempts to stave off the inevitable were implemented. Large numbers of Kamikaze pilots tried and failed to halt the Allied fleets.

After this last throw of the dice the Japanese tried to get a peace settlement via negotiations through Sweden. But after all the Japanese had done in the past there was only one settlement the Allies would accept. Unconditional surrender, the bitter pill they had so gleefully imposed on the Allies at Singapore.

All these things had taken their course while the POWs struggled on mostly in ignorance living from one day to the next. In rare instances such as at the Changi camp, Tanjong Priok and Sandakan, signalsmen had managed to put together basic radio receivers to listen to the world news and knew something of what was happening in the outside world and more importantly the state of the war. There was a system for disseminating this round the various other camps, but giving away news that they should not have known would put their Japanese captors on their guard. The Japanese made it their business not to divulge information unless it was to extol how well they were doing.

The POWs heard about the ending of the war in various ways. Some were paraded by the Japanese and told they were now free. This was an awkward situation with feelings running high and after years of terrible abuse and neglect you could not blame some of the POWs for wanting to get even.

Roles were now reversed and once the Japanese and Korean guards had been disarmed they had to be secured and fed and supervised, that is, the ones who were still around since many had fled in fear and disgrace. Those most guilty had to be guarded so they could be brought to justice. More than a few senior Officers took the old-fashioned way out of suicide by Harikiri or shooting themselves.

Japan had been stalling since 9 August not believing their new empire had fallen apart.

By 3 September the 7th Indian division had secured the Japanese surrender in Bangkok and begun to release the POWs.

On 12 September the formal surrender of Singapore was taken in a ceremony in the city hall and the number of POWs released was in the order of 32,000, considerably fewer than at the start. So many had been moved away on war work and of course many others had died through neglect and sickness.

POWs and Gunners still remaining in Java at Tanjong Priok camps were just in time to see serious unrest begin once the Japanese had been deposed. The Japanese had for quite some time been whipping up anti-Dutch feelings among the natives, even in some cases arming the locals, and now that the Dutch had been ousted in the main the Javanese and Sumatrans wanted independence. They were led by a self-appointed leader called Dr Soekarno who had seized his chance to take power and he convinced them he was the man to fall in behind.

Even as late as 6 October some POWs were still awaiting repatriation. By this time the civil unrest had got to the state of having curfews imposed to prevent murders and the settling up of old scores.

British troops had been rushed in to aid the Dutch authorities to regain control but it was obvious that with millions of locals clamouring for independence it was not going to be long before they got what they wanted.

As these scenes were unfolding the last of the POWs were starting their homeward journeys, often via Singapore before onward transit to the UK. Australian prisoners were also rescued and then taken to hospital camp facilities before being shipped back to Australia to await a rapturous welcome.

Chapter 11

End Game and Incidents

————

Once the Burma railway had been completed surplus manpower was withdrawn to go to Japan as further slave labour. However because of the terrain that the tracks crossed there was always a need for maintenance. Heavy monsoon rains continually scoured and eroded sections of embankments and caused land slips and rock falls. Voracious termites devoured anything wooden they could get their teeth into and helped by the deliberate sabotage of certain sections by the POWs as they worked, there was always a constant need for repairs. Large parties were also employed on cutting down and gathering wood to be stockpiled under temporary shelters to keep it dry for the use of the wood-fuelled engines.

Even when completed the railway only managed an average of six trains a day along its length, considerably less than intended, and towards the end of the war when Allied aircraft were looking for targets it could not be hidden. It was bombed on many occasions resulting in breaches that had to be repaired. The most seriously damaged and hardest to repair were the river crossings, especially the one over the River Kwai which had several spans knocked out. Sadly many POWs were killed during these attacks because the pilots had no idea POWs were being used.

Sgt Newcombe had been at death's door in a camp on the railway as part of this maintenance crew and like many others had succumbed to illness and was laid out on a bamboo bed. He was semi-conscious and not expected to live but one of his mates stuck by him and gave him water and what food he could scrounge and slowly he recovered. But he was no longer the man he had been. He had gone into captivity a strapping 16 stone and now came out weighing just 9 stone, looking like a scarecrow and with sores all over.

While he was in Bombay on his way back to the UK as part of the repatriation process, he wrote to the family he had been billeted with on Penn Common, Mr and Mrs Cole. He had not long been released from his POW camp.

This is the first chance I have had of writing to anyone, I am very shaky and my head is all to hell, so I ask you to excuse any mistakes. It is no good trying to tell you what the lads have been thro'. We have lost pretty heavy. Two lads that were interested in Penn and Wolverhampton have died. Named Price and Rhodes, yes and a lad named Davies. You remember the lady that had the phone just on the other side of the road? Well the lad that was [billeted] there has died. Lots had legs off and big sores. Then after we came back from the Railway they sent a party to Japan. We have not heard how they got on, but the Officers think we lost a lot of men.

Seems funny trying to write. I haven't even asked how you all are and let's hope you are as healthy as when I left you. Three letters I got from you and they were very old though. I hope Jim is fighting fit. If you could see me you would have a roast on straight away. I doubt if I [weigh] nine stone. I have just started to walk, around one month ago. I was laid in a bamboo hut not expected to live but my pal fed me while I was in a serious condition and I came round. I hope to be on the way home in the near future so it will be no use you replying unless by airmail, you may do it that way.

The Army seems so different to us. We being in the jungle most of our time. Anyway they are treating us very well and it's a treat to be with your own people. I tasted my first bread yesterday and was it good? I shall have to dry up as my hand has started shaking ...

Sadly Rhodes had died over a year before and Davies shortly after, both in camps on the railway. (Fig. 11.1) Davies, who was born on 11/3/1911, had previous military service and came from the Mumbles area of south Wales. He had arrived with the Regiment at Penn Common in 1940 and met and married a local girl from there called Ethel. Sadly he was never to return to see the daughter his wife had had after he left England. His widow never remarried, the hurt of losing her new husband being too distressing. She remained in the Penn area, where she had married, till she died.

One of the saddest cases had to be that of Jeffrey Price. He was born in Penn, married a Penn girl and lived in Penn, as well as being stationed there for part of the war in 1941.

He died on 29 May 1945 after being taken to Kanchanaburi for treatment, never knowing that if he could have hung on just ten weeks more he might have made it back. (Fig. 11.2)

Gnr Harry Dawson of 3 Bty was rescued from his camp by American forces, also it a pitiful state. He had been captured in Singapore when the island fell and then spent the next few months in Changi. He then found himself transported to Saigon where he was among those forced to work in the docks

Fig 11.1 The grave of Gnr T. Davies.
Gnrs Davies and Price were both married and lived in the same road in Penn, a few doors apart.

Fig 11.2 The beautifully kept grave of Gnr J. Price (3 Bty 6 HAA Regt) from Penn.
Sadly he died just a few weeks before the war ended.

Courtesy of Rod Beattie, Research Director Thailand–Burma Railway Centre

loading and unloading war supplies from Japanese ships. When there was a need for extra manpower to work on the Burma Railway he was among those selected by the Japanese from the Saigon Battalion and was transported via Cambodia to Thailand. His main camp for the duration there was Kinsaiyok No. 2. This was one of the many camps set up in the jungle and some 168 kilometres from Ban Pong at the southern end, so a little under halfway along the infamous railway. This was one of the camps close to a stone quarry which produced much of the ballast stone for the track bed.

The task of the men here was to drill holes in the rock for the Japanese railway engineers who then charged the holes with explosives and produced the stone. This then had to be loaded into trucks for transporting to the men who rendered it down to ballast-size pieces by hand.

There was a series of camps in the area all called Kinsaiyok and one not far up the line was operated by hundreds of coolies. These unfortunates were mostly Tamils, Chinese, Burmese and Javanese Romushas. Many had been enticed to work on the project after promises of money and rice as payment but of course these things never happened. Instead they died in their hundreds from neglect, disease and overwork. The attrition rate became so bad that work parties of POWs had been detailed off each day to go to this camp and dispose of the dozens of corpses. The situation had become so bad that it even shocked the Japanese and in mid 1943 they arranged for as many medical staff as they could find among the POWs to go to these camps and try and slow the rates of death.

Like many of the others, when the Railway was completed in late 1943 Harry was again moved on but this time to Japan. Here he struggled for the rest of the war carrying out forced labour until he was released by American forces. Like the rest of the Regt he was badly underweight, having suffered from beatings, maltreatment and malnutrition. He had been put on war work by the Japanese and spent the whole time on projects for them.

Once their camps had been spotted, aircraft came over shortly afterwards and dropped leaflets telling the survivors to hang on where they were and not to disperse.

One of the first tasks taken on by the air force was to drop supplies by parachute into the camps when they were found – everything from food and medicines to new clothing to replace the loincloths many had been reduced to wearing.

Sadly for the survivors who had endured conditions quite unheard of before, this was not always the end of the story.

Fig. 11.3 Gnr George Daniels No. 822182 who came back from Kuching.
Courtesy of John Daniels

They were damaged in mind and body and were going to need many months of specialist care after they arrived back in the UK. Unfortunately this specialist care was not really understood at the time and for many it did not exist.

For some, such as Gnr G. W. Daniels (Fig. 11.3), the return was tinged by the awful realisation that when he had been reported missing, perhaps killed, his wife had started a liaison with some one else and had a little boy. He had been away for over three and a half years and no one knew he was still alive. It is hard to judge someone who was put in that situation and it must have been just as devastating for both of them.

Others spent years reliving the nightmare of camp and work conditions as well as fighting imaginary Japanese soldiers.

When men are subjected to such barbaric treatment, who is to know how anyone will react? Most were unable to talk about it to relatives for months or even years and in some cases never. They bottled it all up and tried to carry on as usual. This reluctance to talk has meant many of the stories and incidents have never been revealed.

Two stories that have come down are from G.W. Daniels' family and reveal something of how the POWs lived from day to day in starving and unsanitary conditions. Death was all around them in the camps but of necessity when a comrade died the body had to be carried outside for burial and given as much of a decent burial as the circumstances would allow. One thing the pall-bearers used to argue about was who was to go at each corner of the stretcher. The reason was that nobody wanted to be on the down-wind end.

The second story relates to after the war and showed a little of his black humour. He had returned to Birmingham, his home city, and one day while walking along a street near the city centre with friends they saw a large stray dog walk across the road in front of them. 'That wouldn't have lasted ten seconds in our camp, it would have gone in the pot,' he said.

For Gnr George Daniels the war ended with the two atom bombs being dropped. They waited around in their camp with the British Officers having taken control again from their disarmed captors and those they could find were now under close arrest. Once the camp had been relieved the men were sent to Australia for treatment to injuries and to try and start to put weight back on skeletal frames.

Behind the scenes other men were trying to catalogue all the names of those they had rescued to let their families know they had survived.

Since they had no documentation, which had all been lost or confiscated, they were issued with new temporary pay books with yellow covers by the Australian Military Forces. Under the name was written in pen 'recovered PW from UK Army'. They were treated with the utmost kindness by the 'Aussies', something that had been seriously lacking from their captors for three and a half years.

Shortly after they were given their first pay and the long road to recovery began. Once they were considered fit enough to travel they were shipped back to the UK. After Gnr Daniels got back it took much time to re-adjust to civilian life. He started off working for the Council as a bus driver but this did not suit him and he was advised to try another job that kept him out of doors so he became a milkman for the rest of his working life.

One thing that does come out from the events that are known is the comradeship and help for each other that got most of them through. When you knew it was your mate who was in trouble then your military training took over; it was a battle of wits and if you could get one over on the Japanese then that made your day.

One has to wonder at how the soldiers restrained themselves from taking revenge on their former captors once the war was declared over. In most cases they were too weak to do this but in the camp at Kuching, George Daniels recalled the prisoners immediately went hunting for the camp commandant Lt Col Tatsuji Suga. The camp had been liberated on 11 September 1945 and shortly after this he and some of his senior officers were arrested and transferred to Labuan. By the 16th Suga had denied his captors their satisfaction by committing suicide in a very messy and long drawn out Hara-Kiri (traditional self disembowelment with a knife).

There was another side to the news of relatives who had been imprisoned. Many families never knew till the war had ended that their loved ones had survived. For them it was going to be a happy reunion and trying to come to terms with a changed person, but for those who found out the devastating news that they were now widows the sorrow was hard to bear. This was sadly the case of Gnr Stanley Weston's wife, who had been gamely struggling on hoping against hope even after hearing no news for quite some time and continuing to bring up their three small daughters. On reading the telegram telling her of her husband's death she decided to take her bicycle and ride out for some fresh air to try to come to terms with it.

In one of life's ironies she was knocked off her bicycle in a vehicle accident and spent nearly a year in and out of hospital recovering. Her three children were taken into care for the duration before being returned to her. She was so affected by the loss of her husband that she never really came to terms with it. She always had it in the back of her mind that he would suddenly come walking through the door. She never married again or even went out with anyone else. She had no grave to grieve over, just the thought that his name was carved into a stone in Singapore.

For Gnr Clapp who had survived so many disasters, including the *Singapore Maru*, when he had regained some of his fitness he went to work in the Japanese mines. When he was finally rescued by Americans his weight was down to a skeletal 7 stones. However he was lucky to return to his loving wife and his small children who had grown considerably during his absence.

Maj. McWade and many of those from 3 Bty were lucky to avoid the hellships episodes and were finally rescued from the Burma Railway camps. There then started a programme to heal them and get them back to the UK. Sadly when he arrived in England it was to discover his wife had died two years before from TB and his only daughter was also very sick.

It took him almost a year before he could stand up straight and walk properly again. He was fortunate to marry again and the intention was to make a family life for his daughter but sadly not long after the marriage she too died of TB.

On a happier note he and his wife went on to have two daughters and he remained in the Army till his sudden death in 1969, by which time he had made Lieutenant Colonel.

Col. Hazel, the Regiment's new CO after their surrender in Java, arrived back in the UK on board HMS *Glory*. He was still surprisingly fit and had weathered their time in captivity remarkably well. It was to be his sad duty for the next few months to write reports and letters to the families of those who did not return and to make recommendations for decorations.

Like many he found the Japanese mindset baffling and almost amusing. One of his better anecdotes was from the period when it was obvious to their captors that the tide of war had turned and they were casting around to try and find who might put in a good word for them. The Japanese decided to run a competition called 'the best behaved prisoner' and surprisingly he won first prize, but not as surprised as he was to discover what he had won. The prize was one of their own Red Cross food parcels withheld by the Japanese.

In an effort to make the unpalatable and meagre supplies of rice seem more interesting he and a colleague Lt Ken Attiwill devised a recipe book with whatever items they could scrounge. This book survived their captivity and is now held in the Imperial War Museum archives.

Fig. 11-a Maj. J. R. McWade in happier times with his second wife in 1947. He took over 3 Bty in Singapore. Courtesy of his daughter Sue Ryding.

Fig. 11-b Dvr. William Stone of 3 Bty who survived the Burma Railway. Courtesy of his son Dennis Stone.

Chapter 12

Death after rescue; Sandakan Death Marches; Ballale Island Massacre

---

DEATH AFTER RESCUE

Sadly 'lady luck' had not finished with the gunners yet.

Two men from the RHQ are commemorated on the Singapore memorial plaques but this hides another harrowing story.

BQMS H. Cotterill No. 1018483 and Gnr R. C. Lewis No. 791037 had been captured in the Far East and eventually found themselves working in Saigon on any war work the Japanese considered vital.

Harry Cotterill was born in 1901 and joined the Artillery in 1920 after which he completed 18 years service and retired on a pension. His travels had taken him for a period to India where he had gained promotion. He married in 1932 and went on to have four children. Looking forward to a new life in retirement he least expected that within a few short years the country would be at war again.

Keen to do his duty he enlisted again in the Artillery and found himself in 6 HAA Regt, by now a mature and experienced gunner NCO. He was captured in the Far East in Singapore and became a POW of the Japanese and ended up in Saigon, having been shipped there with the early batches. During the hell that was captivity, and unknown to him, his wife back in England had died of pneumonia leaving four children to be cared for.

Like all the rest of the POWs, for him the war ended after the dropping of the second atom bomb and they were released from captivity, but remained in their camp awaiting repatriation. There were so many men scattered around the Far East in a multitude of camps and in various stages of illness that it took some weeks for the Allies to arrange to collect them and get them back to base hospitals in Burma where their immediate needs could be catered for.

As part of this repatriation process Flight 66 from 117 Sqdn RAF and led by their CO Wing Cmdr A.J. Sampson DFC took off from Rangoon

Mingladoon on 8 September 1945 headed for Saigon. The anticipation of the POWs must have been electric since after more than three and a half years in captivity under unspeakable conditions they were now about to start on the long trip back to the UK and to see their families again. In many cases those families did not even know whether their relatives were still alive or not until shortly after the war ended.

On reaching Saigon the aircraft loaded up with POWs and personnel and Dakota KN 593 took on some 41 persons which included the four crew and five other RAF personnel.

To quote from the RAF report from the time:

> This aircraft took off in the company of others and set out for Bangkok to refuel. They landed some while later and after refuelling took off again headed for Rangoon.
>
> However around 1.00 pm villagers in a village called Nuaungganale some thirteen miles north west of Moulmein remembered hearing aircraft out over the sea.
>
> Not long after there was the sound of an explosion and the next day wreckage and bodies were sighted on the shore line. There did not appear to have been any survivors and those bodies that were found were not identified.

The investigation did not discover why the highly experienced Wing Cmdr with over 2000 hours flying to his credit had flown his Dakota right into a 'well developed cum-nimbus' cloud. Apparently this turbulence caused the aircraft, which was heavily loaded, to break up and crash into the sea with no survivors. What makes this even more inexplicable is that on 6 September, just two days before this incident, another Dakota IV identification number KK 118 and from the exact same 117 Squadron was about 70 miles south of Binhli in Burma and seen to enter a similar cum-nimbus cloud and it broke up in the air with no survivors. On board that time were 21 men of the 1st Battalion Queens Royal Regt plus five crew all on their way to start garrison duty in Saigon.

It seems highly unlikely that the C/O of the squadron who just happened to be flying the second aircraft was not aware of the first incident and its tragic aftermath.

One can hardly credit that after three and a half years in the hands of the Japanese, and having survived that far, both gunners should lose their lives after becoming free men. In Harry's case he left behind four orphans. (Fig. 12.1)

Fig. 12.1 BQMS Harry Cotterill No.1018483 who died after rescue in tragic circumstances. Courtesy of Sarah Carney.

SANDAKAN DEATH MARCHES (BORNEO)

Returning to early 1942 , shortly after the capitulation of Singapore, the Japanese could hardly believe the number of POWs they had captured.

The problem was what to do with them all. So a large contingent intended to be around 2700 but subsequently dropped to 1500 were despatched to North Borneo (now Sabah). These were Australians and some months later, to bring up their numbers, around 700 British POWs were sent too. These were then followed by further Australians, such that the totals then reached 2700.

Among the British contingent were men from 6 HAA Regiment. The intention was for them to go to Sandakan to help build an airfield for the Japanese military which was to help protect the recently captured oilfields of Borneo.

The aim was to construct two runways and associated taxi ways and the necessary infrastructure to make the airfield operational.

With typical Japanese ruthlessness their captors expected them to carry out this work with not much more than their bare hands. The conditions as always were horrendous – poor accommodation, lack of clean water and food, long hours of back breaking work under sadistic guards, and typical rain and monsoon conditions, all within the primary jungle landscape.

Many of the men were suffering various forms of sickness or had untreated wounds. The Japanese never provided any sort of medical facilities and kept rations at starvation levels. Sandakan was a small town with its own harbour and a population of Malays and a few Europeans with Malay and Indian Police to keep order.

The Australians had arrived at their site after a march from the harbour and noted that the camp was surrounded by barbed wire fences. There were already huts which suggested a previous military use.

The camp that was set up by the predominantly British POWs was located close to the future airfield. Initially conditions were tolerable though mighty unpleasant, but in mid 1943 the guards somehow found out that the prisoners had managed to make a radio and were listening to world news. The basic set had been put together by some of the signallers from parts scrounged from every conceivable sort of location.

As a result of this some 250 men, including many of the Officers, were removed to go to another camp and the regime for those left behind went down another notch. Things remained in this deplorable state for at least a further year as the airfield took shape.

Towards the end of 1944, and with the Allied advances in the war, the airfield was subjected to bombing. Now that it was obvious to the Japanese that the war was going against them, they brought further troops into Borneo to help defend the oilfields and areas that might be used by the Allies for an invasion and these needed large quantities of stores to maintain them.

With this in mind it was decided to move the prisoners and march them to Jessleton well to the west. The airfield had been rendered unusable by bombing so the men were surplus. Japanese thoughts were that the prisoners were just another source that had to be fed; they were no longer able, or in a fit state, to carry out any sort of resistance so marching them away might resolve the problems. Some 470 of the fittest, and this was something of a euphemism, were selected for the first march out.

They set off towards Jessleton in small groups of about fifty with each group guarded by a few Japanese soldiers, and used tracks and trails through primary jungle but the terrain was so severe that even the Japanese guards found it difficult. Many POWs were suffering beriberi, malaria and dysentery and some even had no footwear to protect them against the terrain.

After many days and about 100 miles a halt was called at the town of Ranau. By this time there were only about 190 prisoners alive. The guards had had their instructions that anyone who could not keep up and all those who collapsed sick were to be disposed of. This they carried out with relish by either shooting or bayoneting them or in some cases clubbing them to death with rifle butts.

Those that had survived were immediately put to work on building a new camp for themselves and their guards. This included humping heavy stores and collecting water from a nearby creek.

By May another batch had been selected by the commandant back at Sandakan and some 536 men set off. These were predominantly British POWs. These suffered the same attrition rates from sickness, beatings and disease and only 183 survived to reach Ranau.

Once these emaciated skeletons got there they found only a handful of men alive from the previous draft. They were all put on tasks that involved carrying heavy stores across country for the Japanese supply lines. The death rates soared even faster.

Because the Australian 26th Brigade group had landed on Tarakan Island and overcome the Japanese resistance by 28th May, the Japanese commandant now realised that help might arrive to aid the remaining POWs if nothing was done to move them out. In June yet another selection was made at Sandakan from those still able to stand and 73 men set off for Ranau. Hardly surprisingly, none of these got beyond about 50 miles, having all either been murdered or died from exhaustion.

Those that had been left behind were now so weak that it was intended by the Japanese to let them die from starvation. Before the end of the war when Japan surrendered in August 1945, most had died and the rest were murdered and the camp set on fire to hide the evidence.

Of those that had reached Ranau none survived except 6 Australians who had managed to escape earlier on, and with the aid of local natives to stay alive and out of Japanese hands. They could see how things were going and the probable outcome, and then decided that anything was better than that so they made their bid for freedom. It is by their courageous decision that we now know most of the details of these events.

This has got to be one of the worst atrocities committed by the Japanese amongst many during the Second World War. Of some 2700 prisoners initially detailed to go to Sandakan, only 6 survived. They had been systematically starved, beaten, shot, abused and over worked.

It is possible to say that amongst the POWs were men from the 12th, 15th Btys and the RHQ of 6 Regt. They all died under these terrible conditions

Fig. 12.2 Gnr S. Weston No. 797493. Murdered on Sandakan.
Courtesy of Mr and Mrs Harrison.

Fig. 12.3 The author in the Commonwealth War Cemetery at Kranji in Singapore, where many of those from the Regiment are buried or commemorated.

and certainly at least 5 were involved on the marches, the remainder dying in the camps either before they set off or on arrival at the new area.

It is not possible to say with complete certainty when Gnr Stanley Weston (POW 2994) actually died. However from her excellently researched book, *Sandakan: A Conspiracy of Silence*, Lynette R. Silver has compiled extraordinarily accurate lists. From the date of death given by the CWGC as 07/05/45 this would mean he died while still at Camp No 1 and not on one of the marches. His cause of death is given as malaria which was a catch-all put down by the Japanese to conceal all manner of abuse as to why a man had died.

He would have been buried in No 2 Cemetery where after the war some 427 bodies were recovered for reburial in the Labuan War Cemetery. Of these only 82 could be identified and sadly Stanley is not one of them. Suffice to say that anyone who could survive that length of time under those conditions must have had extraordinary resilience and courage. (Fig 12.2)

However Stanley is not forgotten and for him and the many others who have no known grave their names are etched into the stone panels in Kranji Commonwealth War Cemetery in Singapore.

Two other names are revealed from Lynette's lists of researches. Although she did not know their Regiment I can confirm that these two are some of the very last to be murdered on the Sandakan marches. To have survived so long and yet be killed days before the end of the war beggars belief. Both men came from 6 HAA Regiment, 12 Bty.

Lt P.H. Young   No 109991 was murdered on 26/07/45 while in one of the temporary camps set up after the general move out of POWs and was the last British officer to die. Shortly after this Sgt J.H. Rooker No 818029 was murdered on 04/08/45 and the last NCO from the British POWs.

After the war, as teams of men searched for evidence of the bodies and their whereabouts, a pack was found in No 2 Sandakan Camp which had belonged to Lt Young with a few personal effects, one of the very small number of items recovered that could be positively identified. For all these atrocities no one was ever tried and convicted.

However when the vague locations given by the CWGC are looked at, namely Borneo, Kuching, Labuan and Ranau, it can be pretty certain that the total number to die on the Island of Borneo was nearer 61 which also included a few from 3 Bty who had somehow found their way to those locations. (Fig. 12.3)

BALLALE ISLAND MASSACRE (SOLOMON ISLANDS)

During the months after the surrender of all Allied forces in the Far East, the Japanese realised that they needed to consolidate their gains. They still had intentions of attacking Australia and needed extra airfields to carry this out.

In October 1942 they needed to make up a detachment of men to go to the Solomon Islands to carry out the construction of an airfield. There was already a detachment there from their Japanese Navy 18th Construction Battalion who along with some civilian labourers had made a start.

They trawled through the lists of men under their charge and went to Changi in Singapore to make up the numbers. Having decided on the quantity it was left to the Officers to come up with the right quota and thus around 600 men were selected. Because Singapore housed many of the gunners captured at the fall of the Island, they inevitably formed a fair portion of those selected. They were not told of the final destination but assumed it to be Japan.

They were led by Lt Col J Bassett the former CO of 35th LAA Regt, but additional men were included from various Coast Defence regts and HAA regts too. This made a hotchpotch of men from some 9 different Regts as well as RAMC and RASC. Somehow amongst this motley crew a few men from 6 HAA Regt also got roped in, it would appear at least 20 in number.

Once they had been assembled with their meagre assortment of personal goods they were transported to the docks in Keppel harbour. Here they boarded a ship thought possibly to have been the *Masta Maru*.

Although, as camps went, Changi was one of the better ones, there were still a large number of men there suffering from illness and diarrhoea. The POWs all ended up below decks in the usual cramped conditions, the fit alongside those who were seriously ill.

The voyage started and it did not take long for the men to realise they were not headed for Japan but in an easterly direction. The ship stopped first at Surabaya in Java on 22 October and then proceeded to Timor and Bali. It eventually reached Rabaul on 5 November. Rabaul was a small port on the northern tip of the Island of New Britain.

By this time they had already lost one of their number from dysentery, BSM Lambourne from the 11th Coast Regiment.

Here the POWs were unloaded and forced to march carrying those who were sick on litters. They were headed for Kokopo Camp. There had been a volcanic eruption in 1937 on the island and the men were trudging through a layer of ash with many in just their bare feet.

Once in the camp the usual systematic beatings and sadistic treatment started again. They had an English-speaking camp interpreter who it seemed tried to ease their plight.

However towards the end of November they were paraded again for another selection. This time about 517 men were chosen to move on and those considered too weak or sick to be of any use in labouring were left behind in the makeshift hospital. Of those 80 or so left behind, by February 1943 at least 25 had died from the hardships and by November 1943 a further 36 had died too.

Within the 517 chosen to move on, there were some 15 men from 6 HAA Regt and within the 80 left behind there had been about 5. Because these men had all been selected from Singapore only those men from 3 Bty appear.

It was now that they found out their final destination: the island of Ballale. Ballale Island is a small speck of thinly inhabited land at the southern tip of Bougainville in the Solomon Islands, and the journey there had of necessity to be made by boat (not the *Masta Maru*) and this took two days. Once on the island a camp was set up and work started on the strip. Conditions were as usual diabolical: lack of food and water and no medical facilities and the men guarded by sadistic Japanese and Koreans.

The strip had to be constructed across the island and involved first clearing the scrub and vegetation to expose the ground beneath. For the most part this was comprised of sharp coral. To do this the men were given the barest of tools and much had to be done by hand.

As the war progressed it became a target for American bombers and because the Japanese refused to allow the POWs to dig slit trenches or shelters many were killed in these raids.

Once the strip was complete these men became surplus to requirement and by this time the Japanese were worried about the possibility of an Allied landing. Possibly to prevent the Allies discovering the state these prisoners were in they had all the survivors murdered sometime between March and June 1943.

To cover up the atrocity, when asked about the men's location the Japanese said they had all drowned while in transit in a ship that had been sunk. This information was duly sent to the families of the dead back in the UK and for a long time this is what they believed.

As a matter of fact the murder was not a perfect crime because survivors remained from the party left at Rabaul who knew what had happened.

Those who had been dropped off at Rabaul were the lucky ones although many of these never lived to see the end of the war either. Of the 80 or so who had been too ill to continue, by this time no fewer than 61 had died from various causes.

Of the 19 left alive there was one man from 3 Bty who was the only survivor from the 6 Regt, Gunner Ben Gabbert. His survival was a miracle in itself – too ill to make it to Ballale and he then overcame the dreadful conditions they were forced to work in. Having been left behind in the original draft, when they had recovered enough they were forced to work on Japanese war work.

By February 1944 the few of these still left alive ended up being transported to Watom Island to build defensive works and dig tunnels for the Japanese Army. Their agony only ended when the Americans landed and they were lucky enough to be rescued.

Details did not come to light of the fate of the POWs till after the war when interrogation of Japanese prisoners disclosed the massacre. This was also corroborated by a few of the natives who lived on the island.

Later two mass graves were excavated and the bodies removed for proper interment. A total of 438 bodies were recovered but since the Japanese had at the time of burial removed all traces of ID tags they could only be interred in separate graves, each marked by a blank headstone: 'Known only unto God'.

With the deaths from other causes and the massacre, some 500 plus prisoners who had gone to Ballale Island had died; not a single man survived.

The difference in the numbers of bodies found in the mass graves compared to the numbers of POWs known to have gone to the island can be explained by the fact that in many cases when a prisoner died from a serious disease, the Japanese had a habit of throwing the body into the sea to get rid of it. Sadly for these men there will never be a known grave site.

Records suggest that out of 3 Bty a total of 15 men died from all causes (and the massacre) and a further 4 died at Rabaul.

[As an aside, when it was decided for Admiral Yamamoto to go on a routine tour of some of the islands to review his troops on 18 April 1943 he was on his way to visit Ballale Island when his plane was shot down and he was killed. Unknown to the Japanese, their naval codes were being read by the Allies and his flight was disclosed. They arranged for fighter aircraft to intercept the Admiral and his escorts. It must have given the Americans great satisfaction since it was he who had orchestrated the attack on Pearl Harbor in 1941.]

Chapter 13

The Japanese Hell Ships

SUEZ MARU MASSACRE

Around April 1943 the Japanese were still desperately trying to build up their air bases to resist American bombing attacks and maintain control of the territory they had captured already. They had a trawl through POW camps in various locations on Java in order to accumulate sufficient men to be sent to Ambon to help construct a new airfield. They managed to scrape together some 4000 men mostly from the three camps at Tanjong Priok, another camp near Bandung and the rest from a camp at Surabaya, the port on the north east coast.

Amongst these men there was the usual long list of those too sick to work and many others ill with a multitude of tropical diseases including beriberi and malaria. Also amongst these men were a few from 6 Regt who just happened to be included because they were available. They had to work under the usual horrendous conditions to finish this airstrip, and by November the work was done.

There was now no need to keep the vast number of men there, especially since many were sick. Large numbers were not much more than skin and bones and so unable to carry out any sort of heavy manual work, so the decision was taken that they would be transported back to Java so they could be better looked after and have some chance of recovering.

However by this time four men from 6 Regt had already died from the terrible conditions during the course of the construction: Gnrs M. Fitzpatrick, S. Brookes, F.H. Creedy and H.P. Walshe, who may have been buried on the island. The survivors were now prepared for a move back to Java.

Men were collected from outlying camps, some arriving in a coal barge from a nearby island. Those on Ambon island in Liang Camp are marched down to the docks where both parties met up to board another ship called the *Suez Maru*. She was about 6400 tons and one of many used by the Japanese merchant fleet to carry POWs. She was not tied up alongside but anchored out in the harbour so the laborious process of transporting sick prisoners out to her began.

While this was slowly progressing a large detachment of sick and injured Japanese soldiers arrived who also needed embarking, and immediately these were given preference.

The area around Ambon was known to be well patrolled by Allied submarines and in some trepidation the Japanese commander of the POWs, Lt Koshio, asked his superior officer Lt Col Anami what would happen if they were torpedoed. It was very obvious that the two small minesweepers which were going to be the escorts were not of sufficient size to take on board all the men now embarked.

He was told curtly by Lt Col. Anami that it was his duty to ensure that no POW survived to be rescued, they were all to be killed to prevent this happening.

By 26 November 1943 the *Suez Maru* was loaded and set sail out to sea. She was escorted by two minesweepers called *W11* and *W12*.

On board were some 559 POWs composed of Army, some RAF personnel and a contingent of over a hundred Dutch. The men were crammed into two holds (3 and 4) under the most awful conditions. The Japanese sick were in holds 1 and 2, in somewhat slightly better conditions.

They were due to reach Surabaya in several days' time, but the Japanese obviously expected some men not to make it because of their physical state. The most ill were allowed to be left on deck so that if they died they could be easily disposed of over the side without the need for having to pull their corpses up from the depths of the holds.

They had not been steaming for long when reports came in that magnetic mines had been dropped in Surabaya harbour and one escort, the *W11*, left. Meanwhile the *Suez Maru* and its single escort now continued alone.

During the 27th and 28th the two continued together but without zigzagging, which was the normal procedure to try and confuse submarines. For whatever reasons the *W12* did not have active sonar operating and briefly disappeared for one day, only to reappear on the 29th having left the *Suez Maru* on its own.

In the meantime the Submarine USS *Bonefish*, which had arrived in the area on the 28th late in the evening, managed to get a radar return at about 17 miles. She started to shadow the two craft in the early hours of darkness of the 29th. Come 0800 hrs it was now daylight and she launched four torpedoes at what she could see as two overlapping targets.

At this time the US Navy was experiencing trouble with their torpedoes which had magnetic fuses. These were designed to explode on entering a magnetic field generated by the ships passing and so did not in fact have to actually make contact with the hull. In this case out of the four fired, two missed and one exploded prematurely, and the remaining one hit the *Suez Maru* squarely towards the stern.

On the *Suez Maru* the watchmen had seen the bubble trails fast approaching the ship and shouted warnings. The Captain ordered hard to port and so combed the first two. The third was a premature explosion but the fourth struck home. The area of the explosion was number four hold and the damage considerable, causing many casualties. Water started to pour in at once. In the immediate panic men started to come up from hold number three onto the upper deck. They were ordered to go down into hold number four and try to aid those still alive.

The ship lost way as the propeller had been damaged and the engines had stopped. It was obvious that the ship was mortally wounded and started to sink. The emaciated POWs could do little to help those seriously injured and when it came to heaving life-rafts and Kapok floats over the side they didn't have the strength and it was left to the guards to do this. The minesweeper *W12* called desperately for help and then circled round trying to pick up survivors. She had to be wary in case the submarine tried to attack her too.

By 0940 hrs the *Suez Maru* had sunk, stern first, taking with her many of the Japanese soldiers and a large proportion of the POWs. Many of those who survived the explosion were too sick to get out from the holds and so drowned.

As the last of the large air bubbles burst on the surface and any bits that would float came bobbing up too they found themselves floating in long lines amidst trails of debris and fuel oil. Estimates put their number at around 200–250 men.

It was noticed that the W12 kept stopping to pick up men from the water and floating life-rafts but as was the usual Japanese custom they only collected Japanese personnel, leaving all the POWs to their fate.

By about 1400 hrs the last of the Japanese was picked up and the Japanese Captain Kawano had a dilemma. The decks were full with survivors and still another 200 plus men are in the water. He confronted Lt Koshio and wanted to know what he was to do. After a short discussion he gave the order that they had to obey the High Command's instruction that no POW should fall into Allied hands. They were all to be killed.

At this time feelings were running high since they had witnessed the destruction of the *Suez Maru* and a large number of sick and injured Japanese soldiers had been drowned. Men were issued with rifles and machine guns and lined the decks of the W12 and as she slowly sailed along the line of floating men they opened fire, killing every single one. This carnage took about two and a half hours till they were satisfied no one had been missed. The sea had turned red and many of the corpses bobbed about on the surface completely lifeless, held up in some cases by their Kapok life jackets.

The *W12* deliberately rammed any lifeboats that were still intact and then turned about and steamed off, but this time in the direction of Batavia since the mines at Surabaya had not been cleared.

Thus a total of some 549 POWs died, many during the sinking and then the survivors were murdered. Sadly among them, 6 HAA Regt lost 15 men. These were made up from 12 Bty which had lost five men and 15 Bty who had lost nine and there was one additional casualty, a signaller, who came from the attached ranks.

The Japanese W12 eventually reached the port at Batavia and unloaded some 298 survivors. They were all Japanese, not a single one was an Allied POW.

THE TRAGEDY OF THE *JUNYO MARU*

During the early part of 1944 the Japanese realised a landing on Sumatra was a strong possibility. They also realised they would have to move large quantities of men and equipment about, and rapidly at that. [In the event the landing never happened because the landing craft and ships had been needed for the invasion of Italy.] Roads were few and far between and in many cases halted at rivers where the only way to cross was by the use of ferries.

Their answer to the problem would be to construct a railway from the town of Pakan Baroe and link to Moera. There was already a railway from Padang to Moera and the new section would join to it forming a continuous track from south to north across the island. This railway would also help to solve the problem of an acute shortage of trucks that the Japanese army was experiencing. Once complete it would not just stand idle awaiting an invasion but could be used for transporting coal and freight.

Work had started in May 1943 with thousands of slave labourers, the ubiquitous Romushas, who were brought in from many outlying areas. They had started at the Pakan Baroe end in the north and were driving it towards the south west.

The line of the railway had to cross the watersheds of the Siak and Kwantan rivers and would be something like 138 miles in length. Large areas of mangrove marsh, creeks and mosquito infested swamps and multiple rivers had to be negotiated. The line was not flat and had to cross mountains and gorges and extremely difficult terrain. It was the worst sort of ground for laying a railway that could be imagined. The climate was incredibly hot and humid as one would expect for somewhere right on the equator.

In the meantime, as on the Burma railway, a series of camps would be established from which the various groups would push the track. There would be some 15 camps in the end and the railway was to be pushed from both ends.

Trees were cut down to be used for the piles of the river bridges, many of them rubber trees from nearby plantations. Cuttings and embankments were going to have to be constructed because the Japanese had no intention of constructing tunnels. They even sent in Japanese engineers to carry out blasting of rock to form the cuttings and shelves cut into the side of hills.

After many months, work was not going as fast as the Japanese wished, so it was decided to gather surplus POWs from Java and ship them to Sumatra to bolster the workforce. From a variety of camps around Java men were paraded and set off for destinations they could only guess at.

A large contingent of well over a thousand had come from the 10th Infantry Battalion camp formerly occupied by the Dutch East Indies Army on Java. These men marched via the roads to reach the central railway station and were then crammed into carriages for the trip to Tanjong Priok. Here they were joined by another 700 who had come from a camp at Makassar. As usual rumours of their destination abounded, the favourites being Japan or Thailand.

Once at the docks they were paraded again and waited to board a ship. As usual there was little or no food or water provided. They had arrived early in the morning and spent some hours just lounging around waiting for orders; all the time the sun had risen higher and the temperature had risen.

As the POWs sat about trying to avoid the heat of the sun, long straggling files of Romushas appeared and were forced to climb the gangplank of one of the two ships lying berthed against the quay. She was called the *Junyo Maru*.

They were directed towards the front of the ship and those who could not find space on deck were herded down into the two forward holds. There were some 4200 of them and the crush was life threatening. There was not even space to lie down and hundreds sat with their knees drawn up to their chins. The toilet facilities were as usual totally inadequate for such a vast number of men.

Once they were loaded it was the turn of the POWs to be embarked. Among these were men from 6 Regt who just happened to have been caught up in the trawl for labour. The POWs could not help but notice the derelict state of the docks and lack of ships, an indictment to the Japanese system of control. It seemed that once they captured a place little effort was expended to try and put right the damage, perhaps because they did not have anything like enough skilled men to carry out this work and it was beyond the skills of the POWs.

The POW spaces were in holds three and four at the stern. As usual to accommodate some 2300 men composed of British, American, Dutch and Australians the Japanese had constructed a mezzanine level using bamboo shelving. To make more space the POWs had been told to leave their packs and belongings on the deck above where they covered the meagre life-saving apparatus.

The inside of the holds was dark and only lit by light filtering through the gaps where several of the hatch planks had been moved to one side. There was some sort of sticky substance remaining on the tarpaulins covering the deck and this seemed to have been part of the previous cargo, which looked like it may have been sugar. Added to this was the obvious remains of coal dust which stuck to just about everything. Once the Japanese guards came on board they were all wearing their life jackets but for the POWs there was no such luxury.

The ship sailed later that afternoon but had not gone far before it dropped anchor in the harbour and here they stayed overnight. There was no breeze and next day those in the open fried under the sun all day. The conditions in the holds became unbearable and claustrophobic; the long queues for the toilets became a nightmare and many men with dysentery could not wait.

On the 17th they finally sailed again and were joined by two escorts, one a Corvette-sized ship and the other a somewhat smaller gunboat carrying asdic and depth charges.

Around 18 September and still with no clear idea of where they were headed, they were subjected to tropical storms. Those on deck tried to get below for protection and those below were glad of the chance for some fresh air above.

They still had no idea of where they were headed but from the direction, which was westerly, they thought it might be Singapore, that is until they entered the passage between Sumatra and Java and continued westwards up the south coast of Sumatra, all the time staying about twenty miles off the coast, which led the men to believe the destination was now Padang.

Around 0530 the ship was rocked by a violent explosion at the bow. While they were coming to terms with this a second explosion occurred towards the rear section. By now it was obvious to all that they had been torpedoed. In the ensuing panic men fought to get out from the holds but of course there was no space on deck for them to assemble. The Japanese ran about shouting and trying to launch the few lifeboats available. The engine had stopped and steam was coming from the bowels of the stricken ship. Water was rapidly filling the damaged compartments, and overshadowing the whole scene was the ship's siren, which was sounding loudly.

The Corvette slowed to pick up men who had jumped overboard while the gunboat started to circle, frantically dropping depth charges at random. To those in the water the depth charges were a death sentence if they were too close to the point of detonation and even those some distance away suffered severe hydraulic shock effects.

Men continued to throw anything over the side that would float heedless of the fact that there might be others floating alongside the hull. Long lines of men queued up and jumped to get away. Those already in the water managed to swim to rafts and debris to get a hold on something that floated and looking back saw the ship was settling slowly deeper in the water. By this time there was not long to go; she had settled deeply at the stern and the bows started to lift out of the water revealing her hull.

The remaining men panicked when this happened because it was obvious she had only a short time before she sank. As the bows rose ever higher the surviving Romushas clung forlornly to whatever they could at the bows. It was probable that most could not swim anyway. As the bows reached the point of no return the Romushas started to slide down the deck into the water and ended up smashing into the central bridge of the ship. Within an hour she had gone, taking with her some 5600 men, most trapped within the holds. Death under those conditions must have come as a relief.

For those struggling in the water the name of the game now was to stay with something that would continue to float. The lifeboats had of course been commandeered by the Japanese.

The rescue ships continued to pick up men until they were full. Although those rescued were predominantly Japanese, some POWs did get collected. Once full to bursting they then steamed off for Padang some hours away.

As silence settled over those still clinging on, they must have wondered what was to come. All through the night many hundreds held on and in the morning they were greeted by a thick mist, but then quite surprisingly the gunboat reappeared out of this mist. It circled slowly gathering men on the end of ropes thrown over the side. When they deemed they had collected all who were still alive they sailed off to Padang to unload at the port.

The final tally of POWs was 680 Allies and some 200 Romushas, a pitiful 880 out of over 6500. Simple maths shows this to have been the highest death toll of the war regarding POWs and slave labour in transit.

What made the tragedy worse was that the submarine that caused the disaster was the British submarine HMS *Tradewind*. In good faith she had attacked a legitimate target without knowing it was carrying POWs. Having dived deep to escape the inevitable searches she never realised the mayhem she had left behind.

For those who survived this terrible ordeal there was only one outcome. Once they had been rescued, counted and sorted they were sent to work on the Sumatra railway, the intended project from the outset.

Among the casualties were three men from the 6 Regt, one from 12 Bty and three from 15. It can be seen that having survived combat and been taken prisoner, in many cases it was far more dangerous to be in the hands of the Japanese as a POW, especially in transit.

Having lost so many potential workers for the Railway the Japanese now had to collect POWs from elsewhere.

TAMAHOKO MARU

By the early part of 1944 it was obvious to the Japanese who were prepared to admit it that the war had turned against them and there was an ever greater need for more slave labour to be sent back to Japan to work in their war industries. So in May 1944 an order went out to gather extra POWs from Java and a large group were assembled from various camps such as Adek, Buitenzorg, Bicycle camp and Kampong Macassar by 10 May.

The final total was some 41 officers and 731 men and these were composed of 197 British, 42 American, 258 Australians and 281 Dutch. Among this motley crowd were men from 6 HAA who happened to be roped in. Unusually for the time there was very little sickness amongst the men; included in the draft were some 90 doctors and medical orderlies.

They embarked on 19 May in the 3500 ton *Kiska Maru* and after a three-day voyage reached Keppel Harbour in the south of Singapore. Here they managed to view with great interest a German submarine which was tied up alongside and obviously suffering from damage to the hull at the aft end, before they were driven off to Havelock Road Camp.

During the next few days they were all subjected to the obligatory glass rod up the rear end. This produced five positive results and these men were removed from the draft.

On the morning of 2 June the remaining 772 men marched down to the docks having left the sick men behind.

Singapore had limited docking facilities so they were loaded onto barges and transferred to their new ship the *Miyo Maru* (4000 tons) which was lying at anchor out in the 'Roads'. The ship was already loaded with bauxite and the POWs were loaded into the two forward holds. Since there was not the usual crush some 300 men could sleep on deck which also meant that those below could also sleep lying down.

The *Miyo Maru* sailed on 3 June 1944 and formed up as part of a convoy of 11 ships bound for Japan via Manila. She was not the only ship carrying POWs as part of a mixed cargo and they had an additional four small corvettes as escorts.

There was of course great concern about the possibility of submarine attack which turned out to be well founded when one of the escorts was torpedoed on 6/7 June. There were on board a large quantity of Kapok life jackets which the Japanese sergeant in charge refused to issue. This was too much for the senior officer, Maj Morris, and after much complaining the sergeant relented.

On 11 June the remainder of the convoy arrived safely at Manila and anchored in Subic Bay. Unknown to the POWs the American submarine USS *Tang* had left Pearl Harbor on 8 June for her war patrol in the China Sea under the Command of Lt Cdr O'Kane.

After two days at anchor in the bay the 10 remaining cargo ships set off for Takao (in Formosa) on 14 June escorted by 3 corvettes, a minelayer and a whaling ship. Initially the convoy sailed northwards within sight of land but then struck out into the open sea. It then ran into a typhoon which severely buffeted the convoy and the *Miyo Maru* sustained serious damage. The conditions down below for the POWs who were 'hold bound' was nothing less than horrendous. Many were violently sea sick and many were injured by being thrown against the bulkheads. Their only route out was via a metal ladder against one side. The convoy eventually reached Takao on 18 June in a badly shaken state and immediately the *Miyo Maru* started to unload its cargo.

Because of the serious damage to the ship it was decided to offload the POWs and they were transferred to another ship already there called *Tamahoko Maru* (6700 tons) which was already loaded with sugar and rice and some 500 Japanese soldiers. The POWs were put down in the two forward holds while the Japanese had the aft end. To ease the crush some 300 men were again allowed to sleep topsides. The rest spread out where ever they could find a space. The ship carried life jackets but again they were not issued, being left stacked up against the side forward of where the guards were. There were also a few balsa rafts tied to the guard rails.

This new convoy plus escorts and whaling ship left Takao on 20 June and after the heat of the tropics the cooler air made things more comfortable for the first few days.

However on 24 June the USS *Tang* came across the convoy and started to shadow it. They were well south west of Kagoshima (the south west tip of Kyushu island) and in the dark Lt Cdr O'Kane could make out at least six large cargo ships. He crept in to attack and selected two large silhouettes in the starboard column. Just before midnight he fired a fan of three torpedoes at the first and then after waiting for the sights to come on fired another fan of three at the next. He then dived deep to escape and reload. They heard and felt several loud explosions.

The first the POWs knew in the *Tamahoko Maru* was when they were all jarred awake by the ship in front suddenly blowing up after two torpedo strikes. Hardly had they recovered from their surprise than they themselves were hit in quick succession by two more. The blasts were so enormous that all the forward hatch covers were blown to pieces and the men resting on them too. Hundreds had been killed and others badly hurt by flying debris. As men ran to try and get to the life jackets in the dark they fell down the newly opened holes in the deck and landed in the holds.

The ship had been hit hard with two enormous holes in the hull and started to sink almost immediately. So rapid was the inrush of water that many men were actually washed out of the holds as it sank. Survivors reckoned she sank within two minutes of the attack and many men had no chance of getting out of the holds in that time. Hundreds were drowned or killed in the explosions.

In the pandemonium and shock of the situation the survivors found themselves floating in a sea of debris. They managed to find some of the life rafts and life jackets and then along with the Japanese survivors settled down to see how long before they would be rescued. There did not appear to be the same attitude to the POWs this time as had been experienced during other ship sinkings. Everyone was in the same situation.

The escorts did not seem to know where to look for the attacker and mercifully they dropped no depth charges. (Lt Cdr O'Kane claimed two ships sunk in his report but postwar research into Japanese records showed in fact he had sunk four. Some of his torpedoes had missed those in the front column and gone on to hit ships in the next column.) With four sets of crews and many POWs to rescue in the dark it is no wonder the escorts were totally confused. When it became light one of the corvettes came back and stopped and lowered boats and began to pick up only Japanese survivors.

Around 0700 hrs the whaling ship also appeared and lowered rope ladders. These the POWs were allowed to climb and they huddled forward on the deck close to a gun platform. The whaler was well handled and cruised up and down collecting all she could find. When it was deemed there were no more alive she prepared to sail off.

The only unfortunate incident at this time was when some POWs who had been picked up by the corvette, which did not wish to take them, came along side and threw them over the side expecting them to swim across to the whaler. Sadly two of these men were non-swimmers and drowned.

Once a final check had been made for any more survivors the whaler set off for Nagasaki carrying 211 men. They were duly unloaded, shocked, cold and hungry and many covered in oil at 1800 hrs. Sadly amongst those who did not survive were four men from 6 HAA:

Grs Barker and O'Shaunessy from 12 Bty, Gnr Minton from 15 Bty and Gnr Irving from RHQ.

The POWs were collected by lorry from the docks and driven to a camp called Fukuoka 14 where they were given dry clothes and bedding and some hot food. The camp was in the Mitsubishi factory area and close to Nagasaki, a name they would all come to know later.

The results of this sinking were some 560 men had died. Lt Cdr O'Kane had no idea of the terrible results of his attack until much later. (Lt Cdr O'Kane had a highly successful career but during a later convoy attack in which he sank several ships the last torpedo fired turned out to be a rogue and circled round and struck his submarine USS Tang sending her to the bottom. He was one of only seven survivors who were picked up and interned for the duration of the war.)

Chapter 14

The *Hofuku Maru*; the Haruku Island Atrocities and the Sumatra Railway

---

ANOTHER TRAGEDY – *THE HOFUKU MARU*

In mid June 1944 the Japanese decided to reduce the numbers of men in Singapore, many of whom had returned from the Burma railway earlier in the year. They were held for the most part in River Valley Road camp in the south of the island.

They arranged for a ship called the *Hofuku Maru* to collect them and the intention was to ship them to Takao. They had already chosen those they considered fit enough to work from the Burma railway survivors and these were the ones who could just about stand up unaided.

So in early July 1944 some 1286 POWs were loaded into the holds in the usual horrendous conditions. Amongst those selected were several from 6 HAA Regt.

The *Hofuku Maru* was a transport ship of about 5800 tons and once loaded they put to sea on 4 July and joined nine other ships to become convoy SHIMI-05. They were not the only ship carrying POWs as the convoy was transporting about 5000 men, one of the largest movements of POWs in the war. The convoy was escorted by a torpedo boat and two minesweepers which carried depth charges for use against any submarines detected.

The first stop was to be Miri in Borneo which they reached without incident on 8 July. Here there was a change of plan and two ships were detached to await another convoy. The *Hofuku Maru* was one of them and the other was a supply ship that did not carry any POWs.

While they waited for their new convoy the remaining ships set off for the Phillipines as part of a new convoy designated MI-08. These ships arrived safely but by the time they had reached Manila many men were suffering serious health problems, exacerbated by the lack of food and water and proper sanitation. Many had in fact been suffering a variety of illnesses even before being loaded.

Meanwhile back in Miri the *Hofuku Maru* had joined its other convoy and set off for Manila following behind the previous one. She was the only ship carrying POWs out of them all. The remainder carried war supplies.

They arrived there on 19 July which meant that both parts of the original convoy were now back together again and anchored in Subic Bay. The ships from the first part then left again for Takao which they all reached safely.

While still anchored off Manila further ships joined the second part of the original convoy and some of these set off again some days later for the longer trip across the China Sea to Japan.

Out of the 19 ships involved two were torpedoed and sunk by US submarines during the transit but luckily they were both supply ships and no POWs were lost.

Around 13 August this convoy docked at Moji, a large port at the northern end of the island of Kyushu. Here there was a large hospital facility and many of those who were extremely sick were transferred there for treatment. The remainder were dispersed around outlying camps.

While this was all happening to them the remaining ships were still in Manila, and unfortunately the *Hofuku Maru* was one of them since she had developed engine trouble and needed time for repairs. The POWs were still cooped up in their holds and gradually getting weaker and sicker. Food and water as always were in very short supply.

The senior medical officer and the senior officer in charge argued heatedly with the Japanese in charge to try and get the most seriously ill men taken ashore for proper treatment in the base hospital at Subic Bay. Initially it was all to no avail but the Japanese did eventually see how sick some of the men were and allowed a few to be offloaded on stretchers. Not to be outdone they then made up the numbers by putting Dutch POWs on board, some of whom were almost as sick as those removed. Conditions below decks were now absolutely horrendous. Lack of space, little or no water and food and no medical supplies at all. The air was fetid and the smell horrendous.

Eventually the engines were repaired and on 20 September some two months after they had started, they sailed again, now designated as convoy MATA-27. This time they were part of an eleven-ship convoy, but only the *Hofuku Maru* was carrying any POWs. The convoy steamed out of Subic Bay and anchored for the night.

Next day, 21 September 1944, they turned north, this time carrying about 1300 POWs. Some of the critically sick had been left behind and their places taken by the extra Dutch POWs. They were headed for Takao in Formosa and they had not been at sea for long and were still within sight of land when a force of US airplanes found them and attacked. This was the carrier based task force No. 38 of bombers and torpedo-carrying planes. Once they had started they just kept up the attacks and with 100 aircraft it was relentless. One ship after another was hit and sunk until by the end of the day they had all gone.

It was estimated that only some 200 POWs escaped, either by being picked up by Japanese rescue craft or swimming ashore. Sadly many men were drowned in the holds because they were too ill to climb out and others were killed in the air strikes. These survivors were then loaded onto another ship and this set off for Formosa arriving on 25 September. Once again the Regt had casualties amongst those lost – three men of whom two were from RHQ and one from 3 Bty.

The Japanese at least attempted to rescue men this time but of those who managed to swim ashore it is thought about 13 were found by guerrilla forces and spirited away from the search parties. With the exception of one who died some time later the rest survived till the war's end.

Once again those who reached Japan were transferred to POW camps where they met up again with colleagues from the first convoy and all were used for slave labour duties.

THE HARUKU ISLAND ATTROCITIES AND THE SUMATRA RAILWAY

The Japanese had further ideas for consolidating some of the smaller islands off the island of Seram which lay well to the north of Timor. They not only wanted to be able to supply emergency airstrips for aircraft in trouble but to improve existing strips and have new bases close enough for their bombers to be able to reach Australia.

With this in mind, around April 1943 they gathered together a large quantity of POWs from various sources to make up the working parties. They were looking to find some 4000 men and the majority were assembled from Java comprising men from three different camps.

They were designated a suffix letter to show where they had come from and formed into three separate parties sent on different dates. The suffix letter 'A' meant they had come from the camp at Tanjong Priok, the letter 'B' from Tjimahi Bandung and the letter 'C' from the large camp at Surabaya.

Those in the camps round Surabaya had been used extensively on war work, something the Japanese didn't seem to be troubled about despite it being contrary to the normal regulations governing POWs. They spent their days being taken to airfields to repair damaged runways and infrastructure and in some instances to build gun and aircraft protective bunds. Much of the material was clay and the work heavy, especially for those not used to hard manual tasks.

Another of their tasks was to build air-raid shelters in local towns. This seems a strange idea because the Japanese had captured all the islands they wanted, but there must have been a deep rooted fear that at some stage the US forces would come back again.

Around April 1943 the first party was assembled and marched down to the docks in Surabaya to make up what was going to be about 4000 men. The first draft was composed mainly of RAF personnel. These men had been captured in various theatres and had been, for the most part, non-combatants such as aircraft fitters and armourers and signals specialists or medics.

They were loaded as always into ships totally unsuited for the journey. Two of these were called the *Amagi Maru* and the *Matsukawa Maru* and they set out for the island of Ambon on 28 April. This was not just a short journey across the bay but an ocean trip of over a thousand miles and would take nearly two weeks. On the way they would make a brief stop at Madura island off the coast of Surabaya.

Walter Mear and his mate Robert Digg, a cook by trade, were still together having been moved across to Surabaya some time before. They had avoided the first selective drafts in October of men to go to Japan completely by chance. (Among those chosen to go to Japan was Walter's friend Albert, the Dutch soldier, and he too survived the war.) Fate decreed those who went by the simple expedient of being in the wrong place at the time of selection or being perceived as fitter than others around them.

As the POWs waited, one item that held their attention was a sudden fire aboard a nearby ship lying out in the harbour. What started as dense clouds of smoke rapidly turned to flames. The harbour floating fire tender was in close attendance but did not manage to control things. Sparks rushed up into the sky to be followed by minor explosions and more dense smoke and then a cataclysmic explosion tore the ship apart, scattering huge sections of steel plate over a wide area.

After this rather alarming start to the voyage they finally reached the island of Ambon several days later and as they approached the harbour they could see a Japanese navy sea plane base which was a hive of activity with float planes bobbing at anchor.

The airstrip that some of them were going to be employed on was some way out from the town and close to the shore on a relatively flat piece of ground on the far side of the inlet. It was a great relief to get out of the cramped hold because the usual sickness of the men had been compounded by the lack of sufficient rations and precious little drinking water.

The first duties they found themselves on were to unload the cargo which turned out to be hundreds of 40-gallon drums of fuel. In addition to this they had to unload large numbers of munitions including bombs. As was usual, the Japanese had no ideas for the safety of the men and just shouted and screamed at them to work faster.

Two days later the groups were split so that half of them were loaded to go on to a smaller island further to the east called Haruku and because of the shallow depth of water they were transferred to smaller craft so that they could be landed. Haruku was a small coral island to the east of Ambon and covered in jungle vegetation; it was not completely deserted but was home to several villages of native peoples. It was known rather romantically as one of the Spice Islands because of its history of producing such exotic produce as nutmeg.

Those who stayed behind were going to be used to repair and maintain the airstrip on Ambon; those that went to Haruku were to be used specifically to construct a new airstrip from scratch.

(There was yet a third party of about 1000, mostly Dutch, who went further east to work on an airfield on Seram.)

Among those who were detailed off for Haruku and who numbered about 2000 was Walter Mear and his old mate Robert Digg and a few others from 3 Bty. They also left other men from the Bty back at Ambon having been unable to all stay together.

Once they had made their way ashore under torrential rain they were counted and marched away to the site of the new camp. Counting was always carried out in Japanese as part of their humiliation. Here they got their first shock, there was nothing there. So some set to and started to clear an area of all vegetation while others got fires going for the cooking and Robert joined in this detail. The sick were made as comfortable as possible and temporary shelters made out of whatever materials they could find. Then tired and exhausted and extremely hungry they bedded down for the night to await the morning.

The next day a large number of local natives arrived carrying bamboo, rattan and hut-making material and got on with the task of constructing a camp. The POWs carried on with the clearing and they levelled off various areas to take the huts and even a large enough piece of ground to be able to parade on. Because of the natural desire to stay with their fellow country-men the groups divided up so that each nationality had its own area. Thus there were the Dutch in one place and the British in another.

After a few days of organising, the huts had come on well and these were the standard design they had become so used to – a rectangular structure with bamboo poles supporting attap walls and roofs, sleeping benches down both sides, a central walkway, push open attap shutters over the window openings and a door in each end. These also had the luxury of a verandah down each long side and the whole thing was suspended above the ground on stilts, the normal native way to try and keep the inside dry and free from bugs. They had also dug several pits to be used as toilets and constructed a path down to the local river to set up the cook house some distance away.

Each morning during the *Tenko* the Japanese commandant's latest instruc-tions were translated for them all to digest by the camp interpreter Kassyama, who did his best with his limited knowledge of English.

It was not long before they found out why they were there. The aim of the exercise was to build an airstrip across the island. At that time the ground was virgin jungle and covered a small coral hillock, on both sides of which were two long natural pronounced hollows. The engineering feat was to remove the top of the hillock and use this material to infill the two long hollows and so arrive at a flat surface for the runways. As usual the tools provided for the task were totally inadequate: hammers and steel chisels of varying lengths, and the ubiquitous *Changkols*. Even the Japanese realised the difficulty of the task and sent in their own engineers to supervise. Some time later they installed a narrow gauge railway to carry material around the site.

Like the men on the Burma railway the same system of forming the holes for the blasting was adopted. One man held the metal chisel while another man struck it with a sledge. The holder then twisted the chisel ready for the next strike and this was repeated till a hole of suitable depth had been produced. The broken coral had to be loaded by hand and for men without proper gloves or in some cases even footwear, there was the added danger of severe cuts.

While some POWs were used to clear the undergrowth the rest were involved in the tedious task of making the blast holes and carrying the broken material to where it was needed. What made their life sheer hell was they were always being required to work harder and faster. Any perceived laziness was rewarded by beatings and punching and throughout the whole period the food rations were kept at starvation levels.

Once the work was well under way the groups were split again so that a roadway could be constructed from the site down to another river where the intention was to build jetties so ships could unload stores.

There were no proper medical supplies for illnesses such as malaria or dysentery or for treating cuts and ulcers. Men whose feet were badly cut by the coral had no option but to wrap them with whatever they could find. The medical men with the party managed to work wonders with scant equipment or supplies and one was well known for concocting his own medicines from local produce in the form of leaves and barks.

The guards were the usual mix of second rate troops but in this camp was one who was famed for his sadistic treatment of all those beneath him. He was their commander and quite adept at beating up his own men if he thought they were not doing their job as he saw it. He had taken it on himself to be the one to hand out any serious punishment and he relished this duty so much so that the POWs considered him not only highly dangerous but a psychopath. He went by the name of Gunso Mori and was Japanese by birth. (In fact the POWs later nicknamed him and the camp interpreter Blood and Slime because these were two symptoms of dysentery in the bowels.)

Besides working on the runway they were called on to help unload stores delivered by ship for the construction site. Very often these were drums of fuel which were thrown overboard from anchored ships and had to be dragged ashore and up the beach.

The work progressed slowly as sickness reduced the labour force drastically, and then an epidemic of dysentery swept through the camp. Men died by the score and a temporary cemetery had to be dug close to the beach and still the Commandant refused to help the doctors with medicines. As with most Japanese camps, disease, malnutrition and death were all around. A lot of the problems within the camp were caused by the very unsanitary toilet facilities where huge maggots crawled about in the pits and enormous bluebottle type flies buzzed everywhere spreading the germs. Gunso forbade the camp staff to construct a toilet structure over the sea which would have certainly helped because he considered it would contaminate and defile what was in effect part of the Emperor's sea.

More and more men went down with all manner of diseases and the workforce dwindled to such an extent that even the hardened Japanese became worried. The men themselves were skeletal in many cases and suffering from all kinds of ailments including beriberi and ulcers.

The death rates soared and still the food rations were not improved. The only consolation was that in some places where the men walked to work from their camp, which was a distance from the construction site, it was possible to pick wild fruits and berries and collect edible leaves. These at least helped provide some vitamins but never enough for them all.

One of the most debilitating aspects of their existence was the continual beatings by any guard, sometimes for no discernable reason other than to relieve their sadistic tendencies. Like all the others Walter was not immune and many times was severely injured by ferocious thrashings from a cane across his body. The heavy wheals and scars from this treatment were clearly visible on his back some 60 years later. The secret was to try and stay standing during this hellish treatment because falling down was a sign of weakness and would invite prolonged torture.

Month after month the work went on under a relentless sun and the glare from the coral made some men temporarily blind. After many months the strip was so well advanced that it was bombed on several occasions by American aircraft. This damaged the surface which had then to be repaired but also killed some of the POWs and local villagers who the American pilots had no idea were working there.

As the brutal treatment continued to be meted out and the death toll rose the strip was finally considered to be ready for use and a few Japanese aircraft practised landing and take-offs.

At this point of the war the Americans had by-passed the area with the intention that it be left for later operations. The Japanese now realised they had become a bit of a backwater and with the need for so many men elsewhere they greatly reduced the numbers and made plans to ship them out and back to Java. By this time, of the original 2000 men, not far short of 400 had died from disease and neglect and the appalling treatment. Walter Mear and his best mate Robert had thus far managed to stay together and survive the conditions, emaciated and in very poor health but fit enough to stand.

So it came as a surprise when one day in late November 1943 the Japanese paraded the whole camp and told them some were to be shipped out to Ambon. 750 men from the camp at Palao made their way to the harbour area where they were collected by small boats and transferred to Ambon, a journey of more than a day across a very rough open sea.

Once at Ambon the groups were split again with some of the fitter ones being detailed off to stay and work on the strip there. The remainder waited to be loaded onto a ship that was anchored further out in the harbour. By this time the original group had been joined by a large contingent from Liang camp in Ambon and they all sat around and waited.

It was a mixed bunch with men from the Army, some Gunners, RAF and Dutch personnel, many severely ill and being carried on makeshift stretchers. The RAF men who were for the most part skilled technicians had been particularly hard hit by the unusual ardour of the work. Their war had come to an end when in many cases they had been ordered to surrender and in one case betrayed by the Dutch who had handed them over to the Japanese.

The transfer of POWs out to the ship anchored off had to be done via the use of small craft and home-made rafts made up by securing bamboo poles and frames to native dugouts. These latter were notoriously unstable and in more than one case turned over spilling the unfortunate occupants into the water.

The loading continued at a slow rate all morning and then a large detachment of sick and injured Japanese soldiers appeared and they took priority.

Eventually Walter and his mate made it to the ship and witnessed the struggle to force POWs down into an obviously full hold. By this time a little over 550 men had been taken on board and the hold covers could not be shut properly so some of the POWs were told they would have to disembark and make their way back to shore and await the next ship.

From such instances is history made and Lady Luck had played her part again. Walter and his mate went back to the wharf and saw the ship sail off on 26 November with a full load, which included a few men from the Regt. This was supposed to be the start of a journey of more than ten days. The remaining POWs who could not get on were returned to Liang Camp on Ambon to await the next available ship.

The ship they had seen sailing away was named the *Suez Maru* PS 45 and her story is told in chapter 13. Suffice to say Walter and his mate had had an extremely lucky escape. There were no survivors from this ship after she was torpedoed. Every POW who had survived the sinking was machine-gunned to death while in the sea by Japanese navy seamen.

Despite this narrow escape Walter was not yet out of the woods. It was to be several months before another ship arrived, the delay being caused by the severe shortage of available ships, and when this arrived it took the survivors back to Java to await further transport to Sumatra. What Walter was not to know was that amongst the other POWs was one who would later become famous as an explorer after the war by the name of Laurens van der Post.

Walter Mear had luckily avoided the *Suez Maru* by a whisker and so too the *Junyo Maru* incident (see chapter 13) by being transported via an alternative ship, but by the time he arrived in Sumatra he and all the others were extremely sick and malnourished. There were a few men from 6 Regt in the draft out of some 4000 POWs. The largest number were Dutch followed by about 1000 British and a then a couple of hundred Australians. It was a large contingent that had left and there was not a man who was not suffering multiple illnesses and grossly underweight. The usual sores and ulcers were very apparent and in many cases the skeletal frames from malnutrition.

Making up the vast majority of the labour force were native labourers who were something like 16,000 in number. They had been hard at work for many months before the POWs arrived. The POWs were sent to one of the construction camps by rail after disembarking to join hundreds of others, all in dire straits.

It was not long before their malaria and dysentery reoccurred causing many of them to spend much time in the temporary hospital huts. Because the same starvation rations were employed the only way to help the seriously sick was to get better food quality. This was engineered by the simple but extremely dangerous expedient of trying to steal Japanese higher quality rice and replace it with their poorer standard rice. The Japanese had already thought of this problem and whenever ration trains arrived from the coast carrying all manner of food the rice sacks were marked with either a red or blue line. The difficulty for the POWs was to acquire a sack of good quality rice and replace it with the poorer grade usually by hiding it well underneath the rest of the sacks yet to be unloaded. On occasions they succeeded but the penalties for being caught were a life-threatening beating with canes by the sadistic guards.

The construction routine was a mirror image of that employed on the Burma railway. Men went out in advance to cut down undergrowth and clear a path wide enough for the single track line. Others were employed cutting down trees for use in structures and embankments. Further gangs spent all day digging dirt and rocks to make the embankments and track bed, and carrying this in sacks to the designated spot to be dumped ready for compaction. The terrain was as bad as it could get, large areas of swampy ground infested by malaria-carrying mosquitoes, snakes and crocodiles and with strength-sapping rainfall and humidity from being almost on the equator.

Gangs were used to cut up the trees into suitable sleepers while others brought in the rails and spiked them down. Because of the severe nature of the ground a large number of bridges had to be built. Their construction was at best precarious and when it rained heavily the list on the piers was quite noticeable, to such an extent that the POWs were scared for their own safety when the time came for the work trains to cross.

Blasting was used to remove rock from cuttings and the relentless pressure to maintain progress created many serious accidents. In one such accident a train full of native labourers was passing below an overhanging section of cliffs when the whole lot came crashing down in a landslide, derailing the train and wagons. Many were killed and there was then the gargantuan task of trying to get the engine and wagons back onto the track which they eventually did. Derailments were not that unusual and always required a mass of labour to lever the trucks back on again using timber fulcrums and wedges. Besides the dangers of falling trees there was another unpleasant side effect, being attacked by red ants who had just lost their homes. They would bite with ferocious jaws and inflict nasty wounds.

The Japanese had already devised a sadistic method of determining who might be malingering to avoid work. They had set up some poles in a swampy area and this was where the sick were sent. If the man was able to hang on during his time there he was obviously strong and fit enough to work. If he fell off he was left to die. Walter, a young man of 22, through sheer strength of character and will-power grimly held on with the result that he was returned to the work details. By this time he had seen many men drop off and drown and had the nightmare vision of seeing their bodies gradually covered with flies before being allowed to be taken away for burial.

The Japanese set up a series of camps from which the railway could be constructed (about 15 in total) and as each section was completed the camps were moved further along the line.

One of the worst nightmares for Walter and the rest was to find that their old adversary from Haruku by the name of Gunso Mori had also arrived in Sumatra and was meting out the same sort of discipline as before, and he had not mellowed in the least.

Around January 1945, as the war progressed and the Japanese were finally being pushed back into their homeland, an Allied carrier group was detailed off to attack oil installations at Palembang and Pladjoe which they did with limited success. Planes took off from HMS *Victorious* and other carriers and these attacks so stung the Japanese that they retaliated with a series of kamikaze attacks against them but without serious damage. Whether the POWs were ever aware of this action is not known, but if they were it would have helped morale no end.

The conditions were so serious that eventually Walter and many others were so sick they were unable to work and got moved to a special hospital camp to try and let them recover.

The work went on for another eleven months under these dire conditions after their arrival before this railway was finished and when it was finally opened the date was early August 1945, just in time for the war to end by the dropping of the atomic bombs.

The railway was never used by the Japanese for their intended war effort. In fact it had one major use during its life and that was after the Japanese surrender when the surviving POWs were ferried along its length towards the north end to Pakan Baroe where they could be given medical aid and then repatriated.

Sadly during the construction there were some 700 deaths among Commonwealth prisoners. As was normal these were from disease, malnutrition and the usual bestial treatment from their guards. The death rate among the natives was considerably higher.

Walter recalls that the end of the war came quite suddenly. One day they were being brutally treated by the guards and the next they woke up in the morning to find complete quiet, no shouting, no screaming. All the guards, the heroes of the Rising Sun, had fled.

It was some time later towards the middle of August that they heard aircraft flying in the area in an obvious search pattern. In order to make sure they were discovered as soon as possible they broke into one of the camp stores and got hold of some sacks of tapioca powder. Because they were near to a beach they had to make out the letters POW in this powder spread out in an open area not far away.

Not long after this the aircraft flew over and saw the message. It flew back again, and unknown to the prisoners there was an RAF photographer taking pictures for record purposes in the back. Eventually the rescue operation was put into effect and they were all collected and taken to hospitals for assessment. This was the start of the long road back to recovery in the UK including a trip by hospital ship.

For Walter Mear, release meant that he could now get proper medical treatment for his many illnesses. He eventually arrived back in the UK. and started a long period of recuperation. Having been demobbed from the Artillery he then spent time learning a trade and became an electrician, something at which he excelled. He next started working at a company in South Wales called Chrome Leather and while there found out just how small the world really is. During the course of a conversation he was told that someone else who worked there had also been out in the Far East in the

RAF during the war, but was not in fact a POW. They met and it turned out that this man had been a photographer and in fact the very same one to have flown over Walter's camp taking the pictures!

Walter later married and had a family of four and continued his lifelong skill at invention and resourcefulness. He joined the National Coal Board where he won recognition for his inventiveness and then retired for a life helping his family and son to run a successful garage business. He was dogged all his life by poor health and had to have a series of major operations to correct damage caused by his treatment as a POW and even after 60 years the wheals and scars on his back and body were still obvious. However despite these hardships, in true Gunners tradition, Walter's spirit never gave in and he was active to the very end.

Once the multitude of camps had been located strung out around the Far East the task was to get everyone away as quickly as possible. The only thing on the POWs' minds was home and family; however those that rescued them, in many cases Americans, were horrified and astonished at the condition of the men they now saw. It was patently obvious that systematic brutality and starvation had been used to reduce fit servicemen to living skeletons. Many were quite lucid enough to tell their stories and name names.

For many there was one other duty to be done and that was to fill out forms they had been given so they could describe the conditions of their captivity and name anyone who had been responsible for 'war crimes'. Hundreds of these were sent to investigating centres and the pattern was the same from each camp. Certain names kept coming up along with serious accusations.

By 1948 these had resulted in numerous Courts Martial where the Japanese had the opportunity to defend themselves. There were so many names that only a percentage could ever hope to be tried and as a result of the evidence over 1700 trials were held with some two-thirds being found guilty. Those with the worst records were sentenced to hang and others received long terms of imprisonment. Among those with horrendous records was Gunso Mori and he was subsequently hanged in Singapore prison. It was never going to be possible to try everyone who was guilty but at least the POWs had the satisfaction of knowing that some of the worst perpetrators were given their just deserts.

Even during the trials one thing continued to be avoided by the Japanese guards – no one ever acknowledged guilt or showed any sign of remorse.

In fact so bitter were the Japanese soldiers that they had suffered the dishonour of surrender, that there were many recorded cases of them still murdering POWs up to three weeks after they had been told of the cessation of hostilities.

Those men who returned were scarred for life and in many cases never regained their former physical and mental state.

Trying to determine where every POW who formed part of the Regt ended up is made most difficult by the lack of any reliable records. Men were transported from place to place at the whim of the Japanese, sometimes by ship and sometimes by train and even in extreme cases on foot.

However it is possible to say that certain men ended their careers in different theatres many miles apart or even in separate countries, despite the fact they had been captured for the most part in only a few places. Many of those captured in the fall of Singapore were moved to Changi from where they were later shipped to Thailand, Saigon, Taiwan and Borneo. Many of those captured in Sumatra and Java ended up in Borneo and a large contingent went to Japan.

In many cases where men were known to be dead either at sea or elsewhere and there was no known grave, they are remembered on memorial plaques in Far East cemeteries. The CWGC shows where memorials or grave markers are now located but not necessarily where the person died. They have records of grave site locations or positions on memorial walls. Taking things in chronological order for the Regt, there are several men shown as being buried in Belgium and France, mostly in the Dunkirk Cemetery. There are several shown as being buried in the UK and presumably these are casualties of the Blitz or other causes.

As would be expected the largest number who died on the Burma railway were from 3 Bty who had been left on Singapore, then shipped to Saigon from where they were moved to Thailand. Many of those from 12 and 15 Btys appear in Sumatra, Java and in Borneo which is where they ended up after the islands fell (also in Japan where they were transported to). Many of the incidents were actually continuing at the same time but in widely different locations and overlapped.

During the immediate action that occurred after 3 Bty of the Regt landed in Singapore on 13 January 1942 and reading extracts that remain from witness accounts it is known that the Regt lost at least 40 men killed (including those attached men at HQ such as RE, RAOC, RASC and Signallers) during the final days before the capitulation. Another 20 or so seem to have died in the days that followed or within a few weeks, and it can be assumed these deaths were most probably from serious wounds or other similar causes.

None of the Btys was immune to casualties from their transportation on the so-called 'Hell Ships'. They all at some time or other endured the terrible conditions aboard, conditions that could so easily have been eased by the simple expedient of painting red crosses on the hull and treating the men as human beings rather than expendable cargo or by ensuring that there were medical men on board sufficient to cope with the vast numbers of sick men, or even by supplying the basic medical supplies required and not loading men in such tight conditions. However this was not the Japanese way.

After trawling through the CWGC site and numerous records from odd sources Robert McAllister and I think the final total is now 495 names from all causes. The members of the Regiment who did not return are buried or commemorated in the far-flung corners of the world.

They stretch from the UK through France and Belgium to Singapore and Thailand. Others have their final resting places in Sumatra, Java and Borneo with many in unknown graves in remote islands after being murdered. Some can be found in Japan as a result of long-term systematic malnutrition, overwork and untreated diseases. Sadly for the many who died in transit in the hell ships their remains were committed to the sea.

There were several buried in the UK in the months after repatriation and presumably they died as a result of their experiences. If we include those who died in the blitz and from other causes and accidents we arrive at 19 names. 29 lie in France and Belgium from actions and the retreat to Dunkirk, but the vast majority are in the Far East and comprise 447 names.

This equates to a ratio of about one in three from the total in the Regt who did not make it.

Annex A

The following story was researched over several years by Keith Jenkinson, son of L/Bdr T. Jenkinson. It is an opportunity to give details of the fate of some of 3 Bty and is appended here. So many men died in unknown circumstances it is rare to be able to add further details to an already sparse canvas.

My thanks go to him for allowing me to include the text and photographs of a very brave man.

L/BDR THOMAS JENKINSON NO.1073904

Fig.A.1 L/Bdr T. Jenkinson 3 Bty.

L/Bdr Tom Jenkinson was born at Lancaster on 22 December 1910. He spent the first part of his life at 10 Ramsden Street, Carnforth in North Lancashire, in a tiny terraced house without bathroom or indoor toilet or hot water, which he shared with his parents, two brothers and four sisters.

About one month before his seventeenth birthday he enlisted in the Royal Artillery at Lancaster Barracks, headquarters of the King's Own Royal (Lancaster) Regiment. Like many other young recruits in the 1920s and 30s, who saw enlistment as a route to self-improvement, he gave a false age. Consequently his Army Record shows his date of birth as 22.12.08. Many years later this would prove to be a problem in relation to the age recorded on his headstone.

According to MOD Records he was posted to a Depot Brigade 2nd Training Battalion, 22.11.27 and after three years was transferred to the Army Reserve. (see Fig. A.1) No details survive of his employment before 1927 or between 1930 and 1935, the 'Civil Trade' entry of his service record showing simply 'Labourer'. However, some time in 1935 he became a postal worker at the GPO delivering mail by motorcycle to local villages before eventually moving to the Post Office in Carnforth. By now he was engaged to Mary Wilson, a machinist at Morphy's dressmaking factory in Carnforth.

Tom and Mary were married on 12 September 1936 and set up house together at 9 Highfield Terrace. They were to have barely three years of normal married life before the German invasion of Poland precipitated the beginning of hostilities in a new world war. Tom received his call-up papers on Friday 1 September 1939, two days before the declaration of war and reported immediately to a Reception Depot at Aldershot. He and his friend Alec Mashiter, also RA, were the first Carnforth men to be called up. Apparently half of Carnforth turned up to wave them off.

Having been a trained gunner (but in the reserves) he had in fact only a few weeks left before being discharged. However the dire situation of the time guaranteed he would have been called up anyway.

On 6 September he was posted to 3 Bty 6 Heavy Anti-Aircraft Regiment at Blackdown and by 15 September was in France where the Regt were deployed. His records show a change briefly when his Bty was attached to 4th AA Regt on 29.01.40, before rejoining his own unit again.

In this 'Phoney War' phase, relations with the local population seem to have been mostly good. Tom Jenkinson and some of his comrades were billeted in the barn of farm in the village of *Izel-les-Hameaux*. He obviously got on very well with the Belval family who owned the farm because when he was granted compassionate leave to visit his wife back in England, after the birth of their son Keith on 29 February 1940, they gave him a bottle of champagne to take home for the christening. He arrived home on 4 March for seven days; however the family doctor was able to secure a further week so he returned on 19 March.

He remained with 3 Bty during the multiple moves until being rescued from the beaches at La Panne. In words taken from his wife's diary: '... *he was very lucky to survive such an experience. He used to say that he could never go through such an ordeal as that again*'

After ten days survivors' leave Tom Jenkinson reported to Aberystwyth where 6 HAA was re-forming. By 18 June it had resumed its original composition of 3, 12 and 15 Btys.

3 Bty then moved down south for port defence and he found himself at Falmouth. During the following months Tom made regular visits home on leave. His wife's diary entries note that some of these may have been at least partially 'unofficial' because she lost count of the times she had to sew on, remove and sew back on again the L/Bdr stripes that he occasionally lost and regained after going temporarily AWOL.

He moved north with the Bty from London in November 1940 after Coventry was hard hit. Then later during redeployment further north 3 Bty was stationed at Beverley and it was here that the group photograph was taken. (See Fig. A.2)

Mary Jenkinson remembered receiving a telegram from Tom to say he was in Manchester on Saturday 6 November. This said that they were about to embark for service overseas but that he could get away for a few hours if she could get down to Preston to his brother Leonard's house. She packed an overnight bag and took 20-month-old baby Keith with her on the train. After spending those last few hours together, Tom took a train at about ten o'clock to Liverpool. This was the last time they ever met.

6 HAA Regt sailed from Liverpool on 12 November 1941 on the *Monarch of Bermuda* (Convoy WS12Z) and arrived at Durban on or around 19 December according to the date on a letter-card sent from there. In an earlier letter Tom asked his wife to let him have her brother's army postal address in the hope that he might meet up with him. Because they had been issued with kit suitable for desert conditions he and his mates assumed they were bound for the Middle East where Leslie was already serving. The surprise attacks by Japan on Pearl Harbor, Hong Kong and Malaya meant that they would instead be sent as reinforcements to Singapore.

During his long sea voyage Tom wrote his wife six letters and three letter-cards. In them he was clearly making a big effort to sound cheerful. However, this mood of forced optimism sometime failed him and there was a hint that he feared the worst. For example on 6 December he wrote: '*It's a month since I last saw you for those few hours at Preston darling, it seems a long time but I'll always remember you and baby as I saw you then.*' On the 9th, ashore at Durban, he mentioned his son again: '*I think of him too every day and hope that he will always remember his daddy*'. What his wife did not know until after the war was that he had confided to his brother that he did not expect to come back. In his final letter dated 28 December and written after embarking from Durban on the SS *Aorangi* (Convoy DM 1), he mentioned a friend from Carnforth: '*I was on duty Christmas night on ship's practice so I didn't have much of a time although `Benny` (Gnr Gabbert) and I had a few drinks in the afternoon*

277

Fig. A.2 June 1941. Half of 3 Bty on exercise near Hull.

*and were talking about Carnforth most of the time as we usually do. He's in my
section now and we're often talking about the people at home and wondering what
they're doing.'*

On arrival in Singapore 3 Bty remained to join the defences but because
of the loss or destruction of War Diaries just before or at the surrender, there
is virtually no further official written reference to it. What is known is that
by 15 February, the majority of 3 Bty were either dead or captured. It came
as a stunning blow to Mary Jenkinson to be informed first that her husband
Tom was 'Missing in Malaya' since she had no idea that he was even there,
and then later to be told that he was 'Missing, presumed killed in action'. It
was not until New Year's Eve, 1945 that final confirmation was received
that he had been killed. (See War Office letter Fig. A.3). Like many others
Mary hung on to the slender hope that her husband might still return. This
was because it took some time for all the former Far East POWs to return
and she hoped that he too might have been taken prisoner. One who did
return, although his health was badly impaired by his three and a half years
in captivity, was his friend Benny Gabbert. Unfortunately he could give her
no details of what had happened to Tom. Eventually in late 1945 or early
1946, she received a letter from a Lance-Sergeant Tim Riley. He had recently
been discharged from hospital in Sheffield after being treated for ailments
caused by Japanese brutality while he was a prisoner. His story was a
painful one and she did not tell her son Keith until many years later.

Sgt Riley had come to tell her that there was no hope of her husband
returning because he had seen his body along with the bodies of other men
who had died with him. They had all been bayoneted to death after having
been taken prisoner, apparently as a result of something that one of them
had said to their captors. Sgt Riley had had a few of Tom's personal possessions, including his signet ring, which he had intended to keep for her.
However, the ship on which he was being transported as a POW had been
attacked by US submarines and they had been lost, along with his own
things.

L/Bdr Jenkinson's first official burial was in a collective grave along with
seven other men from 3 Bty in Kranji War Cemetery, Singapore. They were
not reinterred in individual graves until 1951 and even then only with
temporary headstones. Permanent headstones were erected in 1954: families
were invited to contribute towards the cost of the inscriptions. Shortly after
the war ended Dorothy Bleasdale, a young woman who lived on the same
street as Mary and Keith Jenkinson, by an amazing coincidence, happened
to marry Captain (later Major) Jim McWade RA, who had been an officer in

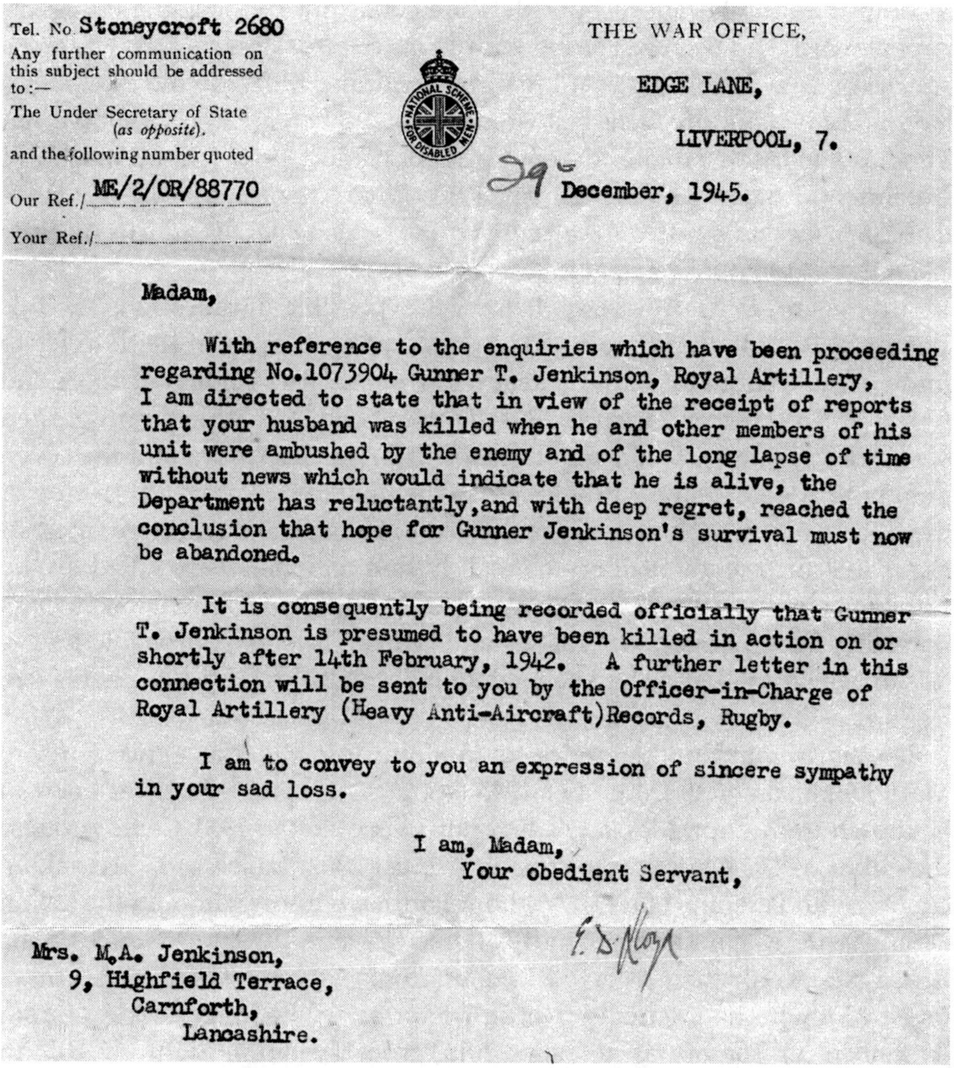

Tel. No. **Stoneycroft 2680**

Any further communication on
this subject should be addressed
to :—

The Under Secretary of State
(*as opposite*),

and the following number quoted

Our Ref./ ME/2/OR/88770

Your Ref./

THE WAR OFFICE,

EDGE LANE,

LIVERPOOL, 7.

29ᵗʰ December, 1945.

Madam,

        With reference to the enquiries which have been proceeding
regarding No.1073904 Gunner T. Jenkinson, Royal Artillery,
I am directed to state that in view of the receipt of reports
that your husband was killed when he and other members of his
unit were ambushed by the enemy and of the long lapse of time
without news which would indicate that he is alive, the
Department has reluctantly,and with deep regret, reached the
conclusion that hope for Gunner Jenkinson's survival must now
be abandoned.

        It is consequently being recorded officially that Gunner
T. Jenkinson is presumed to have been killed in action on or
shortly after 14th February, 1942.   A further letter in this
connection will be sent to you by the Officer-in-Charge of
Royal Artillery (Heavy Anti-Aircraft)Records, Rugby.

        I am to convey to you an expression of sincere sympathy
in your sad loss.

                        I am, Madam,
                        Your obedient Servant,

Mrs. M.A. Jenkinson,
    9, Highfield Terrace,
        Carnforth,
            Lancashire.

Fig. A.3   MOD letter to Mrs Jenkinson about her husband's death.

3 Bty during the war and he remembered Tom Jenkinson very well. From
then on, whenever he was in Carnforth visiting his parents-in-law, he often
visited Mary and Keith and was extremely kind to them. It was a great
comfort for them to have this contact and hear him speak warmly about
Tom. He told Mary that Tom had been very brave in carrying out his duties
in the last days of the fighting and that he had recommended that he be
'Mentioned in Dispatches'. Sadly the War Office would not uphold this

recommendation because Capt. McWade could not produce the necessary papers which had been lost along with so much else. However, and here the subject of Tom Jenkinson's rank re-appears, Capt. McWade did succeed in having the inscription on his headstone amended to read 'Lance Bombardier Thomas Jenkinson'. To quote from Capt. McWade's letter to the Ministry of Defence and dated 13th September, 1951: *'My reason for pointing this out is that L/Bdr Jenkinson was killed because he was carrying out his duty as an NCO and if necessary I can produce a statement on this.'*

Fifty years were to elapse before the possible implications of this statement became the stimulus for an attempt by Tom's son Keith to try to find out more about his father's death, starting with a visit to Singapore and Kranji War Cemetery in April 2001. The first thing to strike an interested observer is the fact that the eight graves of L/Bdr Jenkinson and the seven gunners buried in a line with him are in the final row of graves at the top of the hill, so presumably they were the last to be buried. Even more interesting is that these eight artillerymen, all buried together, were killed on the 13th/14 February 1942 (Gnrs Downend and Hunter, L/Bdr Jenkinson, Gnrs Bareham, Dew, Ledger, McCluskey and Nutty). It is most probable that at this time all the AA guns had been rendered unusable and the gunners were fighting as infantry.

Bearing in mind the reference to an ambush in the War Office letter to Mary Jenkinson of 29 December 1945 (see Fig. A.3) and inferences that can be drawn from Capt. McWade's letter of 13 September 1951 Keith wrote to the editor of *The Gunner* magazine in August 2002, with a view to making contact with veterans of 6 HAA who might have information on the action at Singapore. Major Timbers kindly offered to place a 'Contact Notice' in the next issue. Keith then received a letter from ex-Gunner Arthur Luffman (aged 83), who had actually been a friend as well as a comrade of Tom Jenkinson (or Tommy as he called him) from their time with the BEF in France right through to Singapore. He offered to tell Keith what had happened to his father and a meeting was arranged at Arthur's home in Penn, Wolverhampton, coincidently close to where he had been with 3 Bty before going overseas.

When asked about how 3 Bty had been deployed during the fighting at Singapore, Arthur said that they had manned two gun sites, one above the Alexandra Hospital where he had been, and another at Pasir Panjang. Arthur had been wounded on 13 February during an enemy air attack. He eventually found himself lying amongst the dead and wounded in the hospital and suddenly heard someone utter the sounds 'C.C.S.' (Casualty

Clearing Station). His response in his own words was: '*Arthur, you ain't having none of that. I had enough of that in France.*' So, injured as he was, he made his way out and back to the unit. What he did not realise was this action had probably saved his life. Rogue Japanese soldiers invaded the hospital and murdered hundreds of those there. The next day Arthur went into captivity with the vast bulk of the defending forces. He spent the rest of the war as a prisoner of war, some of it being worked nearly to death on the Burma railway.

Arthur's version of what happened to L/Bdr Jenkinson and his comrades is as follows. They were manning a gun site at or near Pasir Panjang. This was overrun by a Japanese attack. The survivors withdrew and reformed and after a fierce fight they re-took the position only to be overrun by superior numbers of the fanatical enemy. Having been taken prisoner, they were then tied together. One of the men – Gnr McCluskey – was so badly wounded that he begged the Japanese to finish him off, whereupon they were all bayoneted to death. (It is unlikely any of the Japanese could understand English and probably carried out the murder as a matter of course.) Arthur came to know this version of the event because in his version there was one survivor who managed to witness the tragedy from near by and passed the information on to his comrades while they were in POW camp on 15 February. Arthur said that this man was a Scammell driver called Dvr Bone. Unfortunately after 60 years this name may be incorrect and Arthur did not know what happened to Dvr Bone after that.

This account is more detailed than Sgt Riley's, as given to Tom's widow in 1946, and – crucially – Arthur did not know that Keith had heard that story before, so he was not merely confirming an earlier version but was recounting what he remembered. However both accounts contain two identical elements: that at some point the men were captured and then bayoneted to death and that one of the prisoners said something that possibly led to all the men being killed. Given the almost 60-year gap between the two accounts the similarity is remarkable.

Obviously, Arthur Luffman's version introduces a heroic dimension that might seem a bit implausible. Did gun positions really change hands at that stage in the fighting, especially when it seems from other accounts that not many were even in action as late as the 13th or 14th? On the other hand this 'heroic' element does fit rather well with Capt. McWade's commendation of L/Bdr Jenkinson's role in the action.

As with all aspects of the military action in those last few days before the surrender, we are faced with the disappointing scarcity of official records, especially in relation to 3 Bty. So it seems that uncorroborated versions of events are all that we are ever likely to have. What we can say is that men from that unit were fighting up to the end, not always in the role of artillery, and that significant numbers were killed in action. It also seems highly likely that L/Bdr Jenkinson and at least five of those buried alongside him were killed together after capture. This means that their deaths should be counted as war crimes. To the end of his life in 2009 Arthur would return to this aspect in conversations with Keith Jenkinson. Why did they have to bayonet them to death?

L/Bdr Tom Jenkinson ('Tommy' to his mates) had an unlucky war. Recalled to the colours just two months short of the expiry of his Army Reserve status, he served continuously from 1 September 1939 until his death on 14 February 1942, surviving the retreat to Dunkirk but not the fall of Singapore. In those two years and five months, he probably only faced the enemy for less than two weeks at most, but was then killed on the last day of the fighting at Singapore. At the moment he faced death he must surely have felt that the Allies were going to lose the war, the military effort to halt the Japanese had failed badly, and as if all this were not enough, there is no surviving official account of how he and his men died.

After the war Mme Belval wrote several letters from France, first to Tom, asking for news, and then in reply to his wife's letter which had told her Tom had been killed in the Far East she wrote in one letter: '*We did love him so, and quite realize all your sorrow. He has been such a dear friend to us He was so brave too. One night we heard a noise a few hundred metres away from the farm and thought it was German parachutists. Tom and M. Belval went to investigate, Tom was running in front ready to fight.*'

Years later in 1988 Tom's grandson Patrick was spending six months on an undergraduate study placement near Lille. He knew the story of his grandfather's friendship with the Belval family and decided to pay them a visit. Although M. and Mme Belval were no longer alive, their son Edmond, who had been fourteen in 1940, now owned the farm. Because Patrick also knew the detail about the bottle of champagne, he had taken one with him and so returned the compliment that they had paid to the Jenkinson family in 1940. Edmond told Patrick stories about his grandfather and his mates and took him into the barn that had been their sleeping quarters. Incredibly the dartboard that the soldiers had used was still there. Edmond also recounted how the men used to send him to get their beer from the local 'estaminet'. Needless to say Patrick was very moved by this experience. In the first of the Belval letters to Mary Jenkinson they spoke of the bad time they had had under German occupation and how they had only been able with great difficulty to save Edmond from being sent to Germany for 'service obligatoire du travail' (forced labour).

Annex B

L/BDR R CURRIE NO. 843109

I am indebted to Nicholas Currie for the following story about his father's wartime experiences and permission to include it in the book of 6 HAA Regt RA.

Robert Currie was born in Glasgow in 1914 as the First World War was starting.

He became a stocky lad of 5ft 6 inches and kept himself fit. He joined the Army in 1935 for his compulsory service and ended up joining the Field Artillery where he was trained in gunnery and horse riding since at this time many guns were still drawn by a team of horses.

He loved the horses and became a good rider and a picture remains of him in uniform complete with shiny spurs and swagger stick.

Once his three years had been completed he then went on the reserves for a possible nine year call up in the case of an emergency. His speciality had been as a Physical Training Instructor (PTI) and he had a body that showed this.

However the Second World War came along in 1939 and he returned to volunteer for service under the Colours.

Once he had completed his basic indoctrination since he had been trained on field guns and not Anti Aircraft guns he was posted to 3 Bty of 6 HAA Regt.

Fig. B.1 Gnr Currie in 1933.
Courtesy of Nicholas Currie

They duly embarked for France as part of the BEF in September 1939 and he went wherever the unit was detailed.

Because he had been a driver before the war and was mechanically minded he ended up as a despatch rider carrying messages from HQ to HQ and also directing convoys when they were on the move.

When the BEF were bundled out of France after the German invasion he managed to get to the beaches at La Panne slightly north of Dunkirk.

He recalled later the sheer exhaustion of standing in a long line of troops, up to their armpits in freezing water as they snaked across the beaches awaiting rescue.

Fig. B.2 Gnr Currie in 1940.
Courtesy of Nicholas Currie

They had no defence against attacking planes and after seeing several men killed and blown up by bombing, and in fact being covered at one time by human entrails, they resigned themselves either to being lucky to escape or a quick death and oblivion.

Once back in England he followed 3 Bty down to Falmouth and eventually arrived in the Midlands at Penn Common during November 1940.

The site was a good one with close proximity to Wolverhampton for pubs and dance halls and being a good dancer (or so he claimed) he used to frequent the Palais de Dance in Temple Street.

Here the local ladies who were also discerning dancers and for whom only the best would do, used to turn up. Thus it was that Robert met his future wife. She was a farmer's daughter from Awbridge Farm in the nearby village of Trysull.

Half of 3 Bty went up to Hull for a large exercise in June taking four guns and all their men and on return he married in St Bartholomew's Church in Penn in July of 1941.

Not long after starting married life the unit was detailed off for duty in Iraq in November 1941 and by this time his wife was pregnant. She waved him off for a destination unknown not realising she would not see him again for not far short of four years.

The unit duly arrived in Singapore after having been diverted because of the Japanese invasion of Malaya. The Bty had to be re-equipped from local stocks and then were pushed out to join the defences of Singapore city inland from the area of Keppel Harbour.

They did not have long to wait for the Japanese to arrive. Each day they were subjected to air raids and once the Japanese were across the straights of Johore they pushed all before them into an ever tightening perimeter.

He recalled that towards the end they could see from the high ground they occupied the general fighting going on below them and watch the attackers advancing in their direction. Things were not going well and when an Officer told them there were Japanese troops operating all around them (and even behind them) and they were not taking prisoners, the seeds had been sown.

The Australian troops to their front were putting up a stout resistance but it was no use. By this time their guns were either non-operational or out of ammunition and rifles had been issued to the men with the aim of their becoming infantry. This was a new situation and many were not happy knowing that in a hand-to-hand fight the Japanese and his huge bayonet would always prevail. Some men threw down their rifles and prepared to be taken prisoner, a somewhat risky manoeuvre because the Japanese were not inclined to take men prisoner unless they had fought well.

Over the next few days Robert found himself with other members of the Bty defending a set of slit trenches close to a ridge line. In one trench was a lifelong mate, Gnr Tim Marshall (from Barrow) along with six other men.

During the course of heavy fighting by the Japanese a direct hit landed in the trench at the far end away from Tim and killed the six other men outright. It could have been a bomb, shell or mortar round but it buried Tim under debris and human parts.

Robert was called across in the emergency to help try and rescue anyone who might have survived. They found just one man, Tim, under the bodies, badly traumatised by the explosion and bleeding heavily from mouth and nose. He was also semi-paralysed from the concussion. He was removed carefully and taken down to a field hospital where he slowly regained some sensation in his damaged legs over the next two days.

It was while lying on his bed recovering that an Officer came round saying the Japanese were closing in and taking no prisoners and it was up to every man who could to make his way back to defence lines closer to Singapore centre. Thus Gnr Marshall, using every bit of his strength and helped by mates, made it slowly back a couple of miles to safety. They were to meet again on the Burma railway and remained lifelong 'buddies'.

By 14 February the situation was critical and on the 15th Singapore surrendered and everyone became a POW.

Robert marched with hundreds of others along the rubble-strewn streets to Changi Camp in the north east of the island.

[Once the fall of Singapore was announced in England and what Units were involved, so great was the shock for his wife that she went into labour weeks early and their son Nicholas was born in mid February 1942.]

Here they started to get used to the idea they were now POWs but a couple of months later at a big parade a large number were selected for duties elsewhere.

Because of his obvious fitness he unwittingly got selected to go with the first group out. They were marched down to Keppel Railway Station where after the usual chaos of being counted they embarked in metal-sided cattle wagons. Here started the 7-day trip up country to Thailand. The wagons were so packed that men were lying across each other and the heat was insufferable. Water and food on the journey were almost non-existent and those who had stomach upsets only filled the wagons with their waste.

They eventually arrived at Ban Pong and were then unloaded to march north into the jungle, sometimes having to cut down material to make camps.

At last they reached their destinations which were camps set along the route of the future Burma Railway which they now knew was going to be their work task. Very few men from 6 Regt had been chosen for this so he was rather unlucky.

Now started many months of sheer hell trying to survive on inadequate rations and contaminated water and being worked to death.

Once each section of railway was completed the camp was moved to the next area to start all over again. By the time he had reached another camp further along the line a large number of Australians were already there. These were the famous 'diggers' with their slouch hats whose unbreakable spirit helped maintain the morale of the men.

Everybody was detailed off for various duties and when a man went sick his position was offered to Robert by an 'Aussie'. This man had been responsible for fetching water from the nearby river in open containers and carrying it up from the river via a long flight of steep steps, a never ending task taking many hours each day. He had been warned at first it would cripple his calf muscles which he found quite true, but after a few days the pain eased and he got into the routine.

Another duty for which he was detailed was helping with the clearing of undergrowth and bushes in front of the track line.

The worst part of this was cutting down the ubiquitous bamboo clumps which once severed produced a sharp end to the cut section. One day due to fatigue he let slip a heavy section and it speared into his lower leg causing a bad wound, a wound that would take some time to heal under the climatic conditions.

Other duties which landed on many men were the burial parties. Anyone who had been a miner in civilian life kept very quiet about this to avoid being detailed off on a permanent basis for this strength-sapping duty of digging the holes.

Days and months went by and men died for all sorts of reasons including the many sicknesses. It was a test of human spirit and those with the best mindset had the most chance of coming through. Getting enough food was also a problem and the daily calorie intake was well below what was needed to keep body and soul together.

They were joined by others from 3 Bty in the summer of 1943 and by the end of September 1943, with the railway open, Robert was one of those chosen to be sent to Japan for forced labouring.

They all journeyed by train to Saigon where after being refused passage on the intended ship they hung around for weeks before being sent down to Singapore by the infamous train again.

Once in Singapore there was another long wait before being detailed for a convoy where the POWs were split between two ships for transit.

The ship he was loaded on was the *Kachidoki Maru* which a few days later was torpedoed and sunk by an American submarine with great loss of life. Amazingly he was one of the survivors and eventually rescued by a Japanese corvette and taken to Hainan from where a few days later they were loaded into a whaling factory ship (the *Kabibi Maru*) for onward shipment to Japan.

They arrived in Japan at the start of one of the coldest winters the Japanese had experienced wearing jungle clothes and shorts and many suffering serious diseases and malnutrition. Many were also ill from the effects of being immersed in fuel oil after the sinking. It got in their hair and mouths and stung their eyes and caused difficulty in breathing.

The first thing was to get ashore and then they were separated into groups and spread around a series of camps, none knowing where the others had gone.

His duty now was to become a lumberjack cutting down timber for the war effort, a duty he spent the rest of the war doing. In the early days the Japanese noticed how badly the men were shod and gave them instructions in how to make boots out of straw. At least these helped but once covered by snow they would only last a day. The lucky ones were also given ill-fitting tunics to help against the cold wind.

At last in August 1945 two bombs rescued him and the remainder from captivity.

In the confused state after Japan surrendered American planes flew over the camps dropping leaflets telling the men to stay where they were. The next problem was to drop food in containers to the emaciated POWs and also new clothing to replace the tatters they were wearing.

Once these tasks had been done Allied troops arrived on the ground to find out the true situation and were quite honestly horrified at what they found.

POWs were assessed and immediately some were moved by sea to hospital ships. Others were evacuated by air back to Rangoon and those who were considered slightly fitter were taken by train to Tokyo, a long trip which took them past the remains of Hiroshima. It was a sight Robert said he would never forget, a complete city flattened with hardly a thing standing and virtually no living thing. At the time they would not understand the meaning of the Atomic bomb but they had a first-hand view of what it could do.

Once they arrived at Tokyo Bay they were moved into a huge camp of tents for hundreds of POWs and ultimately back to England to pick up their lives again.

In Robert's case this meant seeing his young son for the very first time, who by now was coming up to four years old.

After the traumas of war Robert returned to lorry driving which he enjoyed till he retired.

Annex C

During his escape by sea Lt Col G.W.G. Baillie (previously Baass) C/O of 6 HAA Regt wrote up a report on 4 March 1942 of his conclusions as to the fighting in Sumatra and Java and some of the points that had been learnt.

How he managed to get away just before the capitulation (and why) has not been established, but he avoided three and a half years of captivity and hellish treatment.

He wrote:

(i) There can be no standard 'lay-out' for the defence of Aerodromes. Each must be treated as a separate tactical problem. In 'bush country' the defence should be based on the following principles

   (a) Troops allotted to the static defence of the perimeter should be in section posts sited for all round defence. The normal platoon and company organisation should be kept but there is no objection to platoons consisting of four sections and companies four platoons.

   (b) A high proportion of the available troops must be kept as a Mobile Reserve. This Reserve must be highly trained in Bush Warfare. Its role is to meet and destroy paratroops outside the area of static defence.

   (c) Posts sited for Perimeter defence must include the defence of Light A.A. Artillery

   (d) The R.A.F. ground staff should be trained and included in the static defence lay-out.

   (e) Close co-operation between the O/C ground defences and the Commander of the Heavy AA Artillery is essential.

   (f) Bren carriers are most useful on large landing grounds but they must be confined to it or to roads not bordered by trees.

(ii) Ground staff RAF should not leave the aerodrome at night to return to billets far away.

(iii) Heavy AA units must be prepared to defend themselves against ground attack.

     W.E. (weapons entitlement) of Heavy Batteries should be increased to allow personnel to be allocated for ground defence while the battery is in action against Enemy aircraft.

(iv) A high standard of weapon training in all AA units is essential.

(v) Unarmed men are a great liability and destroy the mobility and tactical freedom of the armed party. It is strongly recommended that the number of rifles be increased to allow all personnel to be armed.

Tommy guns should be allowed on a scale of one per gun when Batteries are operating in Bush Country.

(vi) It is not practicable to expect Gunners to be well trained infantry men, but there is no reason why a high standard of weapon training cannot be obtained. When operating in Bush Country they should receive elementary training in Bush warfare. At any rate they must know the Bush thoroughly within a radius of 2 miles from their gun sites. The value of this 'Bush Knowledge' is shown by the way 15 Bty were able to fight in the Bush and to withdraw in small parties.

(vii) It is vital that major tactical decisions should not be made on unconfirmed information.

(viii) The priority for A.A. defence tasks should be laid down by the highest formation having full information at their disposal. The method of carrying out these tasks and the allocation of guns to them should be left to the A.A.D.C on the spot who alone can know the local conditions.

Annex D

_____

HONOURS AND AWARDS FOR BRAVERY TO 6 HAA REGIMENT

During the course of their short existence, the Regiment was involved in several theatres of operations, namely as part of the ill-fated BEF, then Home Defence and finally in the Far East against the Japanese.

Nevertheless several awards for gallantry were made to individual members and published in the supplement of the *London Gazette*, the paper used for announcing such awards during and after the war. The awards were made for acts of gallantry which were witnessed and fulfilled the necessary criteria. This list in no way denies that there were also many other acts of bravery by the men of the Regt, just that the man and a suitable witness either both died or there was no suitable witness.

The highest awards made were generally the Military Cross for Officers (MC) and the Military Medal (MM) for other ranks.

In this respect the following awards were made during the course of the war.

Military Cross

Awarded to Lt Edwin Gilby No. 105870 of 15 Bty as part of the BEF. This report is filed at the National Archives at Kew under WO/373/15.

The citation in the *London Gazette* stated:

> On two occasions i.e. 12th and 13th May 1940 his gun position was attacked by formations of enemy aircraft numbering over thirty, in low level bombing. His example and disregard of danger were an inspiration to all ranks and although over two hundred bombs were dropped, no casualties were suffered and he kept his guns in action throughout.

Sadly he would die later in the Far East at the hands of the Japanese.

Military Cross

Awarded to Capt John Stuart Allpass No. 73393 of 6 Regt filed at Kew under WO/373/47.

This award was for a series of operations during the BEF days right through to Sumatra and then capture in Java and where he had risen from Lt to Capt in his career. The medal was awarded after his return from a POW camp in the Far East.

The citation reads:

For conspicuous leadership and coolness in the presence of the enemy on 14 Feb 1942 when the aerodrome at Palembang was attacked by a strong force of Japanese paratroops. This Officer first led a party (which had no grenades or automatic weapons) against a strongly held road block and then when the evacuation of the aerodrome was ordered, he assisted his Battery Commander in organising the evacuation with minimum loss of life. This was carried out under continuous harassing fire from snipers in which Major (then Captain) Allpass showed complete disregard for his own safety.

Both as a Subaltern in the operations leading up to the evacuation of Dunkirk; as a Captain when the Bty was on A.D.G.B. and in operations in Sumatra and latterly as a Bty Commander in Java, this Officer has shown remarkable keenness and organising ability. Indefatigable himself, and with the gift of getting men to follow him he could be relied on in any circumstances to produce the best results possible.

His soldierly qualities and perennial cheerfulness were a continual example and source of inspiration to his men in the Japanese mining camp at Ube, Japan, where he was the senior Officer from July 1943 to May 1945. His combination of firmness and tact in dealing with the Japanese authorities contributed very considerably to making the existence of the men less unhealthy and miserable, and he no doubt helped to reduce the loss of life.

Military Cross

Awarded to 2/Lt Kenneth Andrew Attiwill No. 151869 of 15 Bty. Filed under WO/373/47.

The citation reads:

This Officer was GPO (Gun position Officer) of a 4-gun Hy. A.A.site when it was heavily attacked by paratroops. After landing, the enemy opened fire by snipers who had climbed the trees to the south of the site. It was also threatened by direct fire from [a] Bofors gun which had been captured by the enemy and trained on the site. He directed the fire of his guns, shooting the snipers from the trees and destroying the Bofors together with its captors. His coolness under heavy fire and his determination to use his guns with the greatest aggression both in the sky and on the ground, so encouraged his detachments that both attacks were defeated and the guns were able to be withdrawn and saved.

Military Cross

Awarded to 2/Lt Lionel Derek Andrew No 151926 of 3 Bty 6HAA while attached to 3 HAA Regiment.
Filed at the National Archives at Kew under WO/373/47.
The citation reads:-

During the operations on SINGAPORE ISLAND, after his guns had been put out of action, this Officer commanded, on 13th February 1942 a rear party acting as infantry. In the face of continuous mortar and machine gun fire, and low level bombing by aircraft this Officer held his ground and successfully covered the withdrawal of troops on his flanks. Finally when closely attacked by enemy infantry on three sides 2 /Lt Andrew remained alone to allow his party to withdraw, displaying conspicuous courage and ability throughout the action.

Military Medal

Awarded to Sgt Harold Greenbank No 804010 of 15 Bty 6 HAA.
Filed under WO/373/47 at the National Archives.
The citation reads:-

For devotion to duty, outstanding courage in the face of the enemy, and the setting of a fine example by his display of leadership both whilst performing the duties of G.P.O.A. on the gun position and in action against the enemy in the subsequent evacuation of the gun position. His behaviour was such as to inspire confidence in his section who had little knowledge of infantry warfare, with the result that he was able to seek out and destroy Japanese Parachute troops and materially assist the Battery to reach PALEMBANG in safety. For the above outstanding efforts on 14th February 1942 I recommend he be awarded the Military Medal.

Military Cross awarded to Capt K. Campbell No. 85544 and for the same action a Military Medal awarded to Sgt Gilbert William Allen No 1072668 of 12 Bty 6 HAA.
Filed under WO/373/47 at the National Archives.
The citation reads:-

> For bravery, example and devotion to duty when the SS Subadar was attacked by enemy aircraft in the BANKA STRAITS on or about 2nd February 1942. Capt Campbell with Sgt ALLEN and a small party of men were in charge of some of the Regiment's guns and other heavy equipment being brought by SS Subadar from SINGAPORE to PALEMBANG, SUMATRA when the vessel was attacked by Japanese aircraft. The Indian gunners who were manning the ship's light machine guns fled, and Sgt ALLEN immediately followed Capt Campbell to the nearest gun and engaged the enemy who were both machine gunning and dive bombing. In spite of a bomb which fell into a hold in the immediate vicinity and set up a furious blaze, these two continued to fire their weapons and succeeded in destroying one plane and driving off the remainder. Immediately after Capt Campbell led a party to the blazing hold and succeeded in putting out the fire, thus saving much valuable equipment and possibly the vessel itself.

Member of the Order of the British Empire (MBE)

Awarded to Padre Capt. R Norman Harper-Holdcroft No 42421
Gazetted 30/5/1946 for valuable services in Japanese POW camps.

Military Medal

Awarded to Gunner John Hanson No. 847784 of 12 Bty for actions with the BEF.
The citation reads:-

> On the night 29/30 May 1940 at Bray Dunes although himself wounded by shell fire in the right arm continued to display conspicuous courage and devotion to duty under shell and M.G. fire, by assisting in carrying wounded on the beaches to the boats throughout the entire night.

(Sadly he would die in Java in 1942.)

Member of the Order of the British Empire (MBE)

Awarded to Sgt Powles No. 816995 15 Bty 6 HAA Regt for actions during the London Blitz.

> For rescuing the badly injured Officer 2/Lt Alberry after he was caught in an explosion when a bomb dropped in a raid hit a lorry full of 3.7" shells causing them to catch fire and explode.

Awarded to Gnr H. Orr No. 819108 of 15 Bty 6 HAA Regt for the same action in November of the London Blitz.

British Empire Medal (BEM)

At the end of the war after he had returned from captivity in a Japanese POW camp.

To Sgt Michael Purcell No. 845245 of 3 Bty.
His citation covers a long list of actions:

Purcell was captured on 13th February 1942 at Singapore and was subsequently imprisoned in Saigon in July 1944.

On 1st November 1944 he escaped from the camp with the aid of some French outside helpers and remained with them disguised as a Frenchman for the next three weeks. Then having received arms, he was taken to Phan Thiet and after three days boarded a Japanese troop train at Phan Rang.

He eventually arrived at Gi Lang where the final arrangements were to be made for his safe conduct to China.

About the 1st February 1945 Purcell was joined by some Americans who hoped to be evacuated by the French in a Submarine. This scheme fell through however and the whole party were moved on 3rd Feb to an airport at Pleiku where they waited for an aircraft to pick them up.

Owing to the French and Japanese fighting, the airport was rendered useless and the party were then informed that their only escape was to take to the jungle.

Accordingly they set off travelling from one French out-post to another and reached Tu Non in early March. Here they split up and Purcell and his companion set off to try and locate the Submarine, but were captured by the Japanese towards the end of April.

Having declared himself to be a member of the French Foreign Legion, Purcell was taken to Tourane where he was accused of being an American and beaten up during his interrogation. He escaped from prison that night and having crossed the river at Tourane was picked up by a large party of Annimites, who then handed him over to the Japanese.

This time Purcell was able to convince his captors of his nationality and being in very poor physical condition was taken to hospital at Hue where he remained until July 1945, and was later imprisoned there.

On 13th August 1945, Purcell was one of a number of prisoners being marched to Savanakhet when he and a companion escaped and successfully reached a party of friendly native troops at Phone Sime, who directed them to the Commander of a French guerrilla force who in turn conducted them to the forward allied force at Savanakhet.

Purcell showed tremendous courage and determination in spite of the many 'break-downs' in his escape organisation and was eventually successful through sheer perseverance.

Mention In Despatches (MID)

Normally awarded for actions or service where suitable witnesses were not present or those of a lesser risk, or where it was evident that great bravery must have occurred.

The Regt received no less than 42 of these.

For service during the BEF in France: a large number of awards were made, many to men from 15 Bty while they were attached to 1st HAA Regiment.

Captain AVS Channells
2/Lt Brian Reginald Emmett No. 71288 whose citation reads:

As Ass/Adjt for invaluable work and devotion to duty from the beginning of the war. This young Officer was entrusted with every form of task and performed them all cheerfully and most efficiently.

2/Lt J.A. Hibbert   2/Lt R.A.J Poole
2/Lt B.A.H. Pain
B.Q.M.S. N B. Holder No 1045173
T.S.M. V. Bancroft No 808426
S/Sgt J R McWade No 833552
Sgt C. Baguley No 835404   Sgt L Greystone No 1426503
Sgt W. Jones No 819832   Sgt EWG Breakspear No 1072937
Sgt J. Dougherty No 779231   Sgt Powels No 816995
Sgt F. Holdaway No 863237   L/Sgt F. Cutsforth No 818313

L/Sgt J F Calloway No 842373   L/Sgt A E Powles No 816995
L/Sgt E D Villiers No 7876419

Bdr J S Greatrix No 1425040   Bdr S. Hooper No 819795
Bdr L F Durn No 821217
L/Bdr W J Jones No 819832
L/Bdr W H Knights No 3382993   L/Bdr S.J.Back No 790601
Gnr N D Andrews No 7257484   Gnr B. Blizzard No 784394
Gnr A.G. Buck No 788256   Gnr E. Harrison No 4513616
Gnr A.W. Chapman No 1517766
Gnr S. Fosberry No 828656   Gnr R. Pate No 3382145
Gnr Mitchell No 4746410   Gnr L. A. Smith No 1512936
Gnr F. Pardoe No 788876   Gnr W. Taylor No 3649555

For actions in Sumatra and Java
Maj. E.J. Hazel No 34632 (Java)
Maj G.A. Moxon No 13435 (Java)
Maj. N. Coulson No 67887 (Posthumously Java)
T/Capt W.L. Sherrard. No 74545 (Posthumously Sumatra/Pladjoe)
Sgt. J.J. Keevil No 805169 (Posthumously Java)
Gnr A.F.J. Lewington No 5496011

Annex E

I am indebted to Jocelyn Hayward (née Seager) for details about her late father, 2/Lt Seager of 15 Bty, and for permission to use pictures from her private collection.

In April 1939 when the storm clouds were gathering over Europe, John Ross Seager (b. 1911) enlisted as Gunner 1452324 in the Royal Artillery TA. He was a quiet studious man with striking good looks and working at the time in Insurance in Liverpool. His immediate posting was to 309 Bty of 70 AA Regt and by December 1939, after war had been declared, he was appointed L/Bdr. He had shown aptitude for promotion and was deemed suitable for Officer training. So in November 1940 he was posted to Western Unit 133 Officer Cadet Training Unit. On completion he left with a commission on 22 February 1941 and joined 8 AA Reserve Regt at Cleethorpes. Hardly had he arrived than he was posted to join 15 Bty of 6 HAA who at the time were based on Penn Common in the Midlands.

Fig. E.1 Lt John Ross Seager of 15 Bty marrying Barbara Reeves (postwar). Courtesy of Jocelyn Hayward (née Seager)

They had spent months in France and suffered the fiasco of Dunkirk, then some months on port protection in the south of England followed by the London Blitz.

After the devastating attack on Coventry in November 1940 they had been moved to the Midlands to help protect Wolverhampton and

Birmingham and they had been on the Common for some three months before he arrived.

It was not unusual for local businessmen to ease the hardships of gun site life by asking Officers to visit for meals and relaxation. It was thus that John found himself at Bearnett House, the large palatial home of a successful company director called Frederick Reeves. He owned the production company REVO, based in Tipton, making lighting poles and a great variety of electrical equipment.

John was immediately smitten by Frederick's eldest daughter Barbara and a serious friendship ensued. He had still to move from place to place with his Battery as dictated by AA Command, but by 1941, when the unit was under orders for Iraq, he was engaged to marry Barbara with the under-standing the wedding would take place on his return.

Fig. E.2 Lt Arthur Steeds of 15 Bty (postwar).
Courtesy of Jocelyn Hayward (née Seager)

By this time he had become very good friends with two other Subalterns from 15 Bty, 2/Lt Arthur Steeds and 2/Lt Ken Attiwill, and these three were to remain lifelong friends. The convoy carrying the 18th Division, which included 6 HAA, docked in mid-January 1942 in Singapore having being diverted from Iraq to aid the defences of the island after the Japanese attacked Malaya.

After the briefest of stays ashore it was decided to send 12 and 15 Btys to Sumatra leaving 3 Bty behind. Their remit was to defend two airfields and some refinery installations at Palembang.

As their ship entered the Moesi river estuary leading to Palembang their CO gave a pep talk to all Officers on board making it clear that they were entering a country run by Dutch Military forces, who were to be known as Hollanders, and they were to be respected and saluted as normal protocol. Venereal disease was prevalent and all men were to be warned off from fraternising with the local females. (A not unusual military ploy.)

Once ashore what guns they had were taken north to Palembang Airfield known as P1 while some were sent across the river to another airfield called

P2 some 40 miles away. It was intended to use the rest when they came to defend the refineries.

John and his colleague Ken set up their newly acquired 3.7" HAA guns to the west of the airfield while Arthur and (another subaltern) Geoff Crawford set theirs up to the south. It was a desperate time with the Japanese pushing all before them down the Malayan mainland and they had to try to acclimatise in a hot humid and rain-sodden climate. These scant resources were totally inadequate for the job in hand, and they had virtually no ammunition either. Accommodation was in native-built huts or tents, the latter being regularly flooded out, and mosquitoes in vast hordes made life a misery.

Some of the guns were sited on the edge of rubber plantations and the rest amongst thick scrub. The landscape was generally flat and consisted of jungle interspersed with cleared areas of cultivation and native huts, but much was swampy ground. The only bright spot was they could supplement their bland Army rations with an abundance of pineapples, bananas, limes and vegetables.

They made friends with some Hollander Officers and went into Palembang for drinks and a meal at the Palembang Club. What was rather worrying was the very obvious mutual distrust and lack of confidence between the Hollanders and the British.

By the end of the first week the Japanese raids on P1 were daily occurrences and the lack of ammunition and few fighters based there meant the attackers had the sky virtually to themselves. Once Singapore's dire situation could be seen there was no reason to think the Japanese would not invade Sumatra as well. Attempts were made to teach the men some sort of infantry drills but the issuing of personal weapons was woefully inadequate.

By 13 February ominous warnings from intelligence put everyone on high alert. Heavier bombing raids took place but the Hurricane fighters managed to shoot down a Japanese Zero which crashed in flames close behind the southern guns. John and some of the rest went to look at the charred remains still containing the pilot.

On the morning of Saturday 14 February, whilst Singapore prepared to capitulate, they witnessed a large flight of Hudson aircraft come over. However these were not friendly as expected and almost immediately multiple blobs could be seen dropping from them as Japanese Parachutists tumbled out. Taken by surprise the 3.7" took a little while to react but the odd Bren light machine gun opened up ineffectual firing.

Without the necessary range and height finding equipment John and Ken's guns had to fire over open sights as best they could while Arthur set about gathering together elements of HQ personnel to guard the nearby cross roads. The parachutists were not in the air for long and once landed started to form up but mostly out of sight of the guns. There were sounds of firing of the heavier shells and much small arms fire from different directions showing in the confused state that men were making contact with invaders.

Once sniping started, Ken used the ploy of firing shells at the ground below their positions to shift them. It was a chaotic situation with total lack of information as to what was going on.

By mid-morning the gun crews had sustained casualties and several dead and then orders came through to withdraw what guns could be salvaged and disable the rest. John's crew hastily packed what stores they could and started off down the road on foot and by vehicle towards Palembang. They passed the cross roads which HQ were trying to guard. They had not gone far before they ran into the remains of a road block set up by the Japanese and found themselves taking cover in the road side ditches as the ambush played out.

John met up with Arthur and Ken who were trying to gather men together with personal weapons so as to outflank the Japanese positions which were in some huts at the top of a rise. During this chaotic time and before the Japanese could be dislodged Lt G Crawford was hit and killed by a sniper close alongside the road.

By this time the Japanese had managed to capture a Dutch armoured car and used this to block the road, but once they came under accurate Bren gun fire they fled and most were killed as they ran. This seemed to clear the air for the moment and the shooting tailed off.

Ken, Arthur and John then started to organise the clearing of an over-turned lorry so that the men could start to make their way through to Palembang. Many eventually reached the town while others who had been told to make their way through the scrub kept coming in dribs and drabs during the night.

By next day with one 3.7" gun guarding the ferry across the river all troops were told to make their way to P2 which was being guarded by elements of 12 Bty. By this time most guns had been disabled or abandoned again. The bottleneck of the ferry took many hours to clear but once at P2, later that day, further orders were received for everyone to head for the station with the intention of reaching Oosthaven, the port in the south. Trains made the trip using cattle trucks to hold as many men and stores as possible and finally reached their destination of the docks many hours later.

The troopship *Yoma* was selected for their use and after being loaded to the gunwales set off for Java. Other ships brought further men and stores. The Officers managed to find cabins whereas the men had to find any spot on the decks they could. Rumours abounded as to their destination and many hoped it was Australia.

On arrival in Batavia the next day, John and some of the others left for Meestor Cornelius Barracks to get things ready for the rest. It had been decided that from then on the unit would fight as infantry, a somewhat unusual role for men trained as gunners. Since the *Yoma* stayed at anchor out in the harbour for two days it was not until after this that everyone got off and joined up at the Dutch Barracks.

An attempt was made to try and discover how many casualties they had taken and to tally up missing men. It was then decided to split the remaining forces so that 12 Bty under Major Coulson would go to Kalidjati airfield while 15 Bty would drive the 100 miles to Bandoeng for some more training. 15 Bty arrived at the Dutch barracks of Tijimahi, which they found almost empty. Extra weapons were issued and infantry training began under instructors who had escaped from Malaya. This was all alien to the Gunners but they did their best to follow instructions.

After a short time the next move was to go north to the airfield at Tjililitan using a great variety of loaned vehicles including some Humber armoured cars. They arrived at the airfield to find the Australians who had been there in the process of pulling out to rejoin their main unit. That night John and some off-duty Officers went into town to the Harmony Club for a drink not realising that this was to be the last chance for some considerable time.

Next day the Japanese landed in the north of the island and the Battery was ordered to drive to Soakabemi. Convoys travelled and stopped and started again with no one really knowing what was going on, and eventually they were ordered back to Tijimahi. At this point the Officers were advised that their CO, Col. Baillie, had left and the Unit was now under the command of Col. Hazel (promoted from Major). The next instruction was to go south to the airfield of Andhir. They had seen no Japanese and not even fired any shots. They now found out that 12 Bty had suffered many casualties in its defence of Kalidjati and their OC, Maj. Coulson, had been killed.

It was then decided to concentrate all available forces in the south round Tasikmalaja, so convoys headed in that direction along narrow congested roads. Further wanderings in this chaotic situation found the unit at Garoet. During one stop Arthur recorded that John had been sent off to buy food

Fig. E.3 Some of 6th HAA Officers with other Officers shortly after release from Motoyama Camp, Japan, 1945. Standing at rear from left: -?-, -?-, -?-, -?-, -?-, -?-, -?-, -?-, Lt Ken Attiwill, -?-, -?-, Lt John Seager, -?-, -?-. Their legs display severe signs of malnourishment.

Courtesy of Jocelyn Hayward (née Seager)

and stores and came back with a brand new watch to replace his own which had been left in haste at a Palembang jeweller's for repair.

Not long after the Dutch capitulated, leaving the British forces in a difficult situation; and then the orders went out to stop fighting – somewhat difficult for the Regt which had never really started. This news was heard by John and the others in Garoet while seated having a coffee on the verandah of a house.

The unit now did an about turn and headed north towards Japanese lines. It was a melancholy affair since they knew they were now POWs and had contributed nothing to the defence of Java. When the advance guard was found they then disarmed and with a Japanese escort made for Batavia where they were all directed into a large camp at Tanjong Priok. Men were allocated huts and accommodation and the three Officers managed to stay together, each finding a space on the concrete floor.

One of the first things the Japanese did was to record who they had captured, so everyone was issued a number. John must have been close to the front of the queue because he became POW 13.

As the days drew on a routine developed within the camp, but then the Japanese demanded large quotas of men to work in the docks loading and unloading ships. Because of the large amount of time spent doing nothing many men had to find ways of keeping their minds active. Arthur commented on John's ability to shut the world out and concentrate on playing innumerable games of patience or bridge and chess. He was able to withdraw into silent contemplation and seemed quite happy while doing this. Many people smoked and cigarettes became valuable currency with all sorts of items being traded by those desperate for a smoke. Amazingly Ken still had his typewriter which had been lugged along with each stop and he merrily typed out his diary, letters and plays later on. Hiding this valuable resource kept the best minds occupied.

The poor diet of rice and the lack of vitamins caused many skin infections and it was about three months into captivity that John started to show signs of sores on his arms, fingers and legs. These eventually healed but left permanent scars. The camp was never free from sickness and diarrhoea or the many diseases brought in by mosquitoes. At one point the Padre (Harper-Holdcroft) went down with dengue fever and had to be hospitalised. Despite being seriously under the weather he never lost his composure. His main project was to build a Chapel in the open air to hold services and he used the other men to help him to achieve this.

Later, around September, the Japanese ordered all ranks to have close

Fig. E.4 A group of 6th HAA 15 Bty men and Officers on release from Motoyama Camp, 1945. Courtesy of Jocelyn Hayward (née Seager)

cropped haircuts, this helped with hygiene and also to stop lice. In October large-scale movements of POWs started and John and the rest of 15 Bty found themselves on the *Singapore Maru* and on their way to Japan. Like all those cooped up he suffered sickness, but managed to stay in relatively good shape. (The full details of this period are contained in Chapter 8.)

As the war progressed life in the POW camp at Ube had settled into a regular routine. Men had been divided into shifts and spent long hours working in the local coal mines. This was hard and dangerous work carried out on a diet of rice. And working underground meant everyone breathed in the abrasive coal dust, thus affecting their health. John's attitude was that what was good enough for his men was good enough for him and he spent much time underground supervising and working with them.

One thing they lacked during captivity was fresh produce to go with their daily rice. Gardens were set up on any free space and a couple of pigs reared for their meat. John's contribution was a few scrawny hens which had been acquired but which did in fact supply a regular three or four eggs daily.

After three and a half years as a POW the atom bombs in August 1945 finally brought their suffering to an end. Once they had been found by Allied forces the most seriously sick were transferred to hospital ships or medical camps set up for this purpose. John, although very malnourished as they all were, was examined and thought to have a lung infection brought on by inhalation of dust or possibly TB.

His route home was via Manila on an American ship. Here he started to write letters home, especially to his fiancée. He had no idea whether she was still waiting, since she had no idea if he was alive or dead after such a long delay. His letters which survive are full of hope and expectation of getting home as soon as possible. He realises he is still in the Army but will have to replace his kit. In one from Manila dated 1 October 1945 he says "the only item of my kit I still retain is my service cap" and he requests his brother to loan him some clothes on his arrival. On 9 October 1945 his ship called in at Corregidor, the last fortress on the Philippines to hold out, and he had a brief chance to look round. By 29 October 1945 he says, "we hope to arrive in San Francisco on 1st Nov and take a train across America to catch the Queen Mary on the East coast and be back in the UK by Nov. 20th." However because of the large number of POWs, arrangements were changed and they are off loaded at Vancouver. He is desperate to get a cable off to his Barbara to reassure her.

In another he says how impressed he and Arthur are with Canada and the

Fig. E.5 Part of 15 Bty with their Officers on release from Motoyama POW camp, 1945. Seated, second row from the left: -?-, -?-, -?-, -?-, -?-, -?-, -?-, -?-, -?-, Lt John Seager, Lt Arthur Steeds, Lt Ken Attiwill, -?-, -?-. Courtesy of Jocelyn Hayward (née Seager)

Fig. E.6 More of 15 Bty with their Officers on release from Motoyama Camp, 1945. Seated, Second row from the left: -?-, -?-, -?-, -?-, -?-, Lt Arthur Steeds, -?-, -?-, -?-, -?-, Lt John Seager, -?-, Lt Ken Attiwill, -?-, -?-. Courtesy of Jocelyn Hayward (née Seager)

people's hospitality; they are entertained by the Bishop of Vancouver Island to lunch. He comments, "The Bishop was a very broad minded and entertaining person and did not feel his gaiters required him to abstain from the so called minor vices of life!!"

In another he requests that those at home don't go rushing out trying to obtain special luxuries and spending a lot of money. (Showing how out of touch he was with the situation in the UK.)

The next day there was a farewell party for the CO and some of the other Officers as they were leaving before his group. They spent 5 days crossing Canada by train and arrived at Halifax where he was again medically examined. His worries on TB were relaxed but he still had trouble with his chest. Eventually he reached the UK and finally home where his condition must have caused great anxiety, for he was still not a well man and very underweight. He spent time in several medical facilities before an operation to remove a lung. He did marry his Barbara and his best man was his great friend Arthur Steeds. Thereafter he was paid a pension by the Army before relinquishing his commission.

In 1948 he was offered a sinecure job on the board of REVO and was delighted at the birth of two daughters, one in 1959 the other in 1961. He continued to suffer for the rest of his life from the deprivations of Japanese treatment and to smoke more than he should, and sadly as a comparatively young man he died in 1972.

Annex F

The men from the Regiment who were involved with the ambush at Palembang, Sumatra. 14/2/42:

Gnr Baines	No. 1427339	Wounded
Gnr T. Bishop	No. 1738003	Wounded
Gnr H. Blackburn	No.1892076	Wounded
Bdr J.W. Brackley	No. 786408	Fatally injured
Gnr R. Branter	No.1426530	Fatally injured
Dvr E. Coates	No. 156381	Wounded
Dvr R.C. Earland	No. 812459	Wounded
Dvr W.E Finch	No.1697897	Wounded
Gnr D.A. Hollingsworth	No. 1428422	Fatally injured
L/Bdr S.H. Legg	No. 797787	Fatally injured
Gnr W.J. McVey	No. 1713742	Fatally injured
Gnr T.V. Morrissey	No. 872435	Seriously wounded
L/Bdr L.N. Oliver	No. 1580675	Seriously wounded
Gnr E.R. Owles	No. 794914	Wounded
Gnr J. Rennie	No. 826602	Fatally injured
L/Bdr F. Seabrook	No. 1072029	Fatally injured
Gnr H. Towhills	No. 2065053	OK
Gnr P. Walsh	No. 3382944	OK

The tables that follow have been compiled from many sources but bring the names together for the first time so that an easy search can be made of men from just 6 HAA Regt RA.

3 BTY ROLL OF HONOUR

Name	Other names	Rank	Date Died	Service No.	Death Location/ Memorial site
ALLISON	John	GNR	01/10/1942	1460879	Singapore
AMIES	Sydney George	L/BDR	21/12/1943	1063331	Kanchanaburi
BAILEY	J.E.	MAJ	13/2/1942	47825	Singapore
BALL	Kenneth Stanley	GNR	05/03/1943	1817008	Ballale Island
BANKS	Walter	GNR	12/09/1944	1427472	*Rakuyo Maru*
BARBER	John Henry	GNR	27/08/1944	55914	Borneo
BAREHAM	Harry Walter	GNR	14/02/1942	1764021	Singapore
BARLOW	Henry	GNR	05/03/1943	3857636	Ballale island
BARMBY	Wilfred	GNR	12/09/1944	842520	*Rakuyo Maru*
BARNARD	Harry Reginald	L/SJT	12/09/1944	819377	*Rakuyo Maru*
BARNEY	F.D.	2/LT	11/02/1942	165296	Singapore
BARTON	Francis	GNR	11/10/1943	1695561	Kanchanaburi
BEARD	John	GNR	29/09/1940	4907186	Drowned Cornwall
BERRY	Dare	GNR	18/07/1945	1580612	Kanchanaburi
BLAKEY	Frederick William Thomas	GNR	12/09/1944	2049365	Kachidoki Maru
BURDETT	Avery John Stoke	GNR	22/07/1941	824663	UK
BURNS	Walter Robert	GNR	12/09/1944	791869	*Rakuyo Maru*
CARD	William Frederick	GNR	05/03/1943	1646045	Ballale Island
CARTER	Frank Ernest	GNR	05/02/1942	1696381	Singapore
CHATWELL	James	GNR	13/06/1943	818750	Rabaul
CLARKE	Alfred	GNR	05/03/1943	1818221	Ballale Island
COLHOUN	Richard Campbell	GNR	12/09/1944	819047	*Kachidoki Maru*
CORLETT	Percy	GNR	04/08/1943	1524187	Burma Railway
DAVIES	John Vincent	GNR	07/12/1943	1817055	Kanchanaburi
DAVIES	Trevor	GNR	01/02/1944	798297	Kanchanaburi
DEW	John Walter	GNR	14/02/1942	1789479	Singapore
DIXON	William George	L/BDR	09/04/1945	1425594	Burma Railway
DOBBINS	Alfred Edward	GNR	13–15/02/1942	1817065	Singapore
DOWNEND	Frank	GNR	13/02/1942	1427173	Singapore
EDWARDS	Harry Dudley	GNR	24/10/1944	797196	Kanchanaburi
ELLIS	James	GNR	09/05/1943	1818009	Kanchanaburi
EVANS	William John	GNR	22/12/1943	1817086	Kanchanaburi
EVANS	Evan Gwyn	GNR	21/11/1943	1818014	Kanchanaburi
EVANS	William Ernest	GNR	14/10/1943	1719549	Chungkai
FEATHERSTONE	Albert Edward	GNR	21/09/1944	824772	*Hofuku Maru*
FISHER	Frank	GNR	13/02/1942	3529020	Singapore
FOSTER	Oscar	L/BDR	12/09/1944	797474	*Rakuyo Maru*
FOULKES	Kenneth	SJT	12/09/1944	828643	*Kachidoki Maru*

Name	Other names	Rank	Date Died	Service No.	Death Location/ Memorial site
FROWEN	William John	GNR	05/04/1942	1818240	Java
GARDNER	Leonard Victor	GNR	13/02/1942	6345522	Chungkai
GILLINGHAM	Allan George	GNR	05/04/1942	1757759	Singapore
GINN	Henry Robert	GNR	05/03/1943	1414579	Ballale Island
GREGORY	F.W.	BDR	12/09/1944	827092	*Kachidoki Maru*
GRIFFIN	William James	GNR	07/06/1945	1726216	Borneo (Kuching)
GRIFFITHS	Farnham	GNR	05/03/1943	1817097	Ballale Island
GUDGE	Richard Alfred	GNR	07/09/1942	1427473	Saigon
HABBAJAM	Albert	GNR	29/09/1940	788534	Drowned Cornwall
HALL	Arthur William	GNR	07/11/1943	1725610	Chungkai
HARRISON	Sydney Samuel	L/BDR	18/04/1943	1793693	Saigon. Drowned
HATTER	Walter Allwood	SJT	12/09/1944	781576	*Kachidoki Maru*
HEANAN	John	GNR	05/03/1943	1609683	Ballale Island
HERRING	Horace John	GNR	12/09/1944	822309	*Kachidoki Maru*
HILL	Sydney George	GNR	12/09/1944	1643289	*Kachidoki Maru*
HINSLEA	Frederick Richard	BDR	12/09/1944	1467422	*Kachidoki Maru*
HOLMES	Charles Thomas	GNR	02/05/1943	1720230	Rabaul
HOOPER	Eric	GNR	05/03/1943	2052781	Ballale Island
HUGHES	Charles Edward	GNR	29/09/1940	797795	Drowned Cornwall
HUNTER	William	GNR	13/02/1942	1427112	Singapore
HUNTER	James	SJT	05/03/1943	835260	Ballale Island
HUNTER	John Edward	GNR	14/02/1942	1426245	Singapore
JACOBS	Thomas Henry	GNR	26/08/1945	1580786	Kanchanaburi
JENKINSON	Thomas	L/BDR	14/02/1942	1073904	Singapore
JOHNSON	Frederick	L/BDR	25/09/1943	5044523	Klian Krai
JOHNSON	Albert	GNR	12/09/1944	3855392	Kanchanaburi
JOHNSON	William	GNR	22/05/1940	1071399	France/Belgium
JONES	Norman	GNR	10–11/02/1942	1427229	Singapore
KIDD	George	GNR	29/09/1940	851198	Drowned Cornwall
LAMB	Donald	L/BDR	05/03/1943	815566	Ballale Island
LEDGER	Charles	GNR	14/02/1942	4120319	Singapore
LLOYD	Charles Roger	GNR	05/10/1943	1817153	Chungkai
MacARTHUR	James	GNR	12/09/1944	1517153	*Kachidoki Maru*
MATTHEWS	John James	GNR	12/09/1944	1528640	*Kachidoki Maru*
MAYES	George Henry	GNR	09/08/1944	1643440	Borneo
McAUGHTRIE	Thomas	GNR	05/03/1943	838982	Ballale island
MCCLUSKEY	John	GNR	14/02/1942	797650	Singapore
McGOUGH	James Hartley	GNR	01/03/1943	1610200	Ballale island
McGUIRE	Joseph	GNR	24/02/1943	3308390	Rabaul
MERCER	Frederick William	GNR	10–11/02/1942	1696515	Singapore
MODERATE	James Roger	GNR	05/03/1943	821579	Ballale island
MORGAN	William Cecil	BDR	11/02/1942	809651	Singapore
MOSS	Ronald Arthur	GNR	13/02/1942	1766373	Singapore
MULLEN	Richard	GNR	29/09/1940	809983	Drowned Cornwall
MURPHY	James	GNR	06/11/1942	826416	Rabaul
MURPHY	James Edward	GNR	05/03/1943	1537327	Ballale Island
NICKOLAY	George Arthur William	GNR	16/04/1945	1817324	Kanchanaburi

Name	Other names	Rank	Date Died	Service No.	Death Location/ Memorial site
NUTTY	Edward	GNR	14/02/1942	11053546	Singapore Kranji
OXBY	Owen Reginald	GNR	14/02/1942	323095	Singapore
PADFIELD	Roderick Frank	GNR	21/11/1944	1726135	Borneo
PEARSON	Harold	GNR	14–15/02/1942	877738	Singapore
POWELL	Albert	GNR	02/07/1943	864377	Chungkai
PRICE	Jeffrey	GNR	29/05/1945	839426	Kanchanaburi
READ	George Thomas	GNR	08/08/1942	872454	Saigon
REID	William	GNR	11/12/1943	2872020	Kanchanaburi
RHODES	Eric Peter Geoffrey	GNR	27/11/1943	1427109	Kanchanaburi
RICKETTS	Charles	GNR	25/10/1943	777867	Kanchanaburi
ROBERTS	Edward Arthur	SJT	03/09/1942	545610	Saigon
ROBINSON	Edwin Thomas	GNR	13–14/02/1942	826502	Singapore
RUDDICK	George Edward	GNR	13/06/1943	788969	Kanchanaburi
RUSHTON	Albert	GNR	19/10/1943	781602	Kanchanaburi
SCOTT	James Henderson	GNR	12/09/1944	1489680	Rakuyo Maru
SEDDON	William	GNR	29/07/1943	1733567	Kinsaiyok camp
SKIVINGTON	George Leslie	GNR	02/01/1947	779821	UK after war
SOAR	William Godfrey	Lt	11/11//1943	148038	Tarsao camp
SOUTTER	William Albert	L/BDR	20/01/1943	836697	Rabaul
STADDEN	William	GNR	07/04/1943	1716837	New Britain
STANLEY	Charles	GNR	01/06/1942	1068356	Far East
STAPLES	Albert Edward	GNR	12/09/1943	1643356	Kanchanaburi
STRATTON	William Sydney George	GNR	17/04/1942	1736017	Rangoon
STUART	David Arthur	GNR	12/09/1944	1800894	Rakuyo Maru
STUCHFIELD	Challis Crescens Charles	L/BDR	14/02/1942	4529905	Singapore
TINGLEY	Frank	GNR	11/02/1945	1726151	Yokahama Sentai 9
VAUGHAN	David	GNR	01/12/1943	790353	Chungkai
WARD	Charles William	SJT	06/11/1942	1061364	Rabaul
WATERS	William John	GNR	12/09/1944	1643490	*Kachidoki Maru*
WEAVER	Ronald	GNR	13/10/1943	1749569	Chungkai
WEEKS	Henry Albert	GNR	12/08/1945	1818167	Borneo (Kuching)
WHEBLE	Jack	GNR	07/08/1944	1643497	Kranji
WHEELER	George Henry	GNR	19/08/1945	790021	Fukuoka No 9
WHITEHOUSE	Frederick John	GNR	10/08/1943	790388	Chungkai
WHYATT	Christopher Charles	L/BDR	05/03/1943	1793534	Ballale Island
WILKINSON	Dennis Wilfred	Lt	14/02/1942	85514	Singapore
WILLSON	William John	GNR	05/03/1943	1561724	New Britain
WILSON	William James	GNR	01/10/1943	3646346	Kanchanaburi
WILTSHIRE	Albert Leslie	GNR	09/04/1945	868713	Borneo (Kuching)
WINDOWS	Harry Bernard	LT	05/03/1943	172485	Balalle Island

12 BTY ROLL OF HONOUR

Name	Other names	Rank	Date Died	Service No.	Death Location/ Memorial site
ADAMS	John Edgar	T/Maj.	01/03/1942	151925	Java (commem Jakarta)
BACKWAY	Percy William	GNR	25/11/1942	1426424	Ship 'B' Java–Singapore
BAKER	William	L/SJT	22/11/1942	812965	*Singapore Maru*
BARKER	George Frederick	GNR	24/06/1944	1817009	*Tamahoko Maru*
BARRON	Llewellyn	GNR	01/06/1940	815637	Dunkirk
BECK	Alexander	GNR	31/5 – 2/6/1940	3184334	France
BELSHAW	John Reginald	GNR	04/12/1942	1568459	Fukuoka No 4
BERRY	Herbert	GNR	14/12/1942	842755	Fukuoka No 5/ 6a
BILBIE	Samuel	GNR	02/08/1943	1808154	Burma Railway
BIRDSALL	Charles	GNR	04/08/1942	4264235	Indonesia
BODDY	Herbert George	L/BDR	30/07/1945	781252	Borneo (Kuching)
BOND	Clifford George	GNR	01/03/1942	1817015	Java/Sumatra
BOSWELL	Arthur	GNR	29/11/1943	1734919	*Suez Maru*
BOYLE	Thomas	GNR	28/11/1942	790912	Fukuoka No 4
BRIDGES	Walter Henry	GNR	02/12/1942	822282	Fukuoka No 4
BURDETT	Harry	GNR	01/03/1942	1502840	Java. Kalidjati
BURTON	Ernest	GNR	23/09/1943	1805836	Kanchanaburi
CARR	Frank	GNR	01/03/1942	1676375	Kalidjati (Java)
CASTLE	George Henry	L/BDR	04/08/1945	1817292	Borneo (Labuan)
CHARLES	John	GNR	25/07/1945	1472376	Ranau (Borneo)
CHARLES	Sidney Edward George	GNR	18/07/1945	805194	Borneo (Kuching)
CLARKE	William	GNR	06/12/1942	402224	Fukuoka No 4
CONQUEST	Bertram Edward	GNR	01/03/1942	1502871	Kalidjati (Java)
CORLETT	John	L/BDR	01/03/1942	815098	Kalidjati (Java)
CORNICK	Ernest	GNR	04/07/1945	815103	Sumatra (Jakarta)
COSTELLO	Frederick	GNR	01/06/1940	791060	France
COULSON	Nevil	Maj	01/03/1942	67887	Kalidjati (Java)
CROSS	Ivor John	GNR	02/12/1944	1817036	USA St Louis (**)
CRUTCHLOW	Noah	GNR	01/03/1942	1502883	Kalidjati (Java)
CUNNINGHAM	Kenneth Gordon	GNR	19/08/1943	822663	Chungkai (Burma R'way)
DANIELS	Albert	GNR	30/07/1945	1502885	Borneo (Kuching)
DAVIES	Abraham Isaac	GNR	23/07/1942	1817040	Jakarta (Java)
DEACON	Richard Thomas	GNR	01/03/1942	7144475	Kalidjati (Java)
DEACON	George Arthur	GNR	30/11/1942	1426634	*Singapore Maru*
DECIECO	Lionel	GNR	01/06/1940	826423	France
DEEPROSE	Reginald Alfred	GNR	01/03/1942	1797526	Kalidjati (Java)
DOBSON	George James	GNR	09/07/1945	545292	Sumatra
DUDDY	John James	GNR	25/05/1940	777887	Dunkirk
DYER	Thomas	L/SJT	26/08/1942	856715	Java
EATON	Ralph	GNR	30/10/1943	847359	Borneo (Kuching)
EDWARDS	Frank	BSM	07/03/1940	1419624	France (Self Inflicted)

Name	Other names	Rank	Date Died	Service No.	Death Location/ Memorial site
FAIRFAX	William	BDR	08/12/1942	545131	Fukuoka No 4
FAIRS	Maurice Richard	GNR	01/03/1942	988051	Kalidjati (Java)
FENNEY	George Nicholas	GNR	11/12/1942	4387270	*Singapore Maru* (illness)
FITZPATRICK	Michael	GNR	15/06/1943	847418	Ambon
FORREST	Arthur Stanley	GNR	01/03/1942	1738779	Kalidjati (Java)
FRANCIS	George	GNR	01/03/1942	1580883	Kalidjati (Java)
FRY	William Henry	GNR	01/03/1942	1811648	Kalidjati (Java)
FRYER	Harry	GNR	01/03/1942	822003	Kalidjati (Java)
GARDNER	Thomas	GNR	01/03/1942	4447406	Kalidjati (Java)
GIBBS	Johnson W	GNR	12/06/1945	406212	Sumatra
GORE	Albert Edward	GNR	01/03/1942	1817395	Kalidjati (Java)
GRAVES	Arthur James	GNR	01/06/1940	868752	France
GRIFFITHS	William Samuel	GNR	13/12/1942	1817099	Fukuoka No 4
HAERTOCK	Charles	L/BDR	01/06/1940	6455922	Dunkirk
HAINSWORTH	Ronald	GNR	01/06/1940	808785	France
HALLAM	Joseph	GNR	03/07/1945	1725594	Borneo (Kuching)
HAMMOND	Clarence George	GNR	31/10/1943	1817101	Borneo (Kuching)
HAND	George	GNR	15/10/1944	863337	At Sea
HANRAHAN	James	GNR	04/12/1942	847469	*Singapore Maru* (illness)
HANSON (MM)	John	L/BDR	01/03/1942	847784	Kalidjati (Java)
HARDING	Cyril Frederick	GNR	14/05/1945	2050195	Borneo (Kuching)
HARDING	Arthur Richard	GNR	03/07/1945	1580892	Borneo (Kuching)
HARRIS	Raymond John	GNR	01/03/1942	1811608	Kalidjati (Java)
HARRIS	Henry John	GNR	16/12/1942	1697911	Hiroshima No 8
HARRISON	John	GNR	11/05/1945	1569468	Borneo (Kuching)
HARVEY	Robin Jackson	GNR	06/03/1942	956005	Java. Kalidjati
HARWOOD	Charles Thomas	GNR	22/05/1945	1569031	Borneo (Kuching)
HAWTIN	George	GNR	03/03/1942	822186	Java
HERD	William John	SJT	11/03/1942	1073490	Fukuoka No 6
HERLEY	James Michael	GNR	29/11/1943	1746331	*Suez Maru*
HIGGINSON	Thomas Henry	GNR	01/03/1942	860867	Kalidjati (Java)
HOBAN	Owen	GNR	01/06/1940	1071825	France
HOLLAND	Joseph	GNR	09/08/1945	815067	Sumatra
HORN	Jack	GNR	17/06/1945	1569303	Fukuoka No 6
HORNE	Alfred Bishop	GNR	11/02/1944	895020	Osaka No 14
HOWARD	William	GNR	01/03/1942	872438	Palembang
HURIDGE	Harry	GNR	Post 11/1942	1427260	(Java/Japan?)
HURLSTONE	John Joseph Patrick	GNR	01/03/1942	850383	Kalidjati (Java)
JAMES	Glyn	GNR	01/03/1942	1817116	Singapore
JAMES	Samuel Edward	GNR	08/12/1942	1065758	Fukuoka No 4
JAMESON	Thomas	BDR	01/01/1947	1066095	UK after war
JOHNSTON	William James	GNR	01/03/1942	3239062	Kalidjati (Java)
JORDAN	George Jordan	GNR	10/09/1944	1426161	Hiroshima No 8
KEEVIL	Joseph Jesse	SJT	01/03/1942	805169	Kalidjati (Java)
KING	John Barr	GNR	01/03/1942	1518879	Kalidjati (Java)

Name	Other names	Rank	Date Died	Service No.	DeathLocation/ Memorial site
KISTELL	William Bosanko	GNR	01/03/1942	1591078	Kalidjati
LANHAM	Harry	GNR	26/04/1945	850234	Sandakan (N. Borneo)
LAURIE	Archibald James	GNR	18/06/1945	763289	Borneo (Kuching)
LLOYD	Christopher	2/LT	28/05–02/06/1940	77949	Belgium/France
LOMAS	Walter	GNR	07/12/1942	4527180	Hiroshima No 8
LOWES	Joseph Cuthbert	GNR	24/02/1942	848602	Kalidjati (Java)
MACDONALD	James Alfred William	BDR	21/11/1942	982792	Hiroshima No 8
MACE	Arthur Frederick	GNR	17/03/1945	1719997	Sandakan (N. Borneo)
McCALLUM	Malcolm	Lt.	12/11/1942	156926	*Singapore Maru*
McDONNELL	James Carlisle	GNR	10/11/1942	7008388	*Singapore Maru*
McLELLAN	William Charles	GNR	02/12/1942	1779537	*Singapore Maru* (illness)
McNICHOLL	Sampson	GNR	26/07/1945	1546994	Sumatra
MORTON	Robert	GNR	30/11/1942	1073072	*Singapore Maru* (illness)
NAUGHTON	Henry	GNR	01/12/1942	868364	Fukuoka No 4
NICHOLLS	Thomas William	GNR	01/03/1942	1580671	Kalidjati
NISBET	Charles	GNR	16/07/1945	815147	Borneo (Kuching)
NOTT	George Frederick	GNR	08/01/1945	1829524	Borneo (Kuching)
OSBOURNE	Frederick Charles	GNR	29/11/1943	3184681	*Suez Maru*
O'SHAUGNESSY	Francis	GNR	24/06/1944	1643466	*Tamahoko Maru*
PARSONS	Frederick George	GNR	09/01/1943	1643474	Hiroshima No 7
PIGOTT	Cyril	GNR	01/03/1942	1748911	Kalidjati (Java)
POUNDER	John Smith	GNR	09/08/1945	1748915	Sumatra
POWNEY	Maurice	GNR	10/09/1945	818330	UK
PRICE	James Joseph	GNR	13/05/1944	879897	Borneo (Kuching)
PULLIN	Henry John	L/BDR	18/09/1944	1073830	*Junyo Maru*
QUY	William Edward	GNR	21/08/1945	1817339	Borneo (Kuching)
READ	John	GNR	08/11/1942	1749526	Singapore
RENNARDSON	Arthur William	L/BDR	01/03/1942	1749003	Kalidjati (Java)
REYNOLDS	Leslie Charles	GNR	01/03/1942	1514294	Kalidjati (Java)
ROOKER	Joseph Harold	SJT	04/08/1945	818029	Ranau (Borneo)
SEELEY	Howard	GNR	01/06/1940	1502632	France
SHELLARD	William Henry	GNR	01/03/1942	2069748	Kalidjati (Java)
SHERRARD	William Laurence	CAPT	14/02/1942	74545	Pladjoe (Sumatra)
SIMPSON	John William	GNR	13/03/1945	1065084	Borneo (Kuching)
SKELTON	Harry	GNR	01/08/1943	1643341	Kanchanaburi
SMITH	James	GNR	14/10/1944	1626076	Muna Isles
SMITH	Robert	GNR	10/09/1940	818472	London Blitz
STANTON	Alfred Arthur	GNR	01/03/1942	1745269	Kalidjati (Java)
STEEDMAN	Edward	GNR	29/11/1943	1439392	*Suez Maru*
STEPHENS	Geoffrey Alan	GNR	17/05/1945	4916668	Borneo (Kuching)
STEPHENSON	George	GNR	21/06/1945	1072717	Borneo (Kuching)
STEVENS	Thomas Percy	GNR	03/12/1942	1726146	Fukuoka No 4
SUTTON	Donald David	GNR	23/08/1940	1502675	Southampton accident

Name	Other names	Rank	Date Died	Service No.	Death Location/ Memorial site
TART	Joshua	GNR	01/03/1942	822311	Java
THACKERAY JJ	Alias of JJ Duddy (see earlier)				
TILEY	Joseph	GNR	02/06/1945	401276	Borneo (Kuching)
TITMAN	Horace Albert	GNR	29/04/1945	986617	Borneo (Kuching)
TODD	William Alfred	GNR	01/03/1942	1435926	Kalidjati (Java)
TONER	Arthur John	GNR	30/07/1945	2030965	Borneo (Kuching)
TRICE	Edward Charles	L/SJT	08/12/1942	772441	Hiroshima No 8
TRICKETT	Jack	GNR	01/03/1942	1580909	Kalidjati (Java)
UNDERHILL	George Henry	GNR	01/03/1942	782342	Kalidjati (Java)
UNTERMAN	Francis Rene	GNR	01/03/1942	1427564	Kalidjati (Java)
WAYMAN	Christopher Thomas	GNR	29/11/1943	1065009	*Suez Maru*
WESTON	Stanley	GNR	07/05/1945	797493	Sandakan (N Borneo)
WHITTAKER	David Beavis	GNR	26/11/1942	1687164	*Singapore Maru*
WILLIAMSON	John Herbert	GNR	26/07/1943	847891	Kanchanaburi
WILSON	Thomas Henry	L/SJT	01/03/1942	842112	Kalidjati (Java)
WINKWORTH	Charles Alfred	GNR	24/11/1942	6087473	Ship 'B' Java–Singapore
WYKES	Raymond Walter	BDR	27/03/1944	1437267	Hiroshima No 8
YOUNG	Philip Henry	LT	26/07/1945	109991	Sandakan

GNR IVOR CROSS

** The reason for this unusual location has been sent to me by Brian Green who has researched the actual reason. Apparently Gnr Cross died in captivity in Japan in 1944. As was the norm at the time the Japanese had his remains cremated and these were added to one of a series of large urns also containing the remains of many other POWs. After the war when the Americans came across these urns in the Yokohama Military Cemetery they were identified as coming from Fukuoka No 1 Camp. They also found a long list of names of those whose ashes were contained within each one. These had been inscribed on a shrine nearby.

There were some 250 names, mostly American, British and Dutch and the urn with mostly Americans in was sent back to the States to be interred in Jefferson Barracks National Cemetery in St Louis.It was of course impossible to separate out the individual ashes so Gnr Cross now resides in the USA.

15 BATTERY ROLL OF HONOUR

Name	Other names	Rank	Date Died	Service No.	DeathLocation/ Memorial site
ADAMS	George	GNR	01/12/1942	815241	Yokahama/ *Sing/Maru*
ALLEN	John	GNR	20/12/1945	4690188	UK (Kensal Green)
AMES	Harry	GNR	27/11/1942	865453	Japan
ARMISTEAD	Alex Martin	GNR	14/02/1942	1073966	Palembang.
ASHTON	Frederick John	GNR	02/01/1943	777423	Fukuoka No 4
AYRES	Leonard	GNR	23/12/1942	1726195	Fukuoka No 4 Yokohama
BARTON	George Frederick Thomas	GNR	13/01/1945	1748708	Borneo (Labuan)
BAXTER	Hugh	BDR	14/02/1942	786193	Palembang
BEARD	James William	GNR	30/07/1945	1793880	Singapore Changi
BECKWITH	Charles	GNR	17/03/1945	6004638	Borneo (Kuching)
BEDFORD	Lawrence	GNR	05/06/1945	791677	Sarawak (Labuan)
BENNETT	John	GNR	23/09/1944	809160	Borneo (Labuan)
BENNETT	Steven	gnr	01/07/1942	1713861	Jakarta Cemetery
BESSANT	Thomas Edmund	GNR	29/11/1943	781554	*Suez Maru*
BISHOP	William Arthur	L/SJT	01/07/1942	845539	Ship Java– Singapore
BRACKLEY	John William	BDR	14/02/1942	786408	Palembang
BRANDON	Sidney Charles	GNR	19/03/1944	1426949	Fukuoka No 8 Coalmine
BRANTER	Robert	GNR	14/02/1942	1426530	Sumatra
BROGDEN	William	BDR	01/12/1943	1073124	Fukuoka No 4
BROOKES	Samuel	GNR	02/09/1943	784284	Ambon Island
BURDETT	Robert Victor	SJT	01/07/1942	840410	Java. Tanjong Priok
BURROWS	Percy Wilfred	GNR	04/12/1942	4968035	Fukuoka No 4
BUTLER	Thomas	SJT	09/12/1944	5882787	Java/ Sumatra
CHANDLER	Leonard William	GNR	28/05/1943	1426290	Borneo
COLLINS	Albert James	GNR	19/07/1945	1747978	Kanchanaburi
CONNOLLY	Peter	L/SJT	16/11/1942	1426523	Formosa
COOLEY	Frank	GNR	23/11/1942	847924	*Singapore Maru*
CRAWFORD	Geoffrey H	LT	14/02/1942	79855	Sumatra/ Palembang P1
CREEDY	Francis Henry	GNR	15/09/1943	1747990	Ambon Island
DAVIES	Charles Albert Calvert	GNR	16/06/1945	1618576	Borneo
DAVIS	John Westacott	L/SJT	08/12/1942	1467515	Fukuoka No 4
DAVIS	Leslie Henry	GNR	14/11/1942	1714915	Java
DAVIS	Frederick William	GNR	14/02/1942	1055905	Palembang
DAY	Harold Frederick	GNR	19/09/1942	1632517	Java/ Sumatra
DORRICOTT	Jonathon	GNR	18/09/1944	1811148	*Junyo Maru*

Name	Other names	Rank	Date Died	Service No.	Death Location/ Memorial site
DOUGHERTY (MID)	Jeffrey	SJT	26/11/1942	779231	*Singapore Maru*
DWYNE	Eric	GNR	23/11/1942	1725591	*Singapore Maru*
DYKE	Joseph Henry	GNR	06/01/1945	1818021	Borneo (Kuching)
EASTHAUGH	Frederick	GNR	29/03/1940	780837	France (Bois Carre)
EDGSON	Frank William	GNR	28/07/1941	1580873	UK (St Pancras)
ELLIS	George	GNR	29/11/1942	1063502	Fukuoka No 4
EVANS	Frederick George	GNR	28/03/1943	6009485	Sandakan
FIELD	Frank Eric	GNR	12/12/1942	824967	Hiroshima No 8
FORSTER	Richard Ernest Albert	GNR	06/12/1942	918100	Fukuoka No 4
FOULKES	George valentine	GNR	04/12/1942	816887	Fukuoka No 4
FROSTICK	Ernest	L/BDR	14/12/1942	1525610	Fukuoka No 4
GEORGE	Harry	GNR	31/5/2/6/1940	2214318	Dunkirk
GILBY (MC)	Edwin	LT	23/01/1943	105870	Yokahama No 4
GINGELL	Christopher Sydney	GNR	27/11/1942	1714916	Yokahama No 4
GLEED	Raymond Oswald Edwin	GNR	18/07/1943	1746900	Kanchanaburi
GRAYSTONE	Thomas James	SJT	15/02/1942	1426503	Palembang (P1)
HALLIDAY	Harrold McDonald	GNR	18/09/1944	4190999	*Junyo Maru*
HAND	William	L/BDR	02/05/1942	1551953	UK
HARRIS	Edward	GNR	14/02/1942	1580768	Palembang
HARRIS	Samuel	GNR	15/06/1945	1732109	Borneo (Kuching)
HARRIS	Walter Thomas Ralph	GNR	23/09/1944	5722449	At Sea
HARRISON	Albert	GNR	22/07/1945	1071502	Borneo (Kuching)
HARVEY	Edgar John	L/SJT	10/12/1945	4853474	UK (Leicester)
HIBBERT	William	BDR	01/12/1942	8162149	*Singapore Maru*
HILES	William Richard	GNR	30/12/1942	1817110	Hiroshima No 8
HIRST	Milton	GNR	01–02/06/1940	3384293	Dunkirk
HOLLINGWORTH	David Arthur	GNR	14/02/1942	1428422	Palembang (P1)
HOLMES	Cyril Walker	GNR	01/06/1940	1426935	Belgium
HORSMAN	Frank Wrightson	GNR	14/02/1942	1738219	Palembang
JONES	Lewis	GNR	29/11/1943	1580632	*Suez Maru*
JONES	William John	GNR	30/08/1943	1817140	Kanchanaburi
LAMBERT	John	GNR	18/02/1942	1764423	Sumatra
LAWRENCE	Stanley Walter	GNR	14/02/1942	1426659	Palembang (P1)
LETCH	Alfred Edwin	GNR	01/12/1942	2208787	Yokahama No 4
LEWINGTON	Arthur Frederick John	GNR	07/12/1942	5490611	Fukuoka No 4
LEWIS	Ernest George	GNR	12/05/1942	1732084	Java
LINE	William	GNR	14/08/1945	1719024	Borneo (Kuching)
LOVEGROVE	Albert Parkes	GNR	31–5/2/6/1940		Dunkirk
LUPTON	Jack	L/BDR	14/02/1942	790017	Palembang (P1)
MCDONALD	Duncan	SJT	27/12/1942	835854	*Singapore Maru*
MCDONALD	Thomas	GNR	14/12/1942	1738087	Fukuoka No 4
MCLATCHIE	Hugh Boyd	GNR	23/11/1942	1774707	*Singapore Maru*
MCVEY	William John	GNR	14/02/1942	1713742	Palembang
MEADOWS	James	GNR	29/11/1943	3856946	*Suez Maru*

Name	Other names	Rank	Date Died	Service No.	Death Location/ Memorial site
MELLOR	Harold	GNR	01/12/1942	1072709	Fukuoka No 4
METCALFE	Thomas	GNR	18/02/1942	1073948	Sumatra
MINTON	Robert	GNR	24/06/1944	1530175	*Tamahoko Maru*
MINTRAM	Charles Henry	GNR	01/07/1942	1580799	Tanjong Priok died
MITCHELL	Arthur Albert	GNR	18/09/1944	1643445	*Junyo Maru*
MOSES	Leslie Vincent	GNR	01/01/1943	1817173	Japan
NEVILL	John Louis	GNR	29/11/1943	1475012	*Suez Maru*
NIGHTINGALE	Cyril George	GNR	07/12/1944	3958889	Borneo
NORCOTT	Sydney George	GNR	16/06/1945	1749568	Borneo
ORR	William Swankie	GNR	30/05/1940	776669	Dunkirk
PALMER	Albert Frederick	GNR	29/11/1943	1643469	*Suez Maru*
PHILLIPS	George Sidney	GNR	28/12/1944	1817188	Fukuoka No 6
PITMAN	Sydney Oliver	GNR	18/02/1942	882486	Sumatra
POOLE	Arthur Albert	BDR	19/07/1945	6619382	Borneo (Kuching)
RENNIE	John	GNR	14/02/1942	826603	Palembang
RENTON	Robert	GNR	18/06/1942	1060385	Batavia/Jakarta
RIDLEY	Ralph	GNR	25/07/1945	784188	Borneo (Kuching)
ROBERTS	John Henry	GNR	24–25/11/1942	1817208	*Singapore Maru*
SALTER	Allen Henry	BQ/SJT	19/03/1945	874036	Singapore
SANDS	Richard	GNR	24/11/1942	1748640	*Singapore Maru*
SARGISON	Arthur Lawrence	GNR	27/12/1944	784108	Borneo (Kuching)
SAVAGE	Robert	GNR	13/02/1942	1746426	Sumatra
SEABROOK	Frederick	L/BDR	14/02/1942	1072029	Palembang
SEVIOUR	Hubert Charles	GNR	29/11/1942	777106	*Singapore Maru*
SHARP	Maurice Seymour	GNR	28/07/1945	1643331	Borneo (Kuching)
SIBLEY	Walter Albert	GNR	24/06/1944		Singapore
SIMMONDS	Frederick	GNR	30/11/1944	774380	Borneo (Miri)
STANLEY	Sampson Edwin	GNR	29/11/1943	1770727	*Suez Maru*
STEED	William	GNR	29/11/1943	1502670	*Suez Maru*
STEVENS	Robert Stanley	GNR	01–02/06/1940	3441879	Dunkirk
STEWART	Christopher	GNR	02/11/1942	1738111	*Singapore Maru*
SWALES	John Leonard	GNR	10/05/1940	4383007	France
TATE	John	BDR	07/08/1945	819824	Borneo (Kuching)
TAYLOR	George Horace	GNR	01/11/1944	966663	Singapore
TAYLOR	John	GNR	22/01/1945	1810703	Sumatra
THOMAS	Tom	GNR	14/02/1942	1580723	Palembang
THORNETT	Archibald William James	GNR	14/06/1945	1065901	Ranau
TOOLE	George Michael	SJT	29/11/1943	1427519	*Suez Maru*
TOPP	John Edward	GNR	03/07/1945	1643380	Sumatra
TOWILLS	Herbert	GNR	27/11/1942	2065053	Japan
TURNER	Isaac	GNR	22/10/1944	1502697	Muna Isles Celebes
UNITT	Herbert	GNR	02/11/1942	867307	Borneo (Kuching)
VARNEY	Thomas Edward	GNR	29/11/1943	1502708	*Suez Maru*
WALSH	Patrick	GNR	14/02/1942	3382944	Palembang

Name	Other names	Rank	Date Died	Service No.	Death Location/ Memorial site
WALSH	Stanley	GNR	29/11/1942	843076	Fukuoka No 4
WALSHE	Henry Patrick	GNR	31/08/1943	826266	Ambon Island
WATERHOUSE	Leonard	GNR	14/11/1942	1502722	Formosa
WEAVER	Frederick	BDR	29/11/1942	7877791	Fukuoka No 4
WELLS	George	L/BDR	27/03/1945	1058984	Borneo (Kuching)
WHITE	Tom	GNR	06/12/1942	818020	Fukuoka No 4
WILKINSON	William	GNR	09/06/1945	1810723	Borneo (Kuching)
WILL	Arthur	GNR	01/12/1942	866894	Fukuoka No 4
WILSON	James Stanley	GNR	02/12/1942	1738265	Fukuoka No 4
WILSON	John Matthew	GNR	05/04/1945	856897	Borneo (Kuching)
WOOD	Alfred	GNR	01–02/6/1940	847925	Dunkirk
WOOLF	William Henry	GNR	10/03/1945	808768	Sandakan (N. Borneo)

RHQ ROLL OF HONOUR

Name	Other names	Rank	Date Died	Service No.	Death Location/ Memorial site
ANSTEE	William Edward	GNR	01/02/1942	820116	Singapore
BARNBROOK	Albert Reginald	GNR	27/11/1942	230114	*Singapore Maru*
BRAY	Arthur John	BQMS	16/01/1945	790513	Fukuoka No 14
BUCK	Benjamin Robert	GNR	29/11/1942	1427327	*Singapore Maru*
CASEY	James	GNR	29/11/1942	1569577	*Singapore Maru*
CHORLEY	Wilfred	GNR	11/11/1942	1569040	*Singapore Maru*
COLEMAN	John Joseph	GNR	01/03/1942	847816	Singapore
COPELAND	Herbert Lawrence	GNR	01/03/1942	1760369	Singapore
COTTERILL	Harry	BQMS	08/09/1945	1018483	Burma air crash
FORD	Joseph	GNR	02/12/1942	1065862	Fukuoka No 4
HUGHES	Ernest	GNR	12/11/1942	1817114	*Singapore Maru*
ILES	Bert	GNR	20/11/1944	1714942	Borneo (Kuching)
IRVING	Robert	GNR	24/06/1944	868788	*Tamahoko Maru*
KENT	George Harry	SGT	15/08/1943	1066216	Hiroshima No 8
LANCE	Eric	GNR	23/03/1943	1569486	Rabaul
LEWIS	William Thomas	GNR	05/01/1944	1817274	Hiroshima No 8
LEWIS	Ronald Cecil	GNR	08/08/1945	791037	Burma air crash
MORRIS	George Benson	GNR	22/10/1942	812242	Borneo (Labuan)
OAKLEY	Robert Henry	A/BDR	21/01/1942	1063227	Singapore
PERKINS	Frederick John	GNR	29/05/1940	1517720	Belgium/France
SHERIDAN	Stanley Joseph	GNR	29/05/1940	1438893	Dunkirk
SIPPINGS	William Martin	GNR	30/09/1943	1524972	Chungkai
SMITH	David James	SGT	06/12/1942	791150	*Singapore Maru*
STORR	Henry George	GNR	27/03/1945	815954	Fukuoka No 17
TAYLOR	John	GNR	12/01/1940	1062477	France
WEBB	Daniel Thomas	GNR	02/04/1945	1818166	Sandakan (Borneo)
YOUNG	James	GNR	20/07/1945	805122	Borneo

ATTACHED RANKS AND UNKNOWN BATTERY PERSONNEL ROLL OF HONOUR

Name	Other names	Rank	Date Died	Service No.	Corps	Death Location/ Memorial site
AMOS	Henry	SGT INST	12/05/1942	315313	RAOC	UK (Morden)
ALBERTS	Alfred Harwood	DVR	15/03/1942	T/3390643	RASC	Kranji
ANTHONY	Bruce Edwin Arnold	CPL	03/12/1944	2335321	Sigs	Fukuoka No 14
ASHWORTH	Edgar	CPL	19/11/1942	2341321	Sigs	Singapore
BATES	Edward George	DVR	14/07/1943	T/67550	RASC	Kanchanaburi
BELCHER	Alfred John James	L/CPL	21/09/1944	T/83670	RASC	Singapore
BISHOP	Walter	DVR	10/04/1942	T/155790	RASC	Kranji
BROOKER post	Frederick Charles	BDR	29/07/1946	4912351	RA	UK Bilston war
BRUNT	Richard Allan	S/SGT	13/02/1942	7629856	RAOC	Singapore
BRYAN	Joseph	GNR	29/05–04/ 06/1940	872141	RA	Belgium/ France
BULLOCK	Herbert Patrick	DVR	22/09/1943	T/221848	RASC	Chungkai
BURRIDGE	Edgar Thomas	DVR	18/11/1944	T/193795	RASC	Singapore
CAIRNS	Richard	WO2 (BQMS)	24/04/1945	886233	RA	Thanbyuzayat
CAIRNS	Herbert	PTE	12/11/1943	10559347	"	Thanbyuzayat
CARTER	Thomas Roland	DVR	31/07/1943	T/234722	RASC	Chungkai
CHERRETT	Arthur Edward	DVR	26/02/1944	T/204524	RASC	Chungkai
COOK	Thomas Joseph	GNR	01/03/1942	1600635	RA	Java
DRURY	Harold	L/CPL	21/09/1944	7596785	"	Singapore
EDGE	Sidney Fiest	L/BDR	29–30/05/ 1940	822168	RA	Belgium/ France
EMERY	Harry Marshall	CPL	10/01/1943	10532593	RAOC	Fukuoka No 1
FORD	Harry George	L/CPL	10/12/1943	5441620	RAOC	Kanchanaburi
FRAMPTON	Archibald	PTE	09/07/1943	7633465	RAOC	Kanchanaburi
GALLON	Robert Isaacs	GNR	19–20/02/1942	4271438	RA	Tanjong Priok drowned
HARRIES	William Islwyn	SIG	02/12/1942	2336165	"	Singapore Maru
HEAWOOD	Cecil Lawrence	SIG	01/01/1943	2358574	"	Singapore Maru
HEYWARD	Ronald Sydney	DVR	27/03/1943	T/259177	RASC	Chungkai
HILL	John	SIG	27/05/1945	2351736	SIGS	Singapore
HILL	Harry	S/SGT	13/02/1942	76296276	RAOC	Singapore 3 Bty?
HUME	Allan	DVR	13/11/1943	T/138560	RASC	Chungkai
HUTCHISON	Peter Bolan	PTE	21/09/1944	2191302	"	Hofuku Maru
HYDE	George	SIG	29/11/1943	2351640	"	Suez Maru
IRESON	Leonard Arthur	DVR	26/06/1943	T/62811	RASC	Kanchanaburi
JAMES	Edward Robert	SIG	27/11/1942	2367227	"	Singapore
JONES	James Robert	SIG	02/12/1942	2341465	"	Singapore Maru

Name	Other names	Rank	Date Died	Service No.	Corps	Death Location/ Memorial site
LEGG	Sydney Herbert	GNR	14/02/1942	797787	RA	Palembang (P1)
LORD	Ernest	PTE	23/03/1942	7654985	RAOC	Singapore
MARSHALL	Allan George	CPL	18/07/1943	T/185611	RASC	Kanchanaburi
MARTIN	Edwin John	L/SJT	29/05/1940	1073211	RA	Belgium
MARTIN	Gordon Victor	SIG	06/08/1945	23622136	Sigs	Jakarta
MAYTUM	Alfred Harwood	PTE	16/07/1943	10546148	RAOC	Chungkai
MCDONALD	John Vincent	L/CPL	19/11/1942	2590199	Sigs	Singapore Maru
MCDOWELL	Robert	GNR	03/10/1946	6975524	RA	Ireland post war
MCPHEE	Angus	DVR	27/06/1943	T/220810	RASC	Kanchanaburi
MEADOWS	Samuel	SIG	03/11/1942	2367989	Sigs	Singapore
MENNISS	Charles Walter	PTE	21/09/1944	5443593	RAOC	Hofuku Maru
MILBURN	William	GNR	20/12/1943	794874	RA	Thanbyuzayat
MILES	George	DVR	26/11/1943	T/218243	RASC	Chungkai
MONTEITH	Hugh	SGT	13/02/1942	7642594	RAOC	Singapore
MOODY	Thomas Walter	GNR	26/03/1943	794542	RA	Yokohama
OAKLEY	Robert Henry	L/BDR	21/01/1942	1063227	RA	Singapore
PARKER	Edward Richard	BDR	20–21/02/ 1943	1760495	RA	Ghana
PETRIE	Harry Wilkinson	SIG	09/12/1942	2346516	Sigs	Hiroshima No 8
PEARSALL	Frank Parkes	WO 2	05/10/1940	2314252	Sigs	UK
POWELL	John (Johnnie)	BDR	01/12/1942	2351257	Sigs	Singapore Maru
RICHARDSON	Walter	DVR	03/08/1942	T/230557	RASC	Kranji
SIBTHORPE	Daniel Chas. Edwin	SIG	27/08/1942	2367457	Sigs	Sumatra/Java
SMITH	Benjamin Arthur	CRAFTS-MAN	05/12/1943	7638954	Wk-Shop	Kanchanaburi
TAYLOR	Alfred Linford	SIG	03/12/1942	2366268	Sigs	Yokohama No 4
TURNER	Alexander William	BDR	04/10/1942	1041707	RA	Malaya
TYSON	Henry	CPL	26/09/1944	T/221840	RASC	Singapore
WRIGHT	Leslie Harold Desmond	DVR	09/04/1944	T/139427	RASC	Kanchanaburi
WRIGHT	John	DVR	19/04/1943	T/231495	RASC	Kanchanaburi

During the course of researching for the Rolls of Honour and reading many books on the POWs in the Far East and files at the NA in Kew, names of survivors appear in the texts.

This can in no way be a complete list but the following names are from the 6 HAA Regt. and most survived the war. Where there is no POW camp shown this can be for a number of reasons. Either the name has not so far come up in the researches or in some cases the man was transferred wounded to a hospital outside the Far East and so avoided capture by the Japanese. Sadly in one or two cases the man having escaped the capitulation of the Far East countries then went on to serve in other campaigns and lost his life there.

In many cases their Bty is not given or the details are incomplete.

With the help of Robert McAllister I have cross-checked as many sources as we could, to try and make sure the lists are as exact as possible. Because of the nature of such searches, unfortunately it is still possible that there may be odd errors and for this we apologise.

POWs tended to be moved around at short notice from one camp to another to suit work requirements and camps tended to change their names although not always their location. It is thus possible a man spent many years in the same place but the name changed while he was there. For example the camp called Fukuoka 4 was at Ube and the men there were moved out en masse just before the end of the war when the bombing of Ube put their safety in doubt. (Not in fact a humanitarian move by the Japanese, they wanted to put them to work elsewhere.) There were very few POWs who did not stay in more than one camp during their captivity.

Others had been bombed out of their original camps by Allied aircraft which had no way of knowing they were there. There were no visible identity marks painted on the roofs to warn of the occupants inside. (Several men had been killed in one camp during an air raid when allied planes bombed ammunition wagons in a siding close by.) On Ballale Island more than a hundred POWs were reported killed in Allied air-raids when they were refused the chance to take cover.

So far this list contains 738 names of survivors but it is hoped it will be added to.

6 REGT SURVIVORS

Name	Rank	Initials	Bty	Service No.	POW Camp released from	Survived *Kachidoki Maru*
ABREY	DVR	G.A.	15 Bty	1495859	Motoyama	
ADAMS	GNR	F.T.	12 Bty	1817001	Hiroshima 7	
ADAMS	GNR	J.	12/15 Bty?	1580601	Tanjong Priok	
ADAMSON	L/BDR	J.T.	3 Bty	1073090		
ALLEN	SGT	G.W.		1072668		
ALLEN	DVR	J.	15 Bty	6690188	Kuching	
ALLEN	GNR	T.J.V.	3 Bty	1817004	Saigon	
ALLPASS	MAJ	J.S.	15 Bty	73393	Honshu	
AMBLER	L/BDR	C.A.	3 Bty	806356	Nakom Paton	
ANDREWS	GNR	A.A.	15 Bty	1580603	Kuching	
ANDREW	2/LT	L.D.	3 Bty	151926		
ARCHARD	DVR	D.J.G.	3 Bty	T/193562	Thimongtha	
ARNOLD	GNR	L.R.	15 Bty	1632440	Motoyama	
ARNOLD	DVR	W.A.	3 Bty	T/258958	Nakom Paton	
ASHBRIDGE	GNR	S.	3 Bty	847295	Japan Camp 25	
ASHMAN	GNR	J.C.	3 Bty	797450	Taiwan/Japan	
ATHERTON	GNR	W.	12 Bty	4741330	Sumatra	
ATKINSON	BDR	F.B.	3 Bty	4445842	Saigon	
ATKINSON	PTE	J.	Att	1716001	Nakom Paton	
ATKINSON-CLARK	LT	J.C	15 Bty	77910	Motoyama	
AUSTIN	SGT	G.K.	RAOC	7598805	Chungkai	
AVERY	GNR	R.	12 Bty	854600	Tijmahi Java	
AVIS	DVR	R.C.	12 Bty	2100549	Pakan Baroe	
ATTIWILL	LT	K.	15 Bty	151869	Ube	
BAILEY	DVR	A.R.	12 Bty	2083810	Hiroshima 6	
BAILEY	SIG	S.R.	12/15 Bty	2345234	Tanjong Pagar	
BAILIE	CAPT	J.A.	12 Bty	155188	Kuching	
BAILLIE	LT COL	G.W.G.	RHQ		To Ceylon	
BAINES	GNR	F.H.	15 Bty	1427339		
BAKER	GNR	J.	15 Bty	1477290	Fukuoka 4	
BAKER	GNR	L.E.	15 Bty	1530238	Motoyama	
BALFOUR	2/LT	R.E.P.	3 Bty	166295	Kanchanaburi	
BALL	GNR	A.R.	12/15Bty	1690411	Japan	
BANNISTER	GNR	A.	12/15Bty	1580606	Batu Lintang Borneo	
BANTING	GNR	J.L.	3 Bty	1073230	Saigon	
BARBER	DVR	G.K.	15 Bty	T/139431		
BARFORD	SGT	M.K.	RASC 3 Bty	189490	Changi	
BARK	L/BDR	E.	3 Bty	838321	Taka Butai	
BARKER	DVR	G.E.	15 Bty	T/139431		
BARKER	L/BDR	H.	3 Bty	845571	Nakom Paton	

Name	Rank	Initials	Bty	Service No.	POW Camp released from	Survived *Kachidoki Maru*
BARKER	L/BDR	J.W.	15 Bty	798702		
BARLOW	GNR	E.H.	15 Bty	1714728	Fukuoka 4	
BARNETT	L/BDR	A.	15 Bty	788713	Pakan Baroe	
BARRATT	GNR	H.C.J.	3 Bty	872449	Pratchapkirikan	
BARRETT	GNR	R.H.	3 Bty	1096105	Nakom Paton	
BARTON	GNR	J.H.C.	15 Bty	1582156	Ube	
BATCHELOR	SGT	A.W.	3 Bty	1424730	Changi S`pore	
BATEMAN	PTE	H.		7653787		
BATSON	GNR	S.H.	12/15 Bty	1747264	Sumatra	
BAYES	GNR	R.A.	12 Bty	833537	Fukuoka 4	
BEACHER	L/BDR	S.J.	12 Bty	784378	Sumatra	
BEATTIE	CAPT	T.L.	RHQ	75977	Fukuoka No. 1	
BEDFORD	L/BDR	R.E.J.	12/15 Bty	828688	Fukuoka 4	
BEECH	SGT	G.F.	15 Bty	806130	Japan	
BENNISON	DVR	W.E.	3 Bty	826800	Taiwan	
BEST	GNR	G.H.	12 Bty	5777955	Changi	
BIELBY	DVR/MECH	T.E.	3 Bty	827041	Formosa	
BILSTON	GNR	E.	3 Bty	791941	Formosa	
BIRD	LT	?	15 Bty	?	Motoyama	
BISHOP	GNR	J.W.	15 Bty	1735003	Medevac to Ceylon	
BLACKBURN	GNR	H.	15 Bty	1622078		
BLAIR	DVR	W.R.	12/15 Bty	1818198	Kyushu camp 8	
BLAKE	DVR	H.W.	3 Bty	5498208	Pratchapkirikan	
BLAKEMAN	L/BDR	A.J.	12 Bty	1538401	Sumatra	
BLOWERS	DVR	B.W.	12/15 Bty	5720997	Kyushu	
BOOMER	DVR	W.	15 Bty	1568462	Escaped to Ceylon	
BOOTON	SGT	J.W.	3 Bty	5378606	Honshu 5	
BOWEN	GNR	A.J.	3 Bty	1818206	Honshu 5	
BOWKETT	GNR	C.M.	12 Bty	1780773	Changi	
BOWMAN	GNR	J.L.	3 Bty	1562545	Saigon	
BRADBURY	GNR	J.J.	15 Bty	1734916	Motoyama	
BRADLEY	GNR	J.H.	12 Bty	1745199	Motoyama	
BRADLEY	GNR	W.	3 bty	1713293	Tamarkan	
BRADSWORTH	L/SGT	A.	15 Bty	786712	Tanjong Priok	
BRADY	SGT	T.A.	RHQ	1518853	Ube	
BRAY	GNR	H.J.	15 Bty	1580616	Motoyama	
BRERETON	GNR	G.	12 Bty	868749	Motoyama	
BRERETON	DVR	J.H.	12/15 Bty	1765436	Macassar Java	
BRIGGS	GNR	S.	3 Bty	820895	Thamuang	
BRINDLEY	SIG	R.	Att			
BROADLEY	DVR	E.	12/15 Bty	1519031	Fukuoka No.3	
BROGDEN	DVR	J.H.	12 Bty	82277	Motoyama	
BROOKES	GNR	T.	15 Bty	1749566	Fukuoka	

Name	Rank	Initials	Bty	Service No.	POW Camp released from	Survived *Kachidoki Maru*
BROWN	S/SGT	A.S.	RAOC 3 Bty	7857514	Changi	
BROWN	GNR	D.H.	3 Bty	1817021	Nakon Nai	
BROWN	GNR	G.M.	12/15 Bty	891072	Motoyama	
BROWN	L/BDR	T.	15 Bty	788614	Kuching	
BROWN	L/BDR	T.D.P.	12 Bty	895002	Motoyama	
BUCK	L/BDR	A.G.	15 Bty	788256	Wakayama / Ikono	
BURGES	L/SGT	E.J.O.	15 Bty	819810	Ube	
BURKE	GNR	W.A.	12 Bty	847822	Kuching	
BURNE	GNR	A.C.	3 Bty	826623	Saigon camp 8	
BURNS	GNR	R.	15 Bty	1568466	Kamo?	
BURNS	L/BDR	R.C.	15 Bty	800261	Fukuoka	
BURNS	L/BDR	S.	12/15 Bty	986136	Motoyama	
BURTON	GNR	J.	15 Bty	788462	Ube	
BUTLER	GNR	F.J.	3 Bty	842884	Japan	
BUTLER	L/BDR	L.M.	12 Bty	1501976	Motoyama	
BUTLER	DVR	R.R.	15 Bty	1818213	Motoyama	
BYRON	DVR	J.	3 Bty	3707408	Changi	
CAMM	GNR	L.A.	12 Bty	1464545	Singapore	
CAMPBELL	CAPT	K.	RHQ	85544	Fukuoka No 9	
CARELESS	GNR	T.	15 Bty	10631274	Kyushu Kamo	
CARPENTER	L/BDR	A.	3 Bty	831147		
CARR	GNR	S.	15 Bty	1609789		
CARROLL	GNR	E.J.	15 Bty	4193373		
CARROLL	LT	P.E.	12/15 Bty?	207119	Motoyama	
CARTER	PTE	A.W.	RAOC 3 Bty	891142		
CASIDY	SGT	B.	12 Bty	1427706	Motoyama	
CAULTON	DVR	B.V.	12 Bty	1780730	Motoyama	
CHALMERS	BDR	W.A.	15 Bty	853567		
CHANDLER	L/BDR	T.A.	15 Bty	1066494		
CHARLES	GNR	J.	12 Bty	1472376		
CHAPMAN	GNR	A.W.	RHQ	1517766	Changi	
CHARTER	PTE	J.W.	RAOC12/15	10554347	Changi	
CHESTERS	GNR	J.	3 Bty	1817029	Saigon	
CHITTENDEN	DVR	R.	12 Bty	863246	Ikuno	
CLAPP	GNR	F.G.	12 Bty	5616255	Hiroshima 6	
CLARK	SGT	A.G.	12/15 Bty?	824431	Kuching	
CLARK	GNR	G.H.	12 Bty	800562	Motoyama	
CLARKE	CPL	A.G.	RASC	S/212055	Kuching	
CLIFTON	GNR	J.H.	12 Bty	923557	Sumatra	
CLOWES	GNR	F.S.	3 Bty	1789478	Kaorin	
COATES	DVR	E.	12 Bty	1569381		
COATS	GNR	C.		1645640		
COCKS	GNR	R.B.	3 Bty	1725627	Honshu 5	

Name	Rank	Initials	Bty	Service No.	POW Camp released from	Survived *Kachidoki Maru*
COLE	DVR		15 Bty	11063521	Fukuoka	
COLEMAN	GNR	A.E.	3 Bty	779112	Saigon	
COLEMAN	GNR	W.G.	3 Bty	1817031	Pratchapkirikan	
COLES	GNR	A.	12 Bty	1817051	Motoyama	
COLLETT	GNR	A.N.	15 Bty	1580745	Ube	
COMERFORD	DVR	M.	3 Bty	863260	Nakon Nai	
CONOLLY	GNR	H.E.	3 Bty	1696142	Pratchapkirikan	
CONNORS	GNR	T.A.	3 Bty	1775891	Japan	
COOPER	GNR		15 Bty	818849		
COOPER	GNR	H.S.	15 Bty	819048	Tijmahi	
CORBETT	L/BDR	R.J.	12 Bty	6282766	Fukuoka No 2	
CORY	BDR	H.T.	3 Bty	771652	Japan Sakata	KM
COTTELL	BDR	L.A.	12 Bty	973845	Sumatra	
COUGHLIN	BDR	M.	12 Bty	850117	Kuching	
COX	SGT	A.R.		864476		
CRABB	GNR	W.J.	3 Bty	1783888	Taka Butai	
CRADDOCK	GNR	A.	12 Bty	4911785	Motoyama	
CRAWFORD	L/BDR	C.	12 Bty	816714	Saigon	
CRIPPS	DVR	A.E.	15 Bty	1426512	Ube	
CROMPTON	GNR	W.	15 Bty	1725589	Ube	
CROOKES	GNR	H.	12/15 Bty?	777253		
CROSS	L/BDR	E.		847794	Changi	
CULLEN	DVR	J.	15 Bty	T/129341	Kuching	
CULLEN	GNR	J.	12/15 Bty?	842790		
CULLERTON	GNR	M.J.	12/15 Bty?	891171	Sumatra	
CULLIMORE	DVR	W.J.	15 Bty	1427323	Ube	
CURRIE	L/BDR	R.	3 Bty	843109	Japan	KM
DANGERFIELD	GNR	E.	3 Bty	1426814	Nakon Nai	
DANIELS	GNR	G.W.	12 Bty	822182	Kuching	
DANIELS	L/BDR	H.	3 Bty	6285112		
DANVERS	DVR	E.	RASC 3 Bty	T/139422	Changi	
DARBYSHIRE	DVR	G.	12 Bty	1474466		
DAVEY	GNR	A.B.	12 Bty	1783854	Kuching	
DAVIES	L/Cpl	F.	RAOC 3 Bty	7596716	Thailand	
DAVIES	SGT	G.H.	12 Bty	850840	Kuching	
DAVIES	BSM	H.	12/15?	4442536		
DAVIES	PTE	J.	RAOC 3 Bty	7595447	Changi	
DAVIES	GNR	J.	15 Bty	1737705	Fukuoka 24 Ube	
DAVIES	L/BDR	T.	12/15 Bty?	1580861	Motoyama	
DAVIES	GNR	W.A.	12 Bty	1426642	Wakayama	
DAVIS	GNR	L.	3 Bty	818662	Nakon Nai	
DAWSON	GNR	H.I.	3 Bty	1634325	Nakon Nai	

Name	Rank	Initials	Bty	Service No.	POW Camp released from	Survived *Kachidoki Maru*
DAWSON	BDR	J.T.	12/15 Bty?	1494017	Changi	
DAWSON	BDR	J.T.	3 Bty	815236	Saigon	
DAY	GNR	I.J.	12 Bty	846718	Motoyama	
DEACON	GNR	G.A.	12 Bty	1426634		
DEAN	GNR	G.	3 Bty	1657496	Saigon	
DEAN	L/SGT	J.	3 Bty	2820183		
DELANEY	GNR	J.	12/15 Bty?	6340133		
DENNY	GNR	G.W.	3 Bty	808462	Saigon	
DEWAR	LT	D.H.	12 Bty	145809	Kuching	
DIGG	GNR	R.	15 Bty		Japan	
DILAS	GNR	T.A.	3 Bty	803623	Thailand	
DODDS	GNR	R.	3 Bty	7537211	Chungkai	
DOE	GNR	D.C.	15 Bty	1748053	Japan	KM
DOLAN	GNR	H.	3 Bty	818802		
DOGGETT	GNR	F.J.	3 Bty	1061255	Saigon	
DONACHIE	GNR	E.C.	3 Bty	854663		
DONOVAN	GNR	J.E.	12 Bty	831317	Motoyama	
DOOLAN	L/BDR	M.	12/15 Bty?	794831	Fukuoka 8	
DORLAND	GNR	R.	15 Bty	962363		
DOUGLAS	DVR	C.	15 Bty	4271525	Ube	
DOWSON	GNR	J.C.	12/15 Bty?	859182	Kuching	
DRINKWATER	GNR	H.G.	12/15 Bty?	1746721	Java	
DRYBURGH	GNR	C.	15 Bty	305090		
DUCKETT	L/BDR	B.	15 Bty	786929	Ube	
DUNCAN	DBDR	C.	12/15 Bty?	1072831	Taiwan	
DUNKELY	SGT	A.	3 Bty	1068823		
DUNN	L/BDR	J.W.	15 Bty	1478583	Japan	
DURLSEY	GNR	L.	?	986121	Japan	
DYKES	DVR	H.	3 Bty	1441067	Tamarkan	
EARLAND	GNR	R.C.	15 Bty	812459	Palembang	
EAST	L/BDR	R.F.	12/15 Bty?	2043888	Tanjong Priok	
EDWARDS	PTE	A.N.	RAOC	T/111695	Fukuoka 5	
EDWARDS	L/BDR	C.E.	3 Bty	1427520	Saigon	
ELLIOTT	L/SGT		12/15 Bty?			
ELLIS	SGT	H.	3 Bty	826523	Japan Sakata	
EMERY	GNR	S.	15 Bty	1580756		
EMMETT	MAJ	B.R.	12 Bty	71288	Motoyama	
ENGLISH	GNR	A.J.	3 Bty	7537013	Changi	
EVANS	GNR	G.	3 Bty	1817061	Nakon Nai	
EVANS	GNR	H.	12/15 Bty?	847756	Java	
EVANS	GNR	M.	12/15 Bty	1608952	Kyushu Kamo	
EVANS	GNR	T.	15 Bty	840288	Ube	
EVENDON	GNR	C.H.	RHQ	1466738	Ikono	

Name	Rank	Initials	Bty	Service No.	POW Camp released from	Survived Kachidoki Maru
EVERSON	BDR	K.B.	3 Bty	791084	Selarang S'pore	
EVITTS	GNR	J.	15 Bty	3851676	Japan	
FARMER	DVR	W.H.	12 Bty	828620	Motoyama	
FARRANT	DVR	J.	12/15 Bty?	1580758	Ube	
FARRER	GNR	J.	3 Bty	750104	Saigon	
FAULKNER	GNR	T.R.	3 Bty	1817089	Pratchapkirikan	
FAWCETT	GNR	G.H.	3 Bty	824677	Nakon Nai	
FELL	BDR	G.H.	15 Bty	845741		
FELLOWS	GNR	R.	12 Bty	826196	Motoyama	
FERGUSON	GNR	W.	3 Bty	847229	Pratchapkirikan	
FIDLER	BDR	J.L.	12 Bty	1057309	Fukuoka	
FILER	GNR	W.	3 Bty	1817090	Saigon	
FINCH	DVR	W.E.	15 Bty	1697897		
FINLEY	GNR	B.J.		4269923		
FISHER	GNR	A.T.	3 Bty	1580760	Chungkai	
FITZGERALD	L/SGT	P.E.	3 Bty	6195827	Nakom Paton	
FORBES	GNR	T.	3 Bty	813907	Thamuang	
FORSTER	DVR	J.R.	15 Bty	1629577	Kuching	
FOSTER	GNR	W.	12/15 Bty?	4442219	Ube	
FOUNTAIN	GNR	J.F.	3 Bty	1049955	Saigon	
FOWLER	GNR	W.	15 Bty			
FRANCIS	PTE	R.J.	RAOC 3 Bty	10559049	Singapore	
FREEMAN	DVR	L.G.	12/15 Bty?	1602372	Kuching	
FULCHER	SIGS	B.H.	SIGS	2366866	Ube	
FURNELL	GNR	S.	15 Bty	1580762	Fukuoka no 2	
GABBERT	GNR	B.R.J.	3 Bty	?35296	Ube	
GADD	GNR				Ube	
GALE	LT	V.G.		167252		
GARRY	GNR	J.	3 Bty	1492995	Nakom Paton	
GARTON	DVR	C.A.	12/15 Bty?	1569344	Moji	
GARTON	GNR	W.E.	3 Bty	1818241	Saigon	
GARVEY	DVR	E.	12 Bty	1565459		
GAY	SIG	F.A.C.	Sigs Att.	888576	Palembang	
GEE	GNR	J.H.		1738586	Changi	
GERTON	GNR	W.	RHQ			
GETHING	SGT	J.C.	15 Bty	805562	Kuching	
GIBBONS	GNR	C.A.	3 Bty	1603032	Nakon Nai	
GILL	L/BDR	T.	15 Bty	818025	Motoyama	
GLASS	SGT	W.M.	RASC	T/67948	Fukuoka	
GLAZEBROOK	GNR	A.H.	12/15 Bty?	1817392	Sumatra	
GOLCOUGH	DBDR	T.	15 Bty	788982	Fukuoka	
GOODALL	GNR	T.	3 Bty	791417	Honshu 5	
GOODWIN	GNR	E.S.	3 Bty	842796	Nakon Nai	
GOSNEY	GNR	A.	15 Bty	1726215		

Name	Rank	Initials	Bty	Service No.	POW Camp released from	Survived *Kachidoki Maru*
GRAHAM	L/BDR	A.	12 Bty	1628011		
GRANT	L/SGT	B.	3 Bty	853469	Japan	
GRAY	GNR	D.M.	12/15 Bty?	1764458	Motoyama	
GREATRIX	L/SGT	J.S.	15 Bty	1425040	Tijmahi	
GREEN	GNR	A.E.	15 Bty	1745913	Fukuoka	
GREEN	GNR	A.E.	15 Bty	1778774	Motoyama	
GREEN	GNR	F.S.	3 Bty	1725609	Saigon	
GREEN	SGT	F.W.	RAOC	7641780	Changi	
GREENBANK	SGT	H.	15 Bty	80410	Ube	
GREENWOOD	DVR	G.	12/15 Bty?	1569464	Moji	
GREER	PTE	J.C.	RAOC 3 Bty	402188	Tamuan	
GREGSON	GNR	T.	12/15 Bty?	856637	Kuching	
GRIEVSON	GNR	W.	15 Bty	838878	Kuching	
GRIFFIN	DVR	A.	12/15 Bty?	856931	Motoyama	
GRIFFITHS	GNR	W.	RHQ	1818249	Motoyama	
GUILE	GNR	W.H.	15 Bty	1639558	Borneo	
GUY	DVR	J.W.	12 Bty	5108744	Motoyama	
HADDOM	GNR	J.	3 Bty	800237	Tamuan	
HALFORD	L/BDR	F.A.	12 Bty	1068766	Japan	
HALL	PTE	H.I.	RAOC	10558646	Nakom Paton	
HALL	L/BDR	J.W.	3 Bty	4529987	Taka Butai	
HALL	L/BDR	M.W.	3 Bty	1426662	Japan	KM
HALSTEAD	L/BDR	A.F.J.	12 Bty	850123	Kuching	
HAMER	GNR	P.	3 Bty	1755603	Japan	
HAMMOND	DVR	R.	3 Bty	1059482	Changi	
HANLEY	L/SGT	H.	3 Bty	842885	Japan	
HANMER	GNR	J.	12 Bty	847784		
HANSARD	GNR	G.W.	3 Bty		Taiwan	
HARAM	GNR	W.H.	15 Bty	822859	Motoyama	
HARPER-HOLDCROFT	CAPT	R.N.	PADRE	42421	Japan	
HARPLEY	GNR	J.R.	3 Bty	842995	Wampo	
HARRIS	GNR		12/15 Bty?	1580896	Changi	
HARRIS	GNR	W.	15 Bty	840391	Moji	
HARRISON	GNR	R.	3 Bty	1738933	Nakon Nai	
HARVEY	SGT	E.J.	12/15 Bty?	4853474	Yamata No 3	
HASTINGS	GNR	T.E.	12 Bty	1789070	Kuching	
HAWES	GNR	H.R.R.	12/15 Bty?	1580771	Kuching	
HAWKINS	BSM		12 Bty			
HAXBY	DVR	W.	12 Bty	1559470	Japan	
HAYWARD	BDR	C.M.	15 Bty	826508	Moji	
HAYWARD	DVR	C.V.	RASC 3 Bty	T/60178	Changi	
HAZEL	LT COL	E.J.	15 Bty	34632	Ube	
HAZELL	BDR	E.A.	3 Bty	5988629	Saigon	

Name	Rank	Initials	Bty	Service No.	POW Camp released from	Survived *Kachidoki Maru*
HEARD	GNR	R.	12/15 Bty?	878099	Motoyama	
HEELEY	GNR	N.	12 Bty	1591004	Motoyama	
HEMMING	Craftsman	T.	3 Bty	7638756	Thailand	
HENDERSON	GNR	J.T.	3 Bty	976572	Taiwan	
HERBERT	GNR	R.J.	12 Bty	1726113	Motoyama	
HEWSON	GNR	A.	12 Bty	1774470		
HICKLING	DVR	T.	12/15 Bty?	4798526	Thailand	
HICKS	GNR	C.T.	15 Bty	816877	Ube	
HIDDLESTON	L/BDR	D.	15 Bty	791101	Kuching	
HIGGINS	L/BDR	S.A.	15 Bty	1465193	Ube	
HILL	GNR	T.S.	15 Bty	1055896	Ube	
HILLEN	GNR	A.	att to 77 HAA	1580774	Nakom Paton	
HOARE	L/BDR	W.H.	15 Bty	800250	Ube	
HOBBS	GNR	E.G.	15 Bty	1069520	Motoyama	
HOLLINS	GNR	J.W.	12/15 Bty?	1580778	Japan	
HOLMES	GNR	L.	12/15 Bty?	1426936	Ube	
HOOD	2/LT	F.	3 Bty	197492	Kanchanaburi	
HOPE	GNR	L.	3 Bty	842354	Japan Sakata	KM
HOPKINS	GNR	D.	12 Bty	806239	Motoyama	
HOPKINSON	GNR	S.	12 Bty	828384	Moji	
HORDER	GNR	G.J.	3 Bty	1772174	Chungkai	
HOWSON	GNR	A.E.	12/15 Bty?	1774770	Wakayama	
HUDSON	L/CPL	R.L.	RASC 3 Bty	T/181351	Japan Sakata	
HUGHES	GNR	A.W.G.	12 Bty	1726117	Motoyama	
HUGHES	SGT	C.E.	12 Bty	777164	Motoyama	
HUGHES	WO1	H.		819139	Hiroshima 7	
HULL	SGT	A.D.	12/15 Bty?	5566179	Fukuoka	
HUMPHREYS	DVR	S.S.	15 Bty	809369	Ikuno	
HUMPHRIES	L/BDR	G.	3 Bty	411918	Honshu 5	
HUNT	GNR	A.G.	3 Bty	1636952	Changi	
HUNT	DVR	H.H.	15 Bty	1739554	Ube	
HUNTER	BQMS	E.	15 Bty	1423171		
HURST	BDR		15 Bty			
HYDE	DVR	H.	12/15 Bty?	2350090	Changi	
HYNDS	GNR	J.P.	15 Bty	853938		
INGS	DVR	A.	12/15 Bty?	1380781	Changi	
INWOOD	GNR	R.	3 Bty	1702390	Taka Butai	
IVINS	W/SGT	H.J.	15 Bty	1443209		
JACKSON	GNR	T.	3 Bty	3857613	Nakom Paton	
JACKSON	GNR	T.K.	12/15 Bty?	826517	Changi	
JACOBS	GNR	H.T.	3 Bty	1580786		
JAMES	GNR	G.	15 Bty	1817115	Ube	

Name	Rank	Initials	Bty	Service No.	POW Camp released from	Survived *Kachidoki Maru*
JEAPES	SGT	R.D.	3 Bty	866440	Japan	KM
JEFFREYS	GNR	H.C.	3 Bty	1817120	Saigon	
JOHNSON	BDR	E.	12 Bty	868345	Motoyama	
JONES	GNR	G.G.	3 Bty	1811662	Honshu 5	
JONES	GNR	H.	3 Bty	1738509	Nakom Paton	
JONES	DVR	H.C.	12 Bty	1628935	Motoyama	
JONES	GNR	H.W.	3 Bty	1775988	Honshu 5	
JONES	GNR	J.	15 Bty	1817135	Ube	
JONES	GNR	J.	12 Bty	790308		
JONES	DVR	J.	15 Bty	1070919	Motoyama	
JONES	DVR	J.O.	RASC att	T/131114	Changi	
JONES	SGT	P.S.J.	12 Bty	4073492	Motoyama	
JONES	GNR	R.J.	3 Bty	1695105	Motoyama	
JONES	BDR	R.W.	12/15 Bty?	966685	Pakan Baroe	
JONES	Sigs	S.C.	Att	2350709	Changi	
JONES	L/BDR	W.		806380	Kuching	
JONES	BDR	W.		816491	Motoyama	
KELLY	DVR	W.P.	3 Bty	856912	Changi	
KENWARD	LT	P.M.	3 Bty	197644		
KETCHER	DVR	C.H.	15 Bty	6011373	Moji	
KIDD	GNR	H.			Tokyo 13	
KIMBER	CAPT	R.J.	RASC att	P.34633	Fukuoka	
KING	L/SGT	A.W.	12/15 Bty?	532764	Ube	
KING	GNR	F.C.	15 Bty	1745865	Ube	
KINNEAR	GNR	W.P.	12 Bty	1694891	Japan	
KNIGHT	GNR	D.A.	12 Bty	988057	Osaka	
KNIGHT	SGT	J.	12/15 Bty?	819147	Kuching	
KNIGHTS	L/BDR	D.G.	15 Bty	5933097	Fukuoka	
KNIGHTS	SGT	W.H.	12/15 Bty?	3382998	Kuching	
LACKEY	BDR	J.	12 Bty	1056966		
LAMB	GNR	K.	12 Bty	9045557	Ikuko	
LAMB	GNR	R.	12/15 Bty?	1427434	Ikuno	
LAMBERT	GNR	C.	12/15 Bty?	1787423		
LANE	DVR/MECH	C.	12 Bty	847823	Motoyama	
LANE	GNR	J.J.	12 Bty	1529041	Changi	
LAWSON	BDR	D.	12/15 Bty?	890355	Changi	
LEADBETTER	GNR	W.J.	3 Bty	777182	Tamarkan	
LEE	DVR/MECH	A.	12 Bty	1569488	Kuching	
LEE	L/BDR	C.A.	12/15 Bty?	791676	Fukuoka	
LEES	GNR	J.	12/15 Bty?	1708782	Changi	
LEVEREDGE	GNR	S.A.	3 Bty	1426884	Saigon	
LEWIS	PTE	J.S.	RAOC 3 Bty	7653162	Nakom Paton	
LEWIS	GNR	T.L.	3 Bty	4073168	Honshu 5	

Name	Rank	Initials	Bty	Service No.	POW Camp released from	Survived *Kachidoki Maru*
LEWIS	GNR	W.J.	12 Bty	853916	Changi	
LIDDELL	GNR	R.	12/15 Bty?	784900	Singapore	
LILLEY	GNR	H.	12 Bty	1569141	Motoyama	
LIMERICK	GNR	J.H.	3 Bty	1817151	Honshu 5	
LITTLE	BDR	C.	3 Bty	4610746	Saigon	
LLEWLLLYN	GNR	G.W.H.	3 Bty	2733596	Kuching	
LOAN	DVR/MECH	J.	12/15 Bty?	4265952	Japan	
LOBB	GNR	J.	15 Bty		Ube	
LOBB	DVR	R.	RASC att	T/151398	Motoyama	
LONGLEY	GNR	R.	12 Bty	850151	Singapore	
LONGSTAFFE	SGT	H.	15 Bty	797709		
LOVELESS	DVR	R.G.	15 Bty	1710108	Ube	
LOVELY	LT	P.G.	15 Bty	156857	Kuching	
LOWERY	L/BDR	J.T.	3 Bty	831191	Japan Sakata	KM
LOWRY	GNR	J.J.	3 Bty	1071135	Japan	
LUFFMAN	GNR	A.F.C.	3 Bty	855607	Nakom Paton	
LUNN	GNR	J.	15 Bty	4349253	Kuching	
LYON	GNR	W.	12 Bty	4185537	Japan	
McCAPPIN	GNR	H.	12/15 Bty?	6974963	Changi	
McDONALD	LT	J.	3 Bty	322042	Ube	
McDOWELL	GNR	R.	12/15 Bty?	6965524	Singapore	
McFARLANE	GNR	W.	12 Bty	1579943	Fukuoka	
McILVEEN	GNR	J.T.	12/15 Bty?	1559856	Changi	
McKENZIE	BQMS	H.	12/15 Bty?	816973	Motoyama	
McNIEL	GNR	E.J.	3 Bty	1817163	Nakom Paton	
McWADE	MAJ	J.R.	3 Bty	169549	Kanchanaburi	
MACFARLANE	SGT	J.A.	Sigs att	2325577	Ikuno	
MACKENZIE	BDR	P.	15 Bty	1630009	Pakan Baroe	
MACINTOSH	DVR	?	15 Bty	?	Motoyama	
MAIDMENT	GNR	A.J.	15 Bty	1518284	Japan	
MALLERY	GNR	T.K.	15 Bty	1698268	Macassar Borneo	
MALLOY	GNR	D.P.		1056029		
MALTBY	GNR	C.B.	12 Bty	1591010	Motoyama	
MAN	S/U/BDR	S.C.	12/15 Bty?	1817299	Java	
MANGHAM	L/SGT	T.	12 Bty	863521	Motoyama	
MANSELL	PTE	L.J.	RAOC att	7594770	Japan	
MAPP	L/BDR	O.L.G.	12 Bty	1817158	Motoyama	
MARRIAGE	GNR	H.T.	3 Bty	1817280	Saigon	
MARRIOTT	GNR	H.	3 Bty	871275	Thailand	
MARSHALL	BDR	C.B.	12 Bty	1072712	Kuching	
MARSHALL	DVR	E.	15 Bty	809576	Ube	
MARSHALL	Sigs	E.	Att	??46209	Pakan Baroe	
MARSHALL	GNR	T.	3 Bty	1817281	Nakon Nai	

Name	Rank	Initials	Bty	Service No.	POW Camp released from	Survived *Kachidoki Maru*
MARTIN	DVR	G.T.	15 Bty	967261	Kuching	
MARTIN	GNR	W.D.	12 Bty	6286302	Japan	
MASON	GNR	J.A.	3 Bty	1417129	Taka Butai	
MATHEWSON	GNR	R.G.	15 Bty	1449663	Fukuoka	
MAYFIELD	GNR				Ube	
MEADOWS	Sigs	S.C.	Sigs att	2367989		
MEAR	GNR	W.E.	15 Bty	1818076	NEI	
MEARS	GNR	F.	15 Bty	1595541	Palembang	
MEARS	GNR	R.L.	3 Bty	1817282	Thamuang	
MEDCALFE	L/BDR	W.A.	15 Bty	856770	Kuching	
MELDRUM	Sigs	J.R.	Att 3 Bty	2348838		
MEPSTED	L/CPL	G.F.	Sigs att	2341158		
MERRILL	GNR	W.H.	3 Bty	1817283	Saigon	
METTERS	GNR	J.	12 Bty	843335	Motoyama	
MICHAEL	GNR	D.G.	3 Bty	1817165	Thamuang	
MIDDLETON	GNR	T.	12/15 Bty?	1532227	Nagasaki	
MIER	GNR	A.W.	12 Bty	973133	Motoyama	
MILES	GNR	A.E.	3 Bty	788377	Saigon	
MILLARD	GNR	E.D.	3 Bty	5566887	Saigon	
MILLINGTON	SGT	C.	15 Bty	790325	Kuching	
MILLINGTON	GNR	I.L.	15 Bty	946858	Ube	
MILLINGTON	GNR	J.	15 Bty	802177	Sumatra	
MILWARD	GNR	W.	12/15 Bty?	4909053	Sumatra	
MINTON	GNR	W.M.	3 Bty	1818077	Wampo	
MITCHELL	SGT	R.A.	3 Bty	798659	Pratchapkirikan	
MOONEY	L/BDR	R.G.	3 Bty	872530	Pratchapkirikan	
MOORE	GNR	A.E.	12 Bty	915224	Fukuoka	
MOORE	LT	C.P.	RASC 3 Bty	177247	Chungkai	
MOOREY	GNR	C.J.	3 Bty	1580665	Honshu 5	
MORGAN	GNR	H.B.	3 Bty	1811697	Japan Sakata	KM
MORLEY	SGT		15 Bty		Ube	
MORRIS	GNR	B.	3 Bty	1817169	Japan Sakata	
MORRIS	GNR	E.J.	15 Bty	1427262	Ikuno	
MORRISEY	BDR	T.V.	15 Bty	872435	Medevac to Ceylon	
MOXON	MAJ	G.A.	15 Bty	13435	Jinsen Korea	
MULLIGAN	GNR	J.N.	3 Bty	2755742	Japan Sakata	
MUMFORD	DVR	G.	15 Bty	1426545	Ube	
MUNDY	DVR	L.G.	12 Bty	1471973	Japan	
MURRAY	GNR	J.P.	3 Bty	890940	Honshu 5	
MUSE	SGT	G.	12 Bty	794833	Sumatra	
MYERS	DVR	A.	12 Bty	1605510	Kuching	
NAIRNE	DVR	C.V.	15 Bty	797907	Ube	
NANKIVELL	Sigs	R.S.	att	2342230	Fukuoka	

Name	Rank	Initials	Bty	Service No.	POW Camp released from	Survived *Kachidoki Maru*
NEALE	GNR	J.	3 Bty	1810631	Pratchapkirikan	
NEAVES	GNR	L.G.	3 Bty	1566523	Saigon	
NEILL	SGT	J.A.	15 Bty	1057940	Ikuno	
NEWCOMBE	SGT	S.H.	3 Bty	819125	Nakom Paton	
NEWMAN	L/BDR	B.	RHQ	966708	Moji	
NEWNHAM	GNR	S.W.	3 Bty	1787455	Nakon Nai	
NEWPORT	DVR	G.A.P.	RASC	T/127120	Kuching	
NICHOLLS	GNR	A.R.	3 Bty	816930	Saigon	
NORMAN	GNR	H.A.	3 Bty	863573	Saigon	
NORRIS	GNR	S.P.	15 Bty	1643464	Fukuoka	
NORTH	LT	G.M.	12/15 Bty?	207226		
NOTTAGE	L/BDR	C.V.	3 Bty	784107	Tha Muang	
NOTTINGHAM	GNR	G.W.	15 Bty	1653904	Ube	
NUBBERT	GNR	T.H.	12 Bty	1760793	Motoyama	
OGBOURNE	DVR	G.W.	3 Bty	788375	Pratchapkirikan	
OLDHAM	GNR	R.D.	15 Bty	1444582	Wakayama	
OLIVER	L/BDR	L.N.	15 Bty	1580675		
OLROYD	DVR	S.W.	RASC 3 Bty	T/218859	Pratchapkirikan	
O'NEIL	L/BDR	P.	12 Bty	1749838	Motoyama	
OSBORN	GNR	J.G.H.	15 Bty	2061531	Ube	
ORR	L/BDR	H.	15 Bty	819108	Kuching	
OWEN	GNR	H.J.	3 Bty	908596	Thamuang	
OWLES	GNR	E.R.	15 Bty	794914	Medivac to Ceylon	
PAINE	SGT	A.S.	12 Bty	7258163	Kuching	
PARDOE	DVR	C.F.	15 Bty	788876	Ube	
PARKER	DVR	G.A.	12/15 Bty?	1426139	Motoyama	
PARROTT	L/BDR	T.H.	3 Bty	1427124	Japan	KM
PATTERSON	GNR	A.	12 Bty	1528979	Moji	
PATTLE	GNR	W.B.	15 Bty	891984	Changi	
PAUL	GNR	G.D.	3 Bty	1025928	Saigon	
PAYNE	BSM	S.D.	3 Bty	822404	Nakom Paton	
PEACH	Sigs	N.D.	12/15 Bty?	2337426	Japan Sakata	
PEARSALL	GNR	G.A.	12 Bty	983839	Motoyama	
PEARSON	DVR	A.	3 Bty	2183461		
PEARSON	GNR	A.	3 Bty	1817184		
PENMAN	L/SGT	W.	12 Bty	842863	Motoyama	
PENNINGTON	Sigs	W.	att 12/15	2350815	Singapore	
PEPPIN	BDR	R.W.G.	3 Bty	5699894	Saigon	
PERKINS	GNR	C.V.	3 Bty	3769953	Hunshu 5	
PERKINS	BDR	L.A.	12 Bty	983834	Kuching	
PERKINS	GNR	T.J.	12 Bty	1439100	Motoyama	
PEW	GNR	G.H.		1643301	Moji	
PHILLIPS	GNR	D.H.	3 Bty	1817187	Saigon	

Name	Rank	Initials	Bty	Service No.	POW Camp released from	Survived *Kachidoki Maru*
PILCHER	CPL	R.A.	12/15 att	???41024		
PINNINGTON	L/BDR	T.	3 Bty	843975	Pratchapkirikan	
PIPER	GNR	S.D.	3 Bty	913009	Saigon	
PITCHER	CPL	A.	Sigs	2348156	Fukuoka No 5	
POOLE	CAPT	R.J.	3 Bty			
POOLE	GNR	J.T.	3 Bty	2653077	Saigon	
POWELL	GNR	B.R.J.	15 Bty	1502315	Ube	
POWELL	BDR	J.A.	3 Bty	859782	Pratchapkirikan	
POWLES	L/SGT	A.E.	15 Bty	816995	Thailand	
POWNER	DVR	E.	15 Bty	798134	Ube	
PREEDY	DVR	E.S.	15 Bty	1817193	Ube	
PROBERTS	GNR	R.C.	3 Bty	812647	Japan Sakata	KM
PROCTOR	SGT		15 Bty			
PUCKERING	DVR	W.	12/15 Bty?	1434069	Ube	
PURCELL	SGT	M.W.	3 Bty	845245	Saigon	
PURSEHOUSE	BDR	J.P.	12 Bty	3592734	Kuching	
PURVES	GNR	J.	12 Bty	819074	Ohama	
PYLE	GNR	A.	15 Bty	3193427	Japan Kamo	
PYLE	SGT	G.P.	12/15 Bty?	798259	Japan Kamo	
RAMSEY	GNR	F.F.	12/15 Bty?	1512835	Motoyama	
RAMSEY	GNR	J.	12 Bty	1440501	Kuching	
RAMSHAW	BDR	H.	12/15 Bty?	1064798	Nagasaki	
RAYMOND	GNR	A.H.N.	3 Bty	1726140	Saigon	
RAYNER	GNR	R.	3 Bty	1817196	Pratchapkirikan	
RAYSON	Fitter	R.P.	12/15 Bty	1579081	Motoyama	
READ	GNR	H.N.	15 Bty	1580808		
READ	GNR	J.	12 Bty	1749526		
REEVE	L/BDR	J.E.	12/15 Bty	805584	Changi	
REEVES	DVR	H.T.	12/15 Bty?	2051224	Singapore	
REX	GNR	G.	12/15 Bty?	1817200	Ube	
RILEY	SGT	W.	3 Bty	2692418		
RITCHIE	GNR	J.T.	15 Bty	1643314		
ROBB	L/BDR	J.	3 Bty	1435982	Saigon	
ROBERTS	DVR	A.H.C.	12 Bty	1073822	Motoyama	
ROBERTS	GNR	E.	3 Bty	1817204	Singapore	
ROBERTS	GNR	T.	12/15 Bty?	1811747	Changi	
ROBERTS	GNR	T.E.	3 Bty	1061388	Nakom Paton	
ROBINSON	GNR	A.	12/15 Bty?	1502615	Changi	
ROBINSON	BDR	P.	15 Bty	4531255		
ROBINSON	GNR	T.	3 Bty	1068550	Naom Nai	
ROBINSON	GNR	W.	3 Bty	2037408	Saigon	
ROBINSON	GNR	W.	3 Bty	786509	Thamuang	
ROBINSON	SGT	W.	3 Bty	4531258	Singapore	

Name	Rank	Initials	Bty	Service No.	POW Camp released from	Survived *Kachidoki Maru*
ROBY	GNR	H.	3 Bty	819087	Japan	
ROCK	DVR	F.	12 Bty	850615	Ikuno	
RODGERS	DVR	J.	12/15 Bty?	814310	Kranji Hospital	
ROONEY	GNR	H.	12 Bty	7043059	Ube	
ROSE	GNR	J.C.	12 Bty	1429233	Ikuno	
ROSS	DVR	H.	15 Bty	831333	Kuching	
ROWLEY	L/SGT	O.	12 Bty	843098	Motoyama	
RUMARY	GNR	R.H.	12/15 Bty?	1748631	Ube	
RUSSELL	GNR	A.	15 Bty	1427196	Ube	
RUSSELL	DVR	A.C.	15 Bty	800043	Kuching	
RUTTER	GNR	G.A.	12/15 Bty?	777880	Myata	
RYALL	L/BDR	A.	3 Bty	879014	Nakom Paton	
RYDER	BDR	P.	3 Bty	872645	Japan	
SADLER	L/BDR	A.E.	RHQ	777880	Ube	
SALMON	GNR	C.E.	12 Bty	1745257	Kuching	
SAMPLER	DVR	W.	RASC att	T/193038	Kranji Hospital	
SANDFORD	BDR	G.	3 Bty	840864	Japan	KM
SANSOM	GNR	R.J.	3 Bty	1630532	Tamuang	
SAUNDERS	DVR	A.E.	12 Bty	5377846	Fukuoka No 2	
SAWDON	GNR	H.	3 Bty	1056198	Saigon	
SAWTELL	BDR	G.	12 Bty	788379	Java	
SCHOFIELD	BDR	J.	3 Bty	800554	Escaped to Ceylon	
SCOTT	PTE	C.E.	RAOC att	1642648	Thailand	
SEAGER	LT	J.R.	15 Bty	P/172782	Motoyama	
SEAL	GNR	H.E.	3 Bty	5106145	Nakom Paton	
SEATON	CPL	G.I.	RAOC 3 Bty	7627764	Changi	
SECKER	GNR	S.	12/15 Bty	1643327	Kuching	
SELL	GNR	M.W.	3 Bty	818701	Pratchapkirikan	
SENIOR	L/SGT	G.	3 Bty	1069942	Singapore	
SEWART	Sigs	F.O.	Sigs att	2351710	Fukuoka no 2	
SHARP	GNR	A.W.	3 Bty	1715218	Thamuang	
SHARROCKS	PTE	A.	RAOC 3 Bty	7619735	Kanchanaburi	
SHATTOCK	SGT	W.B.	3 Bty	1057377	Thailand	
SHAW	GNR	R.O.	3 Bty	904493	Honshu 5	
SHAW	DVR	W.	12 Bty	791083	Motoyama	
SHERRATT	GNR	W.	15 Bty	1073824	Sumatra	
SHERWOOD	PTE	E.P.	12 Bty	6135362	Motoyama	
SHIERS	GNR	R.	3 Bty	1726142	Taka Butai	
SHOOBRIDGE	SGT	W.H.	RAOC	7593757		
SHRIVES	LT	S.H.	3 Bty	148105	Kanchanaburi	
SHROPSHIRE	GNR	S.	15 Bty	1609800	Kuching	
SILVERTON	GNR	E.K.	3 Bty	1580710	Taka Butai	
SILVEY	GNR	D.A.	12/15 Bty?	1580814	Moji	

Name	Rank	Initials	Bty	Service No.	POW Camp released from	Survived *Kachidoki Maru*
SIMMENON	DVR	P.	15 Bty	774350		
SIMPSON	LT	E.N.	15 Bty	148034	Kyushu	
SIMPSON	RAOC	J.H.	att 3 Bty	T/139381	Japan Sakata	
SINGLETON	RASC	G.A.	RASC 3 Bty	T/232508	Thailand	
SKILLING	GNR	W.	12 Bty	6405579	Thamuang	
SKIVINGTON	GNR	G.L.	3 Bty	779821	Thamuang	
SLATER	GNR	B.K.	3 Bty	1685586		
SLATER	GNR	W.T.	12 Bty	1519124	Ube	
SLEE	GNR	W.E.	12/15 Bty?	1716836	Borneo	
SMITH	GNR	A.	12 Bty	1767362	Motoyama	
SMITH	CAPT	A.B.	15 Bty	194526	Changi	
SMITH	GNR	C.	3 Bty	427188		
SMITH	GNR	G.	12/15 Bty?	1432248	Motoyama	
SMITH	SGT	H.V.	3 Bty	808799	Thamuang	
SMITH	DVR	J.C.	12/15 Bty?	2089168	Moji	
SMITH	GNR	J.H.	3 Bty	1427335	Thamuang	
SMITH	GNR	L.W.	15 Bty	877477		
SMITH	GNR	P.	3 Bty	1643351	Thamuang	
SMITH	SGT	R.G.	3 Bty	1427518	Saigon	
SMITH	L/BDR	R.G.	15 Bty	873162	Ube	
SMITH	GNR	R.A.	3 Bty	1811528	Saigon	
SNELL	GNR	R.C.	3 Bty	798898	Nakom Paton	
SONNETT	GNR	H.C.	3 Bty	1643352	Japan	KM
SOUTHERDEN	GNR	D.E.	3 Bty	1524971	Nakom Paton	
SPARKS	LT	F.G.	12/15 Bty?	197429	Pakan Baroe	
SPOONER	L/BDR	H.H.	15 Bty	1506346	Singapore	
SPRING	L/CPL	J.W.	RASC 3 Bty	T/249562	Thamuang	
STAINSBY	SGT		15 Bty		Ube	
STARKEY	LT	J.W.	12 Bty	148039	Fukuoka No 4	
STEEDS	LT	A.J.	15 Bty	145839	Motoyama	
STEELE	GNR	G.	12/15 Bty?	1439209	Changi	
STEPHENS	GNR	E.R.	3 Bty	859008	Taka Butai	
STEVENSON	L/BDR	R.M.	3 Bty	819807	Honshu 5	
STEVENSON	GNR	W.	3 Bty	4278816	Japan	KM
STEWART	GNR	M.W.	3 Bty	1811770	Taka Butai	
STONE	GNR	T.	3 Bty	777807	Thailand	
STONE	DVR	W.J.	3 Bty	818653	Pratchapkirikan	
STORR	SGT	C.V.	3 Bty	847117	Nakom Nai	
STREAMES	GNR	J.W.	15 Bty	1643365	Kyushu	
STREET	GNR	E.H.	RHQ		Java	
STRETTON	GNR	S.	3 Bty	1726151	Nakom Paton	
SUGDEN	GNR	A.	15 Bty	1533153	Japan	
SUMNER	SGT	J.	3 Bty	1073742		
SUTTON	GNR	W.T.	3 Bty	1580719	Saigon	

Name	Rank	Initials	Bty	Service No.	POW Camp released from	Survived *Kachidoki Maru*
SWAINSTON	GNR	S.E.	12 Bty	1559526	Motoyama	
SWANN	DVR	S.H.	RASC 3 Bty	T/222255	Japan	
SWINDELLS	GNR	W.	12 Bty	790322	Moji	
SYKES	SGT	L.R.	3 Bty	806405		
SYME	L/BDR	D.A.	15 Bty	848696	Fukuoka	
TALBOT	DVR	E.G.	15 Bty	843309	Motoyama/Ube	
TAPP	GNR	C.H.	12/15 Bty?	982822	Kuching	
TARLTON	GNR	E.W.	12/15 Bty?	966666	Kuching	
TAYLOR	GNR	D.E.	15 Bty	2088988	Ube	
TAYLOR	DVR	J.	12/15 Bty?	1713805	Kuching	
TAYLOR	SGT	S.G.	RAOC 3 Bty	5436859	Thailand	
TAYLOR	DVR	W.	15 Bty	3649555	Ube	
TERRY	GNR	L.G.	3 Bty	5378364	Honshu 5	
THACKER	BDR	J.B.	15 Bty	1427442	Fukuoka	
THOMAS	GNR	G.B.	3 Bty	1818149	Saigon	
THOMAS	DVR	H.J.	15 Bty	1072484	Nagasaki	
THOMAS	DVR	W.J.	15 Bty	1818157	Ube	
THOMLINSON	SGT	T.	15 Bty	875701	Ube	
THOMPSON	BDR	G.W.	3 Bty	1056075		
THOMPSON	DVR/MECH	J.E.	12 Bty	2089832	Kuching	
TIPPLE	GNR	G.	12 Bty	786519		
TODD	GNR	R.H.	3 Bty	2750492	Nakom Nai	
TOWHILLS	GNR	H.J.	12/15 Bty?	2065053		
TULLETT	GNR	F.H.	15 Bty	850845	Ube	
TURNER	GNR	S.V.	3 Bty	1580729	Nakom Nai	
TURNBULL	DVR	E.	12/15 Bty?	1427443	Changi	
VICKERS	DVR	F.	15 Bty	2046872	Ube	
VILLIERS	SGT	E.D.	15 Bty	7876419		
VINCENT	L/SGT	W.H.	3 Bty	826930	Pratchapkirikan	
WALKER	GNR	F.	15 Bty	1502723	Sumatra	
WALKER	BDR	W.E.	12/15 Bty?	818130		
WALLACE	Sigs	P.	att 12/15	6201440	Ube	
WALLAGE	GNR	A.	15 Bty	872626		
WALLER	GNR	R.	15 Bty	1588051		
WALTER	GNR	C.	3 Bty	1726153	Thamuang	
WALTERS	GNR	E.W.	3 Bty	800276	Nakom Nai	
WARD	BQMS	E.	12 Bty	800600	Palembang	
WARD	GNR	K.W.	15 Bty	1502721	Ube	
WARD	GNR	L.J.	12/15 Bty?	1817238	Palembang	
WARD	L/BDR	R.	12/15 Bty?	847980	Kyushu	
WARLOW	BDR	W.J.	3 Bty	7363563	Pratchapkirikan	
WARNER	PTE	J.	RAOC	7619938	Fukuoka no 6	
WARR	GNR	J.S.	12 Bty	1426660	Motoyama	

Name	Rank	Initials	Bty	Service No.	POW Camp released from	Survived *Kachidoki Maru*
WARRINER	GNR	A.A.	3 Bty	1070982	Thamuang	
WATERHOUSE	GNR	C.	RAOC 3 Bty	7618318		
WAYMONT	GNR	E.H.	15 Bty	??32203		
WEBBER	LT	P.StC.	Sigs	89188	Fukuoka	
WEEKS	GNR	L.H.	3 Bty	1817379	Saigon	
WEIR	GNR	T.C.	3 Bty	805148	Thamuang	
WELLER	DVR	B.T.	15 Bty	1588054	Changi	
WELLS	GNR	W.R.	3 Bty	791077	Saigon	
WESTON	GNR	S.R.	3 Bty	819805	Honshu 5	
WESTWOOD	GNR	A.V.E.	15 Bty	1580737	Kyushu	
WETTON	GNR	S.T.	3 Bty	2057704	Nakon Paton	
WHANT	BSM	?	15 Bty	?	Motoyama	
WHEELER	GNR	G.H.	3 Bty		Taiwan	
WHEELER	GNR	P.J.	12 Bty	1440460	Kuching	
WHELON	CAPT	B.C.	RAOC 3 Bty	119826	Kanchanaburi	
WHIGHT	SGT	W.C.	RAOC	6902272	Kuching	
WHITAKER	GNR	H.H.	3 Bty	1643499	Nakom Paton	
WHITE	SGT	A.F.	12 Bty	862245	Ube	
WHITE	GNR	F.	15 Bty	1746847		
WHITE	GNR	J.F.C.	12 Bty	888858	Motoyama	
WHITE	GNR	L.A.	15 Bty	1726156	Pratchapkirikan	
WHITEHOUSE	GNR	J.	15 Bty	1502742	Fukuoka	
WHITHAM	GNR	G.W.	3 Bty	1806101	Japan	
WHITING	GNR	C.	3 Bty	1685838	Changi	
WHITING	GNR	H.	3 Bty	1655154	Saigon	
WHITTY	LT	A.E.	12/15 Bty?	172836	Motoyama	
WHOLEY	GNR	E.J.	12 Bty	1797256	Kuching	
WILDBORE	GNR	S.	3 Bty	5491504	Japan	
WIGGINS	GNR	E.G.	12/15 Bty?	869578	Changi	
WILCOX	L/BDR	W.J.	15 Bty	1073084	Ube	
WILDING	DVR	G.E.	15 Bty	1713847	Kuching	
WILLIAMS	Sigs	A.H.	Att	2343289	Ube	
WILLIAMS	L/BDR	F.U.	12 Bty	841393	Motoyama	
WILLIAMS	DVR	G.	RASC	T/255458	Kuching	
WILLIAMS	L/BDR	T.H.	15 Bty	868799	Ube	
WILLIAMS	GNR	R.V.	15 Bty	1817252	Honshu 5	
WILLIAMS	GNR	W.B.	15 Bty	1817255		
WILLIAMSON	GNR	A.E.	115 Bty	857058	Moji	
WILLIAMSON	Sigs	B.	Att 3 Bty	2365010	Thailand	
WILSON	PTE	F.	RAOC 3 Bty	10631327	Singapore	
WILSON	PTE	S.F.	RAOC 3 Bty	10337410	Thamuang	
WINGFIELD	DVR	H.	RAOC 3 Bty	T/123381	Changi	
WOOD	GNR	C.V.	3 Bty	1640563	Saigon	

Name	Rank	Initials	Bty	Service No.	POW Camp released from	Survived *Kachidoki Maru*
WOOD	DVR	J.	RASC 3 Bty	T/86580		
WOODS	GNR	W.W.	12 Bty	1426972	Kuching	
WOOSNAM	GNR	R.A.	12/15 Bty?	1587280	Thamuang	
WRIGHT	SGT	A.	15 Bty	1425231	Japan	
WRIGHT	GNR	D.J.		1580743	Sumatra	
WRIGHT	BDR	R.	12/15 Bty?	840078	Fukuoka	
WROE	GNR	W.	3 Bty	914275	Tamarkan	
WYATT	GNR	J.	3 Bty	822829	Nakom Paton	
YATES	GNR	C.D.	15 Bty	816925		
YOUNG	BDR	J.W.	12 Bty	1073110	Motoyama	

End Thoughts

Great Britain and her Commonwealth Allies were caught totally by surprise in late 1939.

What few HAA units there were had no chance to be effective. The inter-war years of penny-pinching had left them woefully under strength and having to fight with outdated weaponry.

Germany had been preparing for many years for the chance to take on the opposition and because of their training were unbeatable in the beginning.

Britain found many of her neighbours subdued and isolated and except for her Commonwealth Allies had no one to call on for help.

Britain had no real victories for some considerable time. The Low Countries were lost as were France and Belgium, and then the early days in North Africa and the Med. provided more defeats.

This is what happens when you are not prepared for war.

However the one saving grace was when the Japanese, intent on their Great Asia Co Prosperity Sphere decided they could take on and beat the Americans in the Far East.

For the Allies in 1941 when everything was going against them this was the one bright hope.

The Americans had such an enormous power base for manufacturing that the balance would now be turned. After their initial disaster at Pearl Harbor the American anger was truly awesome.

The Japanese were only really so successful because they were pitted against ill-prepared troops with insufficient equipment and the attitude that British troops ruled the world and were unbeatable.

Over time these failings were redressed and men went out to foreign theatres well prepared and even if it had taken several years to get it right they were now in a position to take on the enemy on equal terms; take him on and beat him in what he considered his domain.

Wherever the Army went the Gunners went too and they provided the supporting fire that was needed to win.

Under the most exacting situations they did not fail. Through thick jungle, hot sandy deserts and mountainous terrain, they were always available.

In the Far East the enemy was ruthless and totally unprincipled and those unfortunate enough to be captured had to live through a hell no others had had to endure before.

By war's end the Gunner strength had risen above 675,000 and in the Far East alone their total casualties amounted to just over 8700 men.

Sadly for those in the Far East it turned out to be more dangerous to be taken prisoner than face the enemy and in a very short campaign their losses were high.

In this respect 6 Regt and its batteries contributed their best and we should not forget that among many thousands of others, many paid the ultimate sacrifice.

As written on the memorial to the Army in Burma at Kohima and which could refer to all troops, in all theatres, who did not make it home, we should never forget,

> When you go home,
> Tell them of us and say,
> For your tomorrow
> We gave our today.

This was not quite the end of the story for 6 HAA Regt.

On 1 April 1946 , once they had recovered from their injuries the fittest survivors reformed along with others from 140 HAA Regt to become the 77 HAA Regt. This comprised three Batteries 209, 221 and 222.

They served with the BAOR (British Army of the Rhine) until 1958.

The name of 6 Regt has disappeared but their heroism remains.

Penn Common golf course in 2011, the site of 8 mobile guns. Now showing no sign of its wartime use.

Lightning Source UK Ltd.
Milton Keynes UK
UKOW01f0147130214

226328UK00001B/7/P